Y0-BKG-031

LECTURES
ON
THE EPISTLE OF JUDE

LECTURES
ON
THE EPISTLE OF JUDE

(TRANSLATED FROM A CORRECTED TEXT)

BY

W. KELLY

NEW EDITION
REVISED BY W. J. HOCKING.

BOOKS FOR CHRISTIANS
Post Office Box 15344
Charlotte, North Carolina
28210

Printed in the United States of America—1970

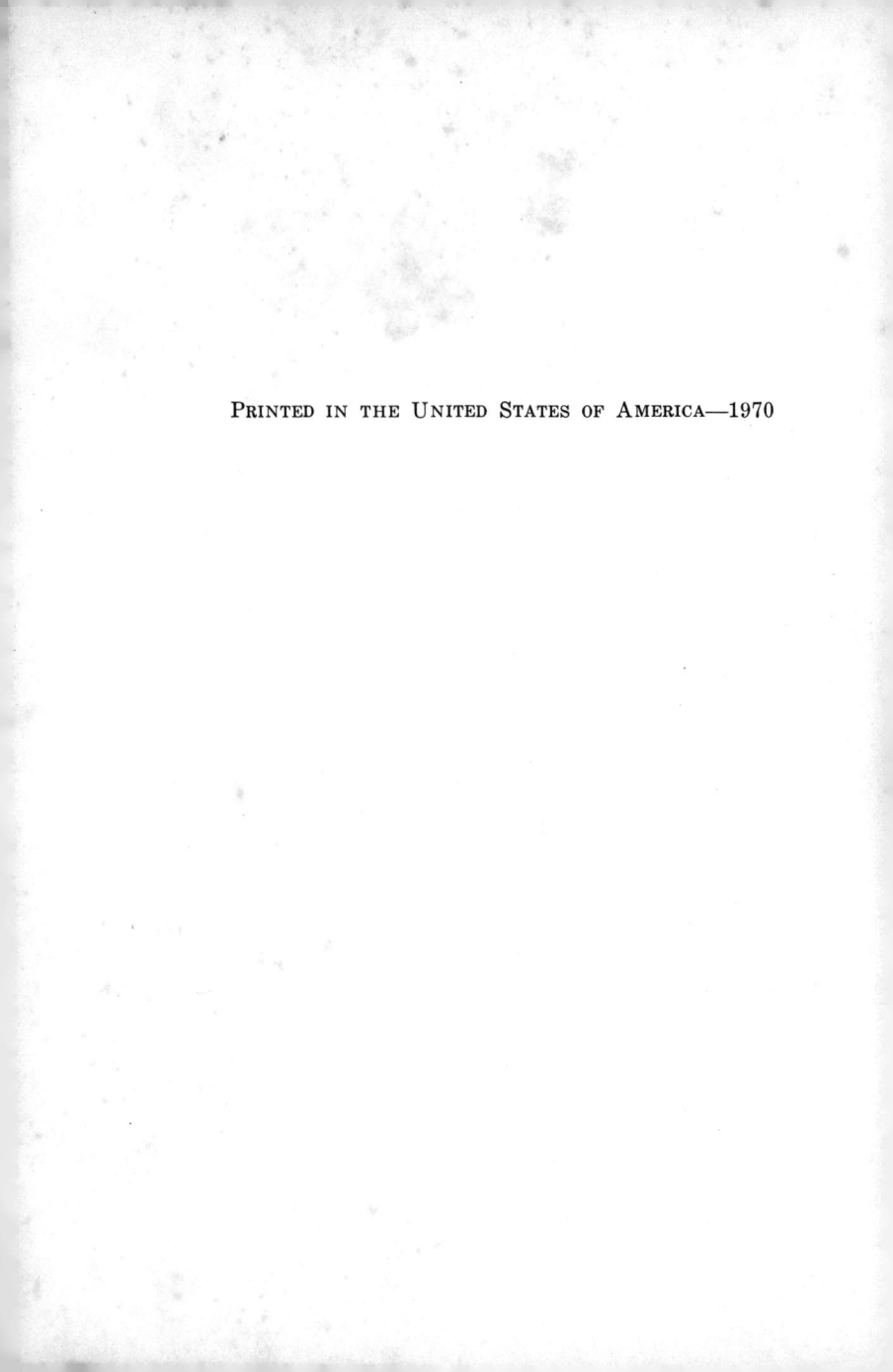

CONTENTS

	PAGE
INTRODUCTION	7
VERSE 1	21
VERSES 2, 3	30
VERSE 3	39
VERSES 4, 5	45
VERSES 6–8	53
VERSE 9	72
VERSES 10–13	95
VERSES 14, 15	113
VERSES 16–19	130
VERSES 20, 21	145
VERSES 22, 23	152
VERSES 24, 25	156
VERSE 25	168

LECTURES ON
THE EPISTLE OF JUDE

INTRODUCTION

WE are arrived at those days now of which the Epistle of Jude speaks. I might say we are further, for the Epistles of John, although they are put before this Epistle, imply from their own contents that they were after. The order of the books in the N.T., we know is entirely human, and, in fact, is not the same in all Bibles. In English ones it is, but abroad it is not so, and in the more ancient copies of the Scriptures there was another order, in some respects even less correct than that which we have; because these Epistles of Jude and John are put before the Epistles of Paul. I need not say that there was no divine wisdom in that. I only mention it for the purpose of emphasising the absolute need of the guidance of the Holy Spirit. It is no matter what it is. The people in early days, it might have been thought, would have had a good sound judgment of how to arrange the books of Holy Scripture, but they had not. I am speaking now of a time long after the apostles, and we are still more distant. But we are at no disadvantage because of this, for the reason that the Holy Ghost Who was given, still abides. The ruin of the church does not affect that gift. It is a very solemn fact, and it does greatly bear upon the practical answer of the church to the glory of the Lord Jesus, and it makes not a small difference for the members of Christ. But the Lord provided for everything when He sent down the Holy Spirit ; and He made known through the apostles that this was the sad history which awaited the church. It is the apostles who tell us what disasters were to flow in with a strong tide—nobody more so than the apostle Paul, who says, " I know that after my decease shall grievous wolves enter in among you, not sparing the flock." Oh, what characters ! What successors ! Apostolic successors !—there are none. The successors were to be grievous wolves and perverse men. Nevertheless, he commended the saints none the less confidently " to God and to the word of His grace."

Well, we have this ; and I do not think that the word of His grace has ever been so deeply enjoyed, as it is now, for many hundreds of years. But then, Who is it that enjoys the " word of His grace " ? We cannot say that all the saints do. All saints ought to do. Can we say that all our dear brethren and sisters enjoy the word of His grace as it becomes them ? I would to God it were so ; and it is of all moment therefore that, knowing the need, we should be most earnest not merely about work—I allow that this has a great place for all true workers, and I admit that many can help the workers who are not exactly workers themselves—but, beloved friends, the first of all duties is that God should have His rights. This is forgotten, even by saints of God. The first-fruits belong to Him always, it does not matter what it is ; and we are never right when it is merely love working outwardly. The first thing is that love should work upward. Is not God infinitely more to us than any converts—as could be said to poor Naomi, who had lost her sons—" better to thee than seven sons " ? Is not He worth more than a hundred thousand converts ? What a poor thing it is, merely to be useful to other people and not to be growing ourselves in grace, and in the knowledge of our Lord Jesus Christ ! How can this be done except by God and the word of His grace ? How does God act now ? By His Spirit. Time was when the great truth was God manifesting Himself by His Son. Well, that abides ; the word and Spirit of God abide for ever. But now the Holy Ghost is sent down from heaven. He is that divine Person with Whom we have to do habitually, and we are either honouring Him, or failing to do so. The great test of honouring Him is that Christ becomes all. This is a truth that got greatly clouded even in apostolic days. It may be a very small comfort; it is a very solemn and saddening comfort, too, if I may use such a conjunction of thoughts, but so it is when we think how everything tends to failure and towards decline, not excepting the testimony of God which was committed to His children.

It is a very solemn thing that the apostles had the

very same experiences themselves. The last of them had to face the fact that the very best of the churches —that which had been the brightest—became the object of the Lord's warning, and the last of the churches of the Lord's threatening; a warning of what soon came to pass, and a threatening to be surely executed viz.—to take away the candlestick of the one, and to spue the other out of His mouth (Rev. ii., iii.).

Now, is that meant to weaken confidence? It was revealed in order to enforce the need of dependence upon the Lord, to encourage us to look up from the earth and things that are here—but not to give up. We are never free to give up anything that is of God. We are never at liberty to plead the state of ruin for carelessness about any expression of God's will. The ruin of the church has nothing to do with weakening our responsibility. It brings in the necessity of greater watchfulness, of more prayer; and particularly the necessity of God and the word of His grace to deal with the difficulties altogether above man. But are they above the Spirit of God?

Now, it is in this very spirit that Jude writes— " a servant of Jesus Christ." For he does not appear to have been the apostle Jude. Most take it for granted that it was only an apostle wrote this or any of the Epistles. This is a mistake. Many of the apostles never wrote any inspired writing, and some that were not apostles wrote both Gospels and Epistles. It is a question of inspiration, a question of a particular work of God, of which vessel the Holy

Ghost would use. Out of the four who wrote the Gospels, two were apostles, and two were not apostles ; so with the Epistles, as it appears to me, for I should not wish to press a thing that is so very much doubted by many persons. But then it is well to remember that almost everything is doubted now-a-days !

It is of interest to consider who is speaking to us in this Epistle. We are told it is " Jude, servant of Jesus Christ and brother of James." He is not the brother of James the son of Zebedee—John was his brother. That James was cut off from very early days indeed, and John was left latest of all ; so different was the issue for these two sons of Zebedee. There was another James (as also another Jude or Judas, besides the Iscariot), " son of Alphæus," who is named " James the Little " (Mark xv. 40). I do not think that this is the James referred to here, but rather that he is the one who has been called " James the Just " ; and I presume that this title was given to him because of his practical pre-eminence. He was a hater of evil and a lover of all that was morally pleasing to God. He comes before us too, in Acts xv., though not for the first time there. In that chapter he takes a great place. He, as far as one can so say, presided, and that is a very proper scripture word. Those " that rule well " means those that preside well. There is nothing wrong in presiding if a man can do it ; it is a mistake if a man cannot, and assumes to do it ; and it is one of the worst things possible when done now by an official, whether there is power or not. But there is such a thing as "ruling" or "presiding" recognised, though it is never confined to one person, "them that have the rule (or, preside) over you" (Heb. xiii. 17) : there we have several.

But we are not anxious about the matter. One might be more prominent on one day, another on another day, but James seems to have been prominent habitually, and this appears to have been quite recognised by the elders at Jerusalem. We find Paul going up to see James, and all the elders were present (Acts xx. 18). This is the man who wrote the Epistle, who also calls himself "a servant of . . . Jesus Christ." Of course, this is true of all, and is said by almost all. The apostle Paul calls himself that continually, and of course so do Peter and John, although the latter calls himself "the disciple whom Jesus loved" rather, but still he calls himself a servant of Jesus Christ in the Revelation (i. 2)— "to His servant John." So you see that it is only a question of the propriety of the case where this word is put forward ; and it certainly was very appropriate in the book of the Revelation, and there accordingly it is. Elsewhere, in his Gospel especially, John dwells rather on the Saviour's love, and in that book he does not call himself anything. We only know by internal evidence that he must be the man whom he describes, not as John, but, as "the disciple whom Jesus loved."

INTRODUCTION 13

But James was not a "disciple"; he was one of the Lord's brethren who did not believe all the time the Lord was living here below; "neither did His brethren believe on Him" (John vii. 5). "His brethren" were sons of Mary after His own birth. Of course we can understand that Romanists have been anxious to make out that they were sons of Joseph and not of Mary. But they were sons of Mary and of Joseph. They would like to make them out sons of a former marriage of Joseph. We do not know anything of a former marriage, nor do they. We do know that scripture is quite plain.

Take Mark vi. 3 for instance, and there you will find that what I have just stated is fully acknowledged: speaking of our Lord, it says, "Is not this the carpenter the son of Mary, and brother" (not the cousin, you see) "of James and Joses, and of Juda and Simon?" We do not know what particular place God gave to Joses and Simon, but we do know that James and Judas, or Jude (it is the same name), were both called to an eminent service.

Now if we look at the first of Acts we get more. It appears there were sisters also, but we need not now pursue that subject. In Acts i. 13 we read, "And when they" (*i.e.* the apostles) "were come in, they went up into an upper room, where abode both Peter and James" (that James is the son of Zebedee), "and John" (his brother), "and Andrew, Philip and Thomas, Bartholomew and Matthew, James [the son] of Alphæus" (that is, James the Little) "and Simon Zelotes" (to distinguish him from Simon Peter and from Simon the Lord's brother), "and Judas [the brother] of James."

Now, in my judgment, the last two names are brought before us in the opening verse of our Epistle, "Jude, the servant of Jesus Christ, and brother of James." But we further read in the same chapter of the Acts, "These all continued with one accord in prayer and supplication, with the women, and Mary the mother of Jesus, and with his brethren" (ver. 14). Who these "brethren" are, we have already seen from Mark vi. James and Jude were two of the Lord's brethren. Simon and Joses were two others. But we do not need to dwell on these, because Scripture does not do so. Yet it says a deal about James; not so much about Jude. As already noticed, although they were unconverted all the time the Lord was on earth they were evidently converted after the Lord died and rose; so that there they were with Mary their mother, and the eleven, all living together and given up to prayer, and waiting for the promise of the Father, the gift of the Holy Spirit. It is certain they were not unconverted now. Nothing would have been more contrary to their mind had they not been believers, but now they are believers for the first time. And very beautiful it is to see that God broke them down by the very thing that might have stumbled them for ever. The crucifying of the Lord might have entirely hindered, but God used that and the Lord's resurrection, not only to awaken their souls, but to bring them in, so that they were there, full of the same expectation of the Holy Ghost as the apostles themselves.

Consequently, when James, the son of Zebedee, was killed (Acts xii.), we find another James, who is not described as the son of Alphæus, and who is the one that has evidently stepped forward, by God's guidance, into a kind of foremost place. For when all the apostles were there, Peter and John amongst the rest, they did not take that place, much less any other of the twelve. James did, and to show you that I am not incorrect in this, I will give you another scripture, (Galatians i. 15–19), which is very convincing and satisfactory. The apostle Paul is showing how he had been kept from mixing up with any other of the apostles in particular, at the time he was brought to the knowledge of the Lord Jesus. " But when it pleased God, Who separated me from my mother's womb, and called [me] by His grace, to reveal His Son in me, that I might preach Him among the heathen ; immediately I conferred not with flesh and blood ; neither went I up to Jerusalem to them which were apostles before me ; but I went into Arabia, and returned again unto Damascus. Then after three years, I went up to Jerusalem to see Peter, and abode with him fifteen days. But other of the apostles saw I none, save James, the Lord's brother " (not the Lord's " cousin ").

Apparently, James, the son of Alphæus, was the Lord's cousin. Now we all know that the word " brother " is sometimes used loosely, but in that case it is always corrected by some other parts of scripture. But this is not corrected by any ; and I do not see any reason why—if the Spirit of God calls Mark, not exactly the nephew, but cousin of Barnabas (the word there used is " cousin "),— James should not be so called here, if he were not really the " brother " of our Lord.

It is true James does not call himself " the Lord's brother," but " the Lord's servant " ; and this is very beautiful. Had there been any self-seeking he would have been the one to say, " I am the Lord's brother ! You must not forget I am the Lord's brother." But that would have been anything but of the Spirit of God, because when he was the Lord's brother, he was an unbeliever. He had been an unbeliever during all the life of our Lord. Indeed, he was so until His death and resurrection. He, therefore, with beautiful grace, never brings up that which was his shame—that he was the Lord's brother after the flesh. The Lord Himself put all that sort of thing down, when He declared that it was not so much the blessed thing to be the woman that bare Him, as it was to hear the word of God and keep it. This is what the writer of this Epistle had done ; he had heard the word of God and kept it. He had received the truth of Christ's Person not as son of Mary but as the Son of God, as the Messiah, the Lord of all. Here then Jude was glad to say, not that he was the Lord's brother, though he was so, but, " a servant of Jesus Christ," and he adds, to make it perfectly clear who he was, " brother of James."

So we have here the plain fact that this James was not the son of Zebedee, who had been killed many years before ; neither was he James the little. We may call him rather, James the great, because he takes such a foremost place wherever mentioned. Acts xv. puts it in a very striking manner which I had better not pass over. After Peter had given his very important testimony, and Paul and Barnabas their evidence, about the reception of the Gentiles, we come to another person (ver. 13) ; " James answered, saying." You see the others are regarded as speaking, but James answers, " Men, brethren " (that is the proper way to read it ; " and " has nothing to do with it). They were not merely men, but men who were brethren. " Men, brethren, hearken unto me. Simon hath declared how God at the first did visit the Gentiles, to take out of them a people for His name . . . Wherefore my sentence is . . ." (vers. 13-19). No one can doubt the place that he took, and that the Spirit of God sanctions his taking it. James was the one who, after having heard all the facts, summed up the mind of God, and quoted a decisive scripture. And this is a very interesting thing that, though they were inspired men, they did not do without the scriptures. When you have facts in the light of scripture, you are then entitled to draw therefrom the truth—what he calls here " my sentence," and what was written in the nineteenth and following verses.

The other striking place where James appears is in Acts xxi. where Paul goes up to Jerusalem. " And the day following "—that is after the arrival— " Paul went in with us to James ; and all the elders were present " (ver. 18). It is evident that this was the great central place of meeting for strangers at Jerusalem, and that the elders also were accustomed to be present on those occasions. These facts give it evidently a very official character, which was perfectly compatible with the position of James at Jerusalem. Tradition makes him the bishop of the church in Jerusalem, but scripture never speaks of " the " bishop, but of " bishops " : and scripture also shows that there were more important persons than the bishops ; and James had a place of evident superiority to any of the " elders " (these were the bishops), a place that none of the elders possessed to the same degree. And this James is the one that wrote the Epistle that bears his name, as that of Jude was written by his brother.

It is instructive to see how God allowed the unbelief of the family of our Lord Jesus. It was not like people plotting together. If you look at the great leader of the Eastern apostasy, Mahomet, it was so. His family were persons whom he induced to take their place along with him, to defend him and stand by him. But in the case of our Lord Jesus Christ,

God allowed that His own brethren should not believe on Him all the time that His mighty works were being done. But there was another work, the greatest of all, and God made that work irresistible. Not indeed the works of His life, but that of His death and resurrection; and these brethren that had stood out so stubbornly against Him were brought out to believe on Him through His work of sin bearing. There was a reason for their unbelief. There are always moral causes, which act particularly in unconverted persons to prevent their reception of the truth. Sometimes it is the fleshly mind, sometimes the worldly mind, sometimes both. In the case of these brethren, their worldly mind came out strongly in John vii. 4, 5, when they said, " If Thou do these things, show Thyself to the world. For neither did His brethren believe on Him." The Lord was infinitely far from doing this. He was not of the world, and tells us we are not. He never sought the world in any form. He only sought to do good to souls in it by delivering them out of the world to make them know the true God, and Himself equally the true God and Life eternal.

Well now, we have this fact so full of interest—that James gives us, according to the spiritual character that was formed in him, a most complete setting forth of practical righteousness in everyday life, in our tempers, in our words, as well as our ways. All this is unfolded by James more than by any other, and it is only from want of understanding it, that some do not like his Epistle. Sometimes great and good men have kicked at the plainness of speech in James. They have not liked it ; but it was a great loss to them, for had they heeded what he wrote it would have corrected many a fault in themselves.

Now in Jude there is another subject altogether. Righteousness is not the point in Jude ; not even the way in which Peter brings it in. Jude does not look at it for personal walk simply, apart from the ruin of those that give it up. He merely shows righteousness to be a necessary thing for every saint. If a man has not got it, he is not a saint at all. But Peter in his Second Epistle looks at it in a large way among the people of God—whether they as His people walk righteously, and more particularly whether the teachers are indifferent to righteousness and are favouring unrighteousness. Therefore his Second Epistle is levelled most strongly at these— the false teachers who, not content with being personally so themselves, encourage others to similar lack of righteousness. Now, this is not what Jude takes up at all, though there is much that is common to them both. It could not be otherwise.

Jude looks at grace. There is nothing like grace ; but what if grace be abused? What if grace be abandoned? What if grace be turned to licentiousness? Now that is what Jude takes up. Consequently, his Epistle is one of the most solemn in the word of God. There is only one writer who is more so—John. John looks at not merely the departure from grace, but the denial of Christ, of the Father and the Son. Well, it is impossible to conceive of anything worse in scripture than denying the glory of Him unto Whose name I may have been baptised, and through Whom I have professed to receive every blessing that God could give. After all that, for a man to be induced by his intellect, or from whatever cause, to deny the Lord, to deny that He was the Christ and the Son of God—there is nothing more deadly—there is nothing more terrible than the state of such a one. And it fell to the lot of him who loved the Lord most, to John, to write about this denial. So that you see that there is a beautiful propriety in all the Epistles.

VERSE I

" Jude, servant of Jesus Christ, and brother of James, to them that are (not exactly, ' sanctified,' but) beloved." This may surprise many who have been accustomed to the Authorised Version, but it is not a question of what we have been accustomed to, but of what God wrote. The Authorised Version is an admirable one. Our translators did not mistake the meaning of the Greek word in the text before them ; but the text which they had was the common text, and this text is as faulty in its way as the common English Version. This text was transcribed by a number of different hands, and if the writing was not very clear there was always a tendency for the copyist to make mistakes.

I have had a deal of writing pass through my hands, but I hardly have seen any, where there is not some mistake made. Particularly when the writing is a copy of another, it is almost always so, and more particularly when the man whose thoughts and words are copied is above the common people. The way to find out the best Greek text is to go up to the oldest of all, and to compare the oldest of all with the different translations made in ancient times, and if these agree, then you have the right one. But they often disagree, and then comes the question, Which is right ? Here the all important question is the guidance of the Spirit of God. We can never do without Him, and the way in which the Spirit of God leads persons who really are not only indwelt by Him, but led by Him, is,—does it express the current of the Epistle ? Does it fall in with the line of the apostle's writing ?

Well, you see the word " sanctified " may be correct in itself, but the word here should be, " to those that are called, beloved," etc. You observe that the word " called " occurs at the end of the verse. This word " called " is very emphatic. Then he describes them in two different ways. First, here, in the A.V., it is " sanctified," but as now generally accepted by those who have studied the text fully, it is "beloved* in God the Father." "In" is very often equivalent to (indeed, it is a stronger expression that) "by." But I now give it literally, "beloved in God the Father." I confess myself that not only is this reading the most ancient, the best approved by the highest witnesses that God has given to us of His word, but it is beautifully appropriate to the Epistle. The assurance of being "beloved in God the Father," or "by God the Father," comes into special value under two sets of circumstances. If I am a young man very young in the faith, when one is proving the persecution of the world, the hatred of men, Jews full of jealousy, the Gentiles full of scorn, and both animated by hatred against the Lord and those that are the Lord's—what a comfort it is to know that I am beloved "in God the Father." This is the way the apostle Paul addressed the Thessalonians as a company, the only one that he ever addressed in this way. They were experiencing persecution, not in a gradual way as most of the other assemblies had done, but from the very start, from their conversion. We know the apostle himself had to flee because of the persecution that had set in there. "These men that have turned the world upside down have come here also," and a deadly set was made upon them, and so the apostle had to escape. The church there had to bear the brunt of it, and in the very first Epistle that Paul ever wrote, the

---

* ἠγαπημένοις (beloved) ℵAB and several cursives, all the Ancient Versions, Origen, &c. ἡγιασμένοις (sanctified) KLP &c.

First to the Thessalonians—that was his first inspired writing—you will find that such is the manner in which he describes them. " Paul and Silvanus and Timotheus to the assembly of Thessalonians in God [the] Father and [the] Lord Jesus Christ " (1 Thess. ii. 1). And that this was studiously meant is shown by the same presentation of the truth in the opening verse of the Second Epistle, where we find there was still the persecution and the danger of their being shaken by that persecution and the error that had come in through false teachers taking advantage of it to pretend that " the day of the Lord " was actually on them, making out that this persecution was the beginning of that" day," and so greatly alarming the young believers there.

Hence the apostle had to write a second letter to establish them clearly in the bright hope of Christ's coming, and in the lower truth of the day of the Lord. Well, in that Second Epistle we have " Paul and Silvanus and Timotheus to the assembly of Thessalonians in God our Father and [the] Lord Jesus Christ " (2 Thess. ii. 1). Now I conceive that the object of the Spirit of God there, by the apostle, was, that as they were so young and so exposed to such an assault upon themselves, which reminded the apostle of the assault which had been made upon himself and his friends, that they should be comforted by the reminder that they were " in God the Father." What could harm them if this were the case ? The apostle would not have ventured from himself to say such a thing. None upon earth would have done so. It was God Who inspired the apostle to let them know that wonderful comfort. There are many people who read this and do not get any comfort from it, because they do not apply it to themselves. They have no idea what it means. You will remember that John, writing in his First Epistle, separates the family of God into three classes —the fathers, young men and the babes (for I give the last word as it should be, literally). They are all " children " of God, but the babes are the young ones of the children of God. The young men are those that have grown up, and the fathers are those that are mature and well established in Christ. Well, it is to the babes—and this will help us to understand what I have been saying—he says, " I write unto you babes " (the proper full force of the word), " because ye have known the Father " (1 John ii. 13).

Well, so it is with this young assembly in Thessalonica. It is described by the Holy Ghost as being " in God [the] Father and in [the] Lord Jesus Christ."

In Jude we have the other side. They are not young saints now. It is addressed to comparatively old saints. There might be young ones among them; there would be such, undoubtedly. But he is looking at them as having gone through a sea of trouble and difficulty, and he is preparing them for worse still. He, as it were, says things are not going to get better but worse, and it is to end in the actual appearing of the Lord in judgment, and what is more, the very kind of people who are to be the objects of the Lord's judgment when He comes have crept into the church already. This is a very solemn thing, and it might be alarming unless people were well read and grounded in the truth, and in love. So, therefore, writing at a comparatively late time (not early as in the case of the Thessalonians, but late), Jude writes in these terms—" to them that are called." You observe that I transpose that word, which is a little spoiled by the interpolation of the conjunction " and " before " called." " To them that are called, beloved in God the Father, and preserved." It is not exactly " preserved *in*." It may be " by " or " for." These are the two alternatives for that word. I do not see how it can be " in " ; so that you see it little differs from what we read here. It brings in another idea, and it is perfectly true either way. We are preserved *by* Christ, and we are preserved *for* Christ. I have not made up my mind which of the two in this instance is right, because they cannot both be the intention of the Spirit of God. One must be right rather than the other, but I cannot say that my judgment is yet formed as to the choice of these two prepositions, whether it should be " preserved for Jesus Christ," or " by " Jesus Christ, He being the great One that does keep us. But in either case, how beautifully it is suited to a time of extra danger, and of danger too that he was not warranted to say would pass ! We say the storm rages now, but the sun will shine shortly. No ; it is to be that blackness of darkness of evil which is now coming in among the professors of Christ to get denser and darker until the Lord comes in judgment on them.

Well, how sweet is the assurance, " beloved in God the Father, and preserved by (or for) Jesus Christ " (either way is full of brightness—and the Lord may give us to learn some day which of the two thoughts is His meaning). But there it is, and full of comfort and sweetness, and eminently suited to the circumstances portrayed in this Epistle beyond any Epistle in the New Testament—an Epistle that shows the departure of Christians, *i.e.*, of professing Christians—of those who were once thought to be as good as any. Sometimes, the people who turn away are those that have been very bright. We should not be surprised at that. It is not always the best fruit that ripens most quickly. Sometimes the earliest becomes rotten very soon. This is often the case with those that seem so bright all at once.

I remember being struck with this in the case of a young woman in the Isle of Wight, some forty years ago. Charles Stanley, our dear brother, in his zeal for the gospel was somewhat in danger of fancying people were converted when they were not. At times of revival, people are often apt to slip in ; their feelings are moved, they are quickly affected. According to the word in the Gospel, " they hear the word, and anon with joy receive it ; yet have they no root in themselves, but endure for a while : for when trial or persecution arises because of the word, immediately they are offended " (Matt. xiii. 20, 21) ; so that we ought not to be surprised. The young woman of whom I speak was employed in a shop, and I was brought to see her as one of these conversions. In a moment she assured me that the old man was all gone, " dead and buried," and other such language she used. This would have been all very sweet had there been any real spiritual feeling ; but she had merely caught the truth in her mind, at best.

Now, a real convert having confessed the truth of Christ for the first time, would be greatly tried by many things, failings, shortcomings, and the like. The soul of such a one would be greatly alarmed to think that, even after having received Christ, he found so little that answered to His love, so easily betrayed into levity or carelessness, or into haste of temper, and ever so many difficulties that a young believer is tried by. But the young woman of whom I have been speaking had no conscience about anything at all. All she had was merely an intellectual idea of the truth that seemed delightful to her, and, indeed, it is delightful. It is like those described in Heb. vi. 5, they " have tasted the good word of God," and there they are, " enlightened " by the great light of the gospel, without being truly born of God. There might be a powerful action of the Spirit of God, and there may be all this without being truly born of God. People who are really born of God are generally tried, and there is a great sense of sin, and they have to learn their powerlessness. All this is a very painful experience ; and it is to this state that the comfort of the gospel applies the knowledge of entire forgiveness and clearance from all that we are ; not only in spite of what we are, but because of what we are, because of all that God has given us—a new life where there is no sin. There never is anything like this true comfort except in those that have felt the need of it, and that sense of need is what goes along with conversion to God. The Old Testament saints were in that state ; and they never got out of it. The New Testament saints began with conversion and came into blessing that was impossible with the law—because the mighty work of redemption was not done. But now it is done ; and can we suppose it does not make an essential difference for a New Testament believer ? Well! " if any man be ignorant, let him be ignorant." Here you have this invaluable comfort for those that have passed through such serious experiences and who have proved their own weakness in meeting it—the liability to be affected by appearances which come to nothing. Fair and smooth words where there is no reality at all—this is what is so trying. And the Epistle shows that people are going to get worse than this.

VERSES 2, 3

THEN (ver. 2) we have, " mercy unto you, and peace and love be multiplied." This is the only place where mercy is wished to the saints generally. When writing to individuals, to Timothy and Titus, for instance, the apostle says " Mercy," but when to the saints generally, " Grace and peace."

Why does Jude bring " mercy " in here ? Because they deeply needed the comfort. An individual ought always to feel the deep need of mercy, especially in the face of danger, and also in the sense of personal unworthiness ; and now Jude gives the comfort of it to all these saints because of their imminent danger. I do not know any saints more in danger than ourselves, because grace has given us to feel for Christ's honour and name, and to have confidence in the scriptures as the word of God. We should not look at a single word in them as a dead letter. I do not suppose that there is a single person here present—brother or sister—that has a doubt of a single word that God has written. It would be difficult now-a-days to find yourself in such a company generally. People think inspiration is a very lively term, and that we must allow for the errors of those good men who wrote the Bible. What could we expect from such men even if learned? They judge by themselves, not by God, nor by the Holy Ghost. Many of these men have not, I think, abandoned Christianity ; but they are darkened by the spirit of unbelief. The spirit of the present day is as bad or worse as in any age since the Lord died and rose. There is one thing that marks it, and, that is lawlessness. A want of respect for everything that is above self, and a determination to have one's own way—that is lawlessness. I do not know anything worse. It is what will characterise the whole of Christendom. Now it works in individuals, and it also works largely in whole companies, but it will soon become the reigning spirit. And that is the distinctive name of the anti-christ, " the lawless one." Christ was the Man of righteousness, Christ is the Man that gives everything its place according to God, and Christ is the One that gives God His place. As to everything and every person, He was the Man of righteousness; lawlessness has nothing but self as its great ambition, a fallen self—man fallen from God. The danger is great in the present day, and so it was when Jude wrote his Epistle. Therefore it is " mercy," not only " peace and love," but " mercy " be multiplied. It is a very emphatic word.

" Beloved, when I gave all diligence to write unto you of the common salvation, it was needful for me to write unto you, and exhort that ye should earnestly contend for the faith which was once delivered to the saints " (ver. 3). It is addressed to those that have learned the value of " the faith." He does not refer to personal faith but to the deposit that the faith holds. It is the thing believed, not merely the spiritual power that believes the testimony. It is therefore called "the faith," distinct from "faith." When did that faith come? The Epistle to the Galatians shows us when faith came and redemption and the Holy Ghost. It is found in iii. 25 : "For after that faith is come." "I live by the faith of the Son of God." ; "Received ye the Spirit by the hearing of faith ? " is a distinct thing (ii.20 ; iii. 2). "The scripture hath concluded all under sin" (Jews or Gentiles—the Jews under transgression, but *all* under sin) "that the promise by faith of Jesus Christ might be given to them that believe. But before faith came we were kept under law," (iii. 22, 23). The law was there until the cross of Christ, but then it was affixed to the tree ; not only was Christ crucified, but the law came thereby to its end, as far as God's people were concerned. We are now placed under Christ. We are now regarded as being " in the Spirit," for Christ is our life and the Holy Ghost is the power of that life.

Well, here then he says that it was needful that he should exhort them to " earnestly contend for the faith which was once delivered to the saints." This is what is on my heart to speak about. How great is, not only " conversion " such as the O.T. people knew before faith came but, the " salvation " which is now, as the apostle Paul says in Ephesians (i. 13), " the word of truth, the gospel of your (not conversion but the gospel of your) salvation " ! This is what was added consequent upon redemption. Nobody could have been delivered from hell without being converted; but the " gospel of our salvation " is to make us perfectly happy on earth, to bring us into cloudless peace and liberty while here in this world. It is this that is new, from the cross of Christ. Why, beloved friends, it is new to many children of God now ! They are not sure at all, even those that are most real; with many it is only a " humble hope." But through God's mercy, I take it for granted that we have all learned this, more or less, the more the better. I do say that this is an all-important thing. Sometimes, when persons are seeking to come into fellowship, there is an idea of the importance of their understanding the church. How they are to understand the church I do not know. I did not understand it when I first began to break bread. I never saw any that did. I have seen persons that thought they did, and they had to correct their thoughts afterwards. We should not expect this knowledge. Possibly, of the saints in communion who have been in fellowship for forty years, there may be many who have not even yet arrived at a true knowledge of what the church is. But to ask it from a dear soul that has not long been saved ! Ah, that is the point—not only " converted," but brought into liberty and peace. I do say we ought to look for that before we get them to the table of the Lord; and we are not on proper Christian ground till we know that we are saved. This is what the gospel gives. It is not a hope of being saved, but knowing it in a simple straightforward, intelligent, Christian manner. However, the word "intelligence" might leave room for our active brethren to find difficulties! I do not want to put difficulties in the way of any, still less in the way of a soul that is trembling and uncertain.

The great requirement for souls seeking fellowship, and, I think, the only requirement, is that they should be settled firmly on Christ and Christ's salvation as a known present thing. Perhaps we find a person that cannot stand that. I recommend them to hear the gospel. There are plenty of saints who want to hear a full gospel. I do not say a free gospel. A full gospel does not convert many souls. A free gospel may do so. A free gospel may be used to awaken many, to cause exercise, but a full gospel will bring the answer to all these difficulties. Peter, I may say, preached a free gospel, and Paul a full one. Most of the children of God have not got a full gospel. It is essential that they should, before they can take their place as members of the body of Christ. Suppose they come in without it: perhaps the first hymn that is given out is an expression of thanksgiving that every question is settled for ever, and they are thus called to sing about themselves what they do not believe, and do not know about. They sing (in, what I call, a slipshod manner, without any conscience) what may not be true of their state, what is too much for them. Well, all that is a very unhappy state of things, and ought not to be. But if they are brought into the liberty of Christ, before they are received, not expecting from them clearness of intelligence, but knowing that their souls are set free (and nothing less than that should be looked for), then things go on happily. They learn quite fast enough when they come in, provided they have liberty in their souls. The lack of it is the barrier against learning. If I have difficulties about my soul with God for ever, it is no good to tell me about other things; and, therefore, wherever that is passed over lightly, there is a barrier. But as to everything else, well, one thing at a time is quite as much as we can bear, and people who grasp everything at the same moment, I am afraid, grasp nothing. All is apt to be cloudy in their minds, and that is not " the faith that was once delivered to the saints."

" The faith " is not a mere mist. Mysteries are not mists or clouds. Mysteries are the firmest things in the Bible. The N.T. is full of mysteries—mystery " concerning Christ and the church," " the mystery of God," " the mystery of the gospel," " the mystery of the faith." Mystery means what was not revealed in O.T. times; now it is. That is just our privilege. Even Christ Himself, in the way that we receive Him now, is a mystery. Do we simply believe on Him as the Messiah? " Great is the mystery of godliness; God [or, He Who] was manifested in flesh, was justified in Spirit, seen of angels, preached among Gentiles, believed on in [the] world, received up in glory " (1 Tim. iii. 16). This is Christ as we know Him now. Everything is mystery in Christianity, even the way Christ is received. He was not known so before. It takes in the gospel, " the gospel of our salvation," the clear riddance from all hindrances. Is not the assembly a mystery ? Is it not a truth of the greatest moment for every member of the body of Christ to know ? And when you have your convert, when the soul is there brought to know the gospel, then show him what the church is, as best you can. Take trouble with him. Do not imagine he knows what he does not know. Where is he to learn if not inside ? He will never learn by staying away. The church of God is not only the great place of incomparable blessing and enjoyment, it is also the great school. Well, the soul wants to go to school. Will he find a better school outside ?

Even the best of those who are outside—that is, those that are not gathered to the name of the Lord, they are mostly occupied about salvation for themselves, or if not that, about work for others. What can you expect better ? They do not know the relationships into which they are brought. Take the question that is now so uppermost in people's minds—priesthood. What an Evangelical would say to meet priestly pretension is, that it is all a mistake to suppose that there are any priests but Christ. Is that where you are ? The truth that God has shown us is, that all Christians alike are priests. When you are only on Evangelical ground, it is not the assertion of positive possession of privilege, it is merely denying an error, a negative way of looking at things. Many would indeed admit that we are all priests, but they do not see how it is applied. If they are all priests unto God, they should be allowed to express their praise, and others join (Heb. x. 22) " Let us " (not you, he puts himself along with those to whom he was writing—let us) draw " near " into the holiest. Were this really applied, people might want to express their audible praises to God sometimes, and this would be considered disorderly. Do you think that we are always as careful as we ought to be ? There are two words of moment in the First Epistle to the Corinthians—the first is, " in order," the other is, " to edification." All things should be done " in order," and " to edification " (1 Cor. xiv. 26, 40). How are we to judge of what is done ? It is laid down in this very chapter. Why do we forget it sometimes ?

A question was put to me, whether it is according to scripture that, at what is called an assembly meeting, or other meeting of a similar character, more than two should speak. What is laid down as to this ? That two, or at most three, might speak (1 Cor. xiv. 27, 29). Where there are more, I should be disposed to get away as fast as possible. You are mistaken about your liberty. We have only liberty to do what the Lord says ; and I can see the wisdom of this limitation. There might be plenty of time for half a dozen speakers, but still the order is clear, " two, or at most three." There can be no question about the meaning. It certainly does not mean that there might not be half a dozen prayers by different people, but that formal speaking, even of prophets, had its limits. And surely the lesser gifts have not a greater liberty than the greater ones! The prophets had the highest gift, and yet it is said, they were only to speak two or three. The plain meaning of it is that there never ought to be, under any excuse, more than two or three. Too much of a good thing is as bad as too little. If you have too much of what is even good, it is apt to make you sick : you must leave room for proper digestion. Hence the wisdom in the restriction as to numbers.

So it is—what seems to me to be so very plain—that we have not got merely the facts given and the commandment of the Lord, but good reason given. There is perfect wisdom, there is not such a thing as an arbitrary word in all the Bible. All the rules and regulations, commandments and precepts, are pregnant with divine wisdom.

It is a long while since " brethren " first began ; but there never was a time when we are more called to see whether we are really " contending earnestly for the faith once for all (not " once on a time," but, " once for all ") delivered to the saints." May God forbid that we should ever swerve in the least degree ! We are not competent to say what a little beginning of divergence may lead to. It might be apparently a little beginning, but alas, a little beginning of a great evil.

The Lord give us simple fidelity, and in all love to our brethren. I never think of my brethren being merely such as are gathered to the name of the Lord Jesus; and I feel most deeply the undermining that is going on everywhere of things that were once undisputed.

VERSE 3

JUDE, then, was in full expectation of a departure from "the faith," and that it would be necessary to defend the faith. He evidently had had it on his heart to speak to them of comforting things, things that are always bright and sweet to the believer; but the circumstances called for alarm, for solemn warning. This is never very acceptable to people. They prefer things smooth; but the apostle himself, or the writer, whether an apostle or not—the writer's whole heart would have delighted in dwelling on all that was comforting and strengthening to the soul. But, my brethren, what is the good of that if the foundations are being undermined? This is what you must look at. Therefore he draws attention to the fact that the faith was "once for all delivered." "Once" is an equivocal word. It might mean "once on a time," once at a particular moment; but this is not the force of the word here at all. It means "once for all." And what a blessing it is that we have in this book (and more particularly in the books of the New Testament), the holy deposit which we are called upon to believe, given us in full, " once for all." There is not a truth to be received that is not revealed in the word of God. There is not a difficulty nor a departure from the truth which is not in one way or another there guarded against. We, therefore, never require to go outside the revelation of God ; and this explains why God permitted, in the early apostolic days, that there should be a deal of evil. Does it surprise us that there should have been gross disorders among the Corinthians, for instance, even at the table of the Lord ? Well, one is naturally struck at first sight by such a fact. How was it that when there was such power of the Holy Ghost, that when there were miracles wrought, that when there were prophets prophesying (the highest form of teaching), that at the same time and place, the saints that gathered on the Lord's Day, broke out into a disorder that we never find even in the present day, or very rarely ? How could God more guard *us* than by allowing it then ? It is always a very delicate matter to deal with evil, either of doctrine, or practice, or service, or government, or worship, or anything that you can speak of. It was of the very greatest moment, therefore, that God, in view of the evils that would, some time or another, appear in the church, should allow the germ of the evils to appear then ; and, for this reason, that we might have divinely given directions for dealing with the evils when they did appear. Consequently, we are not taking the place of setting up to legislate ; but we are not at liberty to depart from the word. This has been given us by the Holy Ghost. We are called to find therein everything that becomes us as saints, and for every part of our work to find a principle, and example too, sufficient to guide us ; so that we may never set up any will of our own about a matter, and that we may always find God expressing, in one form or another, His will. What we have to do is to seek to learn from Him, and to apply the result, either to ourselves for our own correction, or to other people for their warning.

Now that is the reason why there is such great moment in Jude's calling to mind that the faith was " once," and " once for all," delivered to the saints. And, as a point of fact, I do not think we shall ever find in scripture such a thing as a mere repetition. Sometimes you may have scriptures that approach very closely, and in the New Testament you could hardly have it more than in these two Epistles of Peter and Jude. But I am about to point out to you, what will appear as I go along still more completely, that, while there are resemblances between these two writers, who are both speaking of the terrible evil that was about to flood the church ; and who naturally approach each other, yet there is a marked difference between them. It is always the difference that is the special lesson for us to learn. Where the two approach, it confirms. We can say, " In the mouth of two or three witnesses shall every word be established." But where there is a divergence, and a distinction is to be seen in the lessons that they convey, we have evidently more than we might have had if we had only had one of the writers. The same thing is true, not merely in these two Epistles, but in Ephesians and Colossians for example. The resemblance there is so great that a favourite theory of the Rationalists is that the Epistle to the Colossians is the only one that Paul ever wrote, and that the one to the Ephesians is only an enlarged and inflated copy (written, perhaps, by a contemporary of the apostle) ; and, accordingly, that the latter has not the same divine (though I ought not, perhaps, to use that word) value—that it has not Paul's value. These men do not believe in divine value, they do not believe in God having written these Epistles ; but some of them do believe that Paul wrote that to the Colossians, but deny his having written the one to the Ephesians. A very learned man, who translated all the Bible (and, indeed, his is one of the best of the German translations), is one of this school. So that you may learn from this, that there are persons who have laboured all through their lives on the Bible, who nevertheless did not believe the Bible—*i.e.*, really and truly. He, of course, would have entirely objected to such an account being given of him. But what matters what people object to, if it is true ! He was a leading man in his day, and I hope that he was not without looking to Christ before his decease. But at any rate, what he did during his life was a sad departure from the truth of God, from " the faith that was once for all delivered to the saints."

Having then already dwelt a little upon what is one important and primary element of " the faith," I add, further, that believers are brought into great relationships. Not only are we " converted " and " saved," being brought into peace and liberty, but we are called to realise also that we are no longer merely English persons or French, Jews or Gentiles, but that we are children of God, and that we are such now. We, therefore, turn our backs on our boasting in our nation and our city, and our family, and all these various forms of men's vanity, which is merely boasting of something of the flesh. We are called out of that now. This is also part of " the faith once delivered." In Christ there is neither Jew nor Gentile, bond nor free (Gal. iii. 28). What does this mean? It means just what I have been saying.

Well then, again, we are made members of Christ's body; and this is a relationship which so many of God's children are so slow to believe. They think and talk of their being members of the Wesleyan body, or Presbyterian body, or Baptist, of this body, or that body, no matter what it is. Well, they say, to be sure we are members of Christ's body, too! Yes, but if people valued the truth of their membership of Christ's body, what would the other be in their eyes? Simply nothing at all. Where do you find the Presbyterian body, or the Episcopal body, or the Congregational body in the N.T.? Where do you find the Baptist body in the N.T.? There was an approach to this party spirit in the very earliest days—" I am of Paul, I am of Apollos, I am of Cephas " (1 Cor. i. 12). Well, there you have the germ of it. And these germs never perish. It is not only that blessed germs of truth do not perish and are meant to take root and bear fruit, and consequently they are perpetuated here and there ; but alas, evil germs do the same. And what is more, another thing is not a germ exactly, but is a leaven— a corrupt and a corrupting thing that is very palatable, making the wheaten bread to be lighter to the taste and pleasanter for some palates to partake of. And, at any rate, this leaven, whatever may be the case with the bread, is the corrupting influence at work among the saints in two forms. In Corinth it was the corruption of morals ; in Galatia it was the corruption of doctrine. There you have it at work. When our Lord was here He confronted the same thing in the Pharisees and Sadducees. The Sadducees were the great corruptors morally ; the Pharisees were the great religionists, or rather were strong for doctrine. But the Sadducees were sapping all doctrines by denying the truth. There you have the two things again—doctrinal leaven and corrupting leaven ; at any rate there was " the leaven of the Pharisees and Sadducees," however you may describe it. There were also the Herodians—a worldly leaven, a pandering to the Roman court, not merely accepting the Romans as having power and authority from God, but trying to please them in order to make their own position better and their circumstances easier. So that you see what a very weighty truth is this, calling for earnest examination, to take care that we do not infringe upon or weaken our certainty in that faith which was " once delivered to the saints." Are we indifferent about it ? Have we an interest in it ? Have we only partially received it, and are we content with that ? Or are we resolved by the grace of God to refuse everything that is not the faith that was once for all delivered ? Are we resolved to receive and maintain that faith in all its integrity ? That is what we are called to do.

VERSES 4, 5

Now this attitude was the more important ; " for," as he says, " certain men have crept in unawares." Jude is not quite so advanced, in point of time, as John. When John wrote his First Epistle, the bad people went out—the antichrists went out (1 John ii. 19). But the danger here was that they were within. Certain men had crept in, as it were, unawares. That is, they had fair appearances at first, of course. " They, who before of old were ordained to this sentence " (" condemnation " is not exactly the meaning of the word—" to this judgment ") " ungodly men turning the grace of our God into lasciviousness and denying our only Master* and Lord Jesus Christ " (ver. 4).

This, you see, is the prominent thing in Jude's mind : so that, under fair appearances, they were undermining moral principles, they were turning the grace of God into lasciviousness. This was the worst evil, as far as morals were concerned, that Jude warns them against in this Epistle ; but then this evil is connected with a doctrinal error. They denied two things. In Peter they denied only one. There they denied the Sovereign Master that bought them (2 Pet. ii. 1). Peter does not say that they were redeemed. It is a great mistake to confound being " bought " with being " redeemed." All the world is bought, but only believers are redeemed. Universal purchase is a truth of God ; universal redemption is a falsehood. Redemption implies that we have the forgiveness of sins. You see that clearly in the Epistles. Take, for instance, that to the Ephesians, " In Whom we have redemption through His blood, the forgiveness of trespasses, according to the riches of His grace " (i. 7). Now it is clear that the great mass of mankind have not redemption through His blood ; but they are all bought, and the believer is bought too, and we are constantly exhorted on the ground, not only of our being redeemed, but of our being bought. For instance, the Corinthians are told that they were bought. That is the reason why

* Θεόν (God) though added (after "Master") by KLP 31 Syrr., is omitted by ℵABC 13 Vulg. Copt. Sah. Arm. and Æthiopic Versions.

VERSES 4, 5

they should not act as if they were their own masters. We have not any rights of our own (1 Cor. vi.). We are not at liberty to say, I think it quite right to go to a Court of Law in order to maintain my rights. No, I am bound, if I am summoned as a witness, to go ; I am bound, if people go to law with me, to go. But on the contrary, to insist on my own rights ! why do not I rather suffer wrong ? That is the way the apostle Paul looks at it. And who is the apostle ? The voice of God, the commandments of the Lord.

So that you see I come at once to the question of the faith, if really I believe what I may talk very glibly about as if I did. The difficulty is to find faith on the earth. As the Lord has said, " When the Son of man cometh, shall He find faith on the earth ? " Evidently, therefore, this departure from the faith is supposed by that very question of our Lord Jesus. Only here, the solemn thing is, that it is pressed on those who once bore the name of the Lord. They may go on for a while, for years ; and there may be only some little things that one feels here or there, or their departure may not take anything like so terrible a form as here, but the question is, Where will it end ? When once we get on the incline of our own rights, our own will ; when once we abandon His Sovereignty, and, more than that, that He is not only Sovereign Master but our Lord ; who can say what may not ensue ?

Now here we get a closer relationship. Peter, in

his Epistle, only supposes that universal place of our Lord. Why does Jude add, " denying our . . . Lord Jesus Christ " ? Because he looks at that special following of those that are called by His name—on whom the name of the Lord is called. Here, therefore, we find a subtler and a deeper denial than the denial of the Sovereign Master in Peter. That of course was very far outside and very gross—" sects of perdition, and denying the Sovereign Master that bought them." But here, in Jude, it is not only denying the Sovereign Master of the world, of everything ; but " our Lord," the One to Whom we belong, the One to Whose name we are baptised, the One Whom we profess to value and acknowledge to be our life and righteousness, and our all—denying Him !

You must not imagine that these things all come out in a short time. There is a little beginning of departure ; but when your back is turned to the Lord and you follow that path, where will it end ? No man can tell ; but the Spirit of God can and does, and He shows that these little departures end in a fearful ditch of the enemy ; and so He says :

" But I would remind you, though once for all knowing all things*, that [the] Lord having saved a people out of Egypt's land, in the second place destroyed those that believed not " (ver. 5). Here we have again the same word " once," which as we

* πάντα (all things) ℵABC² 13 Vulg. Copt. Syr. Arm. and Æthiop. Vv. instead of τοῦτο (this) KL 31 and Sah. Version.

have already seen is equivocal. It might mean formerly; but that is not the meaning at all, no more than that the faith was formerly given. It means given " once for all."

Well, he says, " once for all knowing," not only " this," but " all about it." The word " this " is now in critical texts changed into " all things," and this is exactly the position of the believer, which is the reason why we are so very responsible. Do you recollect what the apostle John says to the " babes " of the family ? " Ye have an unction from the Holy One, and ye know all things " (1 John ii. 20). How did that come to pass ? We are not in the habit of regarding babes so wise as this ; yet what the apostle says must be true. The only question is—In what sense did he mean that they knew all things ? I think the meaning is this. The babe has got Christ just as much as an apostle. Having Christ, he has the truth—all the truth. There it is ; and he has also got the Holy Ghost—an unction from the Holy One. Therefore, he has got power in the gift of the Holy Ghost ; for a babe has this gift. It is not the privilege only of the advanced learners in the school of Christ. The babes of the family of God have got Christ perfectly. They may draw it out very imperfectly. They may be able to look upon Christ, and speak of Christ in very hesitating terms as far as their intelligence goes, but such is their place and their privilege. Accordingly, Jude presses here their privilege of " once for all knowing all things."

Where were they now? They were in great danger. You often see this in the early beginnings of saints. They are very bright at first; they are not easily stumbled by anything they hear from the Bible; they receive it with simplicity, and delight in it. They, then, are knowing all things, in the sense in which the apostle speaks here. It is not a question of intelligence, but of simplicity and of a single eye, and when the eye is single the whole body is full of light. Thus they had it by the power of the Spirit of God, and it was not at all a question of their being great adepts in controversy, or showing a wonderful knowledge of the types, or anything of that kind. I call that intelligence. But this is the singleness of eye that looks to Christ and sees the truth in Christ, and is not troubled by the difficulties that people are always apt to feel when they begin to reason, when love gets cold and they have questions of duty. Then they cannot see clearly; then a trial is made on their faith to which it is not equal; then they begin to get dark, as well as to doubt. This is just where these saints appear to me to have been, whom the writer is here addressing as "once knowing all things." They knew not only the faith, but these terrible things that are coming in.

However, Jude recalls them to their remembrance: "I will therefore put you in remembrance, though once for all knowing all things, how that [the] Lord, having saved a people out of [the] land of Egypt, afterward destroyed them that believed not."

That fact is a very solemn thing for the writer to bring before them; and it was meant to solemnize them, to deliver them from that careless state of soul which takes for granted that, because we have all been so blessed and led into the truth, no harm can happen. Why, on the contrary, beloved friends, for whom do you think Satan has the greatest hatred out of all on the face of the earth? Why, any that are following the Lord with simplicity; any that are truly devoted to the Lord. His great object is to try and stumble such, to turn them aside, to bring difficulties into their minds and make them hesitate. Now, where souls are simple and single-eyed, they have not these difficulties at all; but when they do not go on cleaving to the Lord with full purpose of heart, they begin to forget what they once knew. It is no longer Christ applied to judge everything here; they allow their own thoughts, their own feelings, their own mind, their own conceit, perhaps to lead them; but, whatever it is, it is not Christ, and now He brings this fact before them. Why, look at the history that you have in the very beginning of the Old Testament. God had a people once before us, and, what is more, God saved that people. That is the very thing—He did save them. It was not only that He passed over them in the land of Egypt, but there was His mighty arm at the Red Sea that crushed their enemies and saved themselves, and brought them into the desert that He might teach them what was in their heart, and let them know what was in His. But they went back to Egypt in their heart, and they could see no blessedness in Canaan, the heavenly land to which the Lord was leading them on—to Canaan, type of heaven, the land of God's delight and glory; they could see nothing in it, and they did see that in the desert there were serpents sometimes to bite those that refused to learn from God; and, further, that the Lord, if He hearkened to their lusting after flesh, made the flesh to come out of them as it were through their nostrils, as a judgment upon their not being satisfied with the manna, the bread of heaven. All these things happened, and what was the result? All perished in the wilderness excepting two men: Caleb and Joshua.

Now Jude says, That is your danger. You must remember that you cannot tell for certain whether a person has life eternal. Every man ought to know that for himself; every woman ought to know that for herself. If a person believes that he or she has life eternal in Christ, they are called to follow the Lord with full purpose of heart. And if they do not follow Him so, or if attracted by anything worldly, or by pursuits of their own from day to day, they neglect the Lord and His word, and neglect prayer and all the helps that the Lord gives us, which we so deeply need for our souls—what will be the end of that? Just what Jude is showing them here: " I will therefore put you in remembrance, though ye once knew all things, how that the Lord having saved a people out of the land of Egypt, afterwards destroyed them that believed not."

It turned out that they were not true believers, after all. The same thing applies now: " These things happened unto them for types ; and they are written for our admonition."

VERSES 6–8

" AND angels which kept not their own original estate, but abandoned their proper dwelling, He hath kept in everlasting bonds under gloom unto [the] great day's judgment ; as Sodom and Gomorrah and the cities around them, having in the like manner with them greedily committed fornication and gone after strange flesh, lie there an example, undergoing judgment of eternal fire. Yet likewise, these dreamers also defile flesh, and set at nought lordship and rail at dignities " (vers. 6–8.)

If we compare this chapter of Jude with the Second Epistle of Peter, we get a very clear view of the precise difference between the two. No doubt there is a great deal that is common in both Epistles ; but it is the difference that is of great account in taking a view of scripture, as has been already observed. In these two Epistles there may be many points in common, but the two accounts are thoroughly different. The same thing is true as regards all the testimony that God gives us. The marks of difference are the great criteria.

You will notice that Peter, after alluding to false teachers, alludes to "sects of perdition" (2 Pet. ii. 1). The word heterodoxy gives a different idea. There was something of this difference in the minds of the apostles that ought to be in ours, viz. :—a very strong horror of the breach amongst those who belong to Christ and the church that He formed in unity here. There is a certain wilfulness that is particularly offensive to God. People now have so little sense of "wrongness" that they think it a natural thing that people should be justified in doing what they like; but to look at the matter in that sense would be to give up God. Perhaps men can be trusted in matters of ordinary life to form a sufficiently sound judgment as regards certain things, such as being careful of their food and careful of their dress, and also as regards other things that belong to this life. We find that God says little on the matter, except to guard His children from the vanity of the world and the pride of life. Still there is nothing technical or narrow laid down in the word of God. But it is quite another thing, when we consider that Christ died to "gather together into one the children of God that were scattered abroad" (John xi. 52), that we should allow ourselves to extenuate a wilful departure from the right course, by allowing our own notions to carry us away therefrom. Persons should not allow themselves to do this kind of thing, nor should they think that they are superior to others, which is generally a great delusion on their part. You will not find that men who are devoted to Christ set themselves up in this way, because we all know that Christ teaches us to count others better than ourselves. That may become merely a foolish sentiment by the separating us from a spirit of power and of love, and of a sound mind. We are to judge of everything by Christ. If we let in "self," we are sure to go wrong. This readiness to see Christ in everything is a happy thing when it is applied to our dealings with our brothers and sisters. It is not that others *are* necessarily better than ourselves, it is that we are to count them so in our spirit and in our dealings with them. When Christ is before us, we can afford to judge our sins as stronger than those of others. We are well aware of our faults; but it is only when we are much occupied with others' doings that we know much about their faults. The great thing is that we are to see Christ as our guide, and we are to judge ourselves in ourselves; we are also to see Christ in others and to love them, and to count them better than ourselves.

There are other senses in which people get into this spirit of sect, and thereby give an improper value to certain views. For instance, with regard to baptism. In modern times, at any rate, and very likely also in ancient times, there is, I suppose, hardly anything that has troubled the church more than this subject. By some people, a superstitious value is given to baptism, causing them, as it were, to despise those who have a reasoning turn of mind, and those who have a strong theory and notions about the Jewish remnant ; but, so far as I know, the Jewish remnant has nothing to do with Christian baptism, because the handing it over to the Jewish remnant means giving up *our* relation to Christ. For Christian people, who are already walking in the ways of the Lord, to be occupied with baptism is, in my opinion, a most extraordinary inversion of all that is wise and right, because Christian people have passed through that experience already. Perhaps, when the ceremony was performed it was not done in the best way, and we may think that, therefore, if we had known then what we know now we might have been more careful in its performance. Baptism is merely an external visible confession of the Lord Jesus, and for persons who have been confessing the Lord for twenty, thirty, or forty years, to be occupied with baptism seems to me to be an extraordinary change from all that is wise. Baptism is an initiatory step ; our Christianity begins when we begin our Christian confession—we should, therefore, be going forward, not backward.

Baptism has even been used as the badge of a sect, and time would fail to narrate the many other ways in this regard. But here, in Peter's Epistle, we have a darker thing referred to—" sects of perdition " (2 Pet. ii. 1). It evidently was not merely a sect, but a sect of perdition. In this case, the sect of perdition was evidently something very dreadful, and it was apparently against the Lord, because the words are "denying the Sovereign Master that bought them." This, as we have already remarked, is not "redemption" but "purchase," and so takes in all men whether converted or not. It is the denial of His rights over all as the Sovereign Master. So, too, Peter begins at once with the flood, the deluge, but there is not a word about that in Jude. This is another great mark of difference to note, the manner in which the denial of the Lord is described, and how we find God's mode of dealing with this matter. So one sees the propriety of the flood being brought in by Peter, because it was the universal unrighteousness and rebelliousness of the whole world. Jude, on the other hand, was not given to look at that particularly, but at the hostility that is shown to the truth and to Christ. Peter looks at the general unrighteousness of mankind, and so he says: "For if God spared not angels when they sinned, but cast them down to lowest hell and delivered them up to chains of gloom reserved for judgment, and spared not an ancient world, but preserved Noah, an eighth [person], a preacher of righteousness, having brought a flood upon a world of ungodly ones; and reducing to ashes [the] cities of Sodom and Gomorrah, He condemned [them] with an overthrow, having set an example to those that should live ungodly; and rescued just Lot" etc. (2 Pet. ii. 4–7).

What makes the reference again more remarkable

is that Jude speaks of the " angels that kept not their own estate," but Peter of " angels that sinned," and who consequently come under the dealing of God. The flood is upon the world of the ungodly, and the cities of Sodom and Gomorrah are turned into ashes for an example to those that should live ungodily; but just Lot was delivered because he was a just man. The want of righteousness brought this punishment upon everyone. It is their general ungodliness, but no doubt there is a particularity which Jude takes up, whilst Peter takes up the universality. This is the marked difference between the two. I have dwelt upon this because it shows what the world of modern unbelief is—what is called higher criticism. For these men have been struck by the resemblance between this Epistle of Jude and the Second Epistle of Peter; but with all their boasting of unbelief they have not got the discernment to see that there is a marked difference between the two. These men have been caught by the superficial resemblance of the two Epistles; but when you, as it were, lift up the superficial veil in which these Epistles agree, you will find that the colours are different. You will find darker colours in Jude than in Peter, although it is bad enough in Peter, most terribly evil. But it is of a general kind; whereas, Jude was led by the Holy Ghost to devote himself to the peculiar form that wickedness takes when it turns from the grace of God, when it turns to licentiousness.

Hence Jude begins with what is not referred to in Peter at all, and it is for this reason that I read verse 5 over a second time to-night. " I will, therefore, put you in remembrance, though once for all knowing all things, that the Lord, having saved a people "—mark that—" out of the land of Egypt "—that is the sovereign grace that shows the salvation. I am not speaking of it now as eternal salvation. It was sovereign grace that chose Israel; they were not chosen for everlasting glory, but only delivered out of Egypt. That surely shows a manifestation of God's goodness, Who, instead of allowing them to be oppressed and terrorised over by the cruel Egyptians, smote the Egyptians and delivered His people. They came into the narrower circle in one sense of what were God's people, in one sense also they were saved; but they gave up the grace, they abandoned God. This latter is what Jude has particularly in view. He looks at Christendom as being about to abandon the truth. He shows that whatever the special favour shown by God, men will get away from and deny it; and further, that instead of using grace to walk morally, they will take advantage of grace to allow of a kind of immorality—they will turn the grace of God into licentiousness.

Peter says nothing about this, but Jude does; so that it is evident that these learned men (who think they are so clever in showing that Jude and Peter are merely imitators of one another, and that it is the same thing in substance in both—that there is no particular difference, that they are in fact the same human picture), do not see God in either. Now, what we are entitled to is to see God in both Epistles, and what is more we should hear God's voice in both. You see then that Jude begins with this solemn fact that the Lord " having saved a people out of the land of Egypt "—I am giving now the strict force of the word—" the second time " (that He acted) " destroyed those that believed not." The first act was that He " saved " them, He brought them out by means of the paschal lamb, which was His first great act of " saving." The first time that God's glory appeared and He put Himself at the head of His people, He saved them out of the land of Egypt. What was " the second time " ? When He " destroyed " them. It is not vague, but it specifically mentions " the second time " ; this is the great point. At the time the golden calf was set up, that was the beginning of " the second time," and God went on smiting and smiting until everyone was destroyed except Caleb and Joshua. That was the second time. This went on for forty years, but it is all brought together in the words " the second time." God " destroyed them that believed not." That is the charge brought against them. Their carcases were falling in the wilderness. In Hebrews iii. (as is very evident also in the book of Numbers and elsewhere) there is this threat during their passage through the wilderness. It is one of the great facts of the books of Moses. As regards those that came out of Egypt, they came under the hand of God; some perished at one time, some at another, but all perished in one way or the other, until all disappeared ; and yet they had all been " saved " out of the land of Egypt by the Lord.

Oh, what a solemn thing to set this before us now ! When I say before us, I mean before the church of God, before all that bear the name of the Lord Jesus here below. This is put expressly as a sample of the solemn ways of God to be recollected in Christendom. Then Jude also refers to the angels. I think the wisdom of that is evident. Peter begins with the angels and then goes on to refer to the flood. I think, therefore, if any person looks at Genesis vi. he will find a great deal of wisdom in Jude's reference. I am well aware, of course, that there are many that view " the sons of God " in a very different way to what it appears to me. They are sometimes very surprised, and expect one to be able to answer all their questions. I do not assume any such competency. I admire the wisdom of God in that God does not stop to explain. He feels the awful iniquity of what occurred in reference to these angels. They are fallen angels, and of quite a different class to those who fell before Adam was tempted.

It appears there were at least two falls of angels ; one was he whom we call Satan—when man was made, Satan tempted man through Eve. Those ordinary evil angels, of which we read in the Bible from Genesis down to Revelation, are not under everlasting chains at all. They are roving about the world continually, and so far from being in chains of darkness, in " tortures " as it is called here, they are allowed access to heaven. You will see that in a very marvellous way in the history of Job. A great many believers do not believe in the book of Job. You will see there " the sons of God " referred to. What is meant by " the sons of God " there ? Why, the angels of God. The angels of God appeared before God. We learn from this that they have access, and include not only the good angels but also the Satanic angels. Satan was a fallen angel, but still he was an angel, and when " the sons of God " came, Satan was there too. So that it is evident, from the Book of Revelation more particularly, that Satan will not lose that access to the presence of God until we are actually in heaven. It has not come to pass yet. People have an extraordinary idea in their heads that whatever access Satan had before that time, he lost it—either when our Lord was born, or when our Lord died—but there is nothing of this in the Epistle to the Ephesians, where, on the contrary, it is expressly stated that our wrestling is not against flesh and blood, but against wicked spirits in the heavenlies. We are not like the Israelites fighting against Canaanites. Our Canaanite is a spiritual enemy in heavenly places, that is, Satan and his host of demons or angels.

But, as we have seen, these are not at all the sins that are referred to here. There is a marked difference. There is a character of iniquity that these angels fell into on earth, and so a distinct difference in their doom. These angels fell into a very peculiar iniquity, which is in a general way spoken of in Peter, but in a special way in Jude. They were put under chains of darkness and not allowed to stir out of their prison. They are not the angels that tempt us now. They did their bad work just a little time before the flood. That fact gives the matter a very solemn character. If people want to know how it was done, that I do not know; but you are called upon to believe, just as much as I am. What Genesis vi. does say is that there were " sons of God " upon earth at that time who acted in a way contrary to everything in relation to God, and which was so offensive to Him that He would not allow the earth to go on any longer, and this is what brought on the flood. No doubt too there was also a general iniquity in mankind that brought the flood upon them. Man was very corrupt and man was vile, but besides that there was this awful violation of the marks that divide the creatures of God in some mysterious manner. Hence God completely destroyed the whole framework of creation, and put an end to them and their offspring, so that every one of them perished. That is what took place then. Of course, you will tell me that they could not perish absolutely. No, I admit that these angels could not perish any more than men such as you; but this is what God did with those angels that behaved in that tremendously wicked manner. They became prisoners, they were put under confinement, not like Satan and his host that tempt us to this day, but these particular angels were not allowed to tempt men any more. They had done too much, and God would not allow these things to go on any longer, therefore there was this mighty interference at the time of the flood, and not only the things that generally inflict men. These are the words, " Angels that kept not their first estate." Their falling was a departure from their first estate. In this very case Satan had not done so, nor had the angels that fell with Satan. But it was quite another kind of iniquity that caused the flood. These angels left their own habitation and preferred to take their place among mankind to act as if they were men on earth, and accordingly, God has now reserved them in everlasting chains under darkness until the judgment of the great day. Nobody can say that this is true of Satan and his host, but if people should think this, I do not see how they can read these verses and give such a meaning to them. Satan will be cast into the bottomless pit for a thousand years, but their years do not run out until the judgment of the great day comes. Then they will be judged everlastingly.

What makes the matter so striking is that Jude compares this conduct, and this awful opposition to all the landmarks that divide angels from mankind, with Sodom and Gomorrah. We know that the enormity of this wickedness exceeded that even of all wicked people. So here their sin brings them into juxtaposition with Sodom and Gomorrah, " Even as Sodom and Gomorrah and the cities about them in like manner to these, giving themselves over to fornication and going after strange flesh, are set forth for an example, suffering vengeance of eternal fire " (ver. 7).

When we come back to Peter and see what he has to say on this matter, it is, " For if God spared not the angels that sinned." Peter does not go further than that. Of course we know how they sinned— that is what Jude looks into. But here in Peter it is general—" angels that sinned." He cast them down into hell and darkness, but that description does not apply to Satan and his host. Therefore it seems there were two different falls of angels ; one, Satan and his followers mounting up in the pride of their hearts to God, the other, these angels sinking down in the wickedness of their heart to man, to man in a very low condition indeed. The difference therefore is most marked. God " delivered them unto chains of darkness to be reserved to judgment, and spared not the old world." There is a connection between the two narratives, as it is about the same time. Peter marks this very point, and puts it along with God's dealing with the angels. This however is entirely left out by Jude. Peter says, " And spared not the old world, but saved Noah, the eighth [person]."

How is Noah described? As "a preacher of righteousness." Noah was not a preacher of grace. The grand truth that Noah proclaimed was that God was going to destroy the world by the deluge. That was exactly the right message. I do not think we are entitled to say he said nothing more, but the characteristic of Noah was that he was "a preacher of righteousness." This is precisely what occurs in Peter; he does not bring out the grace of God at all, in his chapter. He is thundering at unrighteousness. He is giving with that trumpet of righteousness a very clear sound indeed. He is evidently giving out, in very dark and solemn words, the destruction that shall await the wicked at the great change; and he shows that the same thing has happened before, and he begins, as far as man is concerned, not with Israel saved out of Egypt by God, but looks at the whole world destroyed. He is looking at the universality of unrighteousness, and not at the gradual departure of the people that were saved, saved first and lost afterwards. " He saved Noah, bringing in the flood upon the world of the ungodly." Peter then looks at the cities of the plain—more particularly Sodom and Gomorrah. He does not say anything about the special iniquity, but looks at it in a general way. " And turning the cities of Sodom and Gomorrah into ashes, condemned [them] with an overthrow, making [them] an ensample unto those that after should live ungodlily; and delivered just Lot vexed with the filthy conversation of the wicked. For that righteous man dwelling among them, in seeing and hearing, vexed his righteous soul from day to day with their unlawful deeds " (2 Pet. ii. 4–8).

So that instead of these two Epistles being alike, one of them a mere replica of the other, and an imitation in a clumsy way, they are both marked by most peculiarly different characteristics. And this is what deludes some men with all their criticism, and all the doctrine of the working of mind and the reasoning of rationalism is entirely outside the mark. Man's mind sees certain things in a general outside way and reasons upon it, flattering himself that he is doing something wonderful, and that he is bringing light when he is only spreading mist over the precious word of God, nothing but mist and darkness. So that the general difference between the two Epistles is very marked indeed.

Well then, we come now to the bearing of Peter's words upon the present time. " The Lord knoweth how to deliver the godly out of temptations, and to reserve the unjust unto the day of judgment to be punished." That is the practical testimony coming out of it. " But chiefly them that walk after the flesh in the lust of uncleanness, and despise government." It is not, you observe, simply corruptness. No, it is the larger view that is looked at. What would apply to Mahommedanism would apply to Judaism, would apply to heathenism, and would also apply to Christendom. The analogy is, that this particular form of evil requires a particular form of discipline, and that the world will be destroyed not by water but by fire from God in heaven. That is what I think is referred to by the " overthrow," and the reason of it ; " whereas angels, which are greater in power and might, bring not railing accusation against them before the Lord " (2 Pet. ii. 9–11).

But when we come to Jude, it is a great deal closer than all this. What he says is, " Likewise also these dreamers." I do not know any reason for putting in the word " filthy." You will see the word is in italics. There is a great deal of wickedness where there is nothing wrong in word. It is only in the idea, there may be nothing offensive, yet it is sapping and undermining all that is precious in those people who live in the imagination of their own hearts instead of being guided by the word of God. Why ? Because the word of God is an expression of God's authority, and His will is the only thing that ought to guide us, as well as all mankind. If that is true of man because he is the creature of God, how much more is it true of those whom He has begotten by the word of truth ! These latter are therefore called more particularly to heed and learn the word of God. I do not know anything of more practical importance than that. If I were to give, in one word, in what all practical Christianity consists, I should say—obedience ; and that obedience is entirely one of faith, not law. It is characterised in quite another way by Peter, " obedience of Jesus Christ," (1 Pet. i. 2) not obedience of Adam. Adam's obedience was that he was not to touch that particular tree, but now that God has revealed His will we are bound by that revealed will. To him that knoweth to do good and doeth it not, to him it is sin. It is not merely you must not do anything wrong in all those ways of men which show how far their heart is from God, but " to him that knoweth to do good and doeth it not, to him it is sin." Talk about James being legal! obedience is his peculiar grace. He is the very one that speaks about " the law of liberty." The law of Moses was the law of bondage ; it was purposely to convict man of sin which he had in his nature, to crush all self-righteousness out of him. Whereas what James speaks of is the exercise of a new life that God's grace gives us, and of the love that Christ has revealed that we should be after the pattern of Christ. What was the difference between Christ's obedience and the Israelite's obedience ? The Israelite's was, Thou shalt not do this or that. But this is not what Christ says. Of course, Christ never did anything that was wrong. Christ was pleasing to God in every act of His life, in every feeling of His soul, in all that constituted walking with God here below. This is exactly what we are called here to do. This is what Peter means when he says, " Elect according to foreknowledge of God the Father through sanctification (or, in virtue of sanctification) of the Spirit unto obedience, and sprinkling of the blood, of Jesus Christ " (1 Pet. i. 1, 2).

The sprinkling is the sprinkling of the blood of

Jesus, and the reference is to Exodus xxiv., where Moses takes the book of the law and sprinkles it with blood, and he sprinkles the people too with blood; everything being thus brought under death. It was the great mark of death having its sway. The book and the people were sprinkled with the blood shed, meaning death to any who failed to obey that book. Now the Christian in a way stands totally contrasted with that; when he is converted his first desire is to do the will of God. When Saul of Tarsus was smitten down, his first words as a converted man were, " Lord, what wilt Thou have me to do ? " And this is what occurs even before we get peace. It is so with every converted person. His first desire is to do the will of God. He very little knows himself. He does not know how weak he is. He has got a bad nature counteracting him, but he has yet to learn the operation of the new nature that is in him. How does that new nature come ? By receiving the word of revealed grace. I do not say the work of Christ the Saviour, because Saul knew very well that he knew nothing; but mercy and goodness struck him down and gave him a new nature that he once railed at. Paul knew Christ was saving him, but he did not know that we have to learn, not only the word of God, but the experimental way of finding our need of it. It is not only the Saviour that we want, but the mighty work that abolishes all our sins, and brings us to God in perfect peace and liberty through the redemption of the Lord Jesus.

It is not only that I am born again ; that I am going to be saved by and by, but saved now. This is the proper meaning of the Christian dispensation that produces this desire even before I know that the blood of Christ is screening me entirely. I want to obey as Christ obeyed, not merely to do something like the Jew, but I am doing it now because this nature in me impels me to do it. It is the instinct of the new man. We have a great deal to learn about our utter weakness, and, consequently, about the need of deliverance. So we are elect unto the obedience of Christ, and are sprinkled with the blood of Jesus, which gives us the comfortable assurance that our sins are clean gone. Hence the difference is very plain.

Now these " dreamers " referred to, lived in the imagination of their own hearts, and the New Testament is used to help these men very much indeed. When the New Testament is taken up by the natural mind, they proclaim what is called Christian Socialism, which sets up a standard of the gospel and dictates to everybody. You have no right to this large property ! You have no right to these privileges that you assume ! I am as good as you, and better too ! This is the style these men take up with regard to the New Testament, thereby entirely twisting the word in order to gain advantages to themselves and to deny all the truth. It is really dreaming about what ought to be, according to their mind, and to claim everything that they covet from those that are in a dignified position in the world—" likewise also these dreamers defile the flesh, despise dominion and speak evil of dignities." They defile the flesh by what they convert scripture to. They consider themselves the equals of all, and not only so, but speak evil of dignities, so that there is evidently no fear of God before their eyes at all. And this shows that there is something very lamentable in the perversion of the gospel, the perversion of the New Testament. It is their own bad and selfish purpose that causes them to do this. The whole principle of the New Testament is this : what those that are of Christ do. Well, they feel according to Christ. What is that ? Why, it is the principle of love that gives, that does not seek its own. Do you think these kind of men have any idea of giving? They only talk about other people giving. So this is all dreaming, as it is called here. Very justly Jude launches out into these strong terms, " Likewise also these dreamers defile the flesh, despise dominion, and speak evil of dignities."

VERSE 9

" BUT Michael the archangel, when contending with the devil he disputed about the body of Moses, durst not bring against him a railing accusation, but said, The Lord rebuke thee " (ver. 9).

The verse now before us presents one ground of exception taken against the Epistle by men who trust themselves. This introduction of Michael the archangel seems to them altogether inexplicable, as they consider it a mere tradition of the Jews reproduced by Jude or at any rate by one who wrote the Epistle bearing his name ; for they really do not know or care who wrote it. Only nobody must believe that Jude wrote it ! Such talk consists simply of the objections of unbelief, which, doubting all that is inspired of God, sets itself to shake the confidence of those who do believe.

Although it is a fact presented in no other part of God's word, what solid reason is there in that to object ? There is ground for thankfulness that He makes it known here.

Not a few statements may be traced in scripture, which have been given but a single mention ; but they are just as certain as any others which are repeatedly named. The apostle Paul, in 1 Cor. vi. 3, declares that the saints shall judge angels. It is not only that they shall judge the world, which no doubt is a truth revealed elsewhere ; but it is there expressly said that they are to judge angels. I am not aware of any other scripture which intimates a destiny that most would consider strange if not incredible. We do find that the world to come is not to be put under angels ; but that is a different thing. It does assure us that the habitable earth is to be put under the Lord Jesus in that day ; and the saints are to reign with Him. To the risen saints will be given to share His royal authority ; for that is the meaning here of " judging." It has nothing at all to do with Christ's final award of man. It is not a small mistake to suppose that the saints will exercise the final judgment over men or angels. All such judgment is exclusively given to the Son of man (John v. 22, 27 ; Rev. xx.).

When it is said that we shall judge the world, the meaning is plain whether men believe or not. Such judging is to exercise the highest power and authority over the world by the will of God and for the glory of the Lord Jesus. But there is no warrant for the notion that saints will take part in the great white throne judgment. On that throne sits only One, He that knows every secret, that searches the reins and hearts ; and He is the sole Judge when it is a question of judging man in the day when God will judge the secrets of men by Jesus Christ, according to Paul's gospel. No man was ever given to fathom the lives of others ; nor am I aware that we shall ever be called to share that knowledge so essential to the Judge of quick and dead.

In fact, the notion that we are to sit in judgment on people for eternity is a gross and groundless blunder, for which there is no shadow of proof in any part of scripture. But we shall judge the world when the world-kingdom of our Lord and of His Christ is come. He will reign for ever ; and so shall we, as His word assures ; but there is a special display of this joint reign, and this is during the thousand years. This, of course, is no question of eternal judgment, but of the kingdom; whereas, when the earth and the heaven flee, and no place is found for them, eternal judgment follows, and none but the Lord judges. All judgment is given to Him, when the works of men, who despised Him throughout the sad annals of time, come up for His eternal sentence. No assessors are associated with Him; He alone is the Judge.

There remains, however, the plain revelation that we shall judge angels. If this is confined to that one scripture, be it so; one clear word of God is as sure as a thousand. If we have to do with the witness of man, the word of a thousand, if they are decent people, must naturally have a weight beyond one man's. But here it is no question of men at all. What we stand upon, and the only thing that gives us firmness of ground and elevation above all mist, the only thing that gives us faith, reverence, simplicity, and humility, is God's word. It is indeed a wonderful mercy, in a world of unbelief, truly to say, I believe God; to bow before, and rest in, the testimony of God; to have perfect confidence in what God has not only said, but written expressly to arrest, exercise, and inform our hearts.

Assuredly, if God says a thing once unmistakably, it is as certain as if it had pleased Him to say it many times. Indeed, as it appears to me, it will be found that God hardly ever repeats the same thing. There is a shade of difference in the different forms that God takes for communicating truth. Such is one of its great beauties, though quite lost to unbelievers, because they listen to His words in a vague and uncertain manner. As they never appropriate, so they never hear God in it. They may think of Paul or Peter, John or James, and flatter themselves to be quite as good or perhaps better. What is there in all this but man's exalting himself to his own debasement? He sinks morally every time he lifts himself up proudly against God and His word.

Here then we have a fact about the unseen world communicated, not in the days of Moses or Joshua, when the burial of Moses is brought before us. Here Jude writes many years after Christ, and first mentions it. Why should this appear strange? The right moment was come for God's good pleasure to communicate it.

Did not the apostle Paul first give us in his last Epistle the names of the Egyptian magicians who opposed Moses before Pharaoh? No doubt we were told of such magicians; but we did not know their names till the Second Epistle to Timothy was written. Scripture can only be resolved into the will of God. It pleases God to exercise His entire sovereignty in this, and He would therein show Paul given to write of a thing reserved for him to bring out alone. So here we have the Holy Ghost proving His power and wisdom in recalling a mysterious fact at the close of Moses' life. Why should men doubt what is so easy for God to make known?

Is there anything too wonderful for His grace?

Is not He Who works in revealing, God's eternal Spirit ? And why should not He, if He see fit, reserve the names for that day when Paul wrote ? The occasion was the growth of deceivers in Christendom—a thing that many seem disposed to entirely overlook. They yield to the amiable fancy that such an evil is impossible, especially among the brethren ! But why so ? Surely such impressions are not only stupid in the highest degree, but unbelieving too. It ought to be evident that, if anywhere on the face of the earth Satan would work mischief, it is exactly among such as stand for God's word and Spirit. Where superstition is tolerated, and rationalism reigns, he has already gained ruinous advantage over the religious and the profane. If any on the face of the earth at the present time refute both these hateful yet imposing errors, his spite must be against them. The reason is plain. We have no confidence in the flesh, but in the Lord ; and to that one Name we are gathered for all we boast, leaning only on His word and the Spirit of God.

Let these then be our Jachin and Boaz, the two pillars of God's house, even in a day of ruin and scattering. Let us rejoice to be despised for the truth's sake. How can we expect to have any other feelings excited towards us ? Do we not tell everybody that the church is a wreck outwardly ? And do they not say on the contrary that the church bids fair for reunion ? that the classes and the masses are alike won by grand buildings, rites, ceremonies, music, and the like ? that there is on the one side inflexible antiquity for those who venerate the past, but on the other side the device of development to flatter the hopeful and self-confident ? Then think of the modern influx of gold and silver, of which the apostolic church was so short ! Is it not God now giving it to His church that they may in time buy up the world ! And if any tell them that all such vaunts are only among the proofs of the church's utter ruin, what can they be but hateful and obnoxious in their eyes ? Christ has always a path for the saints, a way of truth, love, and holiness for the darkest day of ruin, as much as for any other. It is for the eye single to Him and the ear that heeds His word to find the path, narrow as it is, but its lines fallen in pleasant places and a goodly heritage. But if we, hankering after earthly things, entangle ourselves with man's thoughts or the world's ways in religion, what can this issue be but that we help on the ruin ? Disturbed, uneasy and unhappy we become, like Samson with his hair cut, weak as water, and blind to boot.

Nor is it at all unaccountable that men are busy against an Epistle which is one of the loudest and clearest in the trumpet blast that is blown against Christendom. For it expressly lays down that departure from the truth, and the turning God's grace to licentiousness, are to go on till judgment thereon—not that there may not be such as are faithful and true, keeping themselves in the love of God, and building themselves up on that most holy faith that was once for all delivered to the saints. What can be conceived more remote from men's new inventions? from the vain restlessness which is ever in quest of some fresh effort? From everything of the sort we are bound to keep clear, as being deadly. It is not only from all tampering with bad ways, or false doctrine, but from humanising on what is divine. To this we are bound by the very nature of Christianity, which calls us to entire dependence upon the word and Spirit of God. It is not for us then, to be asking what is the wrong of this? or what harm is there in that? For the believer the true question is, What saith the scripture? How is it written?

It is written here: " But Michael the archangel, when, contending with the devil, he disputed about the body of Moses, durst not bring against him a railing accusation, but said, The Lord rebuke thee " (ver. 9). Here, then, is a grand truth, taught in a striking and powerful manner. The apostle Peter, in the 2nd chapter of his Second Epistle, is said to give exactly the same thing as Jude, but he says not one word about it. He makes no allusion to Michael the archangel. He speaks in verse 4 of angels that sinned, whom God did not spare. But Jude presents it as the angels that kept not their first estate. This clearly has nothing to do with Michael. The reference to the archangel is entirely peculiar to Jude; and the object is to exhibit the spirit that becomes one who acts for God, even in dealing with His worst enemy, that there be no meeting evil with evil, nor reviling with reviling, but on the contrary immediate and confessed reference to God.

What makes it all the more surprising is the power vouchsafed to Michael. He is the angel whom God will employ to overthrow the devil from his evil eminence by-and-by (Rev. xii.). But here the historical intimation given is entirely in character with the future. You may tell me that Rev. xii. was not revealed to Jude, who wrote this. Be it so, yet the same God that wrought by Jude wrought also by John. It is evident from the two scriptures that the antagonism between Michael and the devil is not a truth foreign to God's word. There we have it in the written word. It is the truth of God. Jude was given to tell us what God moved Jude to write, which has not only great moral value for any time, but gives us the fact, full of interest, that the antagonism between Michael the archangel and the devil is not merely of the future. Here the proof lies before us that it wrought also in the past. Thus we can look back fifteen hundred years, and there behold the evidence of this contention between the devil and the archangel. Do you say that it was about the body of Moses, and what is that to anyone? Can we not readily enter into the importance of that dispute? Can we not understand the bearing of that question, when we hold in mind all the history of Israel in the wilderness, as given in Exodus and Numbers?

There is nothing more common among the prophets than this, that while during their lifetime they were hated, after they were dead and gone they became objects of the highest honour; and, what is so remarkable, the highest honour to the same class of people that hated them. They became not objects of honour so much to other people, but were honoured by the same unbelieving class that could not endure the prophets' words when they were alive. They are ready to kill the prophetic messenger when living, and all but worship him when he is dead. Well, it is the same unbelief that acts in both ways; which, when he was alive, scouted the word of God come through him, and condemned and hated him, but when he was dead, and no longer, therefore, a living character to puncture their conscience, the very people who had war with the prophet would build a fine monument to his memory; and so, getting the character of being men who had a great regard for the prophet, men, therefore, that were doing their best for religion, they gave their money to have erected a fine monument, or to have a fine statue made, or as grand a picture as they could pay for! So true it is, the flesh is quite remarkable for being ready to honour a man when he is dead and gone, whom it could not endure when alive. Our Lord drew attention to this very characteristic. It is not an idea of mine at all, it is the truth of God. Our Lord lays this down most strongly against the Jewish people ; and it is not at all confined to Jewish people. If you go now to the town of Bedford—to take an instance from our own country—there you will find a fine monument to John Bunyan, who, when alive, was scouted, imprisoned, and regarded as a presumptuous, bad man. The very same class of people now buy his book, and at any rate are not sorry that the children should read it along with the *Arabian Nights' Entertainments* in the nursery. So there they have the *Pilgrim's Progress* and the *Arabian Nights'* tales, and they are all considered equally entertaining for the children. They thereby show that they think the imprisoned tinker was a genius— for that is their way of looking at it ; and therefore they gain for themselves credit in all sorts of ways, both as being men of taste, and also as men not at all averse to religion when it does not touch their conscience. The thing, therefore, that I am speaking of is always true and always will be true till the Lord come, and then there will be no such thing as " the vile person called liberal, nor the churl said to be bountiful," nor, on the other hand, the unjust treated as righteous. Then there will be righteousness reigning, and everything and everyone will find their level according to God.

Now we all know from the account given of Moses, both in Exodus and Numbers, how constantly the children of Israel were contending with him, murmuring against him, speaking evil of him—hating Moses, really, and Aaron too. And it was only the power of God interfering every now and then that alarmed them, and cut them down, and compelled them at any rate to pay outward respect. But directly he was dead, the same devil that stirred them up against Moses when he was alive—oh, what would he not have given for that dead body ! The dead body would have been made a relic. You know very well that this is a favourite idea of men—the dead body would have been an object of worship. The devil would, therefore, have gained doubly. First, by setting them at war with him while alive, and still more when he was dead by making them idolaters of Moses. So that we can easily understand why it was that the Lord buried the body Himself. But it appears that before he was buried, there was this contention between Michael the archangel and the devil about Moses' dead body ; so perfectly in keeping with the mysterious manner in which Jehovah buried him where none should know, and where even if Satan was allowed to know, God interfered that Michael should guard that grave, that Michael should hinder all the efforts of the devil to get hold of that dead body. So we have the two facts : what is here told us by Jude, and the fact of the xxxivth of Deuteronomy, where we have the account of the Lord's burying Moses—which He never did for any other man. Show me only a single case of the Lord's burying any one. I do not remember one but that of Moses, and there were special reasons why Jehovah should secretly bury that dead body rather than any other.

There never was a man that exercised so remarkable a position towards a whole people as Moses did to the children of Israel, and now that he was gone, a reaction would take place under the devil, not in the least a reaction of faith, but of unbelief, to idolise that very body, the same man whom they continually plagued while living.

So that the fact, here brought before us, goes along with another fact to which I have just now referred in the Old Testament (the two perfectly tally), *viz.*—that there were special reasons in the case of Moses' dead body why the Lord should interfere. Now we learn from this passage in Jude a further very interesting fact, not about the Lord, but about the enemy and the one whom Jehovah thought proper to use. Now, there are others of great weight in heaven besides Michael. Gabriel stands in the presence of God, and, as we know, he was employed for a very important mission by God. It was not Michael, but Gabriel very particularly, who was used in announcing the birth of our Lord Jesus, and we can perfectly understand why Gabriel should be then employed rather than Michael. Michael is the prince that stands up for the Jewish people. Yes, but the Gospel of Luke shows the Lord Jesus born of woman, not merely for the Jewish people, but for man—" God's good pleasure in men," not merely in Jews: and therefore it is not that particular angel, Michael; he was not employed on that occasion. So that it appears to me that there was divine wisdom in Gabriel being employed on that mission rather than Michael; and that this is true will surely be very evident to anyone who reads the xth and xiith chapters of the book of Daniel. I just refer to it now because of its importance in showing the harmony of scripture, and that even in a most extraordinary event that is only once recorded. It shows principles of divine truth that support, and fall in, and harmonise, with what was only revealed once. This is what I wish to show now.

Well, in the latter part of the xth chapter of Daniel (indeed as well the xith chapter), ver. 20, we read, " Then said he " (this is the angel that had to do with Daniel), " Knowest thou wherefore I come unto thee ? and now will I return to fight with the prince of Persia." There you see that it is not quite an unusual thing for angels to contend. Here we have it in still stronger language: " To fight with the prince of Persia: and when I am gone forth, lo, the prince of Grecia shall come."

Now, we shall find a little intimation who and what these princes were in the next verse: " But I will show thee that which is noted in the scripture of truth: and there is none that holdeth with me in these things, but Michael your prince."

We learn here that Michael was pre-eminently the

prince of Israel. In what sense? Not as reigning visibly, but as invisibly espousing the cause of the Jewish people. Now see how this falls in with Michael's guarding the dead body of Moses, with his being employed by God to contend with the great enemy, so that there should be no misuse made of that dead body. Who had so pre-eminently this duty as the prince of Israel? And as to the angel that was speaking with Daniel, of whom we read a good deal in the previous part of the chapter in so highly interesting a manner and in the most glowing colours—he says, " there is none that holdeth with me in these things"—that is, in opposing the princes of Grecia and Persia. Why? It appears that the princes of Grecia and Persia were not favourable to the Jewish people. In the same way, they had interests connected with Greece and Persia that were opposed to the Jewish people ; and in the providence of God the angels are referred to here—angels are the great instruments of providence, the unseen working of God being carried out instrumentally by angels.

This is true now. We are all very much cared for by the angels, more than we are apt to think. We read of them in Hebrews (chap. i. 14) : " Are they not all ministering spirits, sent forth to minister for them who shall be heirs of salvation ? " So we are indebted to angels now. I do not say it is Michael or Gabriel, but I do say that the angels are acting a special part at this present time in Christianity for all the heirs of salvation. You see that at this time, in Daniel, it was not so much a question about the heirs of salvation; it was a question of the Jewish people. They were the great object of God's care in their fallen estate. They had been most guilty, but they were beloved. They were carried into captivity by the Babylonian power. And they were going to be the slaves of other powers on the earth; but for all that Michael stood up for them and this other angel who speaks to the prophet Daniel. There were also other angels that were opposed, whom they had to fight.

Well, people may say that it is all very mysterious. Indeed it is, dear brethren. It is not, therefore, incredible, but of very great moment, that we should have our hearts and minds open to believe what we do not see. There is nothing that adds more to the simplicity of a believer than his having his faith exercised upon the things that are unseen as well as those that are eternal, and we ought to feel our indebtedness to God for these things.

Now, if you want a proof even in detail as to this, take the viiith chapter of the Acts of the Apostles. There you find that the angel tells Philip to go in a certain direction, and he does so; and then we find the Spirit speaks. Not the angel, but the Spirit. I had better refer to it, because there is nothing like the scripture for its precision. Now, in Acts viii. 26 we read: " And the angel of the Lord spake unto Philip, saying, Arise and go toward the south unto the way that goeth down from Jerusalem unto Gaza, which is desert." There were two roads, it appears. One was through a populous part of the land, and the other was desert. Well, a desert is not the place an evangelist would choose. The angel, therefore, acting in the providence of God, says to Philip: "You go that desert road." And it is one of the beautiful features of Philip that he was not a reasoner. Reason is an excellent thing for men who have not got the word of God, and I do not say that there may not be useful reasoning outside divine things, what you may call common sense. But I do say this, that the more the believer can act on divine principles at all times, the better for his soul, and the more to the praise of the Lord. If he is sometimes acting, like a man of the world, on his common sense, and at another time acting on the word of God as a believer, he is in danger of being practically two different persons. And when a man plays the game of two personalities he is very apt to become a hypocrite; there will be a want of reality about the man. We ought only to have one personality. We are bought with a price, not merely for our religious matters, but for everything. We do not belong to ourselves, we are the Lord's; and, therefore, the more a believer can rise above merely what he will do as a man to that which he loves to do as a saint— the more entirely he keeps to this only, so much the more consistent is he with his profession as a child of God. For why should it not be so? What is to hinder his being a saint in anything at all? Cannot he be a saint when serving in his shop? Cannot he be a saint when in his office? Surely he might, and ought to be. There is nothing to hinder, if he were lively in faith and has the Lord before him. But if, on the contrary, he only looks at the shop or the office—" Well, now," he says, " it is not Sunday, nor is it the meeting now; I go there as a man." So there it is. How can he expect anything like faith, or grace, care for Christ and His glory, if that is the case? I deny entirely that we may not be servants of Christ in the commonest things of this life; and this is what, I think, we have all especially to pray for. Of course, we need to pray that we may behave as saints when we come into the assembly, and when we find ourselves at a meeting of any kind; but why we should be off our saintship when we go into business or anything else is another matter, and a very dangerous line to pursue.

Now then, here you see that we have the angel of the Lord providentially dealing with Philip, and Philip acts upon it at once. He does not say, " Ah, I shall not be able to get a congregation, and at any rate I don't like a little one; I want to have a big one." He has not a word about little or big; in fact, he was not going to have a congregation. He must be content with one single soul. That soul is precious beyond all calculation to God, if not even to himself. What would all the world be to one if the soul were lost, as the Lord Himself told men, and which they still refuse to believe?

Well then, the angel gives Philip this word, and he hears, and goes without a question. But when he was there—in this road, " this way that goeth down from Jerusalem "—here this Ethiopian stranger in his chariot was met, returning from Jerusalem, and reading the prophet Isaiah. He was not now going up to Jerusalem to get a blessing there. He may have looked for and prayed for that, but he did not get it there. He was returning from Jerusalem unblest, going away from that city, and this was just what the gospel was doing. It was leaving Jerusalem, driven out by unbelief, and this poor Jewish proselyte was going away unblest by the gospel in that city, for he had not found a blessing there. There was a persecution going on there against it. And now, returning, he was reading in his chariot. " Then the Spirit said unto Philip, Go near and join thyself to this chariot." Now, why is it the Spirit here? Because it was what concerned the word of God and the soul. The angel said not a word about the soul of the Ethiopian. I do not know that the angel knew anything about it. The angel had to do the bidding of God, " Tell that man to go by the road that is a desert." He acted on it; the angel was right, and Philip was right, but it was entirely providential. And then comes the spiritual part, and here the Holy Ghost interposes.

Well, we have not now the angel speaking and the

Holy Ghost speaking, but we have the angels acting. We may not perhaps know how it is, but an angel interposes many a time to prevent us going in a certain way, when, if there had not been that interposition, we should have been killed. We often go where we had no intention of going, or do not go where we meant to go. When I say "often," I mean sometimes; throughout our whole lives it would really bear the word "often." But there is no man but what does from time to time what he never intended to do, perhaps through an impulse given him—he cannot tell how or why—and he goes this way, when he meant to have gone that way.

Here, however, we find that there is another kind of guidance of a more spiritual nature for the soul, prompting (so to speak) the soul to give a word for the Lord. Do you suppose there is no such thing now? Such an idea may be for people who do not believe that the Holy Ghost is come, and that to abide; but He is still here. It is put in Acts viii. in an open objective form, but it is meant to teach us that the same thing is true now, although it does not come out openly in the same manner. It is quite true, and this is not the only case. If you compare the xiith chapter of the Acts with the xiiith, you will see an angel acting in the one chapter and the Spirit acting in the next. I only mention it because the Acts of the Apostles is surely a history of Christianity, a history of Christians, of what Christians have been used for, and what they are meant to live in. Well, then, here, when it was not a question of Christians or the gospel, but of nations and people, we find the part that the angels play—not merely the holy ones, but the unholy ones. This is the very thing that we find at the grave of Moses, and about that same people, Israel. Michael is the prince who stands up for them opposing the efforts of the enemy against them; and this entirely confirms the principles of God's word. They are entirely in favour of this extraordinary revelation made in the 9th verse of Jude, and they are found to support and confirm it in the highest degree.

Now, before we go further, I refer to another scripture in Zechariah iii. There we have a very interesting removal of the veil that we may see the unseen. We read these words: " And he showed me " (that is, the angel showed Zechariah) " Joshua the high priest standing before the angel of Jehovah, and Satan standing at his right hand to resist him " (ver. 1). There you have the same opposition again. In this case, however, it is the " angel of Jehovah." I should be disposed to distinguish him from Michael. The " angel of Jehovah " is an altogether peculiar term. The angel of Jehovah is rather the way in which the Lord Jesus is referred to in the Old Testament—not the only way, but a very usual way. The angel of Jehovah every now and then is shown to be Jehovah Himself. I do not mean that He is the only person that is Jehovah. As we read in

Deut. vi. 4, " Jehovah our God is one Jehovah," that is, it is Father, Son and Holy Spirit, Who are the one God that we acknowledge as Christians. They are all three Jehovah, they are all equally Jehovah, and it therefore helps us to understand why He is viewed as " the Angel of Jehovah." He is Jehovah too, though not the only One that is called Jehovah. This explains what we have here : " He showed me Joshua the high priest standing before the angel of Jehovah, and Satan standing at his right hand to resist him. And Jehovah " (notice that after speaking of " the angel of Jehovah " it is now " Jehovah ")—" And Jehovah said unto Satan, Jehovah rebuke thee, O Satan "—the very words that Michael uses to Satan as reported by Jude !

Well, is not this a very strong confirmation, not only of this remarkable opposition between the holy angels and the unholy ones, but also of Satan's opposition ? We find this antagonism in both scriptures, precisely alike. Even Jehovah Himself, instead of merely taunting Satan, says " Jehovah rebuke thee." The time was not yet for the most terrible rebuke to come, as it will unmistakably when he shall be trodden under foot. He has to be bound for a thousand years in the abyss ; he has to be cast into the lake of fire. All these will be part of the ways in which Jehovah will rebuke him, but till that time arrives we see how God meanwhile guards His own purpose ; He does not allow Satan to interfere with His design. He allows man to show out his insensibility and his sin, and He chastises him. He does not yet put forth His power to deal with Satan as He will do ; but there is that word, " Jehovah rebuke thee," as He surely will. It is a continual warning from Jehovah, which will be accomplished in its own day, and in various places and various stages. But you can easily see that it would be unseemly to have a mere dispute going on between Jehovah and Satan ; and all, therefore, that He puts forth is this solemn warning of what is coming.

Well, the angel repeats that warning to Satan in a very early day, and here, a thousand years after, you have the same truth, the same antagonism even, if not the same persons exactly ; but the same spirit all through.

Scripture is perfectly consistent, perfectly reliable. And although Jude was the first one that brought out this fact, it falls in with the other facts of scripture : both in the early days of Moses, in the later of Zechariah, and now in the days of the gospel, in the days of Christianity.

So that nothing can be more complete than the proof that these learned critics are totally ignorant of God, totally ignorant of the Bible, except of the mere surface, the mere letter that kills, and know not the spirit that quickens.

Well, here then you see how beautiful it is that instead of bringing a railing accusation, Michael simply warned Satan with the solemn words :

" Jehovah rebuke thee "—" The Lord rebuke thee." What would railing do ? If there are two people railing, a good and a bad man, and the bad man's railing provokes the good man to rail, the good man goes down to the level of the bad. It does not at all diminish the railing of the other. I should think at any time that a bad man could gain a good degree over the good man in the way of railing. Surely he is much more practised, and very likely more unscrupulous and more malicious, and therefore it sounds stronger to the ear of man. But, you see, that would be a total lowering of even an angel, and how much more of a saint, I might say. Here we have the beautiful conduct of the angel as a pattern to the saint, that we be not provoked, nor, when we are reviled, revile again, but act as the Lord Himself acted. He committed Himself to Him that judgeth righteously. Well, that is what Jehovah will do ; He will judge righteously, but the time is not yet come for its manifestation.

VERSES 10–13

" BUT these rail at whatever things they know not ; but whatever they understand naturally, as the irrational animals, in these things they corrupt themselves (or, perish). Woe unto them ! because they went in the way of Cain, and rushed greedily into the error of Balaam's hire, and perished in the gainsaying of Korah " (vers. 10, 11).

" But these speak evil "—referring now to the persons who, notwithstanding that they had been baptised and had taken their place in the church, were now yielding to every form of corruption, were abandoning the very things that they professed. I do not say that they were outside. This is the difference between Jude and John. When we come down to John's Epistle they went out; but the corrupting thing in Jude is that there they are poisoning others.

Now it is remarkable that in the Second Epistle of Peter we have only Balaam, and Michael we have not at all; so that nothing can be more superficial than the idea that the one writer has copied the other. It is true that there is much that is common to both Epistles, but the *differences* between Jude and Peter are the striking thing; the points of resemblance are easily accounted for. In the position in which Jude and Peter were, there must have been the closest friendship, and a very near companionship; and there must have been strong links of love between these two elder servants of the Lord. Would they not communicate their thoughts and judgments to each other, even if they are looked at as servants of God? This is nothing, therefore, at all surprising. Nothing more likely than that Peter should communicate a good deal to Jude, and, on the other hand, that Jude should communicate a good deal to Peter; and, besides, the Spirit of God giving them to look at the same, or kindred evil, would give them similar judgments and thoughts. You find that in people who have never met or spoken to one another, if they have to do with the same evil, they often say things very much alike; substantially alike they are sure to be, if guided by the Spirit of God, but there are often surprising verbal resemblances. But this is not where the beauty and the striking nature of the two Epistles of Jude and of Second Peter show themselves. It is in the differences between them.

Now Peter is particularly occupied with wicked teachers—men that privily brought in, what he calls, "heresies," or sects. The word "heresy" in scripture means "a sect." It never means heterodoxy, as we use the word in its modern sense. That is not the scriptural sense at all. No doubt in the sect there might be heterodoxy, and there might be a sect without heterodoxies, or there might be one with a great deal of heterodoxy. So that "sect" admits of all kinds, or shades, of evil and error; but Peter is looking particularly at false teachers, and these false teachers covetous men; greed of gain is one marked feature which he specifies. Well now, where could you get an Old Testament example of greed so marked as Balaam? Consequently, we find Balaam in Peter, just where it should be. It falls in entirely with his purport, and with that Second Epistle and second chapter.

But here, Jude, in this very much shorter Epistle— and far more compact, far more compressed, and far more vehement—writes as in a tempest of hatred of all these bad men. Indeed, I do not know stronger language. Some do not like strong language. But that should entirely depend upon how it is used. Strong language against what is good is infamous, but against what is bad is thoroughly right; and I do not know stronger language anywhere than in this very Epistle of Jude in which he speaks out against railing. But strong language and railing are not the same thing. Railing is abuse of what is good; but here we have the pithiest, the most vehement, and most cutting exposure of what is evil; and instead of this being a thing to regret, it is a thing that we ought to feel and go along with heartily. But I know it does not suit the present age. The present age is an age for trying to think that there is nothing so good but what there is bad in it, and nothing so bad but what there is good in it. The consequence is that all moral power is at a deadlock, and people have no real, burning love for what is good—only a calm, quiet, lukewarm state. They are neither strong for good nor strong against evil; and that is a state which, I believe, the Lord hates—at any rate, it does not agree with either Peter or Jude.

"Woe unto them! because they went in the way of Cain, and rushed greedily into the error of Balaam's hire, and perished in the gainsaying of Korah." In the Epistle of Peter there is not a word about Cain, not a word about Korah. But here you see that Jude, having a different object, compresses in this most wonderful verse—for it is a most wonderful verse—an amount of moral truth, spiritual truth, divine truth, that was here entirely departed from, grace being altogether hated and abused. All this is found in this short verse. He goes up to Cain.

"These are spots (or, hidden rocks) in your love-feasts, feasting together, fearlessly pasturing themselves; clouds without water, carried along by winds; autumnal trees without fruit, twice dead, rooted up; raging sea-waves, foaming out their own shames; wandering stars for whom hath been reserved the gloom of darkness for ever" (vers. 12, 13).

I cannot conceive any but an inspired man venturing to use such decided and solemn language about those that were within the church. That is a marked point of the Epistle. Peter looks at the unrighteousness of man generally, even since Christianity is come, because he is occupied simply with iniquity. This of course is common to both writers; but Jude looks specially at those who took the place of salvation, those that were gathered to the name of the Lord. In this latter case, therefore, the matter had yet more seriousness for the spiritual mind. There is nothing more dangerous than a departure from the faith, the Christian faith. It is not only what man is and has done, but also what grace has made known, for which we are responsible, most of all if we turn from it in unbelief. What is so evil as apostasy?

There are many things that cause truth to lose its power with men. Nothing hastens it more than moral disorder in ourselves, which results from forgetting or abusing grace. We turn our backs on God's authority, as well as our relation to our Lord Jesus; this is followed by our taking up objects that are loved so as to become practically our idols. It is clear that these things have been substantially so from the beginning, as it is also clear from this Epistle that things will go on worse and worse, until the Lord comes in judgment. As to this point we shall have to weigh what is yet stronger than what we have already considered, when it will be ours to seek a divine impression of the words already read. Manifestly they are of the darkest character and full of energy.

Observe here the word, "Woe." I do not know it anywhere in the New Testament except in the very different application which the apostle makes to himself, if he did not make the glad tidings known (1 Cor. ix. 16). Here it is, "Woe unto them." I am not of course speaking of the Gospels, but of the Epistles; where the Spirit of God is testifying of the Saviour and His work to man, or dealing with those who bear the Lord's name. In the Gospels, even our Lord could not but say, "Woe"; but then He was warning those that represented a favoured nation, which was then through unbelief passing under divine judgment. The same One Who began His ministry with Blessed, blessed, blessed, ended it with Woe, woe, woe! Nothing was further from His heart than to pronounce that sentence, but as He said, so was He to execute it in due time. He pronounced it as a Prophet when on the earth, if peradventure they might take it to heart, and He will pronounce it as a Judge on the great white throne when heaven and earth pass away.

What, then, is the explanation of this utterance of Paul, " Woe unto me if I preach not the gospel " ? Paul, who had been a poor deluded soul, by the grace of God had a fearful warning to do His will in preaching, but he does not say " Woe " to them, like Jude. He might have had his great fears for some when he let the Corinthians know how possible it was for a man who preached the gospel nevertheless to become a reprobate (1 Cor. ix. 27). I think there is no doubt that that word " reprobate " means one lost; because salvation does not go with preaching, it goes with believing; and it is quite possible for those who preach to destroy the faith which once they preached. We have known that ourselves from time to time, and it has always been so. But the apostle had such a solemn sense of his responsibility to proclaim the gospel to perishing souls everywhere, that " Woe unto me if I preach not the gospel." Yet he preached it in the spirit of grace beyond any man that ever lived.

Here, however, in Jude it is a very different case. "Woe unto them," he says, "for they have gone in the way of Cain, and run greedily after the error of Balaam for reward, and perished in the gainsaying of Korah."

It is a most remarkable picture of the history of Christendom on its blackest side. There cannot be anything more graphic. It is not the mere order of history. If it were the order of history then the error of Balaam would be put last. It is a moral order, the order of men's souls. It is what presented itself to the apostle in the Holy Ghost. Jude begins with the first root of what is wrong, and I think he is referring to a man (Cain) that ought to be a brother in affection, and who ought to have been a holy brother, because he took the place of being a worshipper. Cain brought his offering to Jehovah, and it was that very bringing of his offering to Jehovah that brought out his wickedness. How little people know what may be the turning-point of ruin for their souls! Cain no doubt went forward with confidence and with a step of assurance in his offering of fine fruit and other productions of the earth that he had cultivated, no doubt, with care. We may be sure he had chosen the very best because *man* would not fail in that. A man of the world is often very careful indeed as to outward appearances. Cain sees nothing defective in the offering itself—in the materials that composed the offering; but there was this vital defect which completely ruined him, that there was no faith. There is no mention of either God on the one hand, which must be, nor, on the other hand, was there any judgment of his own sinfulness. He failed therefore completely as to the inner man, for God never calls upon men who put on any *appearance* before Him. This is what was done here; perhaps no great depth of it, but still Cain took the place of a worshipper and he brought his offering to Jehovah, with no consciousness of his own ruin by sin, nor of God's grace, or of the need of it. But that was not all.

On the same occasion, Abel brought his offering, which was acceptable; his offering was of the first-born of the flock. Not only was it blood that he offered, the acknowledgment of the necessity of death, and of the Saviour to meet his sins, but there was also the sense of the excellency of the Saviour before God—he brought " of the fat thereof." Consequently there was a most decided effect in the case of Abel when he brought his offering before God. His very name shows what was very true of his character, no confidence in himself, for the word " Abel " refers to that which passes away like smoke, whereas " Cain " has the signification of " acquisition," very much like the word " gain " in our language. Abel was a man entirely dependent upon grace, upon the Seed of the woman of whom he had no doubt heard over and over again from both father and mother, with other truths which he had never forgotten. God took care that these truths should be most prominent from the very earliest day, but it made no impression on Cain, and the reason was because he had never judged himself before God, and had no sense of his real need whatever. The opposite of all this was true of Abel, and his offering Jehovah accepted. This at once drew out the character of Cain; plain enough before to God, but it now came out openly in his hatred of his brother. What had his brother done to arouse that wickedness? You may be sure that the general character produced by faith in Abel had shown itself in every way of tender affection to his elder brother; but Cain could not brook that God should accept Abel and his offering, and not look at Cain's. Nevertheless God deigned to expostulate with him and his lack of faith, in order to save him, if it could be, from what his wicked heart was rushing into. But no; Cain failed both before God and man, and what is more, before his brother. Now this is the first great beginning of the ruin of Christendom, and this showed itself in early days. We find such a thing quite common in our own days. We cannot doubt but that there was a powerful impression made on the world by the new life and ways of real Christians; yet there always were persons who have not only no sympathy with God's love, but who even despise it, and who are irritated by it, more especially if they are dealt with faithfully by those that know it. This is another reason why our minds are blinded towards our brothers. There comes a still worse feeling towards God, but this order was reversed in Cain's case. In the root of the matter, I suppose that all evil feeling towards one another springs from a previous feeling towards God. Our feeling in the presence of God breaks out in the presence of one another. Certainly this was the case with Cain.

Here we find the first woe. " Woe unto them ! for they have gone in the way of Cain." It is a departure from faith, it is a departure from love, it is a departure from righteousness. It was the spirit of a worldly man, and therefore he was the first man who began open worldliness. Before that time there was great simplicity. It would be very untrue to say that there was the least of what was savage in Adam and Eve. There was everything that was sweet and beautiful in what God gave them ; but still there were not the delights of civilisation, there was none of those things that people seem particularly to enjoy in modern times. It cannot be wise to disguise from our eyes that the progress of worldliness is enormous. I do not doubt that all the recent discoveries of gold and silver have greatly added both to the covetousness of men, and the desire for " display " one before another according to their means ; whereas Christianity has nothing at all to do with " means " ; it has everything to do with faith. If we care to do so there is always a use for what God gives, that is, to use it to His glory ; but to turn it all to a selfish account, or to a display before others, is a mere vulgar kind of selfishness. This is the kind of thing that we find in Cain. There were, of course, the pleasures of stringed and wind instruments from the very beginning of civic life, and there was also then the beauty of poetry, which began, no doubt, rather poorly. It was all man, and man's reasoning. This is all man's enjoyment, and it is practically very much what we have at the present day. No doubt many things have been invented since the early times. There is always development in human things, and there is our development in divine things, but there is no obedience in development. There is nothing divine in development, but there *is* obedience in doing what the Lord sets before us in His word ; yet the moment you add to that word in any way, or take away from it, it is the reverse of God's teaching. It is setting up to be wiser than God, and this we can do without His power. All this idea that we can do something that will do His work better is the work of unbelief, and is an idea destructive of a Christian's peace, and destructive of the simple principle of obedience contained in the word of God. Oh, what a privilege it is to own and teach this principle ! to hear and do His will ! We are always learners, and should we not always be coming to a better knowledge of the word by faith ? Where there is not faith we do not come to this knowledge.

However, we see in the case of Cain a very fit

and proper beginning of the woe that is coming on and the terrible sin that calls for the woe. Now the solemn thing is that it also refers to the present time. Evil never dies out, but gets darker and more opposed to God—becomes more hardened against God, without the least compunction of conscience.

Taking events out of mere historical order so as to make them exactly suit the truth, we have, as the next thing, the case of Balaam. The incident which brought out the nature of Balaam and the fact of his being a typical enemy of God is a further sample of what was to be in Christendom. This was when he uttered the most glorious truths ; and I suppose, they were the only truths which he had ever uttered in his life. Well, Balaam was drawn to curse Israel, and he was induced to do so by the offers of gold and silver and honour of every kind. And I will even say that he tried to make out that he did not care for money ; he said he was entirely above such a paltry consideration. The sin of Balaam is a very solemn thing. He went out to sin, he went out to meet (as our translators have put it) Jehovah—to " meet the Lord," but there was nothing of " the Lord " in it, the words being merely added (Num. xxiii. 15). The fact is, he went to meet the devil, whom he had been accustomed to meet. He went out to seek enchantment—that is the devil, of course. Our translators have put in " the Lord " (Jehovah), but the fact is it was the enemy of the Lord, the source of all Balaam's wickedness and wicked power. Balaam knew that it was a divine power that compelled him to speak about what he had no thought of speaking about; but when he did so, his vast capacity for eloquence went along with his speaking.

God did not refuse to allow this man's mind to be displayed. This is the way in which God sometimes works by all the writers He employs. The man must be uncommonly dull not to see a difference of style in comparing the different books of the Bible. If it were merely the Spirit of God it would be the same style in all, but it is the Spirit of God causing a man to bring out the truth of God and to give it out with that style and feeling which should justly accompany it. So in the case of Balaam: although he was much moved by the thought of dying the death of the righteous, yet there was not one single working of his soul in communion with God. He was the enemy of God, and the one who came to curse the Israel of God, but he was compelled to give utterance to most glorious predictions. The wonderful effusions of this wicked prophet glorified the coming of the Lord Jesus. There is something of that kind now in Christendom. Sometimes the most wicked of men can preach eloquently, and what is extraordinary too, God has often used the words of unconverted men for the conversion of others. I have no doubt that this is the case at the present time, and it has always been so. Of course, it is altogether one of the side features of ruin.

The normal manner is for those that are saved to be the messengers of salvation to others.

The error of Balaam was that he was the willing instrument of the devil to destroy Israel, and as he could not curse them he did not give it up, yet it was a vain attempt to do so. Jehovah turned it into a blessing. Balaam thought to employ the women of Moab to draw the Israelites after idolatry. He could not turn Jehovah away from Israel, so he tried to turn Israel away from Jehovah. I have no doubt a great many souls throughout Christendom have been converted by these utterances of Balaam. Balaam's eyes were fixed upon Israel—he wanted to damage them; they were the people he hated, they were the persons he wished to bring down, they were the persons he maligned and misrepresented with all his might, but he did not know that they were the people of Jehovah. But God knew.

Then with regard to Moses and Aaron: Moses represented God, and Aaron represented the intercession of the grace of God; but Korah would not submit to such a thing for a moment (Num. xvi.). In the case of Korah, what makes it the more atrocious is that he had a very honourable place; he belonged to the highest rank of the Levites, to that honoured section of the Levites to which Moses had belonged. Moses had first the call of God, Who lifted him up, beyond all question; but Korah belonged to the most honoured of the three families of the Levites who were servants or ministers of the sanctuary, and, as I have said, Korah belonged to the highest of the Levites; but nothing satisfied him. Why? Because he hated that Moses should have a place that belonged to him beyond any other. Satan blinded his eyes, which he always does so that people may feel like this. Korah's object was to achieve what pertained only to Moses and Aaron. There are always many good reasons for bad things, and the reasons sound well, but they are words that strike at God and at Christ. There was a punishment not only of Korah but also of his family, other Levites, and all their families. And the earth opened her mouth and swallowed them up in a way that had never happened on any other occasion since the world began. There may have been something resembling it, as in the case of Sodom and Gomorrha, where it rained fire and brimstone and consumed the wicked, but the converse was the case here. The earth opened and swallowed them up. We find further a remarkable thing: the children of Korah were not consumed. He was the leader of the rebellion against Jehovah, but God in the midst of His judgment showed mercy to the sons. They did not perish through the plague that afterwards set in amongst the congregation. These sons of Korah are referred to in the Psalms, for there is the fact recorded that there are "the sons of Korah," and the right persons to sing such psalms. Well, all these things perish that do not depend upon the grace of God—things like the error of Korah, things that war against God, that cause all those uprisings of falsehood. I think all such things such as the Oxford movement, are wrong. I do not mean the Ritualistic one only, which is extremely vulgar. But what is the error of the Oxford movement? It is very nearly the same error as Korah's. Korah wanted to be priest as well as minister. That kind of thing is what men are doing now who maintain that they are sacrificing priests. It is true that the sacrifice is a perfect absurdity: the sacrifice is the bread and the wine. How could this be a sacrifice? If they called it an offering it would be a better term; but they not only call it a sacrifice, but they fully believe that Christ personally enters the bread and the wine. Therefore they are bound to worship the "elements," as they call it. Such an idea is lower than heathenism, for the heathens never *eat* their God. These men are sanctimonious and exceedingly devoted to the poor. Yes, and they are most zealous in attending their churches, and in attending to their monstrous developments. This is of the same character .as that described with reference to Korah. But the only sense in which these men should preach is when they become really sons of God, redeemed Christians, because that is the only sense in which they will be received; but all this false doctrine of the Oxford School denies that all Christians are priests, and infringes and overthrows the real work of Christ, and substitutes this continual sacrifice, which is a sin. So that no wonder Jude says, " Woe unto them ! for they have gone in the way of Cain, and run greedily after the error of Balaam for reward, and perished in the gainsaying of Korah."

Then note the tremendous words that follow : " These are spots in your love-feasts." Think of it. There were such men at that time in the church. Therefore we ought never to be surprised at anything evil that may break out in the world ; the only thing is for believers to fight the good fight of faith. There is another rendering—" Hidden rocks in your love-feasts, feasting together, fearlessly pasturing themselves ; clouds " they are, and it should be noted they are " without water," without the real work of the Spirit of God, the rich refreshment of it—" carried along by winds." As I said before, I will not deny that God may use any person in a solemn way which is thought to be a good deal of honour in the priesthood, but it is deadly work for themselves who preach. " Autumnal trees without fruit, twice dead, rooted up ; raging waves of the sea foaming out their own shames : wandering stars for whom hath been reserved the gloom of darkness for ever."

May God preserve His saints, and may we by watchfulness and prayer be carried safely through such dangers as these.

VERSES 14, 15

" AND Enoch, seventh from Adam, prophesied also as to these, saying, Behold, [the] Lord came amid His holy myriads, to execute judgment against all, and to convict all the ungodly [of them] of all their works of ungodliness which they ungodlily wrought, and of all the hard things which ungodly sinners spoke against him " (vers. 14, 15).

This is a remarkable utterance, for which we can only account as being in the power of the Holy Ghost.

There is a traditional book of Enoch in the Ethiopic language, which appears to have been known in a Greek form now long lost. We have not got the Greek, but learned men have endeavoured with all possible zeal to try and make out that Jude quotes from this uninspired book; for the book is evidently one of Jewish tradition, and from internal evidence it would seem that it was written after the destruction of Jerusalem. But there is another thing that appears, I think, to anyone that reads it with, not merely learning, but with spiritual understanding, which is, that it differs essentially in this very verse, supposed by some to be quoted from it, from what Jude has here given us by the Spirit of God.

But how was Jude enabled to quote the words of Enoch, who was taken up to heaven before the flood—and nothing can be plainer than that he does give it as Enoch's words? " Enoch prophesied," he says. Well, I think that to us who know the power of the Spirit of God there is no real difficulty in the matter. It is all the same to Him to record what took place three thousand years ago as it would be to record what took place at the time the apostles lived. It may be a little more difficult to those who doubt this power, if they do; but we are the last who ought to do so.

The fact is, that no tradition has any value beyond man, but a prophecy necessarily, if it is a true one, comes from God. We have no intimation that it was conveyed in any written form, and it was quite possible for the Holy Ghost to have given it again to Jude. I do not at all venture to say that it was so; we really do not know, but we do know, however Jude got it, that it is divine. We know that it is given with absolute certainty, and that it possesses God's authority.

There is a peculiarity when it says, " Enoch also, the seventh from Adam." People have made somewhat of that because they do not understand it. But it is very simple. There was more than one Enoch.

There was an Enoch before this one—an Enoch the son of Cain. I do not see any ground to imagine something peculiar and mystical in this. At any rate, if there be such, I confess I do not know what it is. But I do know that there is a plain and sufficient sense to distinguish this Enoch, and to explain how he could prophesy. We should not look for prophecy in a son of Cain. But that Enoch taken up to heaven in a most remarkable way—more so, in some respects, than the case of any other man; more so than Elijah, though that was a miracle of similar import and character—that Enoch should be the medium of prophecy we can quite understand, for he walked with God, and was not. It was not that he died, but "he was not," because he was taken up to God; yet before he left the world, he prophesied. We can hardly doubt that he prophesied about the people of his own day. Prophecy always takes its start from what is actually present, and has a hold in the consciences of those then living. The object was to warn of the terrible consequences of evil that was persisted in, and how the evil then appearing would assuredly be judged of God in due time. But the Spirit of God also launches out to the end from the beginning. This is the common character of all prophecy. We find it throughout all the prophets at any rate. I do not, of course, say that it was always the case where the prediction was about something of a merely present nature, but it was so in the cases of those moral pictures which are not bound to any particular time or person. We can quite understand these being made the vehicle for the Spirit of God to look on to the time of judgment when it would not be providential action of the Lord, such as the flood, for instance, but—much more than any acting after that figurative manner—His real personal coming in judgment.

Now, in that Ethiopic book which I have seen, and of which I have the text and English translation by the late Archbishop Laurence, as well as a French version of the work by a very learned Romanist (perhaps a more excellent scholar than the Archbishop I have named, at any rate one more familiar with Oriental languages)—they both agree in what is totally different from what we have here; and what makes it more remarkable is, they agree in asserting an error which is almost universal now in Christendom.

You are aware that the general view of all Christians who derive their thoughts from traditions, creeds, or articles of faith, is that everyone will be judged alike; and this view falls in quite with the natural thought, particularly of the natural man. It seems to them a very offensive thing that those who are really sinners like themselves, but are believers unlike themselves, should not be judged. It seems, to them, since they think very little of believing, a very hard and unrighteous thing that believers should be exempted from a judgment to which others are fast hastening.

But why? Our Lord puts it in the clearest possible manner in John v. He there describes Himself in two different lights—one as Son of God, the other as Son of man. As Son of God He gives life. And who are they who get life? Does He not tell us that he "that believes on Him hath life eternal"? It is one of those remarkable, short and pithy statements of the Gospel of John. In one form or another it runs through the entire Gospel, I might almost say from the first chapter, though we may not have the literal words, but the same fundamental, substantial sense. And it goes on all through this Gospel, to chapter xx. certainly, if not to xxi. And the same great truth re-appears in his First Epistle; that life belongs to him that believes on the Lord Jesus. Just as surely as we inherit death naturally from Adam, so now there is another man who is also God, and being God as well as Man, He has entirely set aside for us the judgment of our sins by bearing it Himself. But that is not all. He gives us this new life which is proper to Himself that we might be able to bear fruit for God now. There must be a good life to bear good fruit. And there is no good life to bear fruit that God counts good except Christ's life, and all that are of faith have received that life—every Old Testament saint, as really as a New Testament saint. They had faith, they had life, they testified for God. Their ways were holy, which they could not have been had they not a life to produce this holiness; and so it is now.

Well, accordingly, those that believe on Him, the Son of God, receive life. If I reject His divine glory, that is, that He is the Son of God in this high and full sense, then I have not life; because He only gives it to those that believe. But do those who remain in unbelief therefore escape ? No, He is Son of man ; and this is just where their want of faith broke down. They could see that He was a man, and as they had no faith to see anything deeper, they only regarded Him as Son of man. In this very character the Lord will judge them. He will judge them as the Man Whom they despised. They will behold Him as the Man of everlasting glory. Not merely a divine person, but a Man ; and in that very quality—as Son of man—He will judge them.

Now, there would be no sense in, or reason for, judging the believer, even if it were not said by our Lord that the believer shall not come into judgment. Because, what would he come into judgment for ? If any go into judgment, it is a reality. It must be so if God were to enter into judgment with even believers. Were they never guilty of sins ? And if these sins come into judgment, they cannot escape punishment ; and if they are judged, they are lost. But if Christ has borne their sins, where would be the object or wisdom of putting them on their trial after they are acquitted and justified ? And we are justified now by faith. All believers are. Every Christian is. It is not a question of peculiar views. I hate peculiar views. Peculiar views are the errors of men. It would be a most shameful thing to count God's truth to be " peculiar views." The only thing a Christian should care for is God's truth. It is only the language of an enemy to count that " peculiar views." If there *are* those that try to blacken it and call it peculiar views their blood must be on their own heads. The language is the language of an adversary. We have nothing to do with running after new views or innovations of any kind, and God forbid that we should care for one single thing that is an innovation. I call an innovation anything that is a departure from God's word.

It is not the antiquity of sixteen or seventeen centuries, but we go to the very beginning, to the apostles, and to the Lord Himself ; and there is the source from which we may draw and know for ourselves immediately, just as truly as if we had the apostles here before us. The apostles were certainly not more inspired when they spoke and preached than when they wrote ; but it was what they wrote that was made to convey down the stream of ages divine truth with the utmost possible certainty. There is a great advantage in having what is written. You can come and come again. Even if you listened to an apostle, or to the Lord, you might forget. You might slip away from His words and put in some of your own. There is nothing more common than this every day, even with very accurate people ; they do not carry absolutely every word. It is too serious a thing not to have the word of God, and it is of the utmost importance that we have it written. What we want is the truth first-hand—from the people inspired to give it—and this is just what we have. And the simplest man is responsible to weigh and consider it.

It may be said he is a weak soul. Well, we are all too apt to think too much of ourselves. Especially, if men have a little ability, they are apt to overestimate what they have. There is nothing more common than this, and nothing more dangerous. Whereas, if a man is really a weak soul and does not think much about himself there is far more readiness to learn ; unless he is an obstinate man, who, even though he knows but very little, thinks a deal of himself. There is nothing so dangerous as that, especially when such a one lifts himself up against the word of God. When a man is brought to God, he is made nothing of in his own eyes. Would to God we always stayed there, with the sense of our own nothingness ! Would to God that it did not evaporate by our getting peace ! There is always a danger of a person forgetting that there was a time when he counted nothing that he thought, said, or felt, was worth thinking about. We are meant to keep that humility always. The best and truest form of real humility is the sense of the presence of God and of the infinite value of the word of God. There is nothing so humble as bowing to God's authority, there is nothing so humble as obedience—obeying God. And at the same time, nothing gives greater courage, nothing gives greater confidence, nothing gives greater firmness ; and this humility is exactly what we want—to be nothing in our own eyes, and to have perfect confidence in God's word. And faith should produce this in every believer.

Not only, then, does the Lord lay down that the believer, "comes not into judgment," but He declares what the end will be. Not that there will be only one resurrection. Were there but one resurrection, it might be no wonder that there will be only one judgment; but to confirm the fact that there will be no judgment of the believer—no sitting in judgment on him to decide his lot for eternity—there are two resurrections spoken of in that very same passage in the fifth chapter of John; and I would commend that chapter to anyone who has not duly weighed it. There it is shown that there will be a " resurrection of life " for those that have life for their souls already; there will be a " resurrection of judgment " for those that have not life but sins, and not merely sins but unbelief, the refusal of that life. They rejected the Son of God! For them there is judgment, and for them there is a special resurrection at the close of all. For those that have life now, in the Son, there is " the first resurrection," a life-resurrection. Other saints, too, will share in this, for though not at the same moment, their resurrection, nevertheless, will have this character. All that are Christ's who are in their graves when the Lord comes will rise together, and the living that are on the earth at that time will be changed, while others who die afterwards will follow, as we learn from the book of Revelation, which is my reason for guarding the statement. They all have a resurrection of life, except those that do not die, and will be brought into the change without resurrection; but their change will be equivalent to resurrection, so that it may be all called, in a certain way, a "resurrection of life."

But there is also a "resurrection of judgment" for all those that despise Christ, for all that are sinners against God, for all who have refused the Saviour, from the beginning of the world up to that time; and the resurrection of judgment is at the end of all time. Not so the resurrection of life; and the reason why it is not is this—that those who rise in the resurrection of life rise to reign with Christ, before the winding up of all things. The wind up of all will be after all the ages have run their course, so that the last sinner may be included in that awful resurrection—" the resurrection of judgment." We need not call it a "resurrection of damnation," because the word used is distinct from that. In effect it comes to that, but it is not the force of the word. It is always better to stand to the exact word of God, even if we do not understand it. We owe it honour and reverence, whether we understand it or not. His word must be right, it must be wise and the best, the only one that is really good and reliable absolutely.

This may seem a long preamble, but it is necessary,

perhaps, to make the force plain of what I am going to remark here.

In the spurious book of Enoch, from which the learned people maintain that Jude quoted, the doctrine taught is that the Lord " comes with ten thousands of His saints to execute judgment upon *them.*" There you see is the error that betrays the devil in the forger, for from this very verse, I do not in the least doubt that that document has been forged. It has every mark of having been written, subsequent to the destruction of Jerusalem, by a Jew who still buoyed himself up with the hope that God would stand by the Jews.

And so He will in the end, but in a way totally different from what he, the writer, supposed. For there is no true acknowledgment of Christ. He is simply acknowledged as the Messiah from a Jewish point of view, but there never will be deliverance for the Jew in looking for the Messiah according to their thoughts. It is the Messiah of God, the Anointed of Jehovah, the true Messiah that came, and they rejected Him. But when He comes to deliver them by and by they will be brought to say, " Blessed is He that cometh in the name of the Lord." They will then give up all their unbelief, they will welcome Him, and He will come and deliver them, and He will save them out of all that strait of trouble in which they will then be.

But He will not judge His own people. He was judged for them, He bore their judgment on the tree, and He will never judge them. Nor is there one word in the Bible—Old or New Testament—that insinuates in the most distant manner that the Lord will inflict judgment on His own people. That He will judge His people is a common thing in the Old Testament. But that will be, as a King, the judgment of their difficulties, their disorders if there should be any; and He will also vindicate them from their enemies. It is in this sense that He will judge His people.

Moreover, God carries on a moral judgment now in respect to His children. "If ye call on the Father, Who without respect of persons judgeth according to every man's work, pass the time of your sojourning [here] in fear." This is still going on. The Lord dealt with the Corinthians in this way. When they were in such a bad state and profaned the table of the Lord, coming boldly and taking the bread and the wine as if they had been in a good state, the Lord laid His hand on them—some were sick, some fell asleep—were removed by death. All this was a temporal judgment. It is what the Lord does now, and this judgment is for our good and profit.

We see the same thing in a family. It is the judgment that a father carries on in his family, or any person charged with the care of youths put under him—young persons of either sex. Well, there is a judgment for their good. This is a totally different thing from what is called in John v. a "coming into judgment." It is even a different word employed—a different form of the word. From Psalm cxliii. it is evident that the Old Testament saints knew better than that. At any rate, the Spirit of God gave them better knowledge, for there it says, "Enter not into judgment with Thy servant: for in Thy sight shall no man living be justified." If God were to enter into judgment with the believer it would be all over with him, because even the believer himself would be bound to say, I do not deserve to be saved. And if God were to look at all the faults in a believer's life He might say, if that is what I have to look at, I have no reason to save you, you do not deserve it. But the ground of a believer's salvation is not that he deserves it, but that Christ deserves it for us. Christ has completely met all God's nature, and, further than that, He has borne all our sins and iniquities in His own body on the tree. God will not judge them again as if they had not been sufficiently borne, as if the judgment at the cross were not an adequate one. God will never say that about what Christ endured, and this is just what faith lays hold of. Therefore, the uniform doctrine of the Bible—of both Old and New Testament—is this, that believers are not to come into that future judgment which the Lord will execute at the close of all things; but because we now have life, and are God's children, He watches over and cares for us, and carries on a moral judgment; and besides this, the

Lord Jesus carries on now a judgment of the church.

We find, besides the Father judging individually His children, that the Lord Jesus takes up the things that pertain to His name among those that are assembled together. He is Head of the church, and He has a watchful eye that the things that are done under His holy name should be real, should not be hypocritical, that His name should not be profaned. If our ways are unreal, and we go on badly, He deals with us in the way of discipline, and for the very reason " that we should not be condemned with the world." There you have the reason. If He did not do so, you might raise a question as to whether they would be lost.

Now then, the author of this spurious Book of Enoch understood not a word of all this. He was not a believer. He was a false man ; he would never have forged if he had not been. He was a forger of the worst kind. No forgery is so bad as that which pretends to give us the word of God. It is very bad to be deceitful in anything, but if deceit is carried on in the things of God there is none that is worse in its consequences, there is none that more distinctly dishonours God. And that is the case here.

" Behold, the Lord cometh with ten thousands of His saints, to——" what does scripture say ? to " execute judgment upon all." This is not the saints. The " all " are totally distinct from the saints. The saints had been caught up, and now come with

VERSES 14, 15

Him Who executes the judgment on all the sinners to be found in that day. " To execute judgment upon all, and to convince all "—to make it perfectly plain who are meant—all " that are ungodly among them." There it is, to obviate any argument, for there are people who are not great in the truth who are always ready for an argument! Here we see it is " to execute judgment upon all, and to convince all that are ungodly among them " (that is, these " all ") " of all their ungodly deeds which they have ungodlily committed." And not only ungodly deeds; there is another thing that the Spirit of God attaches great importance to—" hard words which ungodly sinners spoke against Him," words that gainsay God's mind, words that say the thing that is false of God. Job's friends did that. Job himself bowed to God. He had not many words, he made a confession of his folly, he said the thing that was right. But his friends had not spoken the thing that was right of the Lord. I do not think that the Lord was putting the stamp of His approval in the same way on *all* that Job said. He often spoke haughtily, and unhappily about God, and fretted about himself, but the Lord does not refer to that. Job broke down and confessed his nothingness. His friends did not break down. Job did, and, in consequence, Job was restored, and had to pray for those, his friends, who were not as yet restored.

But here it is plain that ungodly words are just

as bad in their own way as ungodly deeds. Sometimes an ungodly word does more harm than an ungodly deed. For instance, an ungodly deed might be an act of unrighteousness in a man, but an ungodly word might be a slurring of Christ. This is worse, and particularly if people receive it. People are quite ready to cry out against an ungodly deed. Even worldly men can very well judge ungodly deeds, and the same people would be deceived by hard and ungodly words against the Lord and His grace and truth.

In this Book of Enoch to which I have referred there is not a word about the "hard speeches." This shows that the author was simply a natural man; a man who, no doubt, had this phrase before him, but he did not understand it. He evidently did not understand either about the saint or about the sinner. He did not understand about the saints, because he made them objects of judgment as well as the ungodly. It is just like the theologians now. They do not believe what I am now saying. But there is one word, in leaving that subject, that I wish to add. "We shall all be manifested before the judgment seat of Christ." Everything, good or bad, will come out, for the believer as well as for the unbeliever. But that is a very different thing from judgment. This is not called judgment, but "manifestation," which is not the same thing as judgment. Manifestation of all our ways will be a very good thing for us. How apt we are to overrate ourselves! There may be something that we perhaps flattered ourselves about while we were here alive, and we never saw how foolish we were till risen from the dead and standing before the judgment seat of Christ. There it will all be manifested. Where we thought that we were wise we shall see that we were very foolish. And so in everything where we may have allowed ourselves a little latitude and tried to excuse ourselves, we shall there be obliged to acknowledge it as all wrong. This is for our good. It is a blessing to do it in this life, but it will be all the fullest and richest blessing there. All will be out then. Then we shall know even as also we are known. We shall have no thought different from God's about a single thing in all our lives. But this is not judgment. Judgment is where a person stands to be tried, and to be convicted of his guilt. This will be the case with everyone who has not been justified by the Lord Jesus Christ and His incomparable work on the cross.

But there is a second point where this forger could not copy the text before him aright. He only speaks of "ungodly *deeds*." Hard, ungodlily spoken " words " to him did not seem of very much account, so he left out the ungodly " words." The first part seemed the only right thing to him. Consequently, he mutilated the scripture. He could not even copy it truly, and thus he has given us a false version of it.

In other words, Jude never got his prophecy of Enoch from a mere tradition, or from this book at all. He got it from God. How, I do not pretend to say. But he did.

VERSES 16-19

" THESE are murmurers, complainers, walking after their lusts, and their mouth speaketh swelling things, admiring persons for the sake of profit. But ye, beloved, remember ye the words that were spoken before by the apostles of our Lord Jesus Christ, that they said to you, In [the] end of the time shall be mockers walking after their own lusts of ungodliness. These are they that make separations, natural (or, soulish), not having [the] Spirit " (vers. 16-19).

" These are murmurers." Murmuring is a more serious sin than many think. It could not but be that among Christians there are many things that do not go according to what we like. Suppose it to be even a man of sound wisdom ; but if people are not very well founded they are always apt to be disappointed at something in him. It is natural for people to begin to murmur. The Israelites were constantly at that kind of work.

Now, he says, " There are murmurers," and he adds, " complainers "—not content with their lot (the strict literal meaning of the word). They are persons who like to be something more and greater than they are, than God ever called them to be. They want to be somebody.

" These are murmurers, complainers " ; and what is the cause of that ? " Walking after their own lusts." Lust is not to be supposed to be merely gross lusts. There are refined lusts—vanity, pride, ambition ; what are all these but lusts ? They are all lusts. The lusts of the devil. These are not the same kind of lusts as the lusts of the flesh. Satan was lifted up with pride, and we are warned against falling into the fault or " condemnation " of the devil. It appears that the things mentioned in this verse are very much the same thing : " their mouth speaketh great swelling words, having men's persons in admiration because of advantage." They are fond of having a party, particularly if they can number some rich among the party, " because of advantage."

What I particularly draw your attention to is this. Enoch prophesied of these. I do not know anything more striking than that. There are the same persons now as in Enoch's day. There can be no doubt that these people lived in the time of Enoch. But Jude carried us on to the coming of the Lord. The people who are on the earth when the Lord comes will be the same kind in their wickedness as in the days of Enoch and of Jude. Evil, you see, goes on. Evil retains its own terrible character—malignancy and rebellion against God, and all self-sufficiency, and all the terrible things that are so entirely opposed to Christ. Enoch prophesied of these and of the judgment coming upon them.

"But ye, beloved, remember ye"—to confirm this—"the words that were spoken before by the apostles of our Lord Jesus Christ, how that they told you that there should be mockers in the last time, who should walk after their own ungodly lusts" (vers. 17, 18).

Well, we have at least two of these apostles. Surely, that is quite enough. Very likely the other apostles taught the very same things by word of mouth. But we have this warning about these characters, written down by two besides Jude; one the apostle Paul, the other Peter in both his Epistles. In his First, Peter says that the time is coming when judgment must begin at the house of God, and judgment on just this kind of ungodliness then working up; but in his Second Epistle there is a deal more. And I think that Jude goes still further, and that his Epistle was written after Second Peter, and for this reason, that there is an advance of evil. Peter speaks of unrighteous men, Jude speaks of men that once seemed to have the truth, and through their bad life, bad ways, pride, vanity, or whatever it was, they lost it. That is quite a common thing. By common, I do not mean that any very great numbers break off in this way, but that it is a sin which every now and then breaks out. Why, even since "Brethren" began there

VERSES 16–19

have been the most terrible cases of people giving up all the truth. The greatest infidel of modern days was one of the early " brethren." He was a very clever man, and gave up his fellowship at Balliol to go to the Eastern world, among Arabs and Persians and the like, with the gospel. He seemed to be devoted to the Lord. But even on his way out he betrayed that he was not a true believer at all. How ! By doubting about the full proper Deity of the Lord Jesus ; and when he came back brethren enquired into it. There had been whispers of it before his return, but then he was out of the way, so that till his return it was not possible to deal with him fairly, or to examine him fully, not merely whispers. When he came back he was seen and written to, and his words were the words of an unbeliever ; he was therefore refused any place in our fellowship. After this, he went among the dissenters, who welcomed him most heartily, and he preached in their chapels and was most acceptable among them, particularly as he ran down the " brethren " pretty hotly. At this time, he still appeared to be pious in his outward ways and manner, and still read the Bible. But he gradually gave up everything and gave an account of it in a book which he wrote bearing a very anomalous title indeed, for it would appear that he really never had faith. He was a man who was very impressionable, and he easily took the colour of those with whom he was. He valued and was charmed with the sound of the truth, and thought he had it, but I am afraid he never had. So he lived, and so, I fear, he died. There have been others of no such prominence who have had a similar end; not so marked, perhaps, but as sad. Some had once been in fellowship, and seemed to be very honoured persons for a time, before they were really known. And this kind of thing falls in with what we have here.

There were such persons among them; and not merely the teachers. Peter speaks about teachers, but Jude looks at them more widely; they are evidently responsible even though they are not teachers. If others dishonour the Lord who are not teachers, they are responsible. There is this character in Jude: they are apostate from the truth, and have not gone out of fellowship yet. That is the very thing he says. There they are, although it is likely that no one but Jude who saw these persons could speak of them; and Peter saw them where he was. They appeared fair enough just as there were many such at the time when the person referred to was in fellowship. Many would not believe a word of it. They thought he was a very good man, and that it was a scandal to speak hardly about him. They never could see till the thing came out thoroughly. We are not all " eyes " in the body. We may have an important place. The hand or the foot can do a work that the eye cannot, and there are those who can see far before others; and it is important for people to make use of those who have proved their special competence. Otherwise we are apt to get wrong.

It is an immense thing to say that we have not only teachers now and preachers to spread the truth in spite of their weakness and their liability to err, but we have also those that were kept from error in what they have written, absolutely kept from error; and these are here brought before us as the apostles of our Lord Jesus Christ. They were men of like passions as we are ourselves, but the peculiarity in the case of those apostles and prophets is, that in the midst of their weakness they were preserved—it was not, it is true, like Christ, absolute perfection—but there was the perfect preservation from error in what they wrote. And it was all the more remarkable that this was in one generation only. It was not like the succession that there was in the old dispensation of God. There we have prophets raised up at all times, wherever they were needed; but the great peculiarity for the church and for the Christian is that we have not merely words that were perfect for their purpose, and words that were given faithfully by God in the midst of all the errors of Israel, but now we have a perfect revelation in all respects, by men themselves imperfect, but nevertheless kept and empowered by the Holy Ghost to say the truth without error whatever.

Now, there are two things in the words of the

apostles ; the first is the mind of God for the glory of Christ ; and this we have in all the books of the New Testament. But in the midst of these words, and more particularly in the latter times of giving these words we have the most solemn warnings that are given in any part of the Bible. It was not at all that all these characters of evil came out so that the Christian could discern them, but they came out sufficiently for the apostles to discern them.

Thus we have our lessons for practical guidance in the words of the apostles. They are the persons through whom we have received the full truth of God. There was not an error that ever crept into the church but is provided for here. There is not a good thing that God had to reveal but what is revealed here.

For we are not meant to be inventors, we are not meant to make discoveries, like the men of science. The reason why there are inventions in the arts, and discoveries in science, is, because all is imperfect. But perfection is what marks the word of God—not merely relative perfection, relative to the state of Israel at different times, but—absolute perfection. What brought in absolute perfection ? Christ. There is the key to all that is blessed, to all that is most blessed. There is what explains what is most of all peculiar. It was according to Christ that all the truth should be brought out, unstinted, and perfectly providing for everything that might be through the ages that follow down to the present time. And this in order that we might never have to look outside scripture for the proof of any error, and this also for the provision of everything good. All is in the word; this word that we have got. The Old Testament is full of value, but, nevertheless, it is only general. Our special instructions are in the New Testament, for we can easily understand that there was no such thing as a Christian in Old Testament times. They were believers, but not Christians. A Christian is a man who is not merely looking for the promises, but who has the promises— accomplished in Christ. Well, of course, the Old Testament saints had not got this, and the church was an absolutely new thing. It was not merely promises accomplished, but the mystery revealed: the mystery that was hid in God up to that time. There was no revelation of it in the Old Testament whatever. Now it is revealed, and it is given to us. And how? By these perfect writings of the New Testament, that left nothing to desire, nothing for faith to desire; plenty for unbelief to add, still more for unbelief to depart from; but nothing for faith to desire. We have all here, and it is only for our faith to discern it, and to practise it.

Now for this reason all came out in one generation. John, the very last of all, was the one that saw the Lord from the beginning. He was, not only one of the apostles, but, one of the first two that ever followed the Lord Jesus and entered into living relationship with Him here below. And he was kept here, beyond others, in the wisdom of God. But we have another, also, of those who were eminently favoured, and were conspicuously used. Although Jude wrote a short Epistle, what a great deal there is in it!

Now, turning to what we have already touched upon—" But ye, beloved, remember ye the words which were spoken before by the apostles of our Lord Jesus Christ; that they said to you, In [the] end of the time shall be mockers walking after their own lusts of ungodliness "; that there should be, not merely unrighteous men, or lawless men, but, one of the worst features of evil, " mockers." Why, in the Old Testament, when it was only a question of children that could not resist giving way to their humour—I may call it very bad humour, and very bad manners—but still they mocked the old prophet, they mocked Elisha. And even he, the man of grace, was no doubt led of God to call forth the bears that tore them all.

Here we find that it is not little children in their folly (for we know that " foolishness is bound in the heart of a child "), but the case of men who claimed wisdom; and the way they showed it was by " mocking "! " Mockers in the last time, who should walk after their own ungodly lusts "—their own lusts of ungodly things. It is rather stronger. Their lust was after ungodliness. This is what characterised their lust. It is not a mere vague term; it is a very succinct term—" lusts of ungodliness." Now this is an awful thing. And resulting from what ? I will not say it results from Christianity, from the truth. God forbid. But it resulted from the fact that they were there, and that their hearts got tired of it, and they became the enemies of it. There is nothing more blessed than a Christian man walking in simplicity. There is nothing more awful than a Christian man who casts off Christianity, and who becomes a mocker after the lusts of his own ungodliness. This is what is described here, and what the writer prepares us for. No one could have believed that in early days.

These mockers once looked fair. They once spoke fairly. They were received, they were baptised ; they remembered the Lord Jesus, taking part in the assembly, no doubt. They may have been preachers, very likely ; but here it was evident they were given up to their own lusts of ungodliness and they were mockers ; accordingly, they therefore turned with the greatest spite and hatred upon that truth that once separated them from the world. They were professedly believers, but it is evident they were in reality the emissaries of Satan. And the Epistles (some of the last in the Bible), as well as the apostles of our Lord, laid down this : that these mockers were to come in the last time. The last time was therefore to be a peculiarly evil time, and it is a very solemn thing that we are in that time most fully now. I do not say that it may not be lengthened—that is entirely a question of the will of God. The lengthening of evil may be just as much as the lengthening of tranquillity. There is the tranquillity for one, and it may end in greater departure than ever, or it may be the means of repentance, and extrication from these toils of the enemy.

But here at any rate he declares, "These are they who separate themselves, sensual, having not the Spirit" (ver. 19). It is important to understand this verse, for there are various kinds of separations mentioned in the New Testament. Sometimes, it is separation within; sometimes, it is separation without; sometimes, it takes the character of parties as yet joined with the rest in outward observances, but their spirit alienated. Those are the persons the apostle refers to in Romans xvi.: persons "which cause divisions and stumbling-blocks, contrary to the doctrine which ye have learned" (ver. 17). That doctrine was that we should walk, not only outwardly together but, inwardly, with real love. It is true it may not always be approving of what each may do and say, but with earnest desire that things might go well, and that those even who are in any way caught by the enemy might be delivered.

Now, the persons in Romans xvi. were not to be "put away," but avoided; and the object of that avoiding was to make them feel and reflect upon what they were about. Suppose they were preachers or teachers, avoiding such would be not to invite them, or if they invited themselves, not to accept their offer. Of course, you can understand that they would not like it, unless they were really broken in spirit. In this case all would terminate happily, but if they were bent on doing their own will they ought to be avoided as the apostle says, and if they do not like this avoiding, and grow bitter under it, the effect would be that they would make a division " without " if they could, instead of " within." They would " go out " themselves, and try and lead away others.

There are these kinds of spirits. First, they have an alienated mind within, and are self-seeking ; and because this is blamed by all that have the good of the saints at heart, and the glory of the Lord before them, they resent it strongly, and, instead of breaking down and judging themselves, they become worse, and then it is not a division " within," but " without," that they make. The former is called a schism, the latter a heresy. For I particularly press it on every one here who may not have observed it—that " heresy " in scripture does not mean bad doctrine at all. There may be bad doctrine, of course, along with it ; but this is rather heterodoxy—strange doctrine. There are proper terms for all forms of evil : falsehood, deceit, blasphemy and the like. But heresy means the self-will that does not care for the fellowship of the assembly in the least, and is so bent on its own object that it goes outside. This is what is called

heresy. Now that is what the apostle means in
1 Cor. xi. He says, "There are divisions (or,
schisms) among you. For there must be also heresies
(or, sects) among you, that they which are approved
may be made manifest among you" (vers. 18, 19).

But there is no "must be" in reference to
heterodoxy. People might remain, and like to
remain, with their heterodoxy, but heresy does not
mean bad doctrine, although this might go along
with it. It means that people might get too hot
in their zeal, and, being reproved for their party
spirit, they refuse to stand it any longer, and they
get away. They break loose from fellowship and
form some new thing which has not the sanction of
the word of God. That is what, in scripture,
is called heresy. The doctrine might be sound
enough in a general way. There might be no
blasphemies, nor heterodoxy, strictly speaking, but
there is the heart entirely wrong and seeking its
own things instead of the things of Jesus Christ.

So in the verse before us, "These be they who
separate themselves" means those that separate
themselves "within," not "without," at all. This
is very evident from the early part of this Epistle:
"For there are certain men crept in unawares, who
were before of old ordained to this condemnation,
ungodly men, turning the grace of our God into
lasciviousness, and denying the only Lord God,
and our Lord Jesus Christ" (ver. 4). Certain men
crept in. They are the same people that Jude is

talking about all through. Unawares, they had "crept in," not "gone out." Now this is what gives the true force of the words—" those that separate themselves." We can easily understand it if we bear in mind the Pharisees. The Pharisees never separated themselves from Israel, but the very name of a Pharisee means "a separatist." They were separatists within Israel. These were separatists within the church, and in both cases it was not going out, but it was making a party of pride and self-righteousness within. And who are they? Ungodly men; these were the men that were proud of themselves; these men who had these wicked lusts. They were the persons who assumed to be pre-eminently faithful; and, I believe, you will generally find that it is so, that, when persons are given up to delusion, they always have a very high opinion of themselves. No matter how violent they may be, no matter how evil in their spirit, they claim to be more particularly faithful, and they have no measure in their denunciation of every one that stands in their way. This is exactly the class here described.

"These be they who separate themselves." And what sort of men were they? "Sensual." The word "sensual" is important to understand. Every man has got a soul, converted or not. Now, when we believe, we receive a nature that we never had before; we receive life in Christ. These men here described had nothing but their natural soul. They had not received life in Christ. They were merely "natural" men. "Sensual," in our language, is very often taken to mean people who are abandoned to immoral ways. These people may have been so, but it is not the meaning of the word. The meaning of the word is that they were just simply "natural" men. It is the same word which, in 1 Cor. ii. 14, is translated "natural man," and contrasted with the "spiritual man." So he adds here, "not having the Spirit."

Now, having not the Spirit is to lack the great privilege of a Christian. This is the great difference between a believer now resting on redemption, and an Old Testament believer. They were waiting for the Spirit in the days of the Messiah. Although the Messiah is rejected, the Holy Ghost has been poured down on us, but not on those that are still waiting for the Messiah. The Jews are still waiting, and have not the Spirit. These men, although they had taken their place in the church, had not the Spirit. They were natural men. We are therefore given this further development of the terrible evil that had come in even then, although the great mass of the saints, you may be sure, very little understood it, very little perceived it; and therefore it was of the greatest moment that the apostles should. And that there should be inspired men, or, at any rate, inspired instruction given upon what people otherwise would not have been in the least prepared for, and would have counted it a very fierce and terrible picture without any good ground for it; they would think it was making the worst of everything instead of the best. But the Spirit of God does give the truth just as it is.

VERSES 20, 21

WELL, now we come to a very comforting word. " But ye, beloved, building up yourselves on your most holy faith, praying in [the] Holy Spirit, keep yourselves in [the] love of God, awaiting the mercy of our Lord Jesus Christ unto life eternal " (vers. 20, 21).

So then we are not to be cast down, we are not to be disheartened, even by these terrible pictures of evil. They are revealed in order that we should not be deceived, that we may really know what the actual state of Christianity is before the eye of God, instead of yielding to false expectations and wrong and imperfect judgments of our own. But even in the face of all that, there is this call to these beloved saints to build up themselves on their most holy faith. This is very carefully worded. There is nothing at all said in this Epistle about leaders, or guides, or rulers, or preachers, or teachers either. In a general way, as far as there were any, they have a very bad character, not of course that all who preached or taught were so, but that there were many of this class that were so especially. The saints themselves are here exhorted directly.

They are not to give up their privileges, or to imagine, that because it is a day of such abounding evil, they are not to be very happy. They are comforted with this ; that the blessing is perfectly open to them, and they are called to have more faith than ever. There is no time when faith shines brighter than in the dark day, and there is no time when love is more evidently discerned than when there are not many to love, not many that do love, but where there is the reign of selfishness and indifference, and people care for other objects, and put them before that which is imperishable.

" But ye, beloved, building up yourselves on your most holy faith." This is the only place in all the New Testament where faith is called our " most holy faith." It might have been thought that when things are so evidently wrong we must not be too stringent, that we must not be too exacting, that we must not look for such care as on the day of Pentecost. Why, so far from that being so, we require more care. And instead of its being now called merely the holy faith, or precious faith, Jude calls it, " your most holy faith." The saints, in short, are encouraged to cleave to the truth in all its sanctifying power. We cannot think too much of " the faith of God's elect." I am not speaking now of faith looked at in the saint, but of " the faith " looked at in itself. It is the thing that we believe, which is the meaning of it here. It is not crying up individuals, but what these individuals receive from

God. That is what he calls it—" the faith." There is a great difference between faith and " the faith." Here it is " the faith." Faith is a quality of you, and me, and every believer. But that is not the sense here, which is, " the faith once delivered to the saints," as he says in this very Epistle.

Well, thus you must look at it. When it came, you may say, It came down from God out of heaven, revealed through the apostles—Christ Himself of course in particular. There, was " the faith ": what we are called to believe ; that which separated us to God from everything here below. So here, we have the same faith, only—it is not now said, " once for all delivered to the saints," although this remains true. Here it is called " most holy." What ! has it not got tainted ? Has it not got lowered now? Woe to those that say so! " The faith " is just the same faith now as on the day of Pentecost, the same faith that Peter preached, and also Paul, and all others of the apostles. And we have Peter and Paul, *i.e.* we have their words. We have the most careful words they ever spoke. We have the words that they were inspired to write from God. We do not therefore merely listen, as some of the early fathers talk about a man that saw the apostle and heard the apostle ; and it appears that the man that did so was a poor foolish old man ! Very likely. Well, and what have you got by putting a poor foolish old man between you and the apostle ? Little or nothing. But Peter and Paul and Jude were not foolish, and whatever they may have been in themselves, there was the mighty power of the Holy Ghost Who gave them the truth of God absolutely intact ; and here it is His word now, and we come into personal contact with it by faith. We that believe receive that " most holy faith," and what is more, we are called, every one, to act upon it now.

And what are we to do with it ? It is not only that we impart it to others, we " build up ourselves on our most holy faith." Nothing, therefore, can give a more delightful picture of the resources of grace for as bad a time as can well be conceived as what we have here. " Ye, beloved, building up yourselves on your most holy faith " ; it is not to be on a little bit of the faith, not on the faith that was given to you through the intervention of a poor foolish old man. No, here it is, fresh from God, kept fresh and holy, unmixed with anything that could lower it.

" Praying in the Holy Ghost." What can be better than this ? There were men who spoke with tongues in the Holy Ghost. Do you think that is half as good as " praying in the Holy Ghost " ? Why, the apostle Paul says that the men that spoke with tongues in the Holy Ghost were to hold their tongue, unless there were an interpreter there present so as to give what they spoke in a tongue in a form intelligible to others. It was a real power of the Spirit of God, but it was not to be exercised unless there were an interpreter. But think of the apostle silencing a man praying in the Holy Ghost! No, the very reverse. There is a great deal of prayer that is not in the Holy Ghost. And we are not at all called upon only to pray in the Holy Ghost. Happy is he who does, and happy are they that hear prayer in the Holy Spirit. And where there is prayer in the Holy Spirit all is thoroughly acceptable to God, every word is so. Every word of such prayer expresses perfectly what God means at that time. But there are prayers that begin in the Spirit and do not end in the Spirit. Prayers are often rather mixed, and this is true even of real believers; and sometimes we pray foolishly, sometimes we pray unintelligently! This is never in the Holy Ghost.

And, what is more, we are encouraged to pray at all times, even supposing we say what is foolish. Very well, it is better to say it, than to be silent. Much better. Because prayer is the going forth of the heart to God, and it may be like the words of a prattling child to its father or mother. It is all right that the child should prattle, far better than that the child should be dumb. But the best of all is when it is really prayer in the Spirit of God; yet that is a thing rather to desire than to presume that we have attained to. We have to be very careful indeed that we do not give ourselves credit for more activity in the Holy Ghost than we really possess. This supposes entire dependence, and no thought of self, and no opposition to this or to that.

These are things that, alas! may be, and they all weaken and hinder " praying in the Holy Ghost." But here you see the very same grace that encouraged the saints, even in the darkest day, " to build up themselves on their most holy faith," instead of having the notion, Oh, it is hopeless to look for that now; when Peter or Paul was there we might have the most holy faith, but how could it be guaranteed now? Well, there it is in this precious word. And those that cleave to this precious word will find it out, and if their heart is full of it, their mouth will abundantly speak of it; and there is no ground to be discouraged, but the very contrary.

So, in this twentieth verse, we have two of the most important things possible—the one is, the standard of truth not in the least degree lowered, but maintained in all its highest and holiest character, even in that dark day; and, the second, the most spiritual action that could be in any believer here below, viz., " praying in the Holy Ghost." Why, this is even more than preaching or teaching, because the heart is sure to be in the prayer. A man that can speak well and knows the truth—this may often be a snare. There is a danger in such a case to say the truth, and speak it out, and earnestly too, without there being present the power of the Spirit of God. But to pray in the Holy Ghost is another thing altogether. This cannot be without the immediate action of the Spirit in this most blessed way.

"Keep yourselves in the love of God." Here Jude is looking at the practical result of these two things. "Keep yourselves in the love of God." Now, could we keep ourselves in anything better? Was there ever anything higher than the keeping ourselves in the love of God? Love is of God, and we are to keep ourselves in it, instead of being provoked by the evil things around us, instead of yielding because of others yielding. This necessarily supposes great confidence in God, and delight in what God's own nature is—the activity of His nature. Light is the moral character of God's nature; love is the active character of God's nature. Light does not allow any impurity; love goes out to bless others. We are called to keep ourselves, not merely in the light of God—we *are* there, we are brought there as Christians—but, in the love of God. We are not meant to have that doubted. We are to keep ourselves fresh and simple and confident in His love.

And he further adds, "Looking for the mercy of our Lord Jesus Christ unto eternal life." I think that mercy is brought in here especially because of the great need, because of the distress, because of the weakness, because of everything that tended to cast people down. No, he says, do not be downcast, look for the mercy of our Lord Jesus Christ. Is it only by the way? No, it is all along the way, to the very end—" unto life eternal," the great consummation. This could not be unless they already had life eternal in Christ now; but this mercy of God, "of our Lord Jesus Christ unto life eternal," looks at the full heavenly consummation.

VERSES 22, 23

Now we come to a passage which I feel to be unusually difficult to expound; and the reason is this. The original authorities and the best authorities are all in confusion about it. This is very rarely the case in the New Testament, but it is the case here. All the great authorities are at sixes and sevens in the testimony they give of these two verses (22, 23). And, to show you how great that is, our Version—the Authorised, so-called—looks at two cases only, "And of some have compassion, making a difference"—that is one class; "and others save with fear, pulling them out of the fire; hating even the garment spotted by the flesh"—this is the second class.

Now I believe there are three classes, and not two only. That will show how uncertain it is. Although, as I have said, I am very far from presuming to give more than my judgment as far as the Lord enables me to form one. I am certainly open to anything that might be shown to the contrary, but as yet no one has shown it. No one at all. I think that those who know best about it are those that have spoken most cautiously as to it.

Many who trust themselves are apt to speak more confidently.

First of all Jude says, "And some convict when contending."* That is the idea—"when they dispute"; not, "making a difference," as of the man that shows compassion. The fact is, compassion belongs to another class, not to this one at all, as far as I am able to judge, which depends upon looking at all the authorities and using one to correct another. That is what it comes to in this singular case, which is a very exceptional thing in the great original witnesses; but God has been pleased in this particular instance not to hinder their difference.

Some then "convict when they dispute." I think that is the meaning of it. "Making a difference," as in the Authorised, should rather be, "when they dispute." It is the people that are being convicted who of course make the dispute, instead of the person that shows compassion making a difference among them. It is quite a different idea. The first class, in this twenty-second verse, has been given (in my belief) very wrongly indeed.

Well, then, the next is, instead of "convicting" people so as to leave them without any excuse for their disputatious spirit, another class is looked at—
" others save, pulling them out of [the] fire "; then,

---

* ἐλέγχετε AC*, the best cursives, and Vv., διακρινομένους ℵABC, good cursives, Vulg., Syrr., Arm.—Text. Rec. ἐλέειτε διακρινόμενοι KLP, etc.

a third class, " and others pity with fear*, hating even the garment spotted by the flesh " (ver. 23).

These then are the three classes : a disputatious class to be convicted and silenced—then, those that are to be saved, snatched out of the fire—and, others to be compassionated with fear, hating the garment spotted by the flesh. So that this all tends to complete the picture of the danger to souls. There is the all-importance of grace in the midst of it, but the truth maintained in all its power. And, you observe, it is for the same persons who are building up themselves on their most holy faith to do this. It is work that is thrown on the responsibility of those that were thoroughly happy and walking with God. These are the persons that would be able to silence the disputatious if they would be silenced by any one. But even apostles could not always do that. The apostle John speaks of the " malicious words " of Diotrephes. These words were directed against himself, and even an apostle could not alter that. The apostle Paul complained of " evil workers " who pretended to be quite as much apostles, if not more so, as himself. He refers to them in very trenchant terms in 2 Corinthians xi. He could not hinder that. And when there was the great meeting in Jerusalem, where all the apostles were present, there was a deal of disputation and

---

* σώζετε ἐκ πυρὸς ἁρπάζοντες ℵABC, best cursives, Vulg., Memph., Arm., Aeth., οὓς δὲ ἐλεᾶτε ἐν φόβῳ ℵA (ἐλεεῖτε) B, Vulg., Memph., Arm., Aethiop.—Text. Rec. ἐν φόβῳ σώζετε ἐκ τοῦ πυρὸς ἁρπάζοντες KLP, etc.

discussion there. It was only after it burst out in a noisy meeting at first, that Peter, as well as Barnabas and Paul, gave their testimony, and then James summed up the decision of the assembly (Acts xv.).

I only mention it to show that a like state of things existed at that time as now. We often look on the apostles as the painters represent the Lord. If you look at the pictures of the Lord Jesus, He is generally represented as going about with a halo of glory about His head. Well, if that were true, one might expect all the multitude to be down on their knees looking up to the man with this golden halo around him. But that is just what imagination does. It puts a halo around the Lord, and it puts a halo around the apostles; so that people do not realise at all the terrible evils that had to be faced by them. This was the portion, too, of those that were serving God, even in the best of times. How much more may we expect it now! As the Psalmist said, Time was when the work of the sanctuary was regarded as a good thing for a man to have put his hand to: all that fine carved work, all that grandeur of gold that gleamed in the sanctuary; but now it came to that pass, that a man was prized because he brake it all to pieces (Ps. lxxiv.).

Well, this is what we have in the increasing lawlessness of Christendom, but let us not be downcast. Let us remember that the prize is coming; that the Lord puts especial honour on those that are faithful to Him in an evil day. The Lord grant us that great privilege.

VERSES 24, 25

In the body of the Epistle we have already had the coming of the Lord in judgment, that is to say, bound up in the awful departure from the truth which was to be found in the Christian profession. This is what many souls are very unwilling to face. It is natural for man to think that everything must be progressive—the truth as well as all else. No one ever drew that from the Bible, and every part of the Bible, from the first book till the last, shows us man set in a place by God, and abandoning it for Satan. And there is the same story here. No doubt it is unspeakably terrible to find that what bears the name of Christ should turn out worst of all. I need not say the guilt of it is entirely man's, and that the secret source of that evil is still Satan, as Satan is always behind the scenes in his antagonism, not only to God, but more particularly to the Lord Jesus. He is the One that Satan hates, and hates most of all because He became Man to glorify God where man had failed, and as Man to glorify God even about sin. Therefore, there is, what we might call, a natural antagonism in the devil, being what he is, against the One Who is to crush him at last. He well knows this, and there will come a time when, as he knows, he will have but a short time.

That time has not yet come, but it is coming, and coming fast.

So Jude introduces the coming of the Lord in a very remarkable manner—not by a new prophecy, but by the recovery to us of one of the first prophecies ever uttered, and, certainly, the first prophecy that took shape, the ordinary shape, which gave its character to all others that follow. For nothing could be more in the prophetic character than these words: "And Enoch also, the seventh from Adam (to distinguish him from the Enoch who was the son of Cain) prophesied of these, saying, Behold the Lord cometh with ten thousands of His saints, to execute judgment upon all, and to convince all that are ungodly among them of all their ungodly deeds, which they have ungodlily committed, and of (what people think little of) their hard words which ungodly sinners have spoken against Him." "Words" are the common expression of man's iniquity, because he cannot *do* all that he would like to do, but there is nothing he cannot "say." Consequently, it is said, "For by thy words thou shalt be justified, and by thy words thou shalt be condemned." This character of evil, so far from being a light thing, is one which is presented with the utmost gravity, and that by Enoch before the flood: and it is nowhere else preserved. Here, thousands of years afterwards, Jude was enabled to disclose this to us—by what means we do not know. The Holy Ghost was perfectly capable without using any means. Whether there were any, we know not, but we know that here it is, and that this is the certain truth, not only of God, but through Enoch before he went to heaven.

But there is another connexion with Enoch that we have now to look into, in the verses that close the Epistle. This is, that we may regard a latent connexion *in* them with the blessed manner in which Enoch was taken out of the scene altogether. Now, this fell to Jude and not to Peter. I have already compared the very great marks of distinction between Peter's and Jude's treatment of these very cases. Peter's view is purely as a question of unrighteousness, and he looks also at the teachers as being the most guilty parties in that unrighteousness—generally done for gain, or fame, or for some earthly motive of the kind that is not of God. Jude looks at it in a still deeper light; for he does not make so much of the teachers. The awful thing to Jude was that the church, that the body of the saints, who ought to be the light of God—the heavenly light of God in a world of darkness—that they were to become the seat of the worst evil of Satan; and this through letting in (no doubt, by carelessness, by lack of looking to God) these corrupters. That is his point of view. Not so much unrighteousness as apostasy. There is nothing so terrible as apostasy. In the case of unrighteousness it might be merely that of men going on with their badness. But apostasy always supposes that people have come out of their badness professedly, that they have received the truth professedly, that they have professedly received grace from God in Christ the Lord, and have turned their back upon it all. There is nothing so bad as that. So that you see, if there were not the gospel, and if there had not been the church, there could not have been so bad an apostasy as that which Jude contemplates here, from first to last.

We have, first of all then, as I have already shown, the trace of that apostasy as it presented itself to Jude by the Holy Ghost. And he takes his great figures of it from Israel, which after it was saved became the enemy of God, and fell under judgment. Peter does not say a word about that; he looks at merely wicked men; consequently, he is more occupied with the evil that brought on the deluge. Jude does not say a word about the deluge, because there was no question of a people being saved. There was a family—a few individuals—but there was not a people. Jude looks at the church, and compares the church getting wrong and losing everything after, having apparently gained everything: according to the picture of Israel, saved out of Egypt, and nevertheless, all coming to nothing.

We see how beautifully the figures employed and the illustrations used are all perfectly in keeping with the great differences between the two Epistles of Peter and Jude. And I mention it again, as I have already done, as a proof of the blindness of men in our day, in what they call "higher criticism." They will have it that the one Epistle is only a copy of the other. Why, they are perfectly contrasted the one with the other. There are some points, of course, that must be common—the wickedness of man, the grace of God, the truth of God. All that must be common to the two Epistles.

But the character of the truth in the one case is simply, men corrupting righteousness into unrighteousness—that is Peter. In Jude it is men, who were blessed by the revelation of grace, turning it into licentiousness, men who had not merely the authority of God, but the authority of our Lord Jesus Christ. Peter does not say a word about this. It is God's authority. Even the Lord is there looked at as Master—a Sovereign Master—not in the attitude of "our Lord Jesus Christ." Jude adds that. So Noah is the great figure in Peter; whereas Enoch, and not Noah, is the figure before us in Jude.

Now, I ask, how could the wit of man ever have done this? Even when people have read the two Epistles, many Christians have not noticed these differences, yet there they are. What learned men see is the apparent resemblances between the two. But that is an altogether unintelligent way of reading anything. Because, even if you look at all the men of the world, well, they all agree in being men, but just think how foolish a person must be who can see no difference between one man and another because they are both men! That is just the way these learned men talk. They see no difference between Peter and Jude, the one copied the other! Whereas the striking thing is that, although they both go over the same ground, they look at it in different ways—both full of instruction, yet such instruction as only the Holy Ghost could give.

Oh, how solemn when we read this last Epistle, which bears upon the apostasy of Christianity, or rather of Christendom, of those that were introduced to the richest blessings of God's grace and truth in Christ, yet turning to be the bitterest enemies of it (not only abandoning it, but) treating it with contempt and disdain, and with hatred to the last degree.

This is exactly what we have in the middle of the Epistle. We saw the characters that it takes, particularly Cain, Balaam, and Korah—the beginning, middle and end, I might say. The unnatural brother that hated, not a mere man only, but his own brother, and slew him. The bitterest enemies of the faithful are always those who profess to be faithful and are not. There is no bitterness so deep as that of an unworthy bearer of the name of Christ. Well, that is Cain. Not a word of this in Peter. That belongs to Jude, and is here.

Then Balaam appears in Peter because he is a false prophet that figures the false teachers, who are more the thing in Peter, but not in Jude; for here it is the saints, the body of the saved ones—at any rate in profession. That is what alarmed and shocked him. And he puts it forth for us, that we might now understand it, that we should not be too much perplexed by any of these terrible things which may break out at any time in our midst. There never was a more foolish idea, perhaps, entertained by some of us, that whoever might go wrong this could not happen amongst those called " Brethren." Oh, foolish Brethren, to flatter themselves in such a way as that! Why you, we—for I take my place along with you in it altogether— we are the persons most liable to have the highest flown expressions and pretension to the greatest piety, while there may be an enormously evil thing going on. How are we to judge of such things? By the word of God. And you will always find that those that are carrying on in that way slip from the word. They do not want the word. They want something new, something that will go on with the times, something that will make the " Brethren " more popular, something that will get bigger congregations, and all those things that are flattering to human vanity ; the consequence is they are naturally afraid of the word. No wonder. No one ever quarrelled with the word of God, if the word of God did not condemn them. Every person who loves the word owes to it all his entrance into blessing ; he derives all from that precious word and that precious word reveals Christ. Consequently we should not be occupied about pleasing others and about their work, but with Christ. And we want all God's children also to be occupied with Christ as the only ground of any solid and sure peace.

In Enoch's prophecy we may observe once more that it is not exactly "the Lord cometh," but, "Behold, the Lord came." This manner of speaking is quite usual in the prophets, and that is why they are called "seers." What they described they saw as in a prophetic vision. John saw all the various objects which he describes in the Revelation. He saw the heaven opened, and the Lord coming out, and the throne set. But it does not mean that all this was accomplished then. He saw it all before it took place. So did Enoch. He saw the Lord come; and he presented it in that way. In Isaiah liii. we see the same thing. "He is brought as a lamb to the slaughter, and as a sheep before her shearers is dumb, so He openeth not His mouth." It does not mean that there was any doubt about its being all future; but that the prophet saw it before his eyes, the eyes opened by the Holy Spirit. It is the same thing here. The Lord is seen at the close of the age coming with ten thousands of His saints to take judgment, to inflict judgment on these apostates; and the Spirit of God here intimates that the same family likeness of departure from God has been going on since the days of Enoch, and that it was to go on, not only in Jude's day, but in the future till the Lord comes. It was all one in character—hatred of God. And you see how entirely this falls in with what I have been saying, that man always departs from God. It is not only that he is rebellious, not only that he behaves himself badly, not only that he violates this and that, but he turns his back upon God altogether and His truth. This is apostasy, and the spirit of it is already come. It will, come out thoroughly, and then the Lord will come in judgment.

But now the hope ! What is that ? Well, it is implied in what we saw. " Behold, the Lord came with ten thousands of His saints." The question is, How did they come with Him ? If the Lord comes *with* His saints, He must have come before to fetch them to Himself, and this is just what He will do. But that is a thing entirely outside the prophetic introduction of the Lord's coming. The Lord's coming for His saints is not a matter of prophecy at all. It is a matter of love and hope ; we may say of faith, love and hope. They are all in full play in the wonderful prospect that grace has opened out before our eyes. Therefore it is that the Lord does not introduce this prospect except in a very general way, in any of the Gospels so much as He does in John : " In My Father's house are many mansions : if it were not so, I would have told you. I go to prepare a place for you. And if I go and prepare a place for you, I will come again and receive you unto Myself " (John xiv. 2, 3).

There is nothing about prophecy in that passage. It is future, but its being future does not make it prophecy. It is an abuse of terms to think that prophecy is essentially bound up with judging a wrong state of things and replacing it with a better. But in this case, as in John xiv., the Lord, when He comes to put us in the Father's house, does not judge a wrong state of things. It is consummating His love to the dearest objects of His love, not merely on earth but for heaven; and it is in that way that the Lord speaks. It is the same thing in the Revelation. After He has done with all the prophetic part, He presents Himself as "the bright and the morning star." And when the church has that before her, we find a new thing, "The Spirit and the bride say, Come." That is not prophecy; that is the church's hope, and it is strictly the church's hope. Because when you say, "The Spirit and the bride," it is not merely an individual, it is the whole—personified—of the saints that compose the bride. "The Spirit and the bride!" What a wonderful thing that the Spirit should put Himself at the head of it! "The Spirit and the bride say, Come." It might have been thought, Oh! that is only a sanguine hope that the bride has got. But, no; you cannot talk about anything sanguine in the mind of the Holy Spirit. "The Spirit and the bride say, Come." Hence you see that the great object of the Lord, in that close of the Revelation, was to show that you must not mix up the hope of the Lord's coming to receive us to Himself with the accomplishment of prophecy. The hope is entirely apart from any prophetic events. It is not in the seals, it is not in the trumpets, still less is it in the vials. It is after all these things that the Spirit of God, in the conclusory observations, gives there what the Lord had given, when Himself on earth, to His disciples. The Spirit of God takes up there what was suited to the then condition of the church. The church then knew that she was "the bride" of Christ. This had been clearly shown in more than one chapter of the Revelation. In chapter xix., the marriage of the Lamb had come, and the bride had made herself ready. That could not be the earthly bride. How could the earthly bride celebrate a marriage in heaven? And how could the heavenly bride celebrate it there unless saints composing it had been taken there before? This is just what I am about to come to.

Well, then, this coming of the Lord, which is "our hope," is exactly what Jude takes up here in the closing verses.

"But to Him that is able to keep you without stumbling, and to set you with exultation blameless before His glory; to an only* God our Saviour through Jesus Christ our Lord† [be] glory, majesty, might, and authority, before all times,‡ and now, and unto all the ages. Amen" (vers. 24, 25).

* σοφῷ (wise) is omitted by ℵABC Vulg. Copt. Arm. Æthiop. and Syrr. Vv.—T.R. inserts with KLP and many cursives.

† διὰ 'Ιησοῦ Χριστοῦ τοῦ κυρίου ἡμῶν ℵABCL Vulg. Copt. and Syrr. Vv.—T.R. omits with K.P.

‡ πρὸ παντὸς τοῦ αἰῶνος ℵABCL Vulg. Copt. Arm. and Æthiop. Vv.—T.R. omits with KP and most cursives.

"Now unto Him that is able to keep you from falling." How appropriate when thus presenting the dangers, the evils, the horrible iniquity of apostasy from all Christian grace and truth that might have the effect of greatly dispiriting a feeble soul ! No one ought even to be dispirited ; not one. "Now unto Him that is able to keep" clearly refers to every step of the way, and there is power in Him to keep. It is we who fail in dependence. Never does He fail in power to preserve. "Now unto Him that is able to keep you from falling and to present you faultless." Where ? "Before the presence of His glory." Where is that ? Is not that the very glory into which the Lord has now gone ? And does not He say, "that where I am there ye may be also " ? Here we find that the hope of the Christian and the hope of the church is entirely untouched by all the ruin that had come in. Spiritual power remained intact. And not only that : this glorious, blessed hope remains for our consolation and our joy in the darkest day.

" Now unto Him that is able to keep you without stumbling and to set you faultless before the presence of His glory with exceeding joy." There we have what falls in not with Peter, but with Jude. Jude, of course, entirely agrees with Peter, and confirms Peter as to the judgment that is to fall on those that were not only unrighteous but apostate. But then Jude does not forget that there are those that are true, that there are those that are faithful, that there are those that are waiting for Christ, that there are those that are even more appreciative of the blessing because of the unbelief of man. Therefore it is that he brings in this present power which depends entirely on the Holy Spirit's presence to keep us; and, further, he speaks of the blessed hope depending upon Christ's coming to receive us to Himself, " and to present us faultless." That will only be because we are glorified; that will only be because we are like Himself. He was the only One intrinsically faultless, and He is the One Who, by redemption, and then also by its accomplishment for the body—for redemption now is only as far as the soul is concerned, but when He comes it will be for the body as well—will present us faultless both in soul and body " before the presence of His glory with exceeding joy."

VERSE 25

" To the only [wise] God." The word "wise" has crept in here. In all correct texts the word " wise " disappears in this place. It is perfectly right in Romans xvi. 27. And I just refer to that text to show its appropriateness there : " To God only wise." I presume that it was this passage that led the ignorant monk, or whoever he was that was copying Jude, to (as he thought) correct it. But we cannot correct. All these human corrections are innovations, and our point is to get back to what

God wrote and to what God gave. Everything except what God gave is an innovation, but God's word is the standard, and all that departs from, or does without, it is an innovation.

Now, in this chapter of Romans, what made the word "wise" appropriate and necessary there, is that Paul refers to the mystery. He does not bring out the mystery in Romans; but after completing the great subject of the righteousness of God, first, in its personal application as well as in itself, secondly, comparing it with the dispensations of God, and, thirdly, in its practical shape—personal, dispensational, and practical—he here adds a little word at the close, " Now to Him that is of power to establish you according to my gospel, and the preaching of Jesus Christ, according to the revelation of the mystery." The revelation of the mystery—he had not brought this in. But he maintains that this gospel of his was according to it. It was not the revelation of it ; but it did not clash with it. There was no contrariety, but that revelation of the mystery was left for other Epistles, Ephesians and Colossians more particularly ; Corinthians also in a measure, but chiefly Ephesians and Colossians.

Further he says, " which was kept secret since the world began, but now is made manifest, and by prophetic writings " (or, scriptures, namely, those of the New Testament. I understand that what is called here " scriptures of the prophets " are the prophetic writings of the New Testament, of which

Paul contributed so much) " according to the commandment of the everlasting God made known to *all* nations "—that shows that the Old Testament prophets are not referred to here at all—" for obedience of faith ; to God only wise be glory." That is to say, this concealment of the mystery and now bringing it out in due time—not in Romans, but in what would be found to agree with Romans and confirm Romans when the mystery was com municated to the saints in the Epistles that had to be written afterwards—all this showed " God only wise." It is in connexion, you see, with this keeping back for so many ages, and now for the first time bringing out this hidden truth, the hidden mystery, as he calls it, to our glory, which is involved in Christ's exaltation at the right hand of God, and in His leaving the world for the time entirely alone, whilst meanwhile forming the disciples according to the truth of His being in heaven.

In Timothy, however, we have an expression exactly similar to what we have here. " Now unto the King eternal, immortal, invisible, the only God " (1 Tim. i. 17). There the word " wise " is brought in again in our Authorised Version. There is no reason for it there. So that there is the same error introduced in Timothy as there is in Jude, and both of them brought from what we already have in Romans xvi., where it ought to be. Here, we find again, what a dangerous thing it is for man to meddle with the word of God. The apostle is here looking at God Himself, not at what He particularly does. The wisdom of His revelation—that is in Romans. But in Timothy it is, " Now unto the King eternal, immortal, invisible, the only God." There might be all these pretenders, these gods many and lords many that Paul knew very well among the Gentiles, and Timothy also, and particularly at this very Ephesus where Timothy seems to have been at this very time. There was the famous temple (one of the wonders of the world), called the temple of Diana. Artemis is the proper word, for Diana was a Roman goddess, and Artemis was a Grecian goddess quite of a different nature, although there were kindred lies about the two.

Here, therefore, in Timothy the apostle presented with great propriety and beauty " the only God." Bringing in the " wise " God introduces quite another idea which does not fall in with the context, it does not agree with it properly. We find just the same thing in Jude. So that the comparison, I think, of the three scriptures will help to show that " the only wise God " belongs to Romans; that " the only God "—Who is presented in contrast with idols and imaginary beings—brings in to Timothy the force of the " only " true God.

In Jude we have " the only God " for a slightly different reason, but one equally appropriate. He is looking at all this terrible scene and at the greatness of the grace of God towards His beloved ones carried through such an awful sea of iniquity and apostasy.

But if our eye be fixed on Christ, my dear brethren, it does not matter where we are, or whether we are smooth or rough. Some would make a great deal of the large waves, and I have no doubt that Peter was frightened at the big waves on which he found himself walking, and when he looked at the waves down he went. But if there had been no big waves, all as smooth as glass, and Peter had looked down on the glassy sea, down he would have gone all the same. It is not, therefore, at all a question of the particular circumstances. The fact is, there is no power to keep us, except a divine one, and it is all grace ; and the grace that supports on a smooth sea is equally able to preserve on a rough one. Whatever, therefore, may be the special characters of evil and of danger at the present time, all turns upon this : What is Christ to my soul ? And if I believe in His grace and in His truth then what does not my soul find in Christ ?

" Now, unto Him that is able to keep you from falling, and to present you faultless before the presence of His glory, with exceeding joy." For the grace on His part is just the same as if there had been no departure, no apostasy, no wickedness, no unrighteousness of any kind. He wrought His marvellous work of grace for us when we were nothing but sinners. He brought us to Himself when we were no better—unmoved, perhaps, by that wonderful work when we first read and heard about it. But when the moment came for us to believe on Him, how it changed all! And surely the times that have passed over us have only endeared the Lord more to us. I hope there is not a soul in this room but what loves the Lord a deal better to-day than the day on which he, or she, was first converted. It is one of those notions of Christendom that our love is always much better and stronger on the day we were first converted. Never was there greater mistake. There was a feeling of mercy, no doubt; a deep sense of pardoning grace, but, beloved friends, do we not love the Lord for incomparably more than what we knew when converted? Surely that love has grown with a better knowledge of His love, and of His truth. And here we find that His grace is exactly the same, that the grace that brought Him from heaven, the grace of Him, Who lived here below, that died here below, and is now gone back into glory, is without change; and that the exceeding joy or exultation will be unquenched in the smallest degree when the blessed moment comes. " He will set us blameless before the presence of His glory, with exceeding joy." It is not very much to find where the exceeding joy is. I am persuaded it is both in Him and in us. Perhaps we may be allowed to say, " which thing is true in Him and in you " (1 John ii. 8). That was said about another thing altogether —the love that He put into our hearts when we knew His redemption; for until we know redemption there is not much love in a believer. He may have a good bit of affection for the people that he is intimate with, but he is very narrow at first, and till he knows the love of Christ his affections do not at all go out to all the saints. Here then we find, at any rate, this glowing picture of that bright hope, when it will surely be accomplished.

Now, Jude adds, " To the only God." For who could have met all this confusion ? Who could have conceived and counselled all this grace and truth ? Who could have kept such as we are through all, remembering our total weakness, our great exposure, the hatred of the enemy, the contempt of adversaries, of all that are drawn away, of all the enticement to go wrong, all the animosities, worst of all, created by any measure of faithfulness ? Yet He does keep through it all. " The only God our Saviour " ; not only Christ our Saviour. Christ is the accomplisher of it all, but here Jude looks at God as the source, and it is no derogation from Christ. It was the delight of Christ on earth to present God as a Saviour God, and not merely that He Himself was that personal Saviour, the Son of man. So here the apostle desires that we should ever honour God our Saviour, as indeed we find it rather a common expression in those very solemn Epistles to Timothy.

" To the only God our Saviour." All other dependence is vain, all other boast is worthless. We are intended to rejoice, or, rather more strictly, to " boast in God through our Lord

Jesus Christ, by Whom we have now received the reconciliation."

"To [the] only God our Saviour, through Jesus Christ our Lord, be glory, majesty, might and authority, before all time, and now and ever (or, to all the ages)." It is a very interesting thing to note here the propriety with which Jude closes the Epistle. He says, "Be glory, majesty, might and authority, before all time, and now, and for evermore, Amen." He looks at the full extent of eternity. It is much more precise than what we have in our Authorised Version; and is here given according to the reading of the best authorities, and rightly adopted by the Revisers.

Peter also closes his Second Epistle in what is said to be the same. But there is this distinction, that whilst Peter speaks of "glory both now and unto eternity's day" (iii. 18), Jude brings out in the remarkable completeness of his closing ascription what was, and is, and is to be, in all its full eternal character.

NOTES

ON THE

EPISTLE TO THE HEBREWS,

From Notes of Lectures,

By J. N. D.

BOOKS FOR CHRISTIANS

Post Office Box 15344
Charlotte, North Carolina
28210

Printed in the United States of America—1970

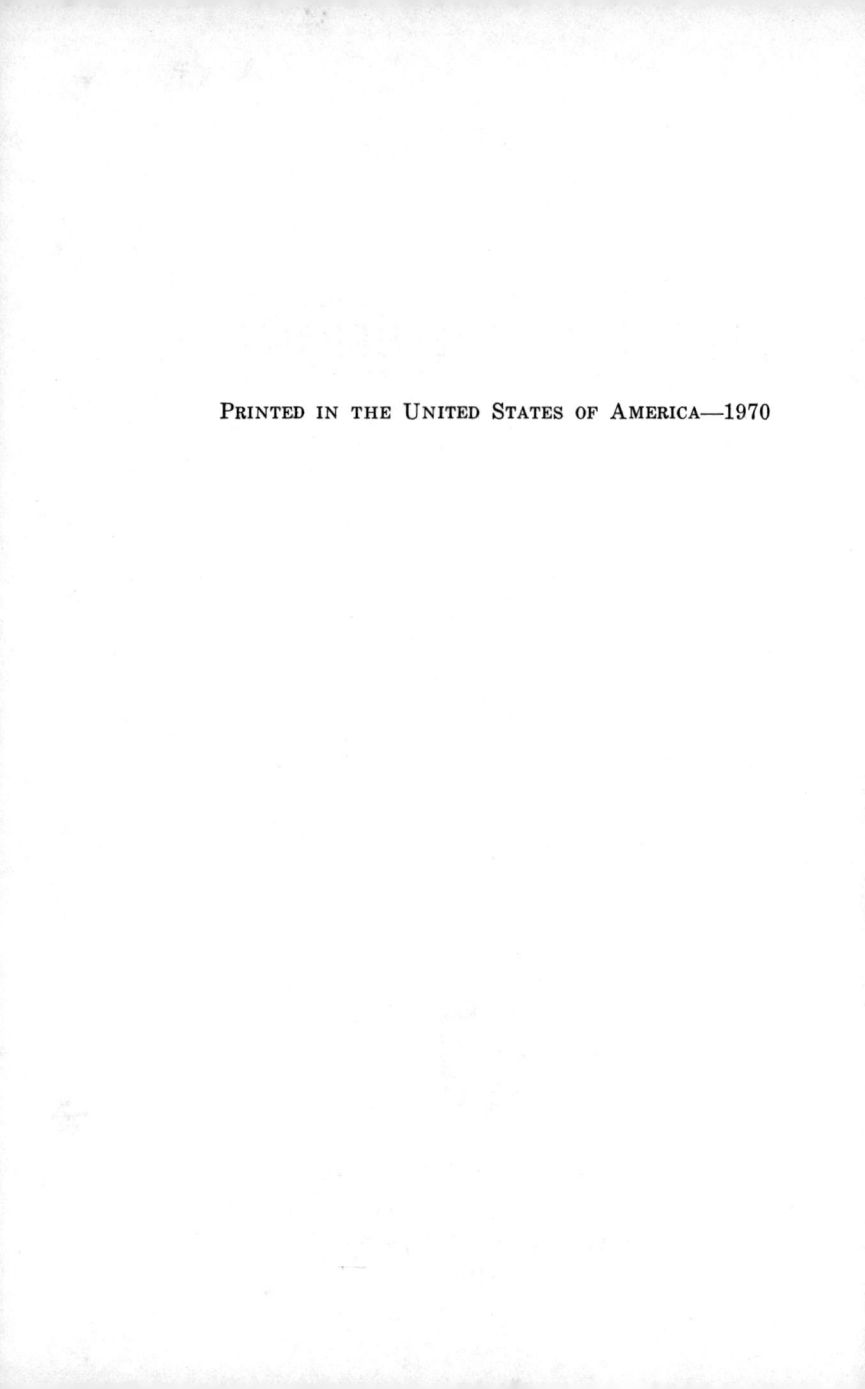

INDEX.

	PAGE
Chapter I., ...	9
Chapter II., ...	18
Chapter III., ...	25
Chapter IV., ...	34
Chapter V., VI., ...	46
Chapter VII., ...	68
Chapter VIII., ...	82
Chapter IX., ...	87
Chapter X., ...	107
Chapter XI., ...	118
Chapter XII., ...	129
Chapter XIII., ...	137

THOUGHTS ON HEBREWS.

CHAPTER I.

THE Spirit of God in this epistle distinguishes between the way in which God spoke, or dealt, in time past and now. So in Romans iii. the apostle speaks of Christ, "whom God hath set forth to be a propitiation through faith in his blood, to declare his righteousness for the remission of sins that are past." There he applies the death of Christ to the sins committed before He came. The day of atonement in Israel was for the putting away of *past* sins. He had been bearing with them all the year, and then when the sacrifice came on, that day the sin was all put away and all bright in the presence of God. There is the day of atonement yet to come for Israel as a nation, when in their land. Then the other part was " to declare at this time his righteousness, that he might be just, and the justifier of him," &c. This is for the present time. By ascending before God on high, He establishes a *present righteousness*—all sins forgiven and we made the righteousness of God in Christ. Romans iii. 25, gives it historically, for the sins of all who were saved in the Old Testament times are put away by this sacrifice; but *we* may apply it immediately, and see that not only *our* past sins are put away, but we stand in righteousness for the present.

Ver. 1., " God who at sundry times," &c. That was before the time came for the revelation of Himself. Messages were sent through others. They had communications from God, for He spake to them through the prophets: but now we have the manifestation of *Himself*. The Son of God has now come. "God hath in these last days spoken unto us by His Son." Thus the word of God is so exalted. "Thou hast magnified thy *word* above all thy name." His name up to that time was exalted—He had made Himself known to Abraham as the Lord Almighty, telling him to trust His *power*, when he had to walk up and down as a stranger, with none to take care of him. Then again He was made known to Nebuchadnezzar as the most High God, higher than any of the gods of the nations; and to Abraham too He was called thus, when he returned from the slaughter of the kings. He will take it again when the kingdom comes. Then, again, He was known by the name *Jehovah*—" I am," the practical force of which is " the same yesterday, to-day, and for ever." All these names were glorious; but the Word He has magnified above all. The *Word* is that which tells all that God is—holiness, love, wisdom, &c. His word expresses His thoughts and feelings; it is the revelation of Himself. God speaks by Christ. Everything that Christ did was the manifestation of God. Who could heal the leper but God? "I will, be thou clean," are His words. Who could raise the dead but God? "Lazarus, come forth!" (John xvii. 8.) "I have given unto them the words which thou gavest me." He has committed His words to us, to be the vessels of His testimony according to our measure. "He that hath received His testimony hath set to his seal that God is true."

We are not only brought to God now, but to God *revealing* Himself, God manifest in the flesh. Christ came declaring the Father. "Believe me that I am in the Father . . . . or else believe me for the very works' sake." What a blessed place we have in Christ, having Him as the revelation of God to us! The mind of God is brought before us in Christ. "The word is nigh thee, even in thy mouth and in thy heart." This is what makes Scripture so precious. It is indeed the written word, but the revelation of God. "No prophecy of Scripture is of private interpretation." You have got the mind of God in *writing*, and there it is stable and imperishable—in contrast to traditions merely handed down from one to another. There cannot be the Church speaking, without Scripture. If the Church can say anything itself, then Christ's words go for nothing. I have another master over me. I am speaking of authority now, not of *gift*, which of course there is in the Church for the bringing out of truth. But *authority* in the Church trenches on the lordship of Christ over His house. It is a great thing to treasure in our souls that we have this revelation of God in Christ; and the beginning of the next chapter takes us up on the ground of possessing it. "Therefore we ought to give the more earnest heed to the things which we have heard, lest at any time we should let them slip." These were Jews to whom the apostle was writing, and they had heard the Lord Himself speak, and afterwards His apostles; and that is the reason why Paul did not put his name to this as to other epistles, when inditing them. You Jews hear what God Himself had said to you. You have heard Him. Thus, the apostle only confirmed what He had said. It is blessed thus to see how Paul drops his own apostleship, (he was not, it is true, the apostle of the circumcision,) and only speaks of the twelve who confirmed Christ's own words.

In this chapter we have first the glory of Christ shown in His being "heir of all things." He was the Son of the Father, and the everlasting Father, by virtue of His own power; and He will take everything. He will inherit all things. If a Son, we may say, then an heir; and it is even said of us, "If children, then heirs." All that is the Father's is His. "He shall take of *mine*, and shall show it unto you." Psalm viii. is alluded to in chap. ii., when in the counsels of God it is appointed that as a man He should take all things; but in this chapter we have this same One as the Son of God and "heir of all things;" and for this glorious reason, He "made the worlds." In Colossians we have it, they "were created *by* him and *for* him." There it is His title over creation, but as "the image of the invisible God, the first-born," &c. So here it is "heir of all things, by whom also *he made* the worlds." He is distinguished from God the Father—the right hand of His power. By wisdom He planned and by power He wrought. Christ is that wisdom and that power.

Ver. 3. "The express image of his person." Christ was the outshining of God's glory. That is more than testimony made by the prophets in other ages. John xii. 38-41, in connexion with Isaiah vi., shows the shining out of His glory very remarkably. See also Heb. xii. 27 in connexion with this word, "the express image of his person."

"Upholding all things," &c. Of course this is a divine act. Who could keep the universe going? How could it all go on without God, so that not a sparrow falls to the ground without Him? How could it be without Him who made it? Though He has established the order of all things, it is He who is keeping it all going. The one actually acting and possessing all is Christ. We see His *glory* in all this.

Another divine work there is spoken of in His having "purged our sins;" and it is just as much a divine act to purge our sins as to create a world, and in one sense far more difficult, because sin is so hateful to God. It would be easy enough for Him to create another world out of nothing. He could look at His creation and say it was all "very good;" but

He is so holy, He cannot look upon sin. Therefore, there is something He must take away, and he does come to put sins away. We have sinned against God, and it is impossible for any to forgive the sin but the person sinned against. We have sinned against God, not man primarily, and man cannot forgive sins. This is another reason why God should be the only one who can forgive sins.

Mark another thing. He must *purge* before He can *forgive.* In passing through this world, man has to pass over a great deal, and get through as well as he can; but God cannot do that. He "is of purer eyes than to behold iniquity." Then if God is to have anything to do with us, He must purge it. There is this dreadful necessity, that God should be occupied with our sins; and He had love enough and power enough to do it. If He passed it over, He would have to give up His holiness. Therefore there was this moral necessity of His holiness, that if He is to have any such poor sinners in His presence, He must cleanse us. So there must also be the feet-washing, if we are to have part with Christ.

"When He had by Himself purged our sins"—it must be by Himself. No one could help Him in it; angels could have nothing to do in it, though they were sent to minister to Him when engaged in the work. Man could not, for man can do no more than his duty; if he did more, it would be wrong. It must be a divine work to purge away sin. There is a divine necessity upon God to do it—and that by

Himself, because He could not allow sin. This is how I am purged. Because He could not bear sin, He must take it away Himself, and "the blood of Jesus Christ cleanseth from all sin." It is a work that has been done : not anything that He will do, and may do—not something yet to be done. *It is done*, and He has sat down. We then no longer have a prophet coming to tell us He will do it, but there is the testimony of the Holy Ghost that it has been done.

"The brightness of God's glory," it is said, not the Father's. Sin is connected with God as its judge, not with the Father. He "sat down on the right hand of the Majesty on high." The whole work is accomplished, and so perfectly done that He can take His own place again, and with the blessed difference, that He goes back as a man, which He never was before. Stephen saw Him as the "Son of man," standing on the right hand of God. Here He is "sat down on the right hand of the Majesty on high," He has taken our sins, and yet is on the right hand of the throne of God. This shows that the righteousness wrought out was so perfect and divine, that though he has taken our sins, He could sit down on the throne of God, and not soil it. He had a right, of course, on the ground of His divine person; but there is more than that here. Divine righteousness is presented to God, as an accomplished thing, just as the Divine Son was manifested to man when He came down amongst us. It is all divine glory throughout.

Psalm ii., "Kiss the Son," &c. Blessed is the

man who trusteth in God; but cursed the man who trusteth in man. (Jer. xvii.) We find in the prophets certain traits in mystery, as it were, to display the divine person of the One who was coming in humiliation. See Isaiah l. 3—5. The same glorious person who said " I clothe the heavens with blackness," &c., says, "The Lord God hath opened mine ear, and I was not rebellious," &c. In Daniel vii. again, see ver. 13, "the Son of man," brought before "the Ancient of days," and in ver. 22, He is giving out Himself to be "the Ancient of days." Heb. i, 7. "Who maketh His angels spirits," &c., but He does not *make* when speaking of the Son. "Thy throne, O God, is for ever and ever." (See Psalm xlv. 1—7; Heb. i. 9.) He whose throne is for ever and ever has been put to the test; and He loved righteousness and hated iniquity while amongst us, and has brought us up as *His* fellows out of our iniquity. See the contrast in the connexion in which "fellows" is mentioned here, and in Zech. xiii. 7, where Jehovah speaks of the man, His fellow who has been "wounded in the house of His friends."

Thus we see the glory of *Christ* shining through the Old Testament continually, but in this chapter it is fully brought out. He is owned as God, though a man, and glorified above all others.

Ver. 10, 11, &c. See Psalm cii. "Thy years are throughout," &c., is in answer to ver. 23, and first clause of ver. 24. This is still more pointed and precise. Jesus, in His humiliation, breathes out His broken heart to Jehovah. The psalm anticipates the rebuilding of Zion. If so, where would this smitten Messiah be? If cut off in the midst of His day, how could He be there? God's answer is, that *He*, the holy sufferer, is Jehovah, the creator and disposer of all things. What a testimony to His unchangeable deity!

This is the time of grace, when those who are to be His companions in the glory are being gathered out (His fellows, ver. 9). Ver. 13. Angels have a very blessed place and office, but it is never said to them, " Sit on my right hand," &c., but Jehovah did say so to the man, Christ Jesus. He has His own place there.

What a blessed Saviour we have! The *Lord* Himself has come and taken up our cause. The One whom we look to, and lean upon as a Saviour, is the Lord Jehovah.

Then, besides the glory of His person, there is the other blessed truth, essential to our peace, to see what a wonderful salvation we have: our sins completely purged away! There is a wonderful and divine glory in this salvation, and divine and ineffable love—the love of One who is not like an angel, who could only do his work when told.

Our souls are thus called to worship *Him* who clothes the heavens with blackness, who indeed made all things: even Jesus, the Son of God.

CHAPTER II.

THE first four verses of this chapter are an exhortation founded on the preceding one. Observe, this epistle does not begin with an apostolic address, as the others do; but Paul puts himself entirely among these Jewish believers, and speaks of *Christ* as their Apostle, not himself; and, throughout, he is unfolding all the riches of Christ, to keep them from sliding back into Judaism. Though the gospel of the uncircumcision was committed to Paul, as that of the circumcision was to Peter, yet is Paul the one used to these Hebrew believers. In chap. i. 1, 2, God hath "spoken to *us:*" that is, he puts himself among them. In the Hebrews, the Church is not addressed as such, but the saints *individually*—not in their aspect of oneness with Christ. Even in the Epistle to the Romans it is said "whom he justified, them he also glorified;" but here we get *Him only* "crowned with glory and honour." Further, I would remark, as it is not of union with Christ of which the apostle speaks here, responsibility is pressed; continual "ifs" and warnings flow from this. These warnings do not one whit touch the final perseverance of the saints, as the doctrine is called; though I would rather say, the perseverance of *God*, *His* faithfulness, for He it is who keeps us to the end. " If you continue," does not throw a doubt on your continuance. The quickening work of the Spirit of God is scarcely referred to in this epistle save in one or two cases. (Chap. ii. 2.) "The word spoken by angels," means the law given at Sinai. In these verses the whole Jewish nation is addressed, while those only who had faith would receive the warning. And I would notice that the warnings of God are not merely against sin, but not to let slip truth, &c. Christ came into the world, not imputing their trespasses unto them, but they added to their rebellion of heart by rejecting Him who came to warn them. *Neglecting* salvation is despising it. By the rejection of Christ the Jews bound their sins upon them. To have broken the law was bad enough, but to reject grace was worse; and these first four verses press this upon them.

God's purpose for man (ver. 5, and following), is to set him over everything; but that purpose is still unfulfilled. "The world to come," is not heaven, for that does exist now; but it is the *habitable earth to come*, not this earth in its present state. The Jews expected a new order of things; they looked for blessing and peace, and they were right, for so it will be. The present world is in subjection to angels. God's hand is not seen directly, but His angels are ministering spirits to the heirs of salvation. Everything in this world, however mercifully ordered in providence, is a proof of sin—the clothes we wear, the houses we live in, &c. All this was not God's purpose. He is not, as I said, *now* acting *directly*.

He permits and overrules, but He draws His own people from the world (delivering us " from this present evil world "), and then teaches them to walk through it, as not of it. He protects us through His angels; they are His ministers in His providential dealings. (Ver. 6.) But it is a man who is to be set over the world to come. *Once* (in Adam) dominion was committed to man, but he lost it. (Ver. 8, &c.) God's purpose, that is, His order of things, is not thereby touched. *Now* we see *Jesus* crowned, and when *we are*, then all things will be accomplished. The Head is now glorified, and the members are down here in suffering. Christ is sitting at God's right hand, waiting till His enemies are made His footstool. Take Psalm ii. and compare it with Psalm viii. God says, " Yet have I set my king upon the holy hill of Zion." Christ is come, and is not yet set there as king. Now Psalm viii. shows that, though rejected as Messiah, Jesus took the place of Son of man. So when Peter confesses Him as the Christ, Jesus charges him straightly not to tell any, for the "*Son of man* (His title in Psalm viii.) *must* suffer many things," &c. Sin must be put away before God could set up His kingdom. We are now passing through that order or state of things which is not yet put under Jesus. Christ has gone through this very world, and been tempted before He took His place as priest, that He might succour them that are tempted. This is not *sin*, for we do not want sympathy in sin, but help and power to get out of and overcome it, and all this we have in Him. He went perfectly through reproach and tribulation. All that Satan could do to stop Him in His godly course Satan did; but all was in vain. The Lord " resisted unto blood." We need to pray God for help to judge sin, each in himself. Sympathy in distress and suffering is another thing, and this we have as well as forgiveness.

I began by saying there were two things—the *purpose* and the *ways* of God. Now, the latter it is our privilege to trace, while the former remains still unaccomplished. Instead of being merely Son of David, Christ is Son of man. He takes possession in our nature—not, of course, in the state in which it is in us, but still in our very nature. Now, as to the *ways* of God, we get these in ver. 10 : " By the *grace* of God he tasted death," &c. Mark this well—our *sin* brings us to the same place which, by the *grace of God*, He took. Perfect grace and perfect obedience we find in Him. When Christ came, as in Psalm xl. to do the will of God, God's majesty needed to be vindicated ; and I would say, unhesitatingly, that God's truth, His righteousness, His love, His majesty were all vindicated by the death of Christ, aye, far more than they would have been, had we all died. In anticipation of this, He said, " I have a baptism to be baptized with ; and how am I straitened till it be accomplished ! " His love could not fully flow forth till then. In the words, " It became him," I find the character of God ; while in the expression, " many sons," I find the objects of his love. He could not bring us to glory in our sins. We get Christ taking up the cause of this remnant; and where, *historically*, did he begin? It was in John's baptism that He outwardly identified Himself with His people, that is, with the sanctified ones. (Ver. 11. See Psalm xvi. 2, 3.) His association was with the saints; and there cannot be a step in the divine life in which Christ does not go along with us. Christ, in all that he is, is with us in the smallest fibre of divine life, from the repentance which is at the beginning. Not, of course, that he had aught to repent; yet His heart is with us in it. This is as true now, as it will be when manifested in glory. (Ver 16.) There was no union of Christ with the flesh. The associates of Christ are the excellent of the earth; while in grace one of His sweetest titles was "the friend of the publicans and sinners."

Verse 12 is a quotation from Psalm xxii. 22, where Jesus in resurrection takes the place of leader of the praise of His brethren. Our songs should, therefore, ever accord with His. He has passed through death for us; and if our worship express uncertainty and doubt, instead of joy and assurance in the sense of accomplished redemption, there can be no harmony, but discord, with the mind of heaven.

Verse 13 is quoted from Psalm xvi., where as also elsewhere, Christ on earth takes the place of the dependent man. He is specially thus described in Luke's gospel, where it is so frequently recorded that *He prayed.* Again, "Behold I and the children," &c.

This passage from Isaiah viii. 18, is particularly applicable to these Hebrew believers. While waiting for Israel, He and His disciples are for signs.

In ver. 14 we find the consequence of His association with us. In these latter verses we have these two things: He took our nature that He might die, and also that He might go through temptation. We were alive under death; then Christ comes, and He takes upon Him all the power of Satan and death, and destroys thus him that had the power of death. By His death He made propitiation for sin. The feelings of His soul, the temptations of Satan, were before His actual death, in the garden of Gethsemane, where His language was, "My soul is exceeding sorrowful, even unto death." This was because of Satan's power; for He said, "This is your hour and the power of darkness." But all this He went through, as part of His appointed sufferings. In the three first Gospels, we have His cry in Gethsemane. In John we have His remembrance of His Mother, and His other cries ("I thirst!" and "It is finished!") *on the cross*; and this is in character with that Gospel in which His divine aspect is given. After the conflict with Satan was over, Christ took up the cup from His Father's hand. They who were sent to secure Him had no power against Him for they all fell back; but He gave Himself up. Satan pressed the cup upon Him; but He took it from the hand of His Father.

As regards temptation, I shall hope to speak more about it another time. I would only now say that succouring is not dying instead of me; but now that I am going through this world, I need succour. The ark in Jordan was like Christ preceding us through the waters of death, which to Him overflowed its banks, while we follow dry-shod. For what is dying to the Christian? It is passing away from all sorrow into the presence of the Lord—the happiest moment in a Christian's existence.

CHAPTER III.

THE first title of our Lord in this chapter is connected with the first part of the epistle; the second, viz., the priesthood, refers to what follows afterwards. In chapter i. also we have His qualification for being the Apostle; in chapter ii., His qualification for the priesthood. He was the Divine Messenger for the testimony He was to bring to earth; and He is gone up on high to exercise His priesthood on behalf of a needy people down here where He has been. " God manifest in flesh, justified in the Spirit...received up in glory," referring to His having come down and become man. He must be in the holy place in order to carry on His work as Priest; but He must be a man. Therefore what He was on earth fitted Him, as it were, for this work. There is a third character connected with Christ brought out in this third chapter; Christ set " over His own House." In this epistle we do not get the unity of the body at all; we get a Mediator speaking to God for us, and speaking from God to us: " Let us hold fast the profession," &c. If He spoke of the unity of the body, that is inseparable; there is one Holy Ghost uniting the members to the Head,— " ye in me, and I in you." It is not so here. Therefore, profession is spoken of, and the *possibility* of that being not true profession; yet assuming it might be sincere, " we are persuaded better things of you," &c. (Chap. vi.) There might be all these privileges and no fruit, but falling away. These Hebrews had made a public profession of having embraced Christ, and received a heavenly calling. In speaking of the body of Christ, we know it is perfect—no possibility of a false member getting in; but in a living congregation, I may address them as hoping they are all saints, but the end proves. No man can tell the end, whether they will all persevere; but if there is life we know they will.

" Apostle of our profession,"—it could not be said Apostle of life. We never can understand this epistle properly, unless we get hold of this truth. In Ephesians, where the body is more the subject, I do not get such an expression as this, "that he might sanctify the people with his own blood."

The character of this epistle not being understood is the reason many souls are tried and exercised by passages they find in it. They are addressed with the possibility of their not having life, and so not continuing to the end. The Church supposes a body in heaven. "Heavenly calling" does not necessarily imply that, because they are called to heaven, they are part of the body of Christ. The kingdom and the body are different. "Head over all things to the Church" is wider, too, than the kingdom. Kingdom implies a king; a body implies a head. The Church is precious to God. Everything that Christ has, I have; the same life, the same righteousness, the same glory.

If my hand is hurt, I say it is *I* who am hurt. Paul was converted by this truth, " Why persecutest thou *me ?*" It shows what grace has done for us—taken us out of ourselves. The body of Christ shows out the fulness of redemption, and the purpose of God respecting it. But another aspect of the people of God is down here in infirmity, but having this heavenly calling. In this condition I need One in heaven; and there is not an infirmity, a need, a sorrow, an ache, an anxiety, but it draws out sympathy and help from Christ. This draws out my affections to Him. But before the priesthood is taken up, Moses is spoken of as a type:—" Christ Jesus, faithful to him that appointed him, as also Moses was faithful in all his house." The house is the place where God dwells: and there is another thing here—the Head of the house administering in it.

God has met His people according to the need in which they were. In Egypt they need redemption, and He comes to redeem. In the wilderness they were dwelling in tents, and He would have a tent too. In getting into the land they wanted One to bring them in, and there is the captain of the Lord's host. Then, when they are in the land, He builds His palace, His temple. There is rest. We are not come to the temple yet—we have not rest: we get the tabernacle now, and "there remaineth a rest." There was a temple existing when these Hebrews were addressed, but that was not for us.

The temple is a dwelling for God. There never

was a dwelling-place for God until redemption came in. Scripture never speaks of man getting back to innocency, or the image of God. God did not *dwell* with Adam; though in the cool of the day He came to talk with him. Neither did He dwell with Abraham. "The earth hath he given to the children of men"— "the heaven's are the Lord's." But when redemption comes in, God is forming something for Himself. Thus, in Exodus xv. 13, "habitation" refers to what they had in the wilderness; verse 17 to the rest at the end. (Ex. xxix.)

There were visits to Abraham (Abraham will dwell in heaven), but God could not have a habitation among men until He had made known redemption to them. The nature and character of God require it. Love is God's character: to enjoy God I must be with Him. Holiness is His nature. We are made sons of God ("the servant abideth not in the house for ever," &c.) In the divine nature communicated to us, we are capable of being at home in that house of God, and redemption gives the title.

The individual Christian is a temple now; but the temporary provisional thing is God dwelling with us. The full blessed thing is our dwelling with God. (John xiv.) I go not away to be alone there, but to have you there. "I go to prepare a place for you." In verse 23 the Father and the Son make their abode with us till we are taken to abide with them. God's having a house, as a general thought, is the consequence of redemption. Here in Hebrews it is rather alluded to as to administration than dwelling. "Habitation of God," is the present thing; "temple," is future in Eph. ii. It is spoken of in a larger and more vague way in Hebrews, because here it takes in profession. He that built all things is God. In one sense creation is His house; in another, Christ has passed through the heavens, as High Priest, into the heaven of heavens, (through the two vails, as is represented in the type), into the holiest. In a third sense the body professing Christianity is His house, "whose house are we," &c.—the saints. There may be hypocrites amongst them; but they " are builded together for an habitation of God," &c. Christ administers in it, as Son over His own house. Moses was but servant in the building. There is immense comfort for us in this; first, because it is perfectly governed; second, when we look at the house, we may see all sorts of failures coming in; but though all may be failure, the One who administers in the house cannot fail. Therefore, though all seek their own, not the things which are Jesus Christ's, Paul could say, " Rejoice in the Lord alway," &c. There is One whom nothing escapes. Anyone who has a real care for the Church of God, need never distrust. Paul, in looking at the Galatians, sees so much wrong that he does not know what to think of them : he changes his voice towards them. Ye that are under the law, hear the law. But in the next chapter he says, " I have confidence in you through the Lord." Christ is over His own house. Two things follow then. He will turn everything to blessing—Paul in prison, &c.; and there is present good too. When all the joints and bands do not play as they ought, the immediate ministry of Christ is more experienced. Christ connects everything with His glory; and faith connects the glory of the Lord with the people of the Lord. Moses did so. Faith does not only say, the Lord is glorious, and He will provide the means for His own glory; but it sees the means for it. Moses said, "Spare the people," when with God; and when he came down amongst them, he "cut off the people," because he was alive to God's glory (in the matter of the calf in the camp).

We have to count upon Christ for the Church, not upon itself. Thus Paul, when tried by Nero, passes sentence as it were upon himself; (Phil. i. 23-25;) he settles it that he shall be acquitted. Why? Because he sees it is more needful for them—one single Church. It was divine teaching and faith in exercise which made him to judge thus.

There is failure on the part of the Church down here as to responsibility, but Christ has perfect authority in His Church, and He has interest in it. We have not to make rules for the Church; it is the Master must govern the house, not the servants. There is one Master, and that is Christ. He is over the Church, and not the Church over Him. "Whose house are we, if we hold fast the confidence," &c. Ah! people say, don't you be too confident, because there is an "*if.*" But, I ask, what have you got? What he presses is, that you should not let it go. Is that to be used to hinder my having the confidence? What did they believe? That Christ was come—a heavenly Saviour to them, and this far better than an earthly one. Do not give up that. There is a fear of their *giving up* that confidence, not of their being too confident. What am I to distrust? Myself? Oh! I cannot distrust myself too much. But is it Christ you distrust? Will His eye ever grow dim, or His heart grow cold? Will He leave off interceding? A proof that I am a real stone in the house is that I hold fast the confidence, &c. Those high priests under the old dispensation were continually standing; but He has sat down, because the work is all done. They needed for every sin a new sacrifice: sin was never put away. They needed a fresh absolution from the priest every time sin came up. Now, He says, " their sins and their iniquities will I remember no more." If you are under law, it is another thing; you have not got the confidence. If you talk of distrust, what do you distrust? If you trust in man at all, it is a proof you do not see that you are lost. If you give up confidence in yourself, and say, I am lost already, it is another thing. No one that has really come to redemption, has in the substance of his soul confidence in himself; and no Christian will say, you ought to distrust Christ. Our privilege is to have confidence in Christ as a rock under our feet, and to rejoice in hope of the glory of God. His righteousness has brought Christ into the glory as a man, and the same righteousness will bring me in.

Does another person say, I do not know whether I have a portion in it? You are under the law: God may be ploughing up your soul—exercising it for good; but you have not been brought to accept the righteousness of God. The soul in this state has not accepted the righteousness of God for it, instead of ours for Him. You are still depending on your own heart for comfort and assurance. It is a very serious thing to get the soul so empty of everything that it has only to accept what God can give. It is an awful thing to find oneself in God's presence, with nothing to say or to present. You never get love to Christ until you are saved; and it is the work of God's Spirit. The prodigal found what he was by what his father was. Did the prodigal doubt his interest when the father was on his neck?

The remainder of this chapter takes up the people of Israel—the professing people in the wilderness. They did not get into the land, but their carcases fell in the wilderness. It is speaking of them on the road. The "to-day" quoted from Psalm xcv. never closes for Israel, till God has taken up the remnant at the end of His dealings with them, after the Church is gone up to heaven.

Ver. 14. " Partakers " is the same word as that translated " fellows " in chap. i. You are fellows of Christ if you are of this company. *This place* with the fellows is yours if you go on to the end. This kind of statement does not touch the question of the security of the saints. Both Calvinists and Arminians might say, He will reach heaven, if he holds fast to the end. The certainty of salvation is the certainty of faith, and not that which excludes dependence upon God for every moment. I have no doubt that God will keep every one of His saints to the end; but we have to run the race to obtain eternal glory. Holding fast the faithfulness of God, it is important, along with this, to keep up the plain sense of passages such as the present, which act on the conscience as warning by the way. There is no uncertainty, but there is the working out our own salvation with fear and trembling. In 1 Cor. ix. 27, personal Christianity is distinguished from preaching to others. It is not a question of the *work*, but of the *person* being ἀδόκιμος, and this means disapproved or reprobate, *i.e.*, not a Christian. (Comp. 2 Cor. xiii.) In Rom. ii. eternal life is spoken of as the result of a course which pleases God. No doubt, His grace gives the power; but it is the result of a fruit-bearing course. In a word, it is equally true that I have eternal life, and that I am going on to eternal life. God sees it as one existence, but we have to separate it in time. Walk that road, and you will have what is at the end of it. This does not interfere with the other truth, that God will keep His own, and that none shall pluck them out of His hand. Our Father says, as it were, That is my child, and I watch him all the way, and take care to keep him in it.

CHAPTER IV.

THE word of God is connected with the apostleship. (Chap. iii. 1.) In the last verses the priesthood of Christ the subject. These are the two means of our being carried through the wilderness—the word of God, and priesthood of Christ. Israel were treated as a people brought out of Egypt, but liable to fall by the way. So the warning to these Hebrews, (chap. iv. 1,) "as to seeming to come short." The word is softened. In chap. iii. we have seen them addressed as a body brought out under the name of Christ, but admitting the possibility of hypocrites among them.

There are two distinct things connected with the people—redemption, and being carried on when brought out into the wilderness.

The epistles to the Hebrews and to the Philippians both address saints as in the wilderness. In Philippians it is more personal experience that is spoken of, e.g., "I know that this shall turn to my salvation through your prayer." In both it is as passing through the wilderness, and not yet in the rest.

Ver. 1. We have "*His* rest." Not merely *rest*, but *God's* rest; and this makes all the difference. It is not merely as tired ones, and glad to rest: we are going into the rest *of God*. There is an allusion to creation when God saw all that He had made very good. He delighted in it, and rested. Spiritual labour now is not rest, nor the worry and plague of sin. *God* will rest in His love. (Zeph. iii. 17.) How could He rest here? Not till He sees all those He loves perfectly happy. How can He rest where sin is? Holiness cannot rest where sin is. Love cannot rest where sorrow is. He rested from His works in the first creation, because it was all very good; but when sin came in, His rest was broken. He must work again. God finds rest where everything is according to His own heart. He is completely satisfied in the exercise of His love.

When conflict and labour are over, we shall get into the rest in which He is. That is the promise. "A promise being left us of entering into his rest"—God's own rest. If affections have not their object, they are not at rest. They *will* have this then, and we shall be like Him. There will be also comparative rest, even for this poor creation, by and by.

These Hebrews, who are addressed, are compared to the Jews who came out of Egypt, some of whom fell; but he says, "We are persuaded better things of you," ye " are not of them that draw back into perdition." What had they got? Their Messiah on earth? No. He was gone, and they were left strangers as to what was here below and not having reached heaven either. That is what every Christian is: the state of his heart is another thing.

Ver. 2. "Gospel preached." We have glad tidings preached to us as well as they. The apostle is speaking of the character of those who go in (heaven, God's rest, the promise for us, as Canaan was for Israel). Unbelievers do not go into rest—believers do. That is the door they go in by.

As to God's creation, there is not rest for them in it—it is not come for them. "If they shall enter," &c. . This means they shall not, but God did not make the rest for *no one* to enter. He begins again. (Ver. 7.) David came five or six hundred years after Moses, and in Psalm xcv. he says, "To-day after so long a time," &c. If they did not get into the rest by Joshua, there "*remaineth* a rest to the people of God." That is not come at all yet. It is to be under the new covenant, when Christ comes, the Messiah according to their own Scriptures.

" He that is entered into His rest hath also ceased from his *own works*," not only from sin. When God ceased, it was not from sin, but from *labour*. Godly works are not rest. God rests in Christ. I have ceased from my works, as regards my conscience because I have ceased from works for justification. I have not ceased from godly works; that rest is not come yet. Labouring to enter in here, does not mean as to justification. "There remaineth a rest." We have the former, but there is more we wait for.

The two means of carrying us through, spoken of before, are the Word applied by the Spirit, and the priesthood of the Lord Jesus Christ. We never get union with Christ spoken of here; there is no discerning, judging, &c., connected with *that;* but as

Christians in the wilderness, there is, and the intercession of Christ is needed; as distinct, separate Christians going through the world, beset with snares on every hand, we are addressed.

It is remarkable how the word of God is made to be the revelation of God Himself. "The word of God is quick and powerful, manifest in His sight." Whose sight? The word of God, the revelation of Christ. *He is* called the word of God—"God manifest in the flesh." He was the divine life—the perfection of all divine motives in a man in this world. The word of God brings the application of God's nature. All that He is, is applied to us in going through this world. That begins by our being begotten by the word—born again, of incorruptible seed—the divine nature imparted, which cannot sin because born of God. Then all the motives and intentions of the heart have to be displayed by this word. The written word is the expression of God's mind down here. Divine perfectness, as expressed in the life of Christ, in the written word, is applied to us. What selfishness was there in Christ? I do not now refer to His going about doing good, but as to the feelings and motives of His heart. How much has self been our motive? Not like Christ. It is not gross sins that are spoken of here, but "thoughts and intents of the heart." How much self through the day!

In John xvii. our Lord says, "I sanctify myself." Christ set apart as the perfection of man—Christ, a model man, if I may so speak—all that God approves in a man was seen in Christ. The same should be seen in us. "Sanctify them through thy truth." The word applied to us in all this path, in motives, thoughts, and feelings, is for this purpose. Christ was not only doing good; He walked in love, and He says to us, "Walk in love, as Christ also hath loved us, and given Himself," "forgiving one another, even as God, for Christ's sake, hath forgiven you." What comes down from God goes up to Him. Self may enter in our doing good; but only what is of a sweet savour goes up to God—" *an offering to God.*" What is not done exclusively in the power of divine love, in the sense of an offering, is spoiled—self has come in.

"Dividing asunder of soul and spirit." God has created natural affections, but how much self and idolatry come in! Self-will, too, and self-gratification, how awfully it comes in! That is soul, and not spirit. The word of God comes in, and knows how to divide between soul and spirit, what looks like the same thing, the very same affections, as far as man sees. What a mass of corruption! Can we have communion with God when self comes in? How powerless Christians are now—you, and I, and every one. There is grace, blessed be God! but, in a certain sense, how low we are! "I will give myself unto prayer," said one. All blessing comes from the immediateness of a man's life with God. There are rivers of living water. How are you to get them? "If any man thirst, let him come unto me and drink."

and "out of his belly shall flow rivers of living water." A man must drink for himself first, before there can be rivers, &c. In the time of the prophets they had a message, "thus saith the Lord," and then had to enquire the meaning of the prophecy, but with us, we *drink ourselves first*. We are so connected with Christ, that we have it ourselves from Him, before communicating it to others.

What would make us fall in the wilderness? The *flesh*. It has no communion with God; flesh in saints, as well as in others, is bad. What would make us fall is flesh—the unjudged "thoughts and intents of the heart." The word of God comes and judges all that is of nature in us, after He has brought us out of Egypt. According to the new nature, everything is judged. Everything in Christ is applied to the motives and intents of our hearts—everything is judged according to God Himself. The word is a sword—not healing, but most unrelenting in the character. It detects poor flesh, shows it up, and marks its thoughts, intents, will, or lust. All is sifted. But are there no infirmities? Yes. But whenever the will and intent is at work, the word of God comes as a lancet to cut it all away. For infirmities, weaknesses, not will, we have a high priest, who was in all points tempted like as we are, without sin.

This is beautifully expressed in a figure in the Old Testament. There was water wanted; the rock was smitten, and the water flowed. (There are resources in Christ Himself, the smitten rock, for us; but besides, for us there is the water, a well in us.) They were also tried all through the wilderness. The two-edged sword was wanted. There were murmurings. They must be turned back. God turns back with them. How did they get through? What was on Moses' part, for he was like the apostle here, set forth? How was he to get rid of their murmurings? The rock has *not* to be smitten again. The rods must be put in. There are leaves, buds, blossoms on Aaron's—life out of death—living priesthood. Then go and speak to the rock. Suppose God had only executed judgment! How would they have got through the wilderness? There was the living priesthood come in; grace in the shape of priesthood. That carries us through; and all the infirmities, and even failures, when they are committed, are met by Him who has passed through the heavens, &c.

There is not the least mercy on the flesh. This is judged by the word. Moses, the meekest man, failed in that. Abraham, who had been taught God's almightiness, goes down to Egypt, and fails through fear. God glorified Himself. He glorified Himself at the rock in the wilderness, but Moses did not glorify Him, and He was shut out of the land.

Ver. 14. There are things mentioned, very important, about the priesthood. 1st. The priesthood is exercised in heaven, where we need it; it is the place where God is. When it was an earthly calling, the priesthood was on earth. Ours is a heavenly calling, and Christ, our high priest, has passed through the heavens. Another important part is, Christ in no sense has any of these infirmities while He is exercising the priesthood for us. He has passed through all the course in holiness, obedience, and sanctity. When He putteth forth His own sheep, He goeth before them. He walks the sheep's path, and they follow Him. Christ went through all these exercises of a godly man (e.g, wanting bread, and being tempted to make it, but not yielding to it). Everything that a saint can want as a saint, Christ went through before in perfection. There is the example of perfectness in Him, in the sheep's path; but that was not the time of His priestly work. He has passed through the road, and now can be "touched with the feeling of our infirmities."

In Hebrews we have, as another brother has remarked, more of contrast than comparison. The vail in the tabernacle, and the priesthood of Israel all in a contrasted state to that in which we have them. Our high priest is not compassed with infirmity. Mark the consequence of that: His being in heaven, He brings all the perfectness of the thought and feeling of the place He is in to bear on us. I have these infirmities and difficulties, and He helps me up into all the perfectness of the heavenly places where He is. That is just what we want. He can show a path, and feel what a path is of passing through this world, and bear the hearts down here clean up into heaven.

People often think of priesthood as a means of

getting justified; but then God has the character of a judge in their eyes. They are afraid to go straight to God, and, not knowing grace and redemption, they think of enlisting Christ on their behalf. This is all wrong. Many a soul has done it in ignorance and infirmity, and God meets it there, but it is to mistake our place as Christians. Does our getting the intercession of Christ depend upon our going to get it? It is when I have got away from God—when not going to him—I have an advocate with the Father. Again, Christ prayed for Peter before he committed the sin. It is the living grace of Christ in all our need—His thought for us, or we should never be brought back. It was when Peter had committed the sin that He looked on him. Even when we have committed faults, His grace thus comes in. It is in heaven He is doing it: then how can we have to say to Him if we have not righteousness? The reason I can go is because my justification is settled. He has given me the title of going into heaven in virtue of what He is, " Jesus Christ, the righteous," and what He has done. Our place is in the light as God is in the light—sitting in heavenly places in Christ. Our walk on earth is not always up to this. Our *title* is always the same, but our walk not. Then what is to be done? I am within the vail, and not in a condition to go there at all. The priesthood of Christ is there to reconcile this discrepancy between our position in heaven, and our walk down here. Jesus Christ is the righteous one; and the righteousness I have in Him is the title I have to the place. The priestly work restores me to the communion of the place where I am in righteousness. It is immediately connected with the perfectness of His own walk down here and the place where He now is.

Satan came to Him, when here, and found nothing. He ought to find nothing in us, but he does. I do not want to spare the flesh; then there is the word of God for that. But in all the feelings down here, as He said, "reproach hath broken my heart." In Gethsemane He was in an agony and prayed the more earnestly. He had the heart of a man; and all that the heart of man can go through, He went through but in communion with His Father, no failure possible. Apart from sin, is better than "yet without sin," because there was no sin in him inwardly any more than outwardly. In all these feelings He is now touched for us. Verse 16, "Come boldly to the throne of grace." This is going straight to God, not to the priest. It is to the "throne of grace." We want mercy; we are poor weak things, and need mercy; in failure we need mercy; as pilgrims we are always needing mercy. What mercy was shown to the Israelites in the wilderness! their garments not getting old; God even caring for the clothes on their backs! Think of the mercy that would not let their feet swell! Then, when they wanted a way, Oh! says God, I will go before with the ark to find out a way. That was not the place for the ark at all. It was appointed to be in the midst of the camp, but God would meet them in their need. They want spies to go and see the land for them; fools that we are to want to know what is before us. They had to encounter the Amorites, high walls, giants. A land that devours the inhabitant, is their account of it, even with the grapes on their shoulders. Just like us on the way to heaven. They cannot stand these difficulties. We are as grasshoppers, say they; but the real question is, what *God* is.

As saints we are weaker than the world, and ought to be; but when waiting on God, what is that? When they have not confidence in God, they find fault with the land itself. What a wonderful God He is! He says, If you will not go into Canaan, you must stay in the wilderness; and He turns them, and turns back with them. It is grace, but the throne of grace. God governs: it is a throne. He will not let a single thing pass. See the people at Kibroth-hataavah! In case of accusation from the enemy, as Balaam, there is not chastening, but He says, "I have not seen iniquity in Jacob." The moment it is a question between God's people and the enemy's accusation, He will not allow a word against them; but when there is an Achan in the camp, He judges. Why? Because He is there. It is a throne. If you are not victorious, there is sin.

We may come boldly to the throne, &c. Still it is a throne (not a meditator), but all grace. If I go to the throne, instead of the throne coming to me, so to speak, it is all grace; I get help. I never can go to the throne of grace without finding mercy. He may send chastening, but it is a throne of grace and all mercy—"grace to help in every time of need." If you have a will, He will break it; if a need, He will help you. Do you feel that you can always go boldly, even when you have failed? humbled, of course, and at all times humble, but humbled when you have failed.

CHAPTERS V., VI.

PERFECTION here means the state of a full-grown man. There is much, and, in a certain sense, more, contrast than similarity in the allusions in Hebrews to the Old Testament types. We are now in a different position; those things which went before were only a shadow, instead of their giving us a distinct perception of our position. While they were figures, they did not disclose what we have at the present time. We have boldness to enter into the holiest; with them, the vail was there to separate them from it. In this passage it is important to see the contrast. Christ is the high priest. "Every high priest taken from among men (though He was taken from men, I need not say) . . . can have compassion on the ignorant . . . for that he himself also is compassed with infirmity." Here is contrast, though the general image is taken up. They had infirmity, and had to offer for themselves as well as for the people. If we do not see this, we may make great blunders in drawing these analogies. Absolute analogy in them would draw us away from the truth. There are certain landmarks of truth that guard the soul, e.g., the atonement. The priesthood of Christ is in heaven. It has to be exercised as a continual thing in the place where we worship. We worship in spirit in heaven, and there we want our priest. Those sacrifices were the memorial of sin; we have no more conscience of sins. The priest is there, once for all, in virtue of the sacrifice made once and for ever. While, in point of fact, we fail, our place is always in Christ in heaven. When communion is interrupted, priesthood removes the hindrance.

Observe the dignity of the person called to this office. "Thou art my Son." The glory of His person is owned in order to His priesthood. "This day have I begotten thee." (Ver. 5.) He was as really a man as any of us, without the sinful part of it. He was neither like Adam nor us exactly. Adam had no " knowledge of good and evil." Christ had—God has. But now men have the knowledge of good and evil and, with it, sin. Christ was born of a woman, but in a miraculous way. The spring was sinless, and yet He had the knowledge of good and evil.

We cannot fathom what He was. Our hearts should not go and scrutinize the person of Christ, as though we could know it all. No human being can understand the union of God and man in his person—" no man knoweth the Son but the Father." All that is revealed we may know; we may learn a great deal about Him. The Father we know: "no man knoweth the Father but the Son, and he to whomsoever the Son shall reveal him." We know Him to be holy; we know Him to be love, &c. But when I attempt to fathom the union of God and man—no man can. We know He is God, and we know He is man—perfect man, apart from sin; and if He is not God, what is He to me? What difference between Him and another man? Christ came in flesh. Every feeling that I have (save sin), He had. The quotation here from Ps. ii., "This day have I begotten thee," does not refer to His eternal Sonship, but to His being born into the world in humiliation. He is called to be high priest. He has this calling as a man, not only being taken from men. The glory of His person comes first. Looked at in the flesh, He was born of God; with us, "that which is born of the flesh is flesh." But He in His very nature is associated with God, and associated with man. He is the "daysman that can lay his hand upon us both." Job ix. I may fancy myself clean when away from God, but when I come before God, I know He will "plunge me in the ditch," &c. "Let not his fear terrify me." God takes away the fear through Christ. Christ was perfect holiness, and He was ready for everything. His lowliness was perfect; fear is taken away by Him; He is even as a man, the holy one—on that side He lays hold on God, and on the other He lays His hand on us; thus on both He is the daysman to lay His hand upon us both.

The priest in Israel had to take offerings to cleanse himself. Christ is fitted in Himself, without that. Aaron alone was anointed without blood; his sons after the sacrifice.

As to office, there is in Christ perfect competency. He is the Son, and therefore fit for God. He is man, and so fitted for me. I am not speaking of His sacrifice, but of His person. " This day have I begotten thee;" there is *His person*. Then comes the office, "called of God an high priest after the order of Melchisedec," without beginning of days, &c.; not like man with descent from one to another, " but after the power of an endless life," without genealogies. These great principles are thus laid down concerning His person and office—the Son and a priest after the order of Melchisedec. Before He takes the office, there is another qualification necessary. Here would be a difficulty (not in the earthly priesthood, for it was connected with an earthly tabernacle, and earthly worship, but) now it is in a heavenly place, and the worship is in heaven. Then the priesthood must be in heaven. He could not have experience of infirmity there. What must He do? He goes through all first.

Priesthood supposes a people reconciled to God. There was the day of atonement, and daily priestly offices went on with the reconciliation for the year. The day of atonement laid the foundation for the priesthood for the year. Then on that day the high priest represented the whole people—laid his hand on the scapegoat in order to their reconciliation; (this was not the continued office;) that Christ did on the cross, as the victim and the representative. He gave His own blood. He suffered as well as represented the people, and then He went within the vail, in virtue of the reconciliation He has made. One of these goats was the Lord's lot, (the other was the people's,) and the blood was put on the mercy-seat. There was no confession of sins in that. Christ's blood being on the mercy-seat is the ground on which mercy is proclaimed to all the world, even to the vilest sinner in the world. But suppose a person comes and says, "I find sin is working in me ; how can I come to God ? " I say, Christ has borne your sins; He has represented you there; confessed your sins on His own head, and God has condemned sin in the flesh in Christ. A person is often more troubled at the present working of sin in him than at all the sins past ; but I say to that person, God has condemned your sin in Christ. God's character has been glorified, majesty, righteousness, love—all vindicated on the cross. God's truth is vindicated. He said, "In the day thou eatest thou shalt surely die," and Christ dies instead. Then when I get my conscience exercised, it is not enough to see God has been glorified in the death of Christ ; I feel my own sin before God. Then I see that He has confessed my sins; and now, as Priest on high, He maintains me in the power of the reconciliation made.

Before He made the sacrifice, He has gone the path the sheep trod. It was before He began to represent His people,—" who in the days of his flesh "—a past thing, before He exercised His priesthood. When He putteth forth His own sheep, He goeth before them in the paths of temptation, sorrow, difficulty. Therefore it is said of Him, " the author and finisher of faith," not our faith there. We go through our small portion of exercise of faith. He went through everything. Moses refused the treasures in Egypt; Christ refused the whole world. Abraham "sojourned in the land of promise as in a strange country;" Christ was a stranger in the whole world. In all His path we see him not screening Himself by His divine power, but bearing everything that a human heart could bear. There is not a trial but He felt it. If I speak of a convicted conscience, this is another thing. He did bear that; but it was in our stead, on the cross. In a still deeper way, He took it all upon Himself. What entire dependence! " Prayers and supplications with strong crying and tears unto him that was able to save him from death," &c. Especially in Gethsemane did He realize the full power of what He came to meet. In His walk we are to follow Him, to "walk as he walked." But in Gethsemane it is another thing— He was alone there.

There are three parts in Christ's life. In the beginning He was tempted, first to satisfy His own hunger, and then with all the vanities of this world, but He would not have them, He did not come for that. The next thing was more subtle; the answer He gave, "Thou shalt not tempt the Lord thy God" —thou shalt not try the Lord. Tempting is not trusting. When the people tempted the Lord, they went up to the mountain to see if God would help them. Christ would not take these things from Satan's hands. He bound the strong man, and he departs for a season; then Christ goes on spoiling his goods—healing the sick, raising the dead, &c. A power had come in grace, perfectly able to deliver this world from the power of Satan, to deliver us as to the consequences of sin—all the misery and wretchedness here. But there was something deeper: man had hatred to God—they would not have Him. "The carnal mind is enmity against God." They entreated Him to depart out of their coasts in one place. For His love He received enmity. This world would have been a delivered place, if they would have had Him, but they would not; and man profits by the occasion of God's humbling Himself so as to be within man's reach, by seeking to get rid of Him! That brings out another point. Having taken up the people, He must take consequences. Satan says, if you do not give me my rights over them, you must suffer. Satan comes and uses all the power he has over man to deter Christ from going through. In the garden of Gethsemane, He calls it "the power of darkness," and says, "my soul is exceeding sorrowful unto death; tarry ye and watch," &c.; but they could not watch with Him, they went fast asleep. As Satan has power in death, He brings it over Christ. Does Christ go back? No; but being in an agony, He prayed the more earnestly; He does not defend Himself; He might have driven away Satan, but He would not have delivered us if He had. No other cup did He ever ask to be taken away; but He could not be under the wrath of God, and not feel it. He was heard because of His fear. He went down into the depth where Satan had full power over His soul. He was in an agony, in conflict, but there was perfect obedience and dependence, "Not my will, but thine be done;" only He was crying the more earnestly to God, and then let His soul go into the depth under Satan's power. If He had not given Himself up, they would have gone away who came to take Him; they went backward and fell to the ground. Again He presents Himself to them, "I am Jesus of Nazareth. If ye seek me, let these go their way." He puts Himself forward into the gap. He goes to the cross; and there, before He gives up His soul to His Father, He has drunk that cup; then His soul re-enters the presence of His Father. Having gone through Satan's power in death, ("this is your hour and the power of darkness,") He goes forward; God raises Him from the dead, and gives Him a place in glory. He is the full-grown man, as the second man—perfect. Stephen saw Him as "the Son of man," on the right hand of God.

Now we might suppose that He had come to the end of His service, after humbling Himself and becoming obedient unto death as the servant. What more? See John xiii. He is going to be just as much the servant as ever!

Three things we have seen connected with His priesthood, besides His person. He has walked the same path we have to tread, only unfailingly, through it all, and even unto death. That is one thing. He understands the path. When there is sin, He dies. In His living, holiness is seen. The second thing is

in making propitiation for the sins of the people—
blood is presented. Thirdly, He is a perfect man in
the presence of God. I have, then, the path-trodden,
sin atoned for, and a living man in the presence of
God—an Advocate, Jesus Christ, the righteous. The
foundation is not altered, righteousness remains. He
has made propitiation for our sins. He has gone
through all the trials of the way, and is proclaimed or
saluted ("declared") of God an High Priest for ever
after the order of Melchizedec. The trial is gone
through, and the work is wrought out before He
enters in, and He is perfect righteousness in the presence of God. Aaron's order was not Christ's order
at all. Christ's is Melchizedec's order; but the
analogy is according to Aaron. What was Melchizedec's order? Blessing. He blessed Abraham from
God, and God from Abraham. When the full time
of blessing is come for heaven and earth, He will have
it as Melchizedec had it. It will be praise and power.
We have the taste of it now. 1 Peter ii. 9. When
we are with Christ in glory, we shall shew forth His
praises. While He is within the vail, not yet come
out, He does not publicly take this title; outward
blessing is not come. Why? Is He indifferent?
slack concerning His promise? No; but if He put
all this evil down by judgment, men must perish; but
He is long-suffering, not willing any should perish,
&c. While Christ is within the vail, the operation of
the Spirit is going on, gathering in poor sinners. He
has the title now, but not display. It is, therefore,

after the analogy of Aaron. We enter with Him in spirit, there to offer up spiritual sacrifices. The display of power is not come, but we are within the vail, therefore the apostle presses them to go on unto perfection, full stature growth. What is my measure of a perfect man? In one sense, Adam was a very imperfect man, and what he had in innocence he soon lost, at any rate; (imperfect, therefore, in the sense of being able to lose it;) and certainly man is not perfect now in the Adam state. Where, then, is perfection? In the man in heaven. I have it in the knowledge of my position now in Christ, not in fact there myself yet, but in Him; and we are to "bear the image of the heavenly;" in that sense perfect. The Father has set Him at His right hand. Then, suppose I have the knowledge of that, I am called to walk as such. Then why perfect? Because I have fellowship with Him, association with Him where He is.

Does any Christian say, 'I am at the foot of the cross.' Christ is not at the foot of the cross. The cross puts a man in heaven. Christ is in heaven. You have not come to Him yet. You are labouring about in the thoughts of your own heart, and have not followed Him in faith to where He is, if you are at the foot of the cross. How do I see the effect of the cross now? By being in heaven. I have come in through this rent vail. (The person is not to be despised who is there; but you have not come in by the cross through the vail, if you are at the foot of the cross.) If you were inside the vail you would know yourself worse—not one good thing in flesh. It is precious to see a soul exercised even in that way, as the prodigal son in the far country; but he had not come to his father then: he had not found out where he was. There was a mixture of self, not knowing his father, and talking about being a hired servant. He had not had the Father on his neck, or he could not have thought of being a servant. It is not humility, as people think, to be away from God, saying, Depart from me, for I am a sinful man, as Peter. Is insensibility to God's goodness humility? The prodigal could not dictate and prescribe when his Father was on his neck: he had no business to be in the house at all as a hired servant. It is not humility. It is a mixture of self with the knowledge of having got away from God. Where will you put yourself? You must take Christ's place or none. That is what is meant by perfect here. There is one way of coming in; it is by Christ who is in the glory. We have no title to any other place. How is Christ there? Not in virtue of His High Priesthood, but He is there in virtue of the offering for sin for us. "I have glorified thee on the earth." "Father, glorify thy Son." That is the reason the apostle speaks of the gospel of the glory. Christ is in heaven, the witness of the perfectness of the work that He has done. (Ver. 13, 14.) Milk is fit for a babe and strong meat for a full-grown man; that is all that is meant. Do not let us look for a place the godly Jew had, but the place Christ has. Then he goes on warning them, if they are only on this Jewish ground.

On the cross, Christ was drinking the cup; in Gethsemane, anticipating it. Death and judgment are gone; Christ cannot die again. The victory is complete. Sins are put away and He is gone into heaven in consequence; and that victory is ours.

Nothing seemed to be a greater burden on the heart of Paul than to keep the saints up to their privileges. They saw Christ had died for them, (and this had not the power over them it ought to have had), but they were risen with Him also; they were in Christ in heavenly places, within the vail; and how were they realizing that?—"Are become such as have need of milk." There is a great deal of love in the heart when first converted. And there is another thing. When first converted, all these things are easier to understand than when more used to hearing them, and the world comes in. When there is freshness in the heart, the understanding goes with it. Great force is in that word "*become*," (chap. v. 12,) here. See the state they were in (Heb. x.) when they took joyfully the spoiling of their goods, knowing that they had "a better and an enduring substance." Because they knew they had substance in heaven, they were willing to sacrifice what was here. When Christ had not that place in the heart, they were not willing to give up those things, and the understanding of the heavenly things would be dulled too. Freshness of affection and intelligence go together. When it is bright sunshine, things at a distance are easily seen. If it is dark, there is more difficulty. In the day one may walk through the streets without thinking about the way—one knows it; but at night one has to look and think which way. Just so with spiritual things; there is less spring, less apprehension, less clearness when our hearts are not happy. My judgment is clear when my affections are warm. Motives that acted before, cease to be motives when my heart is right. I can count all dross and dung, when force is given to my affections. "Where your treasure is, there will your heart be also."

"Strong meat belongeth to them that are of full age;" not persons who have made a great progress, but persons of full age. There were things hard to be uttered, because they were dull of hearing. The freshness of affection being lost was the secret of all this. It is serious to think that freshness of affection and intelligence we may lose; but "to him that hath shall more be given." There are *good* and *evil* to be discerned; therefore I spoke of finding the way.

Take this in connection with the beginning of the next chapter, "Therefore, leaving the word of the beginning of Christ," &c., instead of wasting your time with what has passed away, go on to the full revelation of Christ; be at home there, and understanding what the will of the Lord is. We cannot separate the knowledge of good and evil from the knowledge of Christ. When I come to separate between them of myself, how can I? How can I walk as He walked, without Him? I cannot do it. "In Him." What is that? "Ye in me." Where is Christ? In heaven; then I am there too. My affections should be there too; my hope is to be thoroughly identified with Him. The portion I have is what He has—life, glory; what He has; all my associations are with Himself. There is the difference between the principles of the beginning of Christ and the full perfection "being made perfect," (chap. v. 9,) glorified. He went through the experience down here, and then went into heaven to be priest, because our blessings, associations, &c., are all above, perfect up there, not down here. He had not received that point of the counsels of God in glory when down here. Now He is there, and He has associated me with Himself in that place. I can see Christ has been through this world so as to sympathize with us in all our sorrows and difficulties. He has borne my sins; and where is He now? In heaven; and I am there too, in spirit, and He will bring me there in fact. Where He is, is His "being made perfect." The work is done, and now He is showing me the effect of that—showing me the walk belonging to the righteousness He has wrought out. He has taken my heart, and associated me with Himself; and He says that is the "perfection" for me to go on to. Where did Paul see Christ? In glory. If he had known Christ after the flesh before, he did not know Him so now; (that was the beginning when on earth;) but now he knew Him in heaven; and this great truth was revealed to him, that all the saints on earth were as Christ. Paul had been a hater of Christ, had sought to root out His name from the earth; he had gone on in sin, been a breaker of the law, a rejecter of Christ when on earth, and, more than that, he had resisted the Holy Ghost, refused the testimony by the Holy Ghost given in mercy to those people for whom Christ interceded on the cross. They stoned Stephen who bore witness, and Saul was helping in it. He was "chief of sinners," because wasting the Church of God. He discovered the carnal mind to be enmity against God, not subject to God; he proved it in his own experience, and now he found there were saints not in that state—those quickened with Christ, and associated with Christ in glory. "I am Jesus whom thou persecutest." They were not associated with the first Adam, but with the second man, in Christ; that was their position. These people whom he had been persecuting were Christ. What broke him down was seeing Christ in glory, and all these associated with Him. Now he learns that he is dead to law, dead to flesh. The Christ I want to win is a glorified Christ. To win Christ may cost me my life. Never mind. That is my object. As to the first Adam, he was "weighed in the balance, and found wanting." He is out of it; not in the flesh, but in Christ. The old thing entirely past; dead to the law, the world, &c.; dead and risen again, having another object. He is alive from the dead, because Christ is; he is "accepted in the beloved;" he has the consciousness that this work of Christ put him into a new place: (not glorified yet in the body:) this was the "perfection." What was the state of his affections then? "That I may win Christ," was his desire. "As we have borne the image of the earthy, we shall also bear the image of the heavenly." This was his object. His mind was full of it.

The Holy Ghost has come down to bring all these things to our remembrance. Believers are united to Christ (it is never said Christ was united to man) in glory. Then the apostle was living by the power of the Holy Ghost. What a trial for him to see these people going back to their "first principles," "repentance from dead works, faith toward God . . . . . eternal judgments"—all true! but if you stop there, you stop short of a glorified Christ. "Who hath bewitched you?" he says to the Galatians. He says of himself, "I know a man in Christ," and his spirit is broken to find the saints resting with things on earth about Christ. The Holy Ghost was come out to make them partakers of a heavenly calling; to associate them in heart and mind with Christ, and to show them things to separate them from the world; not only to keep them from evil, though that is true, too. They had a temple standing then, where Christ Himself had been. Why should they have left it if Christ had not judged the flesh? The middle wall had been put up: how should they dare break it down, if God had not done it? If God had not said, "I will not have to say to flesh any more," how could they dare leave the camp and go outside? Christ glorified is the end of all the "first principles," and we have to go through the world strangers and pilgrims.

The only thing God ever owned in religion was Jewish. It had to do with the flesh. That is gone by the cross; all is crucified: your life, your home, your associations, are all in Christ. The doctrine of the beginning of Christ was not that. What do I find when Christ is on earth? He is speaking then of judgment to come, which they believe. The Pharisees believed in a resurrection from death; baptisms, which mean washings, &c. All these they had then they formed a worldly religion, and were sanctioned by God until the cross. The Messiah coming on earth was the beginning, but now I leave that. I do not deny these things; they are all true; but I have other things. Saul might have been the brightest saint going under the old things, but not knowing Christ. But suppose persons got into the heavenly thing, being made partakers of the Holy Ghost, having "tasted the good word of God," and then gave it up, what could they do then? Suppose they had received it all in their minds, and then gave it up: what else was there for them? There might have been a going on from faith in a humbled Christ to a glorified Christ, but there is nothing beyond.

There is nothing of life signified here, in their being partakers of the Holy Ghost. It brings very strongly before us the actual presence of the Holy Ghost, and power through Him; a very different thing from life;

and what, notwithstanding, we are in want of knowing. We must have that besides life. Being born of the Spirit, there is power for us through the presence of a person, who may act in another without his having life. There may be light in the soul without the smallest trace of life. In the case of Balaam, we read the Spirit of God came upon him: he had to see the blessedness of God's people, and speak of it. He had light, but there was sleep on his soul, and he has to say, "I shall see him, but not now." That was the opposite to having life. You see a man close to life, seeing all the blessing of it, but not having it. Now, if all the heavenly blessing is seen and rejected, what else could there be?

"Tasted the good word of God"—Simon Magus is an example of this.

"Powers of the world to come" or miracles, putting down Satan's power. In the future day this power will gain the victory over all Satan's power. Simon Magus wanted this power when he saw it.

" Impossible, if they shall fall away . . . . . seeing they have crucified to themselves the Son of God afresh," &c. The nation had crucified Him—they did not know what they were doing. Now these knew what they were doing. The Holy Ghost had poured forth the light, and now they did it for themselves. It was not ignorance, it was will. There are some who anon with joy receive the word—the very thing that proves there is nothing in it. They would have it in joy, and give it away in tribulation. The word of God does not always give joy. When it comes in and reaches the conscience, and breaks up the fallow ground, and judges the thoughts and intents of the heart, that is not joy. It racks the heart when it is to profit, but it is for life and health. Here is not merely the joy of hearing about it, but having tasted of the good word about a glorified, heavenly Christ. It is not quickening that is spoken of here. Moses was quickened, but he was not baptized with the Holy Ghost. The Holy Ghost did not come till Pentecost. He made the house shake where they were assembled, but that was not for giving life. Power is a different thing from giving life. Those already quickened were to be the habitation of God through the Spirit. There were manifestations of God through these things, tongues, &c., anticipative of the setting up of the kingdom. It is after salvation is given, after the soul is born of God, the Holy Ghost comes to the believer as a seal, an earnest, an unction. I might get a taste of the power without being sealed; but as a believer I have the seal, am broken down in myself, not only "with joy" receiving it. I am a sinner—no good in me. It is a direct question between my soul and God; not like Simon Magus, believing the miracles that He did. Before I was converted, I believed there was Christ, as much as I do now. When Christ was on earth, there were those who saw the miracles, and went home again. But when the Spirit of God works in the heart, He shows what we are and makes us submit to God's righteousness. It ploughs up the whole soul and being of a man—makes him submit to the righteousness of God—shows him his place in the risen Christ—shows him that all is his. That is a different thing to merely *seeing* it. If you have rejected these glorious things, there is nothing else for you. If you will not have Christ, there is nothing else. Here this warning is in connexion with the Holy Spirit in the tenth chapter. It is connected with the sacrifice. Then what follows shows no change supposed in the man. " The earth which drinketh in the rain . . . . . receiveth blessing from God ; but that which beareth thorns and briers is rejected," &c. The ground is just the same—the rain comes upon it, but it brings forth briers. So in men, there may be nothing in them to produce fruit. The result of life is seen in fruit, not power. The dumb ass might speak, but that was power, not spiritual life.

"But, beloved, we are persuaded better things of you, and things that accompany salvation." (Ver. 9). There is the work of love here ; then there is life. Perhaps there is only a little bit of fruit; but the tree is not dead if there is any fruit—" things that accompany salvation," not power merely—not joy merely : that might be without a divine nature. But " though I give all my goods to feed the poor, and though I could remove mountains, and have not charity, I am nothing." Judas could cast out devils as well as the rest, but Christ says to His disciples, Rejoice not because the devils are subject to you, but rather rejoice that "your names are written in heaven."

The connexion of your heart with Christ, the consciousness of God having written your name in heaven, is the blessed thing. Here was fruit; love of the brethren was there—the divine nature was there, and the " full assurance of hope to the end " is the thing desired. We may look for that.

When the seed fell into stony places, it sprang up rapidly; there was no root. When the word does not reach the conscience, there is no root, no life, and therefore no fruit. You might weep over Christ, and have no life, like the women going out of Jerusalem. Flesh could go all that length without divine life. There might be working of miracles, without knowing or being known of Him. One atom of brokenness of spirit is better than filling all London with miracles.

Ver. 6. The nominal church of God is just in this state. There is to be a falling away, and they are to be broken off; prophesied of in Rom xi., to be cut off, if they did not continue in His goodness. The apostacy will come, and no renewing them again unto repentance.

Now, a little word for ourselves, what we have got in Christ. We have heavenly things—we are associated with Christ in heaven; " because I live ye shall live also." I have all in Christ. He is my life, my righteousness, before God. Then God rests with delight on me, because in Christ. What place have I in Christ? In heaven, and He has given me the Holy Spirit to know it and enjoy it, so that my soul rests on it as the testimony of God. God cannot lie.

Abraham got a promise, and he believed in it; an oath, and he believed it. I have more than that. I believe He has performed it. I have a righteousness now in the presence of God; and we have more in hope, viz., the glory that belongs to His righteousness. I have life, righteousness, the Holy Ghost as the seal, and more, the forerunner is gone in, and the Holy Ghost gives me the consciousness of my union with Him; not merely the fact that sin is put away. We have the Spirit in virtue of the righteousness. The Holy Ghost has come to tell me I am in that Christ. What is the practical consequence? If the glory He has is mine, I am going after Him. Then all in the world is dross and dung.

"They might have had opportunity to have returned:" that is, where faith is exercised and put to the test. You who have known the Lord some time have had opportunity to have returned, how has it been with you? A stone left on the ground gradually sinks in. There is constantly a tendency in present things to press down the affections—not open sin, but duties, and nothing is a greater snare than duties. We have one duty, that is, to serve Christ. On the side of God, it is all bright.

CHAPTER VII.

THE apostle, being now on the ground of priesthood, shows the excellency of the Melchisedec priesthood of Christ, and uses it to bring back these Hebrews from that which was after the "carnal commandment to that which was "after the power of an endless life."

The order of the priesthood is according to Melchizedec, but after the analogy of Aaron—not yet come out from the holiest. Arguments are drawn from Scripture to show that this priesthood is far more excellent than that of Aaron. One point of importance is its being another—" after the similitude of Melchizedec there ariseth another priest:" that implied the setting aside of the other. Directly the Aaronic priesthood is gone, the whole system connected with it is gone; for that was the keystone. According to their own Scriptures, there was to be another, and now that is come. And wherever *Christ* is concerned the Spirit immediately bursts into all the beauty and excellency of it.

Gen. xiv. and Ps. cx. These scriptures bring us greatly into the history of Melchizedec. They are all we have about him, showing us the mystery of his person and glory. The people, when Christ was on earth, could not understand His being David's Son and David's Lord. In Ps. cx. 4, it is Jehovah, and not in ver. 7. " He shall drink of the brook in the way"—in humbling Himself He shall have His head lifted up.

The history of Abraham is remarkably interesting in Gen. xiv.—his having entirely done with the world, while Lot, in a selfish way, liked the world, and chose the world when he was a believer. Abraham does not this: he gives up the world in the power of faith. Lot was under the world: Abraham had complete power over the world because he had given it up. He would not take from a thread to a shoe-latchet. And then God says, "I am thy shield," &c. He had God. Giving up the world, he had victory over it, and has God for his shield.

It is after this that Melchizedec comes out to meet him. In the future day this will be seen in Christ coming out to His people; it applies to ourselves in a heavenly way now. " Priest of the most High God." In that word, all the peculiar character of Melchizedec comes out. Abraham had overcome by faith. He knew God by faith. Now He is made known to him as " possessor of heaven and earth." The Gentile powers broken, God rules and does what He pleases; and Nebuchadnezzar gives Him the title of "Most High God." He takes to Himself His great power and reigns as Most High. This is not the name known to Abraham's faith; that was Shaddai. " I am the Almighty God; walk before me," &c. Abraham was called to walk before God, and he suffered no man to do him wrong in passing through the world. Jehovah, the one true God, brought His people into relationship with Himself—all the rest were false Gods. We have the relationship of Father in contrast with these; but all these names are for faith to own. Most High is another thing; Possessor; Col. i. " to reconcile all things to Himself;" and Eph. i. "to gather together in one all things in Christ, both which are in heaven, and which are on earth." He will be the possessor of heaven and earth; Melchizedec-priest, in this character of priest of the Most High, He has gained the full victory over the power of the world. The Heir of Promise is the great victor. Psalm xci. He who has got the secret of who this Most High is, (never the Father's name in Hebrews; it is the "throne of grace" spoken of) shall have the blessings of Abraham's God. So Hezekiah (2 Kings xviii. 33) taunted by the enemy, "hath any of the gods of the nations delivered out of my hand," Psalm xci. 2. I will have the Jehovah the God of Israel, now despised, but He will overcome amidst the gods of the nations. (ver. 9.) No secret now in His name. (Luke iv. 11, 12.) And He says, " Thou shalt not tempt the Lord thy God." Tempting God —trying whether He is as good as His word—to see whether it is true. Thou shalt not put God to the test. (ver. 9.) The knowledge of the Most High as Jehovah, is Israel's God. When Christ has taken His real power, He will be Melchizedec-priest: at least He will be Priest on His throne. The counsel of peace, as regards this earth is between Jehovah and this

Priest on His throne—"righteousness and peace have kissed each other." Aaron was never a king.

Melchizedec brought bread and wine after the victory. There is no thought of a sacrifice to secure blessing while living a life of faith; but he brings forth refreshment for the victor, bread and wine, eucharistic, accompanied with thanksgiving; bread, the symbol of that which strengthens, and wine, of that which refreshes the heart of man. The people on earth are fully brought into blessing. Melchizedec blessed the Most High God on the part of Abraham, and blessed Abraham on the part of God.

The earthly priesthood takes the character of joy and gladness on the victory being obtained. Melchizedec was king of Salem, and king of righteousness. This says nothing about divine righteousness; it is righteousness established. He rules according to it— righteousness looking down from heaven—righteousness in His person, and mercy shown to those who do not deserve it. " A king shall reign in righteousness." " A man shall be as an hiding-place, and a covert from the tempest," " righteousness and peace have kissed each other ;" righteousness is the character of the rule, and the effect of it, peace. We have it now in a higher way, a divine way. We have it in our souls ; but it is to be on earth, in Melchizedec, king of righteousness and king of peace. In Ps. cx. Christ is sitting at God's right hand, and we connected with Him during the time He is sitting there—" until " his enemies are made His footstool. His people will be willing in the day of His power—we, through grace, are made willing now,(ver. 3.) "Thou hast the dew of thy youth;" all the new generations of Israel when the fresh blessing comes in on the earth (a figure, of course). He will come in power, and rule over His enemies—He will judge the heathen. "He shall drink of the brook in the way," i.e., willing to get the refreshment by the way, being perfectly dependent. "I have given unto them the words which thou gavest me;" and this is rewarded with exaltation. Looked at as His title, it is after the power of an endless life; but not exercised according to that yet. When "righteousness and peace have kissed each other," it will be. It was necessary that the atonement should have been made. The Jews had rejected promise just the same as law, and now they must come freely, through His grace, like any poor sinner.

But there is more as to dispensation; there is the question of the new covenant. We have to see what our part is in this; the new makes the other old. That old covenant was made at Sinai: it was addressed to man in the flesh, making a claim upon him. The new covenant is on the ground of the law being put into the heart, and forgiveness given. The new covenant was made with Israel and Judah. Have we nothing to do with it? I do not say *that*. His blood has been shed. "This is my blood of the new covenant shed for many," All that God had to do to bring the Jews in was done: their bringing in is suspended because of unbelief. Then what do we get

He was minister of the new covenant, not of the letter, but of the spirit. We have the law in our hearts, and forgiveness. We have all the blessings of the new covenant—God's part all thoroughly laid. We have Christ in whose heart the law was hid; not the letter, that was made with Israel and Judah, though they are now outside. Then another thing: I am one with the Mediator of the new covenant. I am, as part of the Church, a member of His body, (that is not brought out here, but while He is gone in—not seen in the Aaron character) I am associated with Him. He has shed the blood on which it is all founded. He is gone to make good that part which is in heaven, and meanwhile I am connected with Him. I have the effect of the blood. He is there on the throne, a proof of its being accepted. He is the forerunner into the glory I am going into. He is a priest for ever, while I am here in infirmity. He is a priest different to those priests who died, "after the power of an endless life." While He sits waiting till His enemies are made His footstool, He has done everything for His friends, and has sent down the Holy Ghost to associate us with Him in heaven, and to maintain us in communion till He comes out. There is no figure of the temple used here: it is all the tabernacle in the wilderness. He who is High Priest after the order of Melchisedec is gone in. There was provided some better thing for us, and we get *this* heavenly association with Him.

In Heb. vii. the superiority of this priesthood is shown.

(Ver. 3.) "Continually," that is one great thing for us, and that is insisted on much. The constancy of our position comes out in the 9th and 10th chapters. The meaning of it is, without any interruption, not only for ever. Aaron's priesthood could be broken up—pass from one man to another, but this is an untransmissible priesthood. It has the stamp of eternity on it in its very nature; so the value of His blood is *for ever*—continually, perpetually—that is the force. What do we find in the state of souls generally now? Is their peace continuous? or are they, when conscious of failure, wanting to be sprinkled again? The Jew wanted a sacrifice for every sin; but with us there is one sacrifice uninterrupted in its efficacy—not broken in upon. The priesthood goes on continuously. We fail, and there is the Advocate, Jesus Christ the righteous. It is after the power of an endless life— not like Aaron's — not in the temple—but in the "true tabernacle which the Lord pitched, and not man." Always there, untransmissibly, "to the uttermost," right through. "He ever liveth to make intercession."

Melchizedec was a man, no doubt, like any other—a mysterious personage, appearing on the scene without an origin known. Whose son was he? All kinds of suppositions without any conclusion. Why? Because Scripture leaves us in the dark. As a priest, Christ was without genealogy—not as a man. His mother is known. Again, He was not to be cast off at a certain age, as those priests were. He continueth ever. " Made like unto the Son of God "—only as a priest. Royalty is connected with the priesthood. Abraham paying tithes to Melchizedec is another important point. God had given them Aaronic priesthood, promises, &c.; but there was something greater, something behind, which was above and beyond all this. Levi paid tithes in Abraham, showing the superiority of Melchizedec to Levi. (Ver. 12—14.) They must give it all up as applying to Aaron.

Ver. 18—20 give the secret of the whole thing. There was the disannulling of what went before, because not perfect, and the bringing in of a better hope. " Did " is better left out. What is the result of that? We draw nigh to God. (Ver. 19.) Did the Jews do this? Did the priests do it? No. " Now we see not yet all things put under him;" but we have a better thing; " we draw nigh to God." Perfect atonement has been made—the veil is rent— the High Priest in heaven; and when He comes forth, we shall come with Him.

There is a time for Melchizedec Himself when He shall come in glory. To be sitting on God's own throne is the highest thing. Now He is sitting on God's right hand in all the fulness and brightness of His glory; and while there, we get all our associations with Him—dead with him, &c. And when He appears, we shall appear with Him. We may take it as to our union and our association with Him in priesthood, He is the High Priest, and we are priests. The Holy Ghost, being sent down, associates us with

Him, while He is in heaven. We could not receive the Holy Ghost until Jesus was glorified. Then having perfect righteousness, we are seated in Him.

Ver. 25. "He is able to save to the uttermost all that come unto God by him." We do not come to Him, (the Priest,) but He goes to God for us, and we go to God by Him. As Lord, we came to Him; but as Priest, not. He intercedes, and brings us back when we have failed. He is watching always—thinking of us when we are not thinking of Him.

Ver 26. "For such an high priest became us," &c. Why this? It became us! The Jews had worship on earth; we go higher than the heavens. Our priest is there, on the right hand of God. That stamps the character of our worship. "Higher than the heavens" is the place of our worship. In the fullest sense He sanctified Himself (John xvii.) when He went up on high. Instead of a priest joined with us in the place of sin or its consequences (which could not be, He was holy, harmless, undefiled, and separate from sinners, but bore the sin on the cross) He is taking our hearts out of the present world to the scene where He is. The thing that fits Christ for the exercise of His priesthood is, that He can take me where sin is not. He has put it away. It was not put away under the Jewish service; but that is not the character of our relationship with God. We are dead—dead to sin; you cannot connect it with your place on earth. He is gone "higher than the heavens." We have no other connexion with God than that in Christ, out of the flesh (not physically of course, we have the treasure in earthen vessels). Christ made "higher than the heavens," "became us." There is a great deal in the world that is undermining this. Men say we are not dead to sin, and are associating themselves, not dead, with Christ. It is all false. If not dead, I have no associations with Christ at all. The veil is rent, sin is put away —sin in the flesh is condemned—we are dead. I see more and more daily of the danger and conflict there is in connexion with this, and the effort to bring our association with Christ down to flesh. He is risen. We have association with Christ in heaven. Our citizenship is there. Most blessed comfort for us it is, that all I have to go through here, Christ has gone through. He passed through all, "tempted like as we are, without sin." "He ever liveth to make intercession for us," while our hearts are associated with Him through the power of the Holy Ghost.

There are two great foundation principles connected with our coming unto God by Christ. 1st. The place, as giving the character of His priesthood; and, 2ndly, the non-repetition of the sacrifice. "Such an high priest became us," &c. Our place of meeting with God is above the heavens, and the questions of—can I come? how can I come?—are met by His priestly work being carried on there, where we meet with God. He first came down to us in the place where we are as sinners, but in our going to God it must be in the place where He is. The place of the priest was the holy place, under the Jewish order, but with us there is no vail between us and the holiest. God is light. We walk in the light. We must therefore be able to draw near according to the light in which He is. The presence of God is purity itself, and the power of purity.

God has first visited us as enemies. He did not wait for us to go up to heaven; but when we go to Him as worshippers, being partakers of the heavenly calling, we are higher than the heavens. Our intercourse with God is in the sanctuary, in the light where He is; and a high priest is needed for this, who is "holy, harmless, undefiled, separate from sinners, and made higher than the heavens."

The Jews had priests who had infirmity; but in going into the holiest, we could not go in by these. There must be One able to maintain us in the place where divine righteousness has set us. The priest must be holy, harmless, and separate from sinners, *i. e.*, the work is carried on out of the region where sin is going on; the work of Christ on the cross having brought us there. He is separate from sinners (as to His own state, morally, He was always a Nazarite, but) He has set Himself apart as a Nazarite in connexion with us. He is there, where the worship goes on.

Failures are measured by the place where we are. Of Israel it was said to the priests, "ye shall bear the iniquity of the holy things." We are all priests ---there is no separate caste of priests---and all our faults and failings are measured by the place we are in. The place to which we belong, and where our worship is carried on, and where our Priest is, is out of the reach of sin. When we are there in fact, we shall be able to let our thoughts and feelings free; we shall not want our consciences then. Now we must watch everything down here, but there is full liberty with God, there may be the freest, fullest letting forth of every thought and feeling with Him.

The other thing different in our High Priest from those high priests, is that He offered up Himself once, not for His own sins, but for His people's—for the church and Israel's. He has done it fully, finally, and once for all; it cannot be repeated. Once for ever constitutes the full character of the priesthood of Christ. This gives us a very distinct place. Brought into the light as God is in the light, where sacrifice never can be made again, a Priest is there, by virtue of an unalterable condition, in the presence of God. If Christ has not put away sins, they never will be put away. His blood was shed, not sprinkled only. If once you have been sprinkled by the blood of Christ, has anything taken it off? Has the blood ever lost its value? I cannot talk of being sprinkled again, if the blood has not lost its value. I may have my feet washed with water, for renewal of communion; but as to the person, that is never even washed with water again, though the feet may need cleansing.

There were three cases of blood-sprinkling in Israel: the covenant, the leper, and the priest. The covenant was sprinkled once for all: it was never renewed, but is set aside by a better. The leper was sprinkled once, not again, and the priest. There was no replacing of the power of that blood. "We walk in the light, as God is in the light; and the blood of Jesus Christ His Son cleanseth us from all sin." That does not change at all: is heavenly in its character, cleanses and fits for God in light; and it is everlasting in its efficacy. It is a new place where we are set, and set for ever.

Let me stop a moment to ask you how far you have forgotten this? how far you are on Jewish ground? It is connected with "the full assurance of faith." We must be clean before we are there, as God is in the light. It is a different place altogether from that in which the question would arise as to what my state is. How do I get there? By the cross. But if I come by the cross, am I defiled or undefiled? I am brought into God's presence, and cannot be there without having been cleansed. Christ came to us in our sins, or else there would be no hope; but it is by virtue of His blood we go to God. How do you go— cleansed or uncleansed? Do we not know whether we are cleansed or not? We may be ignorant of ourselves, but we know whether we are cleansed or not. The way we get into His presence is by being cleansed. That is quite different from the standing of those whose walk was on earth—finding a sin and getting it cleansed—finding a sin and getting it cleansed. The fruits of the light are such and such things. If we are made children of light, it is not to diminish the light, but to judge everything by it. That is the effect of our being there.

CHAPTER VIII.

"SET on the right hand of the throne of the majesty in the heavens." Why so? Because if we have nothing more to be done, Christ has nothing more to do. (I speak not of the priestly work, but of putting away sin.) He has set down—He is resting, having nothing more to do. (Chap x.) The offering has been made, and cannot be repeated. (Chap. viii. 2, 3.) The whole of the priesthood is carried on in heaven itself. The offering was another thing. The offerer brought the victim, the priest received the blood and carried it in. On the day of atonement there was another thing: the priest had to go through the whole thing by himself—not carrying on the work of intercession, but that of representing the people. Christ took this place. He could say, "mine iniquities," &c.; for He bore our sins. We can never speak of bearing our sins; He, the sinless One, bore them for us. He was the victim, and at the same time the confessor, owning all the sins. Then, as priestly work, He carries in the blood, having offered Himself without spot to God (the burnt offering in that sense). He was "made sin." He offered Himself freely up, and the sins were laid on Him, and He takes that dreadful cup, then goes and sprinkles that place. His priesthood is entirely in heaven.* The tabernacle was upon earth; there was the court of the tabernacle, and inside the court was out of the world, and not inside heaven. He was lifted up (John xii.) to draw all men unto him.

Rejected by the Jews, He was held up by God—the dead Christ, to be the attractive centre for the whole world. As coming in His service and mission on earth, He was coming among the lost sheep of the house of Israel; but when I see the crucified Christ, this is for the *sinner*, and then I get perfect love for the sinner and atonement for the sin—*perfect grace*. Then He goes by virtue of that blood through the rent veil into the holy place; and I come there in spirit into the very presence of God—*not on earth*. Those things were the example and shadow of heavenly things, and our place now is in the holiest of all.

No place is found for the first covenant. Be it remarked, that there is often great confusion about the covenant of grace and law. The law was given at Sinai. All the promises were given without condition—unqualified. When the people came out of Egypt, it was

* There was then on earth, while the Spirit was unfolding the heavenly priesthood to the Hebrews, another priesthood, no longer recognized of God, but going on. Its movement was one of transition; the object was not only to show the actual heavenly privileges of the saints, but to invite them to go forth without the camp. Afterwards came the fall of Jerusalem, when the events themselves spoke to the same effect. Only we can see that the Hebrew believers are treated with great address in this epistle; for the sole conclusion which yet appears is that the promise of a new covenant declares the first antiquated and ready to be done away. We know, from elsewhere, that the cross had, in principle, abolished the old covenant, and that the blood of Jesus laid the basis of the new covenant.

different. The accomplishment of the promise then depended on their obedience; and there was an end of the whole thing, because they could not keep it. Why did God bring in such a principle as this? With the promise, no question was raised of righteousness; but when law was given, there was something required of man: and the effect of this question being raised was to bring out sin directly. Why did the law come in? Because we are excessively proud creatures, we think we can do a great deal.

The law was not a transcript of God, but of what man ought to be; and when applied as a test to man, it brought out the evil there. Given to a sinner to tell him what he ought to be, it was too late—he had failed already: the golden calf was made before they received the words of the law. Christ, instead of requiring righteousness from man, bears the sins and works out the righteousness. It is much more than what the law requires that we have in Christ. The law never required a man to lay down His life—much less the Son of God to lay down His life. He glorified God in the place where He had been dishonoured, not only in a righteous walk upon earth, but God was glorified in Him.

Suppose God had swept away man for sin, in righteousness, where would have been the love? If He had only passed over the sins, without judging them, where would have been righteousness? There was infinite and unspeakable love to poor sinners, and infinite righteousness towards God. The whole ground of the Sinai covenant is gone—we are dead under it: it can go no further. Law puts man under responsibility. Are you standing on your responsibility? You are lost if you are.

It is the whole question of the two trees in the garden of Edom—life and responsibility. Christ, as a man, takes that of good and evil, and dies under it. He puts Himself under the one and gives us the other, for He is life.

Thus, in Chapter viii., there is an entirely new covenant, and the new makes the first old. In the letter, it is made with the house of Israel. But, besides, there is grace. Not I do not remember them, " but their sins and iniquities will I remember no more." I will never remember them any more. That is our place. A covenant made with man, as man, is certain ruin, because his righteousness is required, his keeping it is called in question. But here he says, " I will put my laws into their mind," &c. If man is under the old covenant, he is under an " if." If under the new, there is no " if." This covenant of the letter is made with Israel, not with us, but we get the benefit of it. " This is my blood of the new covenant which is shed for many." This was putting away the breach of all obligation by death. Israel, not accepting the blessing, God brought out the church, and the Mediator of the covenant went on high. We are associated with the Mediator. It will be made good to Israel by and by. Paul was the minister of it in the Spirit, but he could not be as to the letter. They will need no minister of it, because every one will know it, when God writes it on their hearts; the thing is done—God is their minister, (reverently,) when writing it on their hearts. We have it not in the letter, but in the spirit of it, and so have all the value of it, because the way we get it is that the Mediator of it becomes our life—we are forgiven our sins—we are associated with the Mediator. He is our life, and we have all the blessings of the new covenant within the vail. We have all the blessings, for the very reason that it is not executed with the people for whom it was made.

Now the question arises, how far are we standing on this ground? has your faith got hold of this fact that Christ has settled every question against us, and gone in because our sin is put away? The true light now shines: that could not be said while there was a vail and an earthly priesthood.

Can you stand in God's presence without a vail, and knowing that the more the light shines upon you, the more evident that you are without a spot upon you?

CHAPTER IX.

In the preceding chapter, the apostle has touched on a very important point, which, as regarded the Hebrews, (and, indeed, any of us,) was a most absorbing one: I allude to the two covenants. The first covenant made at Sinai had a very distinct character, viz., requiring man's righteousness, and therefore it gendered " to bondage." What distinguished the law as a covenant was, that, instead of promise, it was blessing held out on the ground of obedience. The distinctive character of the ten commandments was, that they required obedience. All the prophets, indeed, spoke of failure in it; but all was connected with the old thing, and went on the ground of their obedience. That must be or not be; there is no question of a new nature. Now, we are told, " without holiness no man shall see the Lord." It is not a question of how he gets holiness : the holy nature will desire to obey, but it is a different thing to the righteousness of obedience. God's nature is holy. I do not speak of God's obedience—it is His nature, and we must have the new nature to be holy. The law showed God holy, but the condition of the law was, " If ye shall obey my voice." The promises of God are connected under the law with the obedience of man. That covenant is now altogether put away.

We are called to obedience, and we are sanctified unto obedience, but that is different to being put under conditions. The new covenant has made the former old. God brings in a new one, not according to the covenant He made with them when He brought them out of Egypt. In chap. ix. the apostle is pressing what the conditions of the new covenant are. If the old had been perfect, God would not have brought in a new one. God will not let man have blessing on that ground, and why? The reason is that He has tried man and found him unable to bring forth any thing good. If it is to be on the ground of my righteousness, I cannot have the blessing at all. Man must be convinced there is no good in himself. Man could never place himself on that ground but as maintaining the pride of the human heart that pretends to be able to gain it. The principle of requiring something from man is entirely set aside, and those who know God's principle, know that it is only in the pride of the natural heart that man could take blessing in that way.

Unless grace, and simply grace, lays new ground, there is no hope whatever. God has brought in a new thing. He had marked out in the provision of bulls and goats, &c., another way of getting blessing. There must be coming to God by cleansing from sin, instead of on the ground of being clean. It was impossible for those things to take away sin. There was no relieving the conscience by these ceremonial observances, which were but shadows, and not the very image of the things to come. Besides the day of atonement, there were continual sacrifices needed to keep them clean; but there was no coming to God (saving in the sense in which He says, " I bare you on eagle's wings and brought you unto myself.") Christ died, the just for the unjust, to " bring us to God." In the tabernacle service there was no coming near by the people or even by the priests. Nadab and Abihu took strange fire and offered that not taken from the burnt offering; and God says, Ye shall not come at all times, &c.; but there was the great day of atonement, and the high priest even could only go in on that day with clouds of incense. There was no revelation of God whatever at that time: there was revelation from God, but not *of* God. He said, " I dwell in the thick darkness." Moses could go into God's presence without a veil. When he came out, he put a veil on his face, but when he went in, he took the veil off. Moses, as mediator, —type of Christ—represented the nation before God, but then the figure dropped; and we find Aaron could only go in once a year. His work was done behind the veil. God could give revelations of Himself to them, but never were their consciences in the presence of God. There was an unrent veil between God and the people and the priests also. This is very important to notice, because of the principle brought out in the contrast of our portion and the Jews'. We are in the presence of God, and we are always there; that is the Christian ground: they never were. Daily cleansing is needed with us, too; but still, we are always in the presence of God. This is very little realized by the people of God now. "If we walk in the light as he is in the light," &c. The work is done once for all, and we are brought nigh by virtue of that work; and if we are not there through that work, we never can get there. I am speaking of God looking for atonement, and our standing in the presence of God, not the children with the Father. Our feelings may be varying from day to day, but our standing before God never changes in Christ. And if we reject this one sacrifice for sin, there is no other.

Verse 3, &c. Within the second veil none could enter. God's reason for it is, "The Holy Ghost this signifying, that the way into the holiest of all was not yet made manifest." The object of the veil was to show that the people could not come to God. He could give them laws, punish them if they broke them, enable them to look to Him; but they could not come near. If it is a question of being in His presence, I must come where He is. In His presence sin is not measured by transgression, but by what God is—"in the light as He is in the light." "Ye were darkness, but now are ye light in the Lord." God's people are now brought into His presence in the light, and always there; it is where God has placed them by faith—not a question of their feeling. As long as the first tabernacle was yet standing, this was not made manifest at all: God was hiding Himself. Directly the veil was gone, He must have let in the Gentiles as well as the Jews; but the very nature of the sacrifices shut out the thought of one eternal redemption. The repetition of them showed that sin was there, or they would not have been repeated. The one sacrifice for sin having been made, shows the sin to be entirely put away. The nature of those sacrifices was never to reveal God, and never to have the conscience perfect.

There is another practical thing to be noticed here. He does not merely say sin is put away, but the conscience is perfect; no more conscience of *sins* (not sinning); that is the same as a perfect conscience. We all have a conscience of *sinning*, but if I have a conscience of *sin* I cannot come to God, but am like Adam hiding from Him. What we have here is not only sin put away in the presence of God, but put away from the conscience, too. Many own the former, but think they need repeated forgiveness, repeated cleansing with blood. How could sin be put away? It could not be but by the suffering of Christ. Must Christ, then, suffer again?

There was piety in the Old Testament, and piety is a blessed thing, but there was never a purged conscience. We never find in the most pious persons under the law the sense of being in the presence of God. The high priest must go once a year within the veil with clouds of incense; but now the holiest *is* made manifest, the veil being rent from top to bottom, and the conscience as perfect as the light in which we stand.

Verse 10. Certain things were imposed on them until the time of reformation. Christ came " an High

Priest of good things to come." What does that refer to? Some may find a difficulty as to whether "to come" refers to what was future for the Jews, while that tabernacle was standing, or to what is now future. I believe *both*. All was *new* in Christ. It was to come on a new foundation. The basis is laid for the entire and perfect reconciliation of man with God.

Verse 7. Under the old covenant, it was only "the errors of the people" that were forgiven. *Now* God takes up the spring of a man altogether. The old covenant dealt with man on the ground of obedience; now God is bringing the sinner himself into a new condition before Him. The old covenant was a partial remedy with the declaration that they could not come into God's presence. While this kept up a testimony for God, now a new thing is brought out, not to patch up the old thing—that was the old even in its remedial character; but now it is the bringing in a new thing entirely—giving a new nature in Christ. The Jewish system provided no remedy for great sins ("keep back thy servant from presumptuous sins"); it was a provision for the old man without seeing God, instead of bringing man perfect, in a new nature, into the presence of God.

Rom. iii. God declares His righteousness for the remission of sins that are past, &c. Righteousness was never revealed under the law—God bore with things, but there was no declaration of righteousness. Now it is "to declare his righteousness." Righteousness was revealed when the atonement was made. Directly it is other ground than promise given to those walking by faith, as Abraham, there is no coming into the presence of God. The old covenant goes on the old ground; the new covenant goes on new ground. The work of Christ and the blood of Christ are not provision for the sins of the old man, but for the perfecting of the conscience of the new man, to set him in the presence of God. We could not be in the presence of God with one spot upon us; we are brought into heaven itself. He is gone in once into the holy place, not gone in to come out again and go in; but by virtue of His own blood He is gone in once. God looking upon the blood cannot see sin. It is not a question of my value of that blood, but the conscience rests on the value God finds in it. "When I see the blood I will pass over." My heart wants to value it more, but the question is, how could I be in the presence of God with a spot upon me? God looks on that blood, and if He looks on the blood, He cannot look on the sin; if He did, it would not value the blood. Where is the blood? It has been presented to God, not to man, and God has accepted it. Impossible that God can impute sin to a believer, it would be slighting the blood of Christ.

Another thing is, it is for ever and ever done. What is faith? It is thinking as God thinks. If I say Christ is gone in once with His own blood, does that ever cease to be there? Then I cannot cease to be perfect; Christ has either done the work for ever or not at all. Another word gives it such power, too, "having obtained eternal redemption," and it is "once for all." How long is it to last? For ever. There is not only cleansing, but redemption. He has taken me up out of where I was, into the presence of God—appropriated me in the presence of God for ever. Has He taken me up in an unclean state? While the veil was there, I could not be taken into God's presence; but now it is a question of the work of Christ bringing me there. Has He brought me there in an unfit state? Impossible! He has " obtained eternal redemption for us," " who, through the eternal Spirit, offered himself without spot to God." We get here, first, His own perfect will in it. He offered Himself; not only, "Lo I come;" but, here filled with the Spirit, He offers Himself up. Christ having become a man, He was obedient in all things; but another thing was, He came to offer sacrifice. As a victim, He was man, spotless man, and the giving Himself up as a sacrifice was His own act; through the eternal Spirit He did it. It is not here the point of sins being laid upon Him, but the giving Himself up, for the whole question of good and evil to be settled on Him in God's presence. He gave Himself up for God to do what He would with Him, to make Him a curse if He would; and He was made a curse; yet it was His own will to come into that place.

It was redemption man needed, not only a little cleansing. Redemption was being taken out of the condition in which we were. God's glory needed to be vindicated where God had been dishonoured. Here was man in rebellion, and in ruin as well as rebellion, under Satan, and He (Christ) must suffer, for God to be glorified—He offered Himself up. Here it was by the power of the Eternal Spirit. There was divine energy in the man, not mere feeling, &c., and it was "without spot," when He was tried even unto death. He became a burnt offering, and that was a sweet savour to God. Every movement of His will was pure, purity in all His thoughts and acts, and there was the unhesitating giving up of Himself to be made even that hateful thing, sin. He would be made sin, made a curse, even unto death; He offered Himself up without reserve; "He was made sin for us;" but He gave Himself up for it: therefore it was a sweet savour. None of the sin offerings were a sweet savour to God: the word used for consuming them is not the same as the burnt offering. For the sin offering, it was merely a word signifying burning, used; in the other it means a sweet savour. It not being imposed upon Him, but His offering Himself up, made it this. All through His life He knew no sin, but on the cross the sin was laid upon Him, and He went through death for it. It led to death—its wages. Therefore we read of the blood, "How much more shall the blood of Christ," &c. Two things there are, the person offering Himself, and the proof of His death for sin; blood being the proof of death. There is a cleansing, purging, daily; but that is with water, and not for forgiveness; and the Father forgiving is another thing. "Without shedding of blood is no remission." How clearly this shows that if it is not done by this, it never can be; the blood never can be shed again. "Purge your conscience from dead works to serve the living God." Here, again, we come back to the conscience. "How much more shall the blood of Christ . . . . so eternal inheritance;" (14, 15,) there is perpetuity spoken of again, too.

Ver. 13. Two things are here alluded to, and not indiscriminately: the great day of atonement, when bulls and goats were offered, and the red heifer, which was for daily cleansing for communion. This was one thing; the other was done once a year, for then it was repeated year by year continually. The blood of the victim was taken into the holy place, and the body burnt outside. This was significant of Judaism done with. Israel was the camp: They had a fleshly religion—flesh in connexion with God; and it could never answer. It was appointed to prove man. Here the blood was carried in. The scape-goat took away the sins confessed over it into the wilderness. Thus the sins were gone. Now our position is having a place inside the veil by the blood, and sin gone. That is our place, shown thus in the type. The " heifer" was for sprinkling the unclean—not with *blood*, but with water and something connected with it, viz., the ashes of the heifer. A heifer was to be taken that had never borne the yoke ; and a clean man was to slay the heifer, and sprinkle the blood seven times, always in the presence of God. Its value always is in the presence of God. But a defiled person, even through touching death, could not go there. The ashes were to be taken with the running water, showing the sin all consumed in the sacrifice offered long ago. The things we have failed about are the very things Christ died for; and the Spirit brings to the conscience the sense of that defilement for which Christ died, and which He put away. This makes me feel the sin much more, while it makes me see it has all been put away. It is not so much the question of *guilt*, but of the terrible nature of sin that occupies me. It is the re-sprinkling with water, not blood; because the re-sprinkling with the blood would call in question its permanent value. The Spirit brings to my conscience and heart the value of Christ's death, and so communion is restored, which is hindered by a sinful thought, &c.

Two instances we have of sprinkling with blood once for all—in the priest and the leper; the whole walk and thoughts consecrated to God according to the value of Christ's blood. But that *never* loses its value. If I do not walk according to the value of it, the Spirit of God brings to my remembrance that my sin brought Christ to ashes. This gives a much deeper sense of the sin. We find out that we have allowed ourselves to be carried away by that which brought God's wrath out, and for which Christ agonized.

" To serve the living God." Under the old covenant, obedience was required from man in his Adam-nature; a veil was before God, and man outside—and he must stay outside. The sacrifices made a temporary provision for intercourse with God, but there was no coming *to God*. Christ, as High Priest of good things to come, brings the new man into the presence of God for ever. The veil is rent, and there is a risen person with cleansing power in the presence of God. Such is the perfectness of the place in which we are set, and every inconsistency is judged according to it.

Verses 16, 17. The word " testament" is rightly used in these two verses. It facilitates the understanding of the passage to see this. Excepting these two verses, read always " covenant."

Thus we find a common event brought in as an illustration of Christ's death. He left us all the blessing in *dying*—it came into complete force directly. We are freed once for all through His death. There is no alteration of it. The blessings of the new covenant became available, valid after His death.

The first must become old if there is to be a new one: the bringing in of the new one involves dying. In this Epistle we get very little of the humiliation part of Christ's work. In the first chapter it is brought in in connexion with His divine person, " when He had by Himself purged our sins, sat down on the right hand of the majesty on high." The purging of our sins is spoken of by the way, and then we hear of His glory on high. The blessedness of Christ's sacrifice, Christ exalted, and having honour put upon Him, are more the subjects in Hebrews. There are three aspects in which the value of Christ's blood is here seen. First, it was the seal of the covenant, connected with its dedication to God. That was also done in connexion with the covenant with Abraham. (Gen. xv.) A person, binding himself to death in the most solemn way, passes through the pieces of the sacrifice. It was the seal of the covenant. Second, it is purifying. Third, the blood is for remission.

First, the enjoining or sanction to it given by the blood. Another thing closely connected with that was consecration by blood. Blood was sprinkled on the leper for cleansing, and on the priest for consecration. The covenant sealed, and the people bound to it by blood; and the leper and the priest are the three cases in which persons are sprinkled. There must be blood, the power of death brought in, or there was entire separation from God. The wonderful efficacy of the blood of Christ is that it brought in death; those separated from God are brought back by His death. " You who were far off are brought nigh by the blood of Christ." The blood was the figure of the life taken. When blood was taken the whole being of man was given up, and the agony of His soul on the cross was the separation from God. " My God, my God! why hast thou forsaken me?" The consequences of it are most important to us. Man with all his perverse will, all his sin, where is it all, if he is dead? It is all gone, if he is dead. " He that is dead, is freed from sin." There is an absolute cessation of the whole will and being in which he was, as a sinner. Christ has taken that place for me. Cain and Abel, as far as appearance went, were equally likely to get the blessing, but in the one was no faith. He did not own that death had come in between man and God. As long as man is seeking good from himself, he does not see himself dead. Are you seeking a dead man or a living man? You are seeking fruit from a living man, and not owning you are dead, if you are seeking fruit from yourself. I cannot search to see whether dead or not, if dead. Abel came by slain beasts to God. He had faith. We do not know how he learnt it, but death came in, and man was clothed in skins of animals. That is, in figure, what makes our peace. "He that is dead is freed from sin." There was nothing done for man while Christ was alive, as to the putting away of sin. "Except a corn of wheat fall into the ground and die, it abideth alone." All that was proved by it was, that man in his natural state could not be reconciled to God.

The first covenant was not made without the sprinkling of blood, but it threw back the man behind death. If you do not obey, all is lost. (Jer. xxxiv. 16, 20.) If they did not obey, they must die; because they promised obedience and sealed the promise by being sprinkled with the blood. In the case of Abraham, God made a promise to him, and sealed it by passing between the pieces, by death. The question was raised by the law of righteousness among living men. There were various figures which intimated the necessity of death coming in, but obedience was the rule and consequently all was failure. Yet all through the principle was brought out—there must be blood. Now, under grace we see the whole putting away of sin. If we had died, judgment must have come on us. Christ coming into it, and bearing the judgment for us, we are free from the whole thing.

When God gave the covenant, He gave it this sanction—the sprinkling of blood. Aaron himself was not sprinkled with blood, typical of Christ, who needed not to be consecrated with blood Himself, but brought blood in for others.

Then you get the sprinkling of vessels—not for forgiveness, but for cleansing. "Almost all things under the law are purged with blood," (not all things are purified with blood,) because there is a purifying with water not connected with blood-shedding. Out of His side came blood and water, representing the effectual grace of expiation and purifying. You could not have man morally purified without death; you must have death. Out of a dead Christ the water flows. Water signifies cleansing by the Spirit with the word. But there must be death—not the cleansing of the living old man; the old man is put to death—I do not own him alive, but there is something belonging to you (your members on the earth) to be mortified and kept in death. The ground is laid for purifying by the blood of the heifer, which was sprinkled seven times before the door of the tabernacle; but water is the figure used for cleansing, viz., " washing of water by the word." " Ye are clean through the word which I have spoken unto you." Reckon yourselves to be dead and to have the power of life in Christ. I have neither life nor righteousness out of Christ. I have nothing out of Him. If I look for water to purify, or anything, it must be by death I get it; then there must be faith. If I look at myself as a living man in the world, I find my will working; then I am not really dead. If I set myself to enquire, I am not walking in faith. I am told to reckon myself dead—that is faith. You cannot mortify your members till you can say, I am dead. If the old man is not dead, it is *sin*. There was no putting away of sin but by death itself—taking life. "Without shedding of blood is no remission"— not sprinkling here; you must have the applying the punishment to the One who takes the sin. In the remission of sin is involved the whole of God's character, majesty, glory. If God does not deal with sin as sin, there is no righteousness—it is indifference. There must be suffering for the sin; then as to death, I am clear of it.

Remission is not connected with sprinkling. This is important in a twofold way. First, there was actual suffering under the consequences of sin; and second, this could be but once. It was done once for all, and if the forgiveness of my sins is not perfect thereby, it never can be accomplished. It will never be done again. We learn more and more the value of the blood; but the work of Christ on the cross has a perfect value, into which the angels desire to look. The thing by which I have remission never can be done again. When I speak of water, it has its importance only so far as it washes; (there is washing and sprinkling spoken of); but not so with the blood; that had to be presented to

God, the offended Judge. The efficacy of the blood is outside ourselves. As regards the man, he is cleansed once for all, but still that is connected with the man. That is not all; the blood has an efficacy in itself, as being the judgment for sin, and tells the tale to God that the judgment is passed over, the sin gone. God says, "When I see the blood I will pass over." That makes the entire full distinction from personal application in cleansing. There is a special value in it for man, because a man when cleansed does not like to get dirty, while one not cleansed does not mind it. True, that as to the *water* when once regenerated by the word, it is done for ever—once for all; but there is besides the constant cleansing of the feet needed. There is no presenting of blood afresh to God—no fresh "shedding of blood." There is increase of spiritual search needed by us to know more of the value of the blood, but there is no fresh searching needed by God for Him to know its value.

Ver. 21, &c. Three things were done on the day of atonement. Blood was put on the mercy-seat, representing Christ gone into heaven, the ground on which we can preach peace to all the world. That was connected with the Lord's lot. His death glorified God, whether one or a thousand are saved.

All was in utter confusion by sin. What kind of world is this? Where is righteousness? Where is love? What folly there is in infidelity! How can men solve the riddle of all the misery we see around, without God? Where is the goodness of God to be seen? How can it be attempted to be explained without Christ? Indifference to sin is not love. Men try to persuade themselves God will be indifferent to sin. When I see God's judgment for sin on Christ, I get at the centre of God's heart—righteousness is satisfied, and what is more, God can rest in His love. And if you come [as a sinner to God, and rest in Christ, it is a matter of the glory of God to see you there because of the blood.

" The heavenly things themselves with better sacrifices." Satan and his angels are there and cleansing is needed. This purging is not remission. God must have His house cleansed as well as His people made righteous. (Comp. Col. i.)

On the people's lot, the scapegoat, the particular sins of the people were confessed. This was substitution. (Ver. 26.) And there is perpetual value in the sacrifice. He once suffered. This suffering was not the mere fact of death. The agony of His soul when he cried, "My God, my God, why hast thou forsaken me," was far deeper than the suffering of the separation of soul and body. Death was looked at as the wages of sin; God's wrath was poured out on Him against the sin. (Death to Christ was not merely going out of the body into Paradise.) That never can be done again. He has gone in once into the holy place. If he went in often, He must have suffered often. " But this man, after he had offered one sacrifice for sins, for ever sat down." This does not mean for ever and ever, but unremittingly He is sitting at the right hand of God. I never can stand in the presence of God, but in the sacrifice of Christ, and that is never remitted. He has put sin away; why should He suffer again? He has put it away according to the glory of God. "Once in the end of the world hath he appeared." That may appear strange, seeing nearly as much of the world's history has gone on since as before Christ's coming; but it does not mean chronologically, but the closing in of the ages. Up to that time God had been trying men as living men in the world. That is ended—man is not alive now (I speak of man morally, as judged by God); therefore it is said to the Colossians, "Why as though alive in the world?" Man has been tried as to life, and now the fig tree is cut down. Did it bear fruit? No! and it was cut down. The fig tree represented the Jewish nation, in whom God made trial of men under the best circumstances. "What have I not done to my vineyard?" Christ came looking for fruit from the fig tree, and finding none, He said, Cut it down; let no fruit grow on thee for ever. The "time for figs was not yet;" the fruit-bearing time not come. God, as it were, said, "they will reverence my Son." No! then there is no fruit from man for ever. Man, looked at as in flesh, is under the sentence of death. "When we were yet without strength . . . . . Christ died for the ungodly." Man is not only ungodly, but without power to get out of that state. Christ must close the history of the old man, by bearing the sin, and must bring in a new thing. Then God makes a feast and invites to the supper; when they not only refuse the Son, but they refuse the supper. Man has been fully tried, and now, if there is to be blessing, it must be not on the ground of responsibility, but wholly of grace, by the second Adam. (Rom. v.) If I believe this, I find out the truth about the old man by little and little. At first we only see gross sins perhaps. 'But what is to be done when I find I can do nothing,' you say. Own you are undone. "In me (that is, in my flesh) dwelleth no good thing." "It is appointed unto men once to die, but after this the judgment." Death is like the policeman to bring us up to the judgment. Then (ver. 28) we have the counterpart of this *in grace*. "*So Christ* was once offered to bear the sins of many," "and to them that look for him," all believers, " will He appear . . . without sin." What does that mean ? As to his own person, He was without sin the first time ; but now the same One comes back—what for ? To deal about the sins ? No ! That He has done the first time : and now, apart from that entirely, He comes to receive them to Himself. For those who trust in His first coming, and look for His second, there is nothing but blessing. There is a work done *in* us to make us sharers in that which has been done outside us, but this is the question of the work done for us, outside of ourselves altogether. What had I to do with the cross of Christ? The hatred that killed Him and the sins that He bore are all that sinners had to do in it; therefore there can never come a shade upon the love of God in the cross of Christ. It is perfect.

CHAPTER X.

THE practical conclusion is drawn in this chapter of what is brought out in chapter ix.—the unity of the sacrifice; one offering by which the foundation is laid for the new covenant.

Instead of finding a man turned out of the paradise on earth because of sin, it is now a new man gone into the paradise of God in divine righteousness; gone in by virtue of a new title, which man never had before. The consequence is, when He comes again in glory, He has nothing to do with sin. He came once for sin; but when He comes the second time, it will be without any question of sin, to complete the salvation wrought out already. When He returns, it is to bring man into the full blessedness He is in Himself. "To them that look for Him, shall He appear," &c.; not only for the church, but it is open for the remnant when He appears to the earth.*

The effect on the conscience of His offering for sin is shown in chapter x. It is not only a statement of facts there. My sin might be put away and I not know it; but Christianity shows us how the conscience

---

* The words do not express the fulness of the Church's hope, which is, the being with Him. This alludes more to the appearing, but it expresses the hope of both, as pilgrims down here.

is purged, not only the sins put away. If the conscience is purged, there is nothing between me and God. I have the full deliverance from all consequences of sin, and a title to glory, by virtue of the new thing. But what is my present state? My conscience perfectly purged. That the *law* could not tell us. It could never make the comers thereunto perfect. That was reserved as a witness for the gospel when the work was done. When a man is in the presence of God, the full effect on the conscience is known. There must be a repetition of sacrifice while the sin was outstanding. There was always a question of sin between God and His people under the law. Israel in the last day will get salvation by virtue of the sacrifice; they will be blessed by Him from Heaven; their thoughts will rest on Christ coming on earth to them. He will bring them blessing where they are, but not take them to heaven. That is not our case at all. We are with Him while He is in heaven. The Holy Ghost has come out in consequence of His being gone in. There was no blood taken within the veil, and the sacrifice not taken without the camp, until after the sin of Nadab and Abihu. After that Aaron was not to go at all times into the holiest, but once a-year, to sprinkle the blood on the mercy-seat. The veil was not rent then; but sin being brought out, the blood must be taken in. The witness of acceptance for Israel is when He comes out. They cannot have it while He is within. We are associated with Him in heaven by the Holy

Ghost coming out and making us know the value of His sacrifice. He will come and receive us unto Himself, that where He is we may be. We are to be associated with Him there.

Up to His death it could not be: God would have put aside the law if the fulness of blessing had been brought in; and the law was given to His own people, not to the Gentiles. The result of Christ's work is, that my constant state in the presence of God is the conscience purged. There is not a revelation, a prophet needed for that. The worshippers, once purged, have "no more conscience of sins." How many Christians there are who do not know they have no more conscience of sins! If you do not, you do not know the virtue of Christ's sacrifice. Are you going to be in heaven with sin upon you? You cannot be there in sins. The old state was that of men living on earth—falling, getting cleansed, and falling again. That is your condition, unless you are in heaven by virtue of that one sacrifice, without sin. The believer is introduced there in Christ—into these heavenly places, cleansed from sin (I am not speaking of what he is as a man on earth, but in Christ). Are you there? That is the question. Are you in the holiest as to your conscience, heart, and spirit, with "no more conscience of sins;" "in the light as He is in the light;" with no remembrance of sin before God? There is remembrance of sins under the law; but here "no more conscience of sins." Christ has not only entered within the veil, because there is no veil now, but I am in heaven by the veil being rent. What is the rending of the veil? The death of Christ. I get there by His death; then I get in without my sins. I get in through that which takes them away. I am there without them. Remark how God takes up all this as His matter. The whole thing is done without us, by God. The thing is done by Him, and the revelation of what is done is by Him too. It is God's work, and it is according to the truth of God.

There were three things needed. If I was full of sin, some one was needed to think about me; some one was needed to do the thing required, and then to tell me the effect. "By the which will we are sanctified." The work of the Spirit in applying the work of Christ, is not spoken of here. But there is, 1st, The will of God—"By which will," &c. 2nd, The work whereby it is done—"By the offering of the body of Jesus Christ, once for all." Before I was born, it was once for all done. Did I do it? No! "By the obedience of one many were made righteous." It was by the offering of the body of Christ once for all. 3rd, There is the knowledge of it given to me. Without this my conscience is not purged. I must be justified by faith: that is, my knowing it, not God's knowing it. Here he says, "the Holy Ghost is a witness to us." That is the ground of the conscience being purged; it is not the quickening here: we have pardon when we are quickened. Peter speaks of being "sanctified unto obedience," &c.; renewed to obedience. It is His (God's) work to quicken my conscience, but besides that, there is the testimony by the Holy Ghost. The thing is settled, and it is not a light thing. We adore Him for it. He says, "Their sins and iniquities will I remember no more." But you say, I sin to-day, to-morrow, &c. God says, "I remember" no more. If there is sin, what can put it away? There is no more offering for sin. If it *is* not put away, how can it ever be done? If He does remember them, there is no hope for me, because Christ will not die again, and "without shedding of blood is no remission." It is very important for the conscience to get into the presence of God, and know our whole condition as to sin there. Looked at as a Christian, there is no sin, for this one reason, that Christ has been in the condition in which I was. By virtue of His being in it, the condition has ceased to exist, and He is gone a man into Heaven, by virtue of the condition having ceased. God has said to Him, "Sit on my right hand until I make thy foes thy footstool." For the sacrifices provided for men in the flesh, there is substituted this one sacrifice of Christ.

Verse 5. "A body hast thou prepared me." Christ came once for all into the place of obedience to put aside all the other appointments. He took ears as a servant. Whatever man did, in offering sacrifices, he could not get out of the condition in which he was. Another comes in. He takes away the first that He may establish the second. They brought of their voluntary will, under the first: that was man. But in the second, all is of God's will, and it is obedience to that. As soon as He has the body prepared, it is not His will at all. It was in the counsels of God long before. "In the volume of the book it is written of me," &c. There was the free-willing of Christ in heaven, to give Himself. He undertakes the whole thing. Then when in it, He goes through all in obedience. "As the Father gave me commandment, even so I do. Arise, let us go hence." There is perfect love to His Father, and perfect obedience at the same time. There is God's will in all its perfection—Christ offering Himself to be the obedient One, and I get not only the fact in purpose, but all the value of a Divine Being giving Himself up. "Lo, I come to do thy will." He is in the place of obedience. "Above, when He said, Sacrifice and offering, and burnt-offerings, and offering for sin thou wouldest not. . . . . Then said he, Lo, I come to do thy will, O God." Here I find the will of man altogether set aside. The will of man is wickedness, the principle of sin. A will independent of God is the very principle of sin. At the first, the will of man was disobedience to God. Christ had a free will, because He was God; but when in the servant's place, He had no will. The horrid pride of man forgets that his independence of God, his will not being moved by the will of God, is rebellion against Him, and that is our natural state. All but obedience to the will of another is sin. We forget we are creatures. Christ came to do God's will, never His own. This would-be independence of man (for, after all, men are the slaves of Satan) is entirely set aside by another Man coming in. He has to learn obedience by the things that He suffered. Every will of His was crossed. There was not a single thing to which He could turn in which obedience was not suffering. He suffered from God, too, for the sins of man. He offered Himself by the eternal Spirit. When tested by Satan's showing Him good and evil, He gave Himself up (becoming specially the burnt-offering from the time of the conflict in Gethsemane.) The first order of things is gone entirely. If I could have righteousness by the law, I would not have it, Paul says, because I have a better—the righteousness of God. If there could have been any righteousness by the law, there was an end to it now. A new thing is brought in.

Verse 11. "Every priest standeth daily," &c. They were always standing, because there was always sin there to be put away. What they did to put it away never accomplished anything. They were dealing with offerings for men in the flesh, and they never did anything. But He has sat down. There was a righteousness fit to sit down on the throne of God, and that is where we are. It is on the throne Christ is, for ever. He is not rising up, like the other priests. The sacrifice was completed and He sits for ever. It does not mean eternally but continuously. The other sacrifices could not have that effect; but now, His being there is the proof there is no interruption. The stopping, in some of the Bibles, makes no sense of it.

It cannot be one sacrifice for sins for ever. He is sitting, never having to get up again, because the value of the sacrifice is uninterrupted in the presence of God, and the Holy Ghost comes out to show me the result of it. The person who had the sins must be shut out of heaven; then Christ is shut out, if they are not gone, for He took them. But the Holy Ghost is the witness that He is there. If you are reasoning about it, saying, My sins are forgiven to-day, but to-morrow, what I may do may be remembered against me, you are away from God. In the presence of God, this is my whole condition, without my sins. In the presence of God, I am either a condemned sinner, or I have a purged conscience. Away from God we may reason. In His presence, there may be awful distress for a moment, but faith brings into the condition of a purged conscience.

Verse 13. " From henceforth expecting." This is the patience of Christ. The conscience has nothing to do with the waiting. Righteousness has nothing to wait for; conscience has nothing to wait for. All is done. He has perfected for ever them that are sanctified. Not merely are those sanctified, sanctified by God, but He has perfected them; they are perfectly set apart, perfected by God, by the very thing He has set them apart by. Then such can say, I am perfect for God, and my heart is happy with Him, because I am perfect before Him. It is so settled with Him that we are thoroughly perfected, that He can sit there quietly.

Now the Holy Ghost declares it all to me showing me the practical consequences: "where remission of (sins) is, there is no more offering for sin." The blood is presented to God, and it abides in unalterable efficacy. This makes nothing, not only of the gross superstitions connected with professing Christianity, but of all forms and ordinances by which men think to attain anything before God. If we are not abidingly as in the presence of God with a purged conscience, we have not got hold of the truth of God about it. When we realize this our place, we have a different estimate of sin; evil is detected, and we know it can have no place, and the good is more understood in the presence of God; sin is judged in a much deeper way, than when there is merely terror and uncertainty.

Verse 19. "Boldness to enter into the holiest." This rending of the veil is altogether ours. We know it is rent by the perfect love of God, and we go into the presence of God without a veil. The way is made manifest. We go where Christ is gone; the holiness that rent the veil has put away the sin. Verse 21: "having an high priest," &c. We do not go creeping in all alone; the High Priest who has done the work is there before us. I cannot go within the veil without finding Him there. The apostle is following Jewish figures, becoming a Jew to Jews. There were other priests besides the great High Priest. Instead of, like the Jewish priests, offering incense outside, we go within. There was the washing of the priests, as for us. The anointing is not in question here, but the sprinkling of blood and the washing of water. So, in substance, it will be for Israel by and by.

Verse 22. "Let us draw near," &c. The next thing, verse 23, is, "let us hold fast the profession of our faith," &c. The exhortation is to be in communion within, and not to be attracted by the world without, ordinances, &c., to which they were in danger of going back. Then, (verse 24,) I am to think of others, walk in the power of the fruits of the Spirit; and (verse 25) not only to have love to individuals, but to remember the assembly. Christ would praise in the midst of the congregation. A person may say, I am very happy in staying at home; but that will not do. To go to the assembly often brings persecution.

The "day" spoken of here is not the catching up of the church, but the appearing. The more the day approaches, the greater the difficulty of assembling ourselves; but the exhortation is to be found assembling as plain evident Christians. It is not said to hear a sermon, but assembling *ourselves*. The way of God's working is not only to make Christians, but to gather together in one the children of God scattered abroad. This is not to be fulfilled in the millennium. There will be different nations then, though they will come up to worship; and in the Old Testament times there was one particular nation, but no gathering together in one—it applies now. Church authority is not what is meant. That is not faith, but assembling ourselves together is faith. Not of man's will, but Christ's; who, through His death, has a church or assembly that is not of the world, and that is manifested by our assembling together.

Verse 26. If you say, 'I give up this assembling to Christ'—there is none other sacrifice for sin but that He has made. If you trample under foot the blood of that sacrifice, knowing what it is, (I do not say being regenerated,) but giving it up wilfully, your portion is the same as adversaries. A person who sees truth and gives it up, is always more bitter than any—he is an adversary. If they chose sin instead of Christ, there was no more sacrifice. It is a case of openly abandoning the Lord for one's own will in sin; not failure nor disobedience, but apostacy.

We see throughout this epistle the importance of the place in which we are set, and the responsibility of walk according to it. Christ is ever in the presence of God for us. Consequently, our title is to enter there boldly; our place never changes, though sin, of course, hinders fellowship till it is confessed.

CHAPTER XI.

WE have already seen in this epistle that the Hebrews, instead of walking by faith, were in danger of turning back to the things they could see—things suited to them as men in the flesh, such as ordinances and objects of outward importance, of which the Jewish system was full. But Christians were called *out* of these; God was leading away from them. The constant tendency of all our hearts is to go back. It is a shame for Gentiles to take up with those shadows, in a measure, it was natural for the Jews, because they had had the beggarly elements appointed for them to observe. *Now* there was something better. They were waiting for Christ to come again, and it is said to them, "He that shall come, will come, and will not tarry." In this epistle we do not have the place of the Church, the body of Christ, brought out at all; in that connexion the Lord comes and takes her to Himself. "I go to prepare a place for you," &c. Here, as pilgrims, there is responsibility before us, and we look for His appearing. In church-character the hope is to be with Him. Here it is the heavenly calling and priesthood between us and God. The apostle goes on to show the power of faith. It is not a definition, but a description of its effects. It is "the substance of things hoped for, the evidence of things not seen." Perfect certainty of realization is the effect of faith. The definition of faith is that it "sets to its seal that God is true." It remains that, what we hope for, we with paitience wait for. The promise is just as certain as if we had the fulfilment of it. We do not see it. If we saw it we should not hope for it, but we realize things not seen. This is the power of faith in the soul.

In this chapter we have faith in its active character —the working of faith when it is there. The thing that produces faith is the spirit of God bringing home the word with power, and when the soul sees anything of Christ it cannot rest satisfied without more. " Of His own will begat He us with the word of truth," is the reception of truth in the soul. Then there follows the practical effect in the walk of the believer. There is a great deal of method in this chapter, more than appears at first sight, for it is not man's method, but God's. The divine mind is always at work according to the measure of divine love. Directly you get the clue to the divine mind, you get beauty and order. Thus, in Exodus, we have the account of the things for the tabernacle, and then the priests, and then again the utensils. The human mind sees nothing but disorder in all this; but when the object of the shadow is known, the most perfect order comes out.

Faith here is spoken of in connexion with creation. That nothing could come out of nothing, is man's wisdom! The philosopher could never of himself have found out how "the worlds were framed," &c.

Creation is absolutely unknown by reason. "*By faith we understand,*" but man's way of accounting for it led to pantheism, &c. *Now* men have got some knowledge of it from the Bible; but without scripture it never could be known simply or certainly.

On the next exampler of faith we see the ground on which man could be in relationship with God. In Abel, the faith that brought a sacrifice: in Enoch, that which led to walking with God, and the power of life in his translation. In the seventh verse, it is faith connected with God in government, and the consequent judgment of the world. In the next example we have that kind of faith that reckons on promise. It takes the promise of God, is satisfied with it, gives up everything, and gets nothing. All that flesh clings to is to be given up. These Jews had to do that. If I have nothing to do with earth I am a heavenly man. If I have nothing on earth, I am not an earthly man. God is not ashamed to be called the God of one whose heart and portion are in heaven; but He would be of one whose heart is on earth. This is the faith that gives character, heavenly character. (Ver. 8-22.) Then you have faith that counts on God, the active energy of life—not merely character, but *energy;* not so much the giving up as the active energy of the new principle in the soul. This is from verse 23 to 31. Then the getting into the land is passed over, the rest promised in heaven. They have possession of the land. It is different to passing the Red Sea and the wilderness.

From verse 32 come out all the various difficulties

and traits of faith in which individuals had to stand against the professing people of God. This is a more difficult thing than any. If you want to live a life of faith, you must often live without Christians. People have to go alone with God and no one else, and if not, they must bring in unbelief to hinder them. Communion of saints is a happy thing, but there are times when you must act alone. Jonathan acted in faith, but Saul's folly spoiled the whole thing. We need the faith that reckons on God, let the people do what they like. This is not so brilliant an action of faith, but it is very valuable. A person who goes to preach in a heathen place knows what he has to do. His difficulty is not nearly so great as that of a Christian with the world, who profess to be Christians.

If not very near to Christ, a man cannot discern what is the world and what is of Christ.

Ver. 37, 38. They had to take what portion they could get here, and they died without receiving the promises, "God having provided some better thing for us," &c. The beginning of chapter xii. is founded on this. The chastening there is connected with the trials of faith: the chastening is against the flesh. (Ver. 2). Our attention is taken off all the other examples of faith in chapter xi., and the eye is to be fixed on Him who has gone through all. "Looking unto Jesus." 'Looking away' is the force of the expression. "He is set down on the right hand," &c. Of the Abrahams, Isaacs, Josephs, Moses, &c., we read, they "received not the promises," but of Christ it is not said, He has not. *He has.* He "is set down at the right hand of the throne of God." He has the reward; and another thing, He has run all the way, bearing mockery, scourging, &c. He has trodden every bit of the path of faith. The others all had their trial in a particular way, but the encouragement for faith now is that He has sat down, having run it all. David has not his reward yet. All these are not made perfect yet, but He is. Christianity was not brought in then. They were not brought into resurrection-glory. There were others to be brought into a better thing. He was the beginner and finisher of faith, and He has the reward.

It is well that we should see what the character of the reward is. Reward is never the motive for conduct: there would be no room for love in that; but it acts as an encouragement, when we are in the path which love has brought into, and encompassed with difficulties and trials.

These Hebrews were going back to the expectation of a Messiah they could see. They are reminded that none of those in whom they boasted did see what they waited for. "These all died in faith, not having received," &c. You want a visible Messiah, but none of these you glory in got what they waited for. With a Jew this was an unanswerable argument. They got nothing but by faith. So with us. What have we but what we have by faith?

Without going into the details of chap. xi. we have, first, the creation—then, respecting sacrifice, "Abel offered unto God a more excellent sacrifice than Cain." One thing to remark here is, how faith meets all cases since sin came in. It has nothing to do with innocence. Innocence does not need faith. When there was enjoyment all around, there was no need of faith. It was when sin came in that faith is known—a most blessed ordering of God; for it brings to us all that is required—righteousness, life, shelter in the judgment of the world. It can wander in a strange country, and bring in a living energy to overcome. It brings in God for enjoyment—communion—want of communion giving the sense of sin, and bringing back. It is the positive bringing in of God when sin had turned out of His presence. It takes out of flesh to God. It brings God in; or, rather, God brings Himself in His word and Spirit. There is no condition in which you cannot have it. The first thing we have it for is for righteousness.

Abel was a sinner: faith brings into a better place than innocency. I can enjoy nothing rightly according to flesh; but the moment I get hold of God, I am out of those things, and am connected with Him. When they were in the land, the occasion for faith dropped through, except where special need brought it out.

When sin had shut us out from God, righteousness is possessed by faith. "He obtained witness that he was righteous." Cain, before his heart was laid bare, was a very decent man: he was labouring in the sweat of his brow, and then went to worship God. What would you have better? It was this very thing that showed he had not one single right thought about God. He thought he could worship God as comfortably as ever. Cain really carried to God the proof of the curse—just what the natural man does. What we find in Abel was entirely different: he brings in *death;* he takes a firstling of the flock, a slain beast, by which he acknowledges he is under the effect of sin, not merely outwardly. He brings *blood* to God—a sacrifice—a slain sacrifice—the only way. He acknowledges by it, he is a *sinner*, and lost unless the death of another comes in. He comes to God with a sacrifice, and that declares, I am lost without. This passage is so clear as to righteousness—" he obtained witness that he was righteous, God testifying of his gifts." This is not only that righteousness is in Christ: *He is* my righteousness—I am "made the righteousness of God in Him." Abel obtained a witness that *he* was righteous, not that *God* was righteous. Not merely that God had given the sacrifice, but there are the actings of God in the man. God provided the sacrifice, but faith acts in bringing it to God. " God testifying of his gifts." It is full of blessing. I have the witness that I am righteous. This is not experience. I do not want a testimony for what I experience. I want a testimony that delivers me from the things I am occupied about in myself, when I am suffering from them. I get it from God's gift that is perfect. I am " accepted in the Beloved." You say, There is something about myself I cannot get over. Remember, the testimony of the Holy Ghost *in* us is the contrary of the testimony of the Holy Ghost *to* us. *In me*, He takes notice of every fault, that is not righteousness; but the testimony to us is, "their sins and iniquities will I remember no more." If a person brings a note to me, he does not ask what I am. In bringing Christ to God, I bring perfection. This is a peculiar figure of Christ, the sacrifice of Abel. Christ made Himself our neighbour: Israel slew Him. They have the mark on them, having cast off Christ. But He is the sacrifice through which they will be restored. Faith says, I go to God by the sacrifice.

In Enoch, life has come in, as well as righteousness. Christ is "declared to be the Son of God with power, according to the spirit of holiness, by the resurrection from the dead." Enoch, before his translation, had this testimony that he pleased God. In the Old Testament it is said he walked with God. If we are reconciled to God, we can walk with Him. Then the life is manifested in walk, and the power of that life is, that he does not die at all. Christ said, "He that liveth and believeth in me shall never die." So, those who are alive when He comes will not die. We may not die. The "wages of sin" for faith are entirely done away. Enoch is not found, for God took him— he is not touched by death at all. That which is the power of death is done away.

Another thing accompanying this is, that "before his translation, he had this testimony that he pleased God." Here I get life before death. That we have as a present thing, and if the Lord comes, we shall not die. His long-suffering is the reason of His not coming. Walking with God, we have the testimony that we please God. It is peace, comfort—joy of the favour in which we stand. The Spirit of God, instead of reproving us, brings the light of God's favour streaming in upon our souls. Glory we now see, through a glass darkly; but it is a real truth that the Holy Ghost is in us, and if we are walking with God, He makes us happy in His favour; not merely I have done right in this or that; I do not think of myself at all, but of God. If I care only for what natural conscience says, I do not get God's mind at all. That does not touch what God is at all, but what man is. It is saying that man may exalt himself— has responsibility to himself; but believing God is a great deal more—it acknowledges responsibility to God. "He that cometh to God must believe that he is, and that he is a rewarder," &c. It is coming to another that is spoken of. Do I come to a person I am with? In coming, I think of what He is—what God thinks of a thing. We have to do with Him in a living way, by faith. He is one who takes notice of everything. If you apply this practically at any moment, what a difference it will make! We are called to judge everything in the light. What do I mind about difficulties, if I know I am pleasing God? Such an one does not despise any, because thinking about God, he goes from strength to strength. Intercourse with God shows him more of God's mind—

he sees what God is doing. " If thine eye be single, thy whole body shall be full of light."

If he fail, there will be distress, thus walking with Him, because he has lost the thing he delights in. If accustomed to walk carelessly, he does not notice it. " Without faith it is impossible to please God." If there is diligence in seeking Him, there is the reward.

Ver. 7. If Enoch's case is that of exceptional translation, like the Church, Noah, like the Jewish remnant of the last days, is found in the place on which judgment was coming, and warned of things not seen as yet, (besides being a preacher of righteousness, as we hear elsewhere,) is moved with fear, and prepares an ark. His is the prophetic spirit; the world is condemned, and himself becomes heir of the righteousness which is by faith. He accepted God's testimony with the provided means of escape, and thus inherited that righteousness on which the new world is founded. Thus we have had faith in creation, faith in sacrifice, walking with God, and testimony.

From verse 8—16 we have, not the great principles of human relationship with God from first to last, as in the preceding verses, but the faith which goes and keeps out as a pilgrim, with all the strength given for fulfilling the promises. And as these realized strangership on earth through faith, lived and died in faith, not in the possession of what was promised, so God regarded them with special favour, is not ashamed to be called their God, and will exceed their hopes of heavenly things. Further, we come (17—22) to the faith that sacrifices the things which apparently accomplish the promise, to receive it from God alone, or confides, spite of all that tends to destroy confidence. This is rather faith's patience, as what follows is its energy. Thus faith in the history of Moses (23—27) abides firm in the face of the utmost difficulties. Moreover, not providence, but faith, should regulate the believer. Again, we may observe in the next verses (28—31) that faith uses the means God appoints; which nature either refuses, or can only meddle with to its own ruin. But if the Egyptians were swallowed up—the type of those who, of themselves, think to pass through death and judgment, the harlot Rahab identifies herself by faith with the spies and people of God, before a blow was struck on this side Jordan, and thus escaped the destruction which fell on self-confident Jericho.

Then follow statements of the actings and sufferings of faith all through the history of Israel after the conquest of Canaan, not detailed as before, but general; but all, like the patriarchs, without receiving the fulfilment of the promise. This was one grand lesson for the Hebrew Christians. Besides, they were to bear in mind that God has provided some better thing for us. *They* are to be perfected, as well as we, in resurrection-glory; but there are special privileges for the saints who are now being called—" for us."

CHAPTER XII.

Two things are the effect of being in the presence of God—alarm of conscience, and encouragement. The presence of God keeps the conscience thoroughly alive, but it strengthens it to look above the evil while seeing the character of it.

He brings us into His presence to judge all that is contrary to Him and to strengthen us against it, and that is encouraging. He delights in us, and He delights in conforming us to Himself; thus grace comes in so blessedly, making us partake of His nature. It is of what He is He would have us partakers, not merely partakers of holiness, but of His holiness. He does not say, You must be holy, *i.e.*, it does not come out in that form: but He communicates the holiness—His own nature. See the contrast of grace and law. Does not God require holiness in His presence? That is true, but it is law. Grace is, that He delights to give it.

Separation from evil and power of good is the character stamped on all God's dealings down here—chastenings, &c. We have the secret of His ways and dealings, if we are near enough to Him to see. The Hebrews were declining in spirituality; therefore they had not the key to understand His ways. The hairs of our head are all numbered. When once the heart has hold of that, it must apprehend that it is of God's *grace* that He is so occupied with us. It is a wonderful check on will to know that He is so occupied. As in Job it is said "He openeth the ears of men and sealeth their instruction that he may withdraw man from his purpose, and hide pride from man."

We have seen the Apostle had named all the worthies in chapter xi.; but then he says "looking unto Jesus." Christ had run the whole course through, the others only a little bit of it. He despised the shame and has sat down; He has reached the end, having gone through the whole course of trouble and difficulty.

Ver. 3, 4,—Addressing them, he says, You are set here in God's behalf in the place where sin is, to get the better of it. We are all set here a witness of divine good in the midst of evil in this world, and that with a power greater than the power of this world. Greater is he that is for us than he that is against us. We are called to be the epistle of Christ—to glorify God in all circumstances;—not to be apostles.

We fail here and we fail there; but we are set according to His will here or there in this world to manifest Christ in it, and not merely to do the work.

In saying this, one immense truth is supposed, viz., that we have this life. Another is, that all questions between us and God are settled; then, whether we eat or drink, or whatsoever we do, do all in the name of the Lord Jesus. To use His name I must be authorized by Him.

All questions connected with us as sons of Adam are entirely done with. "Wherefore, if ye be dead with Christ from the rudiments of the world, why, as though alive?" &c. (Col. ii.) You are not alive in the world at all; "reckon yourselves dead." That is the reason we are freed from the law. We are dead; and the law cannot have authority over our dead man. This position in which we are set as bearing witness, and all God's dealings with us, go on this ground—we are born of God. This is more than receiving life in nature. We do not read of being born of God as creatures, but as a Christian I am born of God. The effect of the communication of this life as having done with all the old life; we have a life "hid with Christ in God." All is settled; not only we have the nature, but perfect peace. "My peace I leave with you." Christ's peace. No cloud of any sorrow was on Him. He has cleansed us to be without spot, and His righteousness is ours.

Having this nature, born of God, which has to be manifested, (and alas! we find in nature many hindrances—temper, &c.) God sets about to do it for us, when we fail to resist "striving against sin," by chastenings, &c. We are set in the place of children and we must look to what God's thoughts are about us. "Whom the Lord loveth he chasteneth," &c. I get the discipline, chastenings, &c., that God sends to those He loves. There is my will to be broken perhaps, and tendencies to be found out in myself that I did not know of before, to humble me. I get exercised about the good and evil. He hates the evil and loves the good, and is breaking us down, subduing the evil, wearing it out, &c. He is bringing us nearer to Himself. God is educating us as children. Sometimes when we do not see what He is doing, we get the blessing. Will works in us; He comes in to smash the will; and we see afterwards that we have got the blessing through it.

A babe does foolish things which perhaps we may be amused at, but it has not been taught better. A Christian is like a babe, to be trained and instructed. God's patience in taking such pains with us should cheer us. It is strange to talk of affliction cheering us; but if our wills are broken, that is a good thing.

There are various ways in which as saints we get tried, (though we live in great quietness, there might be more persecution if there was more faithfulness) but through all circumstances God is threading our way, occupying Himself with us, our particular characters, &c., to break us down and instruct us. What we want is to realize that God loves us so much—we are of such value to God (more surely than many sparrows) as that He should take such pains to make us " partakers of His holiness." We are apt not to believe the activity of His love. Some trouble comes on us; God has been watching us individually for years, weeks, &c., watching us to bring this trouble which He sees needed.

It is of the greatest importance that there should be the consciousness of God's constant dealing with us in love. We are of that family, belonging to Him, God's family, and not of the world; therefore He deals with us as sons. " No chastening for the present seemeth to be joyous, but grievous; nevertheless afterwards," &c. This is all to encourage. Encouragement is given, founded on the bond of grace between us and God. Then He gives us this blessed privilege of being the witness for God in this world. Everything that makes the condition of the heart better is good, and all is grounded on grace. Therefore it is said "looking diligently lest any man fail of the grace of God,"—lest any root of bitterness springing up trouble you, &c. (ver. 15, 16.) Why does He press this? No profane or impure person! Oh, because we are come to God. Grace puts us in His presence, makes us partakers of His holiness; then He says, "looking diligently lest any man fail of the grace," &c., *i. e.*, do not lose this entire confidence in God's love. This is the present practical enjoyment of what God is for you. If you lose that, you fail. There is nothing that links up the heart with God but grace. "Sin shall not have dominion over you, for ye are not under law, but under grace."

Walk in the sanctuary of His presence. You are not come to the terrible mountain Sinai; but having come to the perfect grace of God in the Lord Jesus Christ, take care how you walk. Grace must be the character of our walk. (ver. 22.) This is true blessedness. There is no hindrance of evil by terror. The effect of the fire from Sinai was that they "entreated the word should not be spoken to them any more." Was that getting on with God? We are not to terrify people by our lives. We may warn them if needful and use the law to hammer at people's hard consciences—all is well in its place; but we cannot be a witness in our walk of this. We are come to a different thing. We may speak of the law, but that is not where we are. Now we must be living witnesses of what we are, and where we are. We are come unto Mount Zion, which represents grace. This is the result, speaking of the place we are brought to. It is to God. He speaks of what will be on this earth, and that is as it were looking down. Zion came at the end of the whole course of responsibility. As to the law, the result was, "Ichabod," for the ark was in the enemies' hand. The only link with God was broken. Then God came in and chose David, of the tribe of Judah—not Joseph (which was significant of a full tide of blessing in nature). The Jebusites conquered and gone, David founded the temple on Mount Zion. This was a new link with God in grace when responsibility was ended. The whole of the heavenly, and of the earthly part is spoken of here. Now we have something more—that which was in the purposes of God, which man never had before in any way. God is glorifying Himself in a way angels never thought of. We are come to the city of the living God, the heavenly Jerusalem—to heaven. Then, when there, we find ourselves in the whole company of angels—the universal company of heaven; then "the church of the first-born"—a special assembly registered in heaven. We are that—not merely creatures as the angels are, but those registered in heaven, as having this special privilege—an assembly whom God has identified with Christ, the First-born. It is remarkable how they are singled out here. In the general muster, He cannot let them pass without distinguishing the "church of the first-born, whose names are written in heaven." We are come to that; it is all the grand result. These are all sitting around Him. Then there is another characteristic of the scene, "to God the Judge of all." There is Zion on earth, the heavenly Jerusalem above, the general company of angels, and the church of the first-born. Then God Himself, and in the way of government, "the judge of all;" then the "spirits of just men made perfect," saints of the Old Testament in the character grace had given them, " or just men." They had run their course and they are there. Then begins what is connected with the earthly part—looking at the effect. We are come "to Jesus the Mediator of the new covenant." We are not come to the new covenant, but to Jesus the Mediator of it. I am associated with Him who is the Mediator; that is a higher thing than if merely come to the covenant. He will make this new covenant with Israel on earth.

"And to the blood of sprinkling." The earth will be benefitted by the shedding of the blood of Christ: it cries peace instead of vengeance, as Abel's did.

Having come to the Mediator, I am come to the prospect of all the blessedness for earth. It is sweet to know earth will have it, but ours is the better part. We are to be a witness of whence we are. We come from heaven. In spirit it is true now. What is true in spirit is more real and palpable than what we see. What is passing in our hearts and minds is more what we are really, than what our bodies are occupied in. Christ was a carpenter (as really as any other carpenter,) but that was not what He was. So with us, we are brought into all these things with God. Then the thing is to be always a witness of the place to which He has called us in grace. We are come; then we have God dealing with us in respect of this place to which He has brought us.

Do you say, This trial or that is enough to discourage me? But no; it is God who is bringing you into it, and God is with you in the place, dealing with you in grace, according to the place He has brought you into.

In the midst of the company of heaven, one company is singled out—that is, ourselves. Surely this is enough to make us humble!

CHAPTER XIII.

THE closing exhortations—i.e., of our chapter—are full of importance, and are, as might be expected from all previously seen, in view of the path in this world proper to the saints, who have Christ appearing in the presence of God for them. They do not, consequently, rise to the height of the communications in Ephesians; for the subject throughout has been the heavenly calling, rather than the mystery of Christ and the Church. Brotherly love is to continue spite of obstacles. Hospitality is not to be forgotten, if we would fare like Abraham. Prisoners and the ill-used are to be borne in mind, considering ourselves and our own circumstances. Marriage is to be honoured and purity sought in or out of that state. Our conduct is to be without avarice, contented with what we have; for God will be true to His word of unfailing care, even as to these things; so that we say boldly, "The Lord is my helper and I will not fear. What shall man do to me?"

The Holy Ghost then tells the saints (ver. 7) to remember their leaders who had spoken God's word to them, the issue of whose conversation was worthy of all consideration and their faith to be imitated. They were gone; but Jesus Christ is the same yesterday, and to-day, and for ever. Let them not, then, be carried away by various and strange doctrines. Grace is that which establishes the heart, not meats by which those who walked in them were not profited. It is a mistake that Christians have no altar: they have one, whereof those who serve the tabernacle have no authority to eat. That is, the Jews have lost their place of privilege, which now belongs in an infinitely more blessed way to such as have Jesus. As in Him, so in us the extremes of shame here and glory above are found to meet. It was not so with Israel. They had the camp, and they could not draw within the veil. And yet even they had the most striking type of another state of things. " For the bodies of those beasts whose blood is brought into the sanctuary for sin, are burned without the camp. Wherefore *Jesus* also, that He might sanctify the people with his own blood, suffered without the gate. Let *us* go forth therefore *unto him* without the camp, bearing his reproach. For here have we no continuing city, but we seek the one to come." Christians now must bear the cross, waiting for heaven with Christ. All middle ground is gone with the old covenant. But if we wait for glory not the less but the rather should we praise continually, offering by Jesus to God the fruit of the lips which confess His name, and not forgetting sacrifices of doing good and communication.

Further, we are called to obey our leaders and to submit ourselves; for " they watch over your souls as those that shall give account." It is not that they are to give account of the souls of others, but of their own conduct in respects of others. Obedience on the part of those watched over would be much for these guides, that they might do their work with joy, and not groaning, for this would be unprofitable for the saints.

The apostle asks their prayers, which he could with a good conscience, occupied with the work of grace, and not the weakness and failure of a careless walk. Moreover, he besought it of them, that he might be the sooner restored to them.

And how blessed and suited to their need and comfort is his concluding prayer! "The God of peace that brought again from among the dead our Lord Jesus, the great shepherd of the sheep, in [virtue of] the blood of the everlasting covenant, perfect you in every good work to do his will, doing in you that which is pleasing before him, through Jesus Christ, to whom be glory for ever and ever. Amen."

The name of Paul does not appear at the close any more than at the commencement; and this for obvious reasons in a letter to saints of the circumcision. But who else would have so spoken of Timothy? The writer was in Italy, and sends the salutation of such as were there. The apostolic under-current is apparent to a spiritual mind.

BEHOLD THE BRIDEGROOM!

TEN LECTURES

ON THE

SECOND COMING AND KINGDOM OF THE LORD JESUS.

BY

W. T. P. WOLSTON, M. D.,

AUTHOR OF "THE CALL OF THE BRIDE"; "REST FOR THE WEARY"; "CRUMBS FOR THE HUNGRY"; "RECORDS OF GRACE," &C. &C.

BOOKS FOR CHRISTIANS

Post Office Box 15344
Charlotte, North Carolina
28210

PRINTED IN THE UNITED STATES OF AMERICA—1970

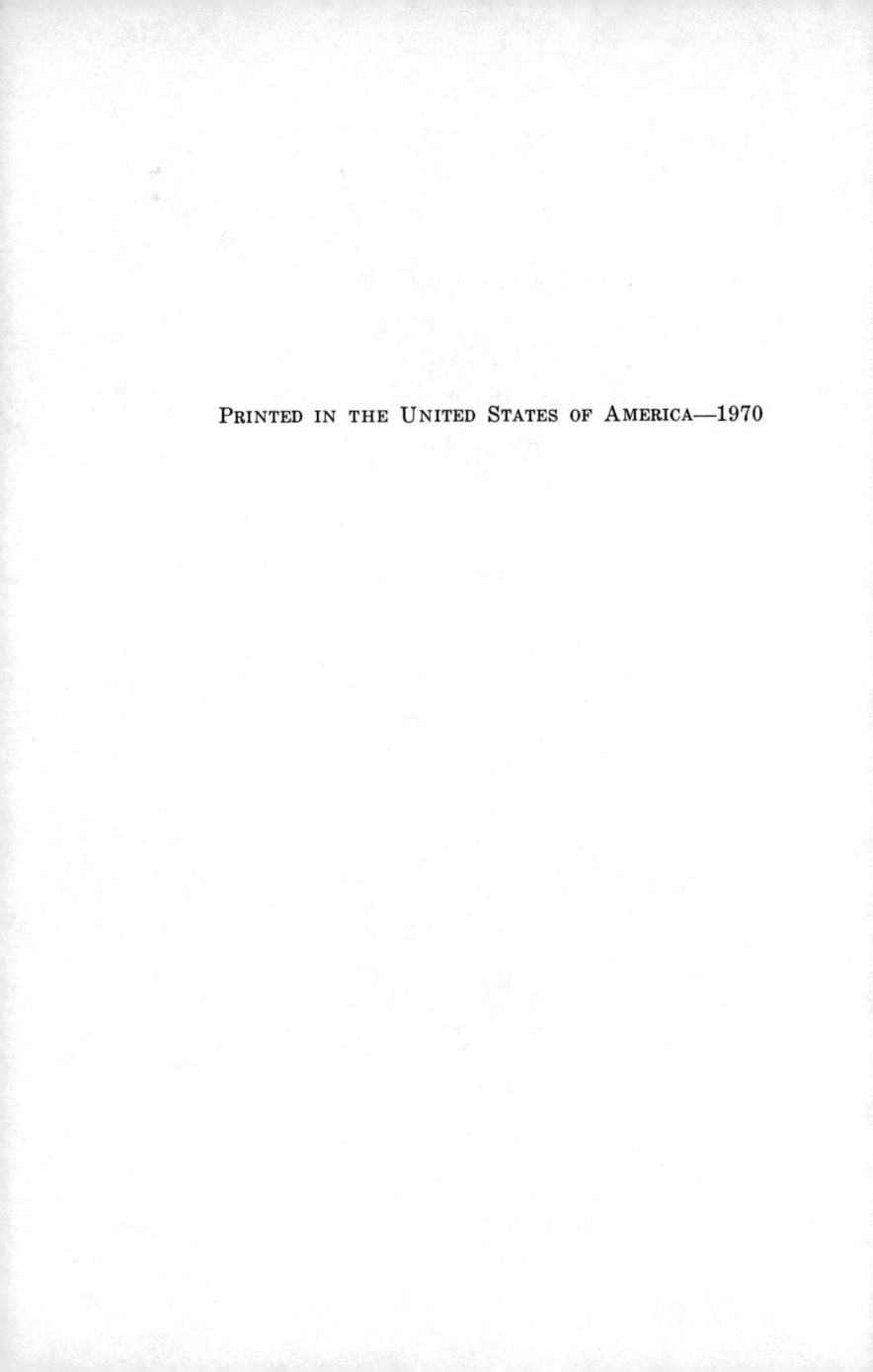

PREFACE TO THIRD EDITION.

THE rapid sale of two large editions, rendering a third so quickly necessary, is happy evidence of the wide-spread interest in the glorious truths connected with the Second Coming of our Lord Jesus Christ.

In no respect does this edition differ from the first, but I take this opportunity of endeavouring to clear up a point briefly touched on in Lecture VI., p. 133, concerning which inquiry has been made, viz., Who are the guests at the marriage supper of the Lamb? Of them it is written, "Blessed are they which are called unto the marriage supper of the Lamb." These clearly are not the Bride, but are "the friends of the Bridegroom." I judge them to be all the heavenly saints—all the risen and glorified saints—other than the Church, which, as being the body—the Bride of Christ—is composed only of believers from the day of Pentecost to the rapture of the saints. Old Testament saints—who are specifically alluded to in Heb. xii. 23 as "the spirits of just men made perfect," will, I apprehend, greatly rejoice in the day of the Lamb's joy, though they be not in the peculiar place of intimacy, which, as the Bride, grace now gives to those who know the Lord, and are, by the Holy Ghost, united to Him in this, the day of His rejection. John the Baptist already anticipated this unselfish joy when he said, "He that hath the bride is the bridegroom; but the friend of the bridegroom, which standeth and heareth him, rejoiceth greatly because of the bridegroom's voice; this my joy therefore is fulfilled" (John iii. 29). So, again, will it be when the heavenly guests sit at the marriage supper of the Lamb. Well may we sing—

> "O day of wondrous promise,
> The Bridegroom and the Bride
> Are seen in glory ever:
> O God! how satisfied."

May the gracious Lord yet further deign to use this little volume to awaken interest in His own near return.

W. T. P. W.

EDINBURGH, *Feb.* 15, 1895.

PREFACE TO FIRST EDITION.

THE origin of the following little volume is this. A year ago a short course of Lectures, on the Lord's Second Coming, was given. Great interest in the subject was evinced, and, by many, a desire expressed, that the truths ministered, might appear in a permanent form, for quiet perusal. As, however, no notes either pre-existed, or were taken, this was then impossible. This spring the Author again felt led of the Lord, to take up the subject of His return, going more into detail, and the shorthand notes, then taken, are now in the reader's hands. They have been revised, and emended, as well as the leisure of a Physician's busy life afforded—subject as it is to constant calls, and interruptions, which do not lend themselves to literary work. To erudition, or scholarship, the book has no claim, and makes no pretensions. That the truth is in it, the Author has no doubt, and the only thought before his mind, in publication, is the profit of souls, if unsaved, and the helping of some of the Lord's dear children, to a better understanding of His prophetic Word, and, a more simple daily waiting, for Him, who says, "Behold, I come quickly."

Delivered, as these Lectures were, to large, and

mixed audiences, of believers, and unbelievers, the felt, and often, expressed need of the latter, made the introduction of the simple Gospel, a necessity, as well as a joy to the speaker. These statements, and appeals, have not been eliminated, for the book may fall into similar hands, and the Lord may be graciously pleased to use the printer's mark, as He did the living voice, to thereby awaken the careless, and bring rest to the troubled. May He do so for His name's sake!

None can be more conscious than the Author, of the many imperfections that exist in his treatment of his subject, so immense is it. But he trusts his attempt, to give a somewhat connected view, of yet future events, will lead the reader to imitate the Bereans, who, when they heard the same testimony as the Thessalonians—the near coming of the Lord—"searched the scriptures daily, whether these things were so" (Acts xvii. 11).

The Lord grant to reader, and writer, to be "like unto men that wait for their Lord" (Luke xii. 36).

W. T. P. W.

46 Charlotte Square,
   Edinburgh, *June* 4, 1891.

CONTENTS.

LECTURE I.—THE MORNING STAR.

Christ's Three Positions—Presentation of His Return in the New Testament Books—Exceptions thereto—The Morning Star—The Christian Hope and its Basis—The Two Resurrections—The Lord, not Death, our Expectation—The Manner of the Lord's Return—The Ten Virgins, and the Bridegroom

LECTURE II.—THE APOSTASY AND ANTICHRIST.

Christians a Delivered People—The Midnight Cry—The Evil Servant—The Post-raptural Condition of Christendom—The Day of Christ—The Apostasy—Its Features—Antichrist—His Names—The Man of Sin—The Man of the Earth—The King—The False Prophet—His Judgment - - - 22

LECTURE III.—THE TIMES OF THE GENTILES.

The Last Week of the Lord's Life—His Testimony as to the Times of the Gentiles—Explanation of the Term in Daniel—*Resumé* of that Book—Nebuchadnezzar's Visions—His Great Image—Its Interpretation—General View of Gentile Empire—The Roman Empire—The Little Horn—The Two Beasts of Rev. xiii. - - - - - 43

LECTURE IV.—THE GREAT TRIBULATION.

The Jews in Relation to the Lord's Return—Are they Cast off?—The Christian's Place—Daniel's Seventy Weeks—Their Interpretation—The Prince that shall Come—The Abomination that maketh Desolate—The Desolator, and the Desolate—The Time of Jacob's Trouble—The Resurrection of Israel—The Lord's Instructions in Matt. xxiv.—The Hundred and Forty-Four Thousand of Israel, and the Gentile Multitude of Rev. vii., who come out of the Great Tribulation—The Church of Christ not to go through it   69

CONTENTS. vii

LECTURE V.—THE SUN OF RIGHTEOUSNESS.

Contrast between the Morning Star, and the Sun of Righteousness—Meaning of the Term—To whom does He Arise?—The Remnant—Their Origin, and Exercises—A Little Book of Psalms—Prayer of the Remnant—Their Double Testimony—Their Call to Israel—Their Summons of the Gentiles—The Gospel of the Kingdom—The Everlasting Gospel—The Appearing of the First-begotten—The Deliverance of Israel—The Lord great in Zion—The Hundredth Psalm—When will it be Sung in the Spirit? - - - 93

LECTURE VI.—THE STONE CUT OUT WITHOUT HANDS.

Nebuchadnezzar's Great Image once more—The Stone that Smites it to Powder—The Kingdom of the Son of Man—Glance at the Book of Revelation—The Worship Meeting of Chapter v.—The Prayer Meeting of Chapter vi.—The Marriage of the Lamb—The Apparel of His Bride—The Lord's Appearing as KING OF KINGS, AND LORD OF LORDS—The Harvest and the Vintage—Christ's Warrior Judgment—Doom of the Beast, and the False Prophet—Christ's Sessional Judgment—The Four Judgments—The Sheep, the Goats, and the Brethren of Matt. xxv. - - - 121

LECTURE VII.—ISRAEL AND THE ASSYRIAN.

The Captivity—Israel's Fall—Salvation come to the Gentiles—God's Faithfulness to Promise—Judah, and Ephraim—The Great Trumpet—Israel's Restoration—Difference between the Two Tribes and the Ten—God's Address to the Land—His Promise to Regather Israel—Meaning of Clean Water—The Valley of Dry Bones—National Resurrection—The Two Sticks—David the King—Ammi, and the Assyrian, Israel's Ancient Foe—Lo-Ammi, and Rome—Gog, Prince of Rosh (Russia)—His Invasion and Downfall—God's Use of the Assyrian—The King of the North—Jerusalem a Burdensome Stone—The Lord on the Mount of Olives - - 143

LECTURE VIII.—A KING SHALL REIGN IN RIGHTEOUSNESS.

A Morning without Clouds—The Lord Jesus as King—The Christian's Relation to Him—The King's First Act—Satan Bound for One Thousand Years—Why—Creation and the

Seventh Day—Features of the Millennium—Death a Rare Thing — The Curse Removed — The Animal Creation Changed—Jerusalem the World's Metropolis—The Temple Rebuilt—Jerusalem the Centre of Worship—The Passover, the Feast of Weeks, and the Feast of Tabernacles - - 172

LECTURE IX.—THE NEW JERUSALEM.

The Heavenly Side of the Millennial Reign—Review of Revelation xix., xx., xxi. 1-8—The Curtain Dropped, to Lift Again —The New Jerusalem, and Babylon—Analogy of Description—The Bride, the Lamb's Wife—The Holy City Descending—Her Place in the Millennium—John xvii.—The Glory of God her Foundation, Protection, and Light—The Place of Angels—The Cube, Finite Perfection—The Precious Stones—The Merchantman and the Pearl—No Temple—The Church the Light of the Earth—The Dispensation of the Fulness of Times—The River, and Tree of Life—Eden, and its Trees and Rivers - - - - - 194

LECTURE X.—THE ETERNAL STATE.

The Two Resurrections—Reasons why the Revelation is so little Read—Satan Loosed—Man's Last Test—Gog and Magog—Their Judgment—Satan's Final Condemnation—The Great White Throne—Who is the Judge—The Two Hours—God's Way of Purifying the Earth—The Resurrection unto Judgment—The Two-fold Ground of Judgment—Death and Hades Annulled—A New Heaven, and a New Earth—A Bride Adorned for her Husband—The Tabernacle of God —God All in All—No more Death—The Fountain of the Water of Life—A Sad Category—The Grandest Thing under the Sun - - - - - - -

Behold the Bridegroom!

THE MORNING STAR.

1st Cor. xv.; Heb. ix. 24-28.

Lecture I.

THERE are three positions in Scripture where the Lord Jesus Christ is presented to us, and all three we have in these few verses of Heb. ix. which I have just read. In the most forcible, and yet the tersest possible language, has the Spirit of God condensed, in these closing verses of Heb. ix., these three positions, in which we behold the blessed Lord Jesus Christ, viewed of course as a man. What He was in eternity is not the question here,—although that was all true,—but we have Him, in these verses, seen in this world, on the cross, dying, yea, dead. You have Him then gone up into heaven, at God's right hand, where He now is; and, finally, He is presented as coming again. You have therefore the whole truth of Christ—known in this world, seen in this world, and to be seen—brought out in this passage. Of course there are many others, which I must refer to, in which the actions of the Lord Jesus Christ are brought before us, but I want just simply to fix this scripture upon the mind first of all. You have here Christ's three appearings.

In verse 26 we find:—"But now once, in the end of the world, hath he appeared, to put away sin by the sacrifice of himself." Then in verse 24 we find this:—He "is not entered into the holy places made with hands, which are the figures of the true; but into heaven itself, now to appear in the presence of God for us." For *us* is an exceedingly blessed word. Whom does it mean? Those of whom the 15th chapter of 1st Corinthians speaks, when it says,—"They that are Christ's at his coming." He now appears in the presence of God for us. He represented us once in death; He represents us now in life; and what is the next thing? "Unto them that look for him shall he appear the second time, without sin, unto salvation." He is coming to take us to glory. The truth of the Lord's coming is one of the happiest things possible for the Christian, while it is a very solemn thing for a man who is not a Christian. By Christian I mean a real believer; I do not mean what you call a professor. When I say Christian, I mean the real thing, one who knows Christ,—one who really knows the Lord Jesus Christ as his Saviour. What a blessed thing to look for that Saviour! People may say,—"But you do not expect the Lord to come yet, do you?" That is exactly what I do expect; and the testimony of Scripture is so clear, and distinct, as to the Lord's second coming, that I desire, with His help, to indicate the salient points thereof.

If you take the trouble to search the Scriptures, you will find that, of the twenty-seven sections of which the New Testament is composed, no less than twenty-two speak to you of the return of the Lord Jesus. All the gospels, the Acts, every epistle of Paul (saving three), James, Peter, Jude, John (except his two minor epistles), and the Revelation, testify to it. Thus in almost every part of the New Testament Scriptures His return is always presented to us, as that which should be daily expected.

But why the exceptions, and what are they? The exceptions are these,—the epistles to the Galatians, Ephesians, and Philemon, and the two minor epistles of John. These do not refer to the Lord's second coming, and the reason, I think, is not far to seek. Why not the Galatians? Because they did not understand the value of His first coming. They were not clear about the Gospel, about redemption. They were going to be saved by law, by works, and therefore Paul has to begin *de novo*, and tell them the value and efficacy of Christ's first coming. Then why not the Ephesians? Because you are exactly at the other end of the line of truth. The blessed truth brought out in the Ephesians is this, that the believer is already "accepted in the beloved"; for, as the 2nd chapter says,—"God, who is rich in mercy, for his great love wherewith he loved us, even when we were dead in sins, hath quickened us together with Christ (by grace ye are saved); and hath raised us up together, and made us sit together in heavenly places in Christ Jesus." The Christian, the believer, is viewed, according to the truth of Ephesians, as now being in Christ, where Christ is, in heavenly places. Then Philemon is a loving little pastoral letter, from the beloved apostle, to a master, about a runaway slave, whom he sends back to his duty. A very nice, good thing to do, and therefore I should not expect Paul to refer to the Lord's second coming in such a case. The two minor epistles of John, similarly, are occupied with specific instructions addressed to an individual.

The teaching of the book of Revelation, above all, is, that the Lord is coming back, and that He is coming back for His people first, and then to set the earth right. I know that the general thought abroad is, that when the Lord comes back, the next time, it is for the purpose of judging the world. There is no doubt He will judge. There is no doubt that the return of the Lord Jesus to deal with the earth is perfectly certain; but let me say this about it—and it was a great help to my own soul when I saw this point—that the return of the Lord, in that character, is connected with what Scripture treats of as prophecy. That is not the Christian hope. The Christian hope is totally distinct from the "sure word of prophecy" (2 Pet. i. 19). We find plenty of prophecy in the Old Testament Scriptures; but, observe, all prophecy relates to the earth, whereas the Christian hope relates to heaven. Now the Lord Jesus Himself has gone, as man, into heaven, and He proposes to take up to Himself there those that belong to Him.

I repeat, then, that the hope of the Christian is not the earth being set right,—although, thank God, it will be set right,—but the hope of the Christian is Christ Himself, and Christ as coming for His blood-bought people. Why have we the Lord presenting Himself to us as the "Bright and Morning Star" in Rev. xxii. 16? Every person understands what the morning star is. It is not daylight. You never saw a man wakened up in the morning by the morning star. You must get up early to see the morning star. What wakes people up in the morning is the sunlight,—it is daylight. What you have in this passage is, that the hope of the Christian is Christ, now known in heaven as the Saviour, and as the One who is coming back for His own people, and the manner of our going up to be with Him is most blessed. The Morning Star is Christ for the watching Christian, *while the world is buried in slumber.*

This expression occurs three times in the New Testament. You will find an allusion in the book of Isaiah to the day-star, but the day-star of the Old Testament is the enemy of Christ, not Christ Himself. The expression is, "O Lucifer! [day-star, *see* margin), son of the morning" (Isa. xiv. 12). He is Christ's enemy, and is to be judged and destroyed. The morning star of the New Testament is always the blessed Lord Jesus Christ Himself. The apostle Peter is the first to speak of it, in his second epistle. He says, referring to the mount of transfiguration (2 Pet. i. 16), "We have not followed cunningly devised fables, when we made known unto you the power and coming of our Lord Jesus Christ, but were eye-witnesses of his majesty. For he received from God the Father honour and glory, when there came such a voice to him from the excellent glory, This is my beloved Son, in whom I am well pleased. And this voice which came from heaven we heard, when we were with him in the holy mount. We have also a more sure word of prophecy; whereunto ye do well that ye take heed, as unto a light that shineth in a dark place, until the day dawn, and the day-star [morning star] arise in your hearts." What did Peter see on that mount? There was the blessed Lord Jesus, with Moses and Elias, the type of two classes,—Moses, a man who had died, and who appears in glory; Elias, a man who never had died, but who passed up to heaven without death. There are these two men with the Lord in glory. Then you have Peter, James, and John, round about, figures of men upon the earth. This is the picture, in miniature, of the coming kingdom of Christ. You have the heavenly side, and the earthly side, of the coming kingdom of the Lord.

One of the most wonderful sides of the Gospel is this, that the believer has title to pass into glory without death, because the One, on whom death had no claim, went down into death for us. This you see prefigured in Elijah. But Peter adds, "We have also a more sure word of prophecy; whereunto ye do well that ye take heed, as unto a lamp that shines in a dark place." A lamp is all very good for a man in a dark night, but lamp-light is not daylight. I can turn to prophecy, which is the lamp, and the light of prophecy will show me how to pick my way through this world, which is under judgment; but there is something better than that. As Christians now, we are brought into the full light. We are children of the light, and of the day. Thus daylight dawns in the heart of the Christian before the day shines on the world; and the day-star—Christ Himself in heavenly grace—is apprehended by the soul, in this character, before He arises as the Sun of righteousness. The lamp of prophecy is good; the light of Christianity is infinitely superior.

Again, in the 2nd chapter of Revelation, the Lord Jesus says to the overcomer in Thyatira, "I will give him the morning star." What is the meaning of that? He Himself, the coming One, gives the Thyatiran overcomer the morning star. It was the darkest age of the Church's declension, and then it was that the hope of the Lord's return was first presented, to cheer the heart of the overcomer.

I turn you now to what the Lord says in the last chapter of Revelation (xxii. 16), "I Jesus have sent mine angel to testify unto you these things in the churches. I am the root and the offspring of David, and the bright and morning star." He presents Himself, His own blessed, glorious person, and "the Spirit and the bride say, Come" to Him immediately. This is the Spirit's cry in the whole Church, and shows what should be the attitude of the Church to the end.

Can you, dear friends, say to the Lord Jesus to-night, "Lord, come"? "Oh, but," you say, "that would be a very serious thing." It would, if you are not ready. But I will ask you that are ready, Would you not like to meet your blessed Saviour? You that love the Lord Jesus, would you not like to meet Him? That is the very thing our hearts are waiting for. Of course it is for the heart that loves Him. The heart must be first won for Christ; and where there is affection for the Bridegroom, but hitherto lack of intelligence, the Spirit adds, "Let him that heareth say, Come." It is not only that the intelligent is entitled to say "Come," but he who "heareth," for the first time, is also to say "Come," *i.e.*, "Lord, come!"

The immediate return of the Lord Jesus is that which is, above all, grateful and suitable to the heart that really knows and loves Him; and in one way or another, nearly all through the New Testament, the coming of the Lord Jesus is thus presented. I will not take you through the Scriptures, because it will take a great deal more time than I have at my disposal to turn to all the passages. Suffice it to repeat, that in every section of the New Testament, save the five I have already mentioned, the truth of the Lord's second coming is presented to us as the next thing before the believer, and nothing is supposed necessarily to intervene to defer that coming.

I will touch briefly on the 14th chapter of John, because there the Lord unfolds this truth most simply, and sweetly, just as He was leaving the earth. " In my Father's house are many mansions ; if it were not so, I would have told you. I go to prepare a place for you. And if I go and prepare a place for you, I will come again, and receive you unto myself; that where I am, there ye may be also." Now people say, " I thought that meant death." I never heard anything so curious in my life. Death has not gone away. "No," you reply, "but I thought that was the Lord coming to the saint in death." The saint, passing away, gets the sweet sense of the Lord's presence, that he may not taste death, which is a very blessed thing ; but He says here, " If *I* go away, *I* will come again." The truth is this, there is the blood-bought mansion, the blood-bought home, the scene of light and glory, in the Father's house on high, bought for us by the blood of the Saviour, and at the fitting moment, He will come, to take up those who are His own—raising the dead, changing the living—and they will be with Him, and in His likeness for evermore. This is the Christian hope.

But, then, what is the basis of the Christian hope? The basis of that hope is the wonderful truth unfolded in the scripture, which I first read this evening, and I ask you therefore to go back to the 15th chapter of 1st Corintnians, because it is absolutely impossible that either you, or I, can quietly, or simply wait for the Lord Jesus, or think of His coming peacefully, and joyfully, if our souls are not clear before God, as to the value, and effect of the work which He has wrought.

It is perfectly impossible for any person to think of the return of the holy, blessed Saviour, unless the conscience is purged, and the heart at rest, in the sense that all sins are forgiven. Now this chapter unfolds the Gospel most simply, and develops the truth of the resurrection, and what was connected with the resurrection. You will see, therefore, what is the basis of our hope, as Christians. By *our*, I mean the whole family of God; I mean every believer in the Lord Jesus Christ. The hope of the Christian is what Scripture presents as the blessed desire of every heart that knows the Lord Jesus Christ. It rests on the fact of His death and resurrection; and therefore I invite your attention to this scripture, to note the way in which the Spirit of God couples the death of Christ, and His resurrection, and the rising of the saints, at the second coming of the Lord, all together. The latter are all connected with Him who died, on whom death had no claim.

What is the way in which the Lord Jesus Christ comes? "In a moment, in the twinkling of an eye." Will the world see, or be aware of that coming? I do not think so. The coming of the Saviour, as the Bridegroom, is for the bride, it is for the saved—His own beloved people.

Let us get hold clearly, and distinctly, of the object, the nature, the effect, and the value of the first coming of the Saviour, and then this truth is as clear as possible. Now see, at Corinth, they had evidently given up the clear hold of the Gospel. Satan came in and denied the resurrection of the body. But observe Paul's argument: Give up the resurrection of the body, and what do you do? You give up Christ. Satan's object always is, in some way or other, to lower the Lord Jesus Christ. The apostle Paul therefore, refutes this error by relating the Gospel, saying, "I declare unto you the gospel which I preached unto you, which also ye have received, and wherein ye stand ; by which also ye are saved." The Gospel, when received, saves men, out and out. But why does he say this :—" By which also ye are saved, if ye keep in memory what I preached unto you, unless ye have believed in vain"? What does he mean by "*in vain*"? He means this. If all this was a myth, or a fable, then there was nothing to rest upon. But, do you not see, it was not a fable, but is the truth, and therefore he repeats it,—" How that Christ died for our sins, according to the scriptures." Wonderful news in a world of death ! Christ died. " How that Christ died for our sins." Well, I believe that. Are you clear of your sins ? Are they forgiven ? He died for our sins. Suppose I were deeply in debt, and you undertook to go, and did go, and pay all that debt for me, what should I be ? I should be accounted clear. Of course, that is the very object for which you paid the debt, you wanted to deliver me, and did so.

Christ, then, was "delivered for our offences." He "died for our sins according to the scriptures." The judgment of God upon man for his sin is that he dies. Consequently men say, There is only one thing you are sure of, and that is death. I stand here, and I say boldly, that is the very thing I am not sure of. And why? Because I fully believe the lovely tidings that Christ died for me. Every believer is entitled to say, " He died for me." " He died for our sins, according to the scriptures." Quite true, that the wages of sin is death, but then what does the 9th of Hebrews say ? " So Christ was once offered."

Look at the "as" and the "so." "*As* it is appointed unto men once to die, but after this the judgment, *so* Christ was once offered to bear the sins of many." There we see the inevitable consequences of man's sin—death, and judgment at the hand of God. But what has taken place? Blessed be God for the news! After our sin, and before the day of judgment, when the whole question of our sins must be raised between God and our souls, what has taken place? The blessed Son of God has stepped in, and He has died for us, for our sins, for sinners. And what is the result? You, who believe in Him, have now crossed the frontier, you have crossed the boundary line, you stand on the other side of death and judgment. It is a wonderful thing to know that.

The man who knows Christ, stands on the very ground where the fire has been. I suppose you all know how to act, if you are in a prairie on fire, and you discover the devouring element coming up behind you. The fire is coming rapidly along. It will not do to run. There is only one way of sure escape,—get the spot upon which you stand burned; set fire to the grass with your own hand. And what is the result? Up comes the devouring flame, and there is nothing to touch, nothing to burn, it has all been consumed. Now, apply that to yourself. How are you going to face God about your sins, if you cannot rest upon Christ? But here is wonderful tidings for sinners—anxious sinners—Christ "died for our sins," and took the consequences thereof, death and judgment, which were our due, and He was buried, and He was raised again the third day, according to the Scriptures. Paul says, "He was seen of above five hundred brethren at once; . . . And last of all he was seen of me."

I have seen Him in glory, and you come to tell me that there is no resurrection? Why, how can that be? "If there be no resurrection of the dead, then is Christ not raised." I think that a most wonderful conclusion. He reasons from us to Christ; because He was once as dead as any man in this audience ever can be. Blessed news! I learn that the One on whom death had no claim whatever, who "knew no sin," whom the Father proclaimed His "beloved Son," goes at length, in the grace of His heart, to the cross, and there, in the darkness of that scene that no eye could ever penetrate, He takes up, between God and Himself, the whole question of our sins—our guilt before God. "For man the Saviour bled." He dies, on whom death had no claim, in the room and stead of the poor guilty sinner. And what is the consequence? Life and blessing for the one who clings to Him, and who looks to Him. The love of Christ constrains the heart to simply trust Him.

Now note, if there be no resurrection of the dead, then, says Paul, "Christ is not raised"; and he argues immediately that if Christ be not raised, our preaching is vain, and, more than that, we have been telling lies about God, for we said that God had raised Him. "And if Christ be not raised, your faith is vain; ye are yet in your sins." But what is the converse? If Christ be raised, for every person who trusts Him, then *you are not in your sins.* That is the Gospel. That is the Gospel I believe in. Thank God, I know my sins are forgiven. Moreover, this forgiveness, this salvation, has been bought for us by the dying agonies of the Son of God; and I love to speak of that blessed Saviour who has gone into death—into the very dominion of death. And what has He done?

He has met the claims of God in righteousness, He has glorified His nature about sin, He has defeated Satan, and broken his power, annulled death, and risen from the dead. Christ has won a victory, that sets every soul that clings to Him free, and brings that soul into the enjoyment of the spoils of the victory which Jesus has wrought for us. What demonstrates the power and the fulness of the Gospel? That the One who died for us is raised from among the dead. If Christ be not raised, ye are yet in your sins; but if He be raised, what then? The two consequences of sin — death and judgment — the blessed Saviour took on the cross, and the result is this, that the veil is rent, the way right up into God's presence is laid open, and there is the blood of atonement that gives you title to draw near to God.

Before this is apprehended there will be a work in the soul. It must be brought to feel itself of no importance—a sinner; and the moment the heart bows before God, with the sense of its guilt, there is the blessed unfolding, by the Spirit of God, of the atoning suffering, and the value of the blood-shedding, of the Lord Jesus Christ. That once finished work avails absolutely, and to the uttermost, for every soul that simply believes in Him, who died and rose again. Why not turn to Him now? Look at that risen Saviour, who has gone up, with the trophy of His victory by His side. He has gone right down into the depths of death, that He might deliver, and bring out every soul that simply believes and confides in His own blessed name.

But the apostle adds, — "Now is Christ risen from the dead, and become the first-fruits of them that slept." The point is this, that the resurrection of the Lord Jesus was the proof, and evidence of the absolute favour of God, towards that blessed One. There are two resurrections spoken of in the New Testament,—there is the resurrection unto life, and the resurrection unto judgment (John v. 29). The resurrection of the Lord Jesus is the pattern of the resurrection of those that belong to Him. As the first man brought in death, by man also came resurrection from among the dead. How? Because Jesus was a man upon whom death had no claim whatever ; He goes down into death, and takes the sting out of it—is the conqueror and victor over it ; and is the risen Saviour. What is the root of the persecution in the 4th chapter of Acts? Why were the apostles put in prison? "Because they taught the people, and preached through Jesus the resurrection from *among* the dead." You tell people that there is a general resurrection, and that all the dead will rise together, by-and-by, and that then things are going to be settled, as to whether they are to be saved or not, and that will be accepted, as very nice, orthodox doctrine; but tell them this, that the resurrection of the Lord's people will be after the pattern of Christ's, and one thousand years before the resurrection of the unbelieving dead, and what will be stirred up? Sometimes a good deal of feeling.

But that is just what Scripture tells us. That is the first resurrection, of which Christ Himself was the first-fruits. In Revelation we read, "Blessed and holy is he that hath part in the first resurrection ; on such the second death hath no power." What about the other resurrection? "The rest of the dead lived not again until the thousand years were finished" (chap. xx. 5, 6). And observe, the Holy Ghost does not call that the second resurrection. What He calls it is "the second death" (see verses 6, 14). God save every soul here from such a resurrection as that, because, mark, it is "the resurrection unto judgment." Nowhere in Scripture is there found the dogma of a general resurrection of saved, and unsaved, all together. The resurrection of the saints is before the millennial reign of Christ. The resurrection after His millennial reign is a "resurrection unto judgment," and the Holy Ghost stamps that as "the second death." I think to die once is quite enough. But I rejoice to stand here this evening, and tell out good news to the man who is troubled about death. There is no need, if you are a Christian, that you should die at all. I do not say, I shall not die. All I say is, I am not waiting for it. Death may come, not must. The Lord *will* come. Death *may* come; not will, not must. The blessed tidings is this, that Christ has gone into death for us, and has come up out of it; and, therefore, those who belong to Him, redeemed with His blood, are brought to God, and stand before Him, on the ground of the work Jesus has accomplished. His resurrection is the proof of the value of that work; and the resurrection of Christ is the pattern of the resurrection of those that belong to Him, in the day of His coming again.

More than that, this very 15th of Corinthians tells us "we shall not all sleep." When does Christ become the head of His body? Not till He is alive from the dead, and gone into glory. It is the risen Christ that your heart turns to. It is not merely that the blessed Saviour died. Quite true; but He rose again. The stone is rolled away, and now He is risen. All who belong to Him are to share the fruit of the wonderful work that He has accomplished. Christ is become the first-fruits of them that slept. Suppose the Lord came to-night—and there is no reason why He should not—what would be the result? All "that are Christ's" must rise to meet Him. There are many in the grave, there are many who have passed away, but they will be raised in the likeness of the blessed Saviour. It is those that are Christ's at His coming, and only those that are Christ's, that have part in the first resurrection. You must be quite clear about that.

But then, when will that be? No one knows. I am not here to indicate to you, in the slightest degree, that any moment can be fixed for the return of the Lord Jesus, but only to point out this, that the hope of the early Christians was the return of the Lord, and our hope is the same. Look at the 51st verse: "Behold, I shew you a mystery; We shall not all sleep, but we shall all be changed." Nothing can be more clear than that. "We must all die," people sometimes say. No; "we shall *not* all sleep," is the distinct testimony of the Holy Ghost; and supposing that blessed Bridegroom were to come this evening in the air, and call up His blood-bought, and tenderly loved Bride, then we should not fall asleep, but we should all be changed, because "flesh and blood cannot inherit the kingdom of God." "We shall all be changed, in a moment, in the twinkling of an eye." No warning! The trumpet shall sound, but that trump is not the trump that is going to raise all by-and-by. No, it only calls those "that are Christ's at his coming." What then? "The dead shall be raised incorruptible, and we shall be changed. For this corruptible must put on incorruption, and this mortal must put on immortality. So when this corruptible shall have put on incorruption, and this mortal shall have put on immortality, then shall be brought to pass the saying that is written, Death is swallowed up in victory" (verses 52-54).

What about those that are not Christ's? The scripture is very plain. "The rest of the dead lived not again until the thousand years were finished." It is an awfully solemn thing not to be Christ's; and therefore, with all the fervour of my heart, would I say, Oh! my friends, decide for Christ; believe on Christ; come to Christ. Turn to Him, and be ready for His coming. In the twinkling of an eye that trump may be heard, and then? The Gospel door closes. No more will news of grace—heavenly grace and pardon—fall on the ear of the sinner. No more Gospel preaching then. The door of heaven is shut, and its ambassadors called home. What a fearful agony of surprise will possess the half-decided soul, that discovers this, just *after* the Lord has come, and all chance of salvation is for ever lost!

The manner of the Lord's coming is most distinctly developed in 1st Thessalonians, chapter iv. In the 13th verse Paul says,—" I would not have you to be ignorant, brethren, concerning them which are asleep, that ye sorrow not, even as others which have no hope. For if we believe that Jesus died, and rose again, even so them also which sleep in Jesus will God bring with him. For this we say unto you by the word of the Lord, that we which are alive and remain unto the coming of the Lord shall not prevent [*i.e.*, anticipate, or go before] them which are asleep. For the Lord himself shall descend from heaven with a shout, with the voice of the archangel, and with the trump of God : and the dead in Christ shall rise first : then we which are alive and remain shall be caught up together with them in the clouds, to meet the Lord in the air : and so shall we ever be with the Lord." When He comes back in glory, then He will bring His people *with Him*, but, before that, He comes into the air, and gathers His own *to* Him. There are two stages,—His coming as the Bridegroom into the air, and our rising to meet Him ; then the coming of the King, in the day of His glory, when He returns to deal with the earth. We rise, at the call of the Bridegroom, and meet the One we love in the air. A little while afterwards, when He appears on earth as Son of Man—as King of kings and Lord of lords— He brings with Him all His heavenly saints.

If her Majesty, coming into Edinburgh from the south, were to send a message, that any, who wished to show their loyalty to her person, were invited to go out and meet her at Portobello, and join her retinue, would not many go to meet her, and come to Edinburgh in her train? Without any doubt. Similarly the blessed Lord is coming, by-and-by, to deal with this earth, but, before that, He is coming into the air, and He gets His followers, true and real,—those "that are Christ's at his coming,"—to meet Him there. I ask you now, Are you sure that you will be "Christ's at his coming"? Oh! make sure, for this moment of rapturous joy draws near. It is most graphically described:—" The Lord himself shall descend from heaven with a shout, with the voice of the archangel, and with the trump of God : and the *dead in Christ* shall rise first." Not a word about the wicked dead— the unbelieving, the unrepentant dead. " The dead in Christ shall rise first : then we which are alive and remain shall be caught up together with them in the clouds, to MEET THE LORD in the air: and so shall we ever be with the Lord. Wherefore comfort one another with these words." I know no greater comfort, than to think that before the clock strikes eight we may meet the blessed Lord in the air. I am persuaded that every Christian in this room would delight to meet the Lord this evening.

But you say,—"I do not know that I am ready." Well, get ready. "Whosoever will, let him take the water of life freely." Have you never drunk of the water of life? Drink it while you sit, to-night. Turn to Jesus. What are you living for? I ask you solemnly, before God, with eternity before you, and the coming of the Lord in view, is it only for self? Ah! turn to Him, and live for Him who died for us. That is the only really right thing to do. Turn to the Lord Jesus, or else what must happen? Why, just what happened in the striking parable in the 25th of Matthew, where we have the coming of the Bridegroom, and the history of the ten virgins. There were ten virgins, five wise, and five foolish; five ready, the others not ready. They all went to sleep while the Bridegroom tarried. The hope of the Lord's coming has been lost sight of for nearly seventeen hundred years, but now the Spirit has sent forth the midnight cry,—"Behold, the Bridegroom cometh!" Why? because the Bridegroom is just coming; because the Lord is coming. Are you not ready yet? What will be the result? Listen:—"At midnight there was a cry made, Behold, the bridegroom cometh; go ye out to meet him. Then all those virgins arose, and trimmed their lamps." What took place? The foolish found they possessed no oil. They had the lamp, quite truly, in their hands—the lamp of profession.

I suppose the great majority of my hearers present to-night are *professors*,—but, are you *possessors* of Christ? Are your sins forgiven? If you cannot answer that question honestly, you will be surprised in the day of the Lord's coming. You will be stirred up, and you will turn and say,—"Give me of your oil." But the answer will be,—"Go and buy for yourselves. And while they went to buy, the bridegroom came." Content with a name to live, and yet dead; content to live without knowing the real Name, they learn He knows them not. Do not lay your head on the pillow to-night without having the matter of your soul's eternal salvation settled,—really, and definitely, and solemnly settled before God. Why? Because the Lord is coming. "While they went to buy, the bridegroom came; and they that were ready went in with him to the marriage: and *the door was shut.*" Ah! how many of us are ready in this hall this evening? Are *you* ready? Are *all* ready? Am *I* ready? Through infinite mercy, yes, through the blood of the Saviour, who died for me and rose again. Dear unsaved one, come now, drink of the living water, and then you will be one of the ready ones; and in the moment when you hear the shout, you will rise and meet the blessed Lord, and say,—This is the Lord that I have been waiting for.

This, then, is the Gospel, and our hope. Christ has died, put away our sins, annulled death, endured judgment; and we, believing in Him, stand on the other side of death and judgment, and just wait for Him. When He came the first time, He took our *sins* away; when He comes the next time, He will take *us* away to scenes of rest and glory, to be the everlasting partners of His joy. As the bright and morning star, He presents His own coming as the next thing before us. May each one be really waiting, and watching for Him.

THE APOSTASY AND ANTICHRIST.

1st THESS. i. 8-10; 2nd THESS. ii.

Lecture II.

THE burden of these verses in the 1st Epistle to the Thessalonians is the Christian hope,—the coming of the Lord Jesus as the Bridegroom, as the Saviour. Most simply, yet beautifully, does the Spirit of God, in addressing the Thessalonians, bring out this hope. Nothing could be more plain, simple, or distinct. The apostle, a few months after he had been at Thessalonica, where he had preached the Gospel for three weeks, and where many had believed it, writes unto them to confirm their faith, and to comfort them concerning some that had fallen asleep, and he says that wherever he went in the district he had no need to speak, because "they themselves show of us what manner of entering in we had unto you, and how ye turned to God from idols." Turned to God from idols, that is conversion of the right stamp. Observe, it is not from idols to God, it is "to God from idols." It is the attractive power of the love of God, it is the attractive blessed power of the grace of God, that touches the heart, and leads a man to drop the things that have been an idol—things that have never really filled him, or really blessed him. To turn to God from idols is blessed indeed, but yet there is more. What? "To serve the living and true God,"—a wonderfully happy thing to do in this world,—and that is what we are called, and saved for—to serve the living and true God. Christianity does not suppose that when a man is brought to God, when his soul is saved through grace, that he then sits down, and folds his arms, and says, "Well, I am saved for glory, and that is the end of it." Not at all. He turns to God from idols, to *serve* the living and true God. Mark, every person who hears my voice to-night, is either serving the living and true God, or serving the god of this world, the devil. Your service is either rendered to the living God, or else you are dominated by the god of this world, who carries men on, in their lusts and passions, to perdition.

There is nothing more grand than to be a Christian—no greater privilege than to serve the living God. I know many a young man thinks it is a dull thing to be a Christian. I will tell you what I think, it is a very dull thing not to be a Christian. Oh! it will be a very solemn thing—a very terrible thing—for a man to find out, at the end of his course, that he has been all wrong, to wake up, in eternity, and find out that his whole past on earth, has been a grand mistake, from end to end. And that is what many a man will find out by-and-by. But, oh! how blessed is it to know the God of all grace, and then to serve Him, the living and true God, and "wait for his Son from heaven whom he raised from the dead, even Jesus, which delivered us from the wrath to come." It is a far brighter, and happier side of my subject, to think of that which is now the portion of the soul,—

present salvation, and deliverance from wrath,—than to indicate coming sorrows. Paul cannot speak of the Lord's second return without weaving in something connected with His first coming. Jesus, he says, is the One you are waiting for. What is Jesus to you? Is He coming as a judge? Thank God, no. Is He coming to deal with our sins? Thank God, no. "Jesus which *delivered* us from the wrath to come" is the One we wait for. Christians are already a delivered people.

The simplest believer in the Lord Jesus Christ is delivered—he knows it—is delivered from the wrath to come, by that which has already come—perfect grace in the person of the blessed Son of God, become a man in this world, and gone down into death, that He might redeem and bring to God, in absolute righteousness, all who trust His blessed name. The immediate hope of the already delivered Christian is the return of the Lord Jesus in the character of the Bridegroom. I know people say, "Of course, the Lord is coming by-and-by,—nobody knows when,— and then it will be a matter of judgment." Yes, He *will* come, and He *will* judge. That is all quite true, but, before the day when He comes to judge the world in righteousness, He comes and meets His own people, and gathers them up out of this world. He comes first for His own loved ones,—some who have fallen asleep, and are in the grave, others living on the earth at the moment of His coming, alive, waiting, watching, serving, and happily looking for His return, and He comes into the air with the assembling shout, "with the voice of the archangel and with the trump of God, and the dead in Christ rise first, then we which are alive and remain shall be caught up together with them in the clouds, to meet the Lord in the air; and so shall we ever be with the Lord."

Now, I defy you to give me anything brighter, or better than that. I challenge you, men of the world, to give me anything to eclipse that. "Oh!" but some one says, "you will have to go through death!" I don't deny that I *may* have to, but I absolutely deny that I *must*, and I truly confess that I am not looking for death, but waiting for Jesus from heaven. The early Christians were called to wait for the Son of God from heaven, and they were waiting. Quite true, while they waited some fell asleep, and therefore the apostle writes to comfort those whose friends had fallen asleep; but, nevertheless, it is apparent that the dominant hope of the Christian, in that day, was the immediate return of the Lord Jesus Christ, in this character, and nothing could be more blessed. He is coming as the Bridegroom, and we saw last Lord's Day evening, at the close of the 25th chapter of Matthew, where the Lord describes what the end of this dispensation will be, when He does come back, that Christendom will be after this sort: "five were wise, and five were foolish," and the wise—" they that were *ready*"—went in with Him to the marriage, and the door was shut, and the others were left outside, very busy *trying to get ready*. No doubt they got thoroughly roused, and were very desirous to be ready; and I have no doubt, dear friends, that if the Lord came to-night at eight o'clock, you would be uncommonly anxious at nine o'clock to get ready; but mark, you would be too late. *Too late!* What a thought! Therefore I say, with all sincerity of heart and affection to every person here now, *You get ready.* "Trim your lamps and be ready." Why? Because the midnight cry has gone out, and the Lord is coming.

But when will He come? say you. Scripture never sets a moment as to when He is to come. No date or no time is ever given. Why? Because if it fixed a date, it would necessarily put the Lord's coming off to the date that had been fixed. Now-a-days some—wiser than Scripture—have been foolhardy enough to fix a date. Now where are such, and all their followers? They have got into the company of those of whom the Lord speaks in the 24th of Matthew, "That evil servant shall say in his heart, My lord *delayeth* his coming." I ask you, would you like Him to come to-night? Let us put it to ourselves clearly, and simply. "No," you say, "I would like it put off for a bit." Then I say you are arm in arm with the evil servant. The evil servant says in his heart, "My lord delayeth his coming," and what is the next thing he does? He begins "to smite his fellow-servants, and to eat and drink with the drunken," *i.e.*, he gets into the world. Then the Lord comes, and appoints him his portion with the hypocrites, because he said, I am waiting for Christ, whereas in his heart he was not doing so. The Lord give you grace to be really ready; get you hold of the wonderful atoning work of the Lord Jesus Christ, and whosoever will is welcome to come to Him, to receive Him, to believe Him, and to know Him. Then what is the next thing? We rise and meet Him in the air, and we pass into the scenes of rest, and life, and joy, that He has prepared for us in His infinite grace; we go to the Father's house, and eternal rest; and oh, what a wonderful thing to be sure about! Can you be sure? Indeed you may. He died that you might be sure. Look at this verse, " Who delivered us from the wrath to come." We have got it,—the believer has eternal life ; he has his sins forgiven. He is ready.

But some person may say, " I thought the world had to be made ready, I thought the whole world had to be converted, and put right, in order to the introduction of the Lord's reign." How do you propose to effect it? I anticipate your answer, " By the preaching of the Gospel." Let us hear Scripture.

The reason why I read the 2nd chapter of 2nd Thessalonians, was to bring to your notice to-night, the distinct and definite statement of the Spirit of God, as to what will be the absolute condition of Christendom,—what would be the condition of Edinburgh—not to go outside of our own circle—if the Lord came into the air, and every Christian was taken up to be with Himself? What would be left? Face the thing, what would be left ? A seething mass of lifeless corruption. Christian profession in abundance, without one spark of Christian life, for every real Christian will have been caught away to glory. I know perfectly well that many a man is full of the idea that the world is to be put right by the Gospel. But what is the effect of this notion? You are playing into the hands of infidels. The man who holds that theory has not got any foundation in Scripture for it, and plays unwittingly into the hands of infidels. In what way? The infidel turns round and says, " You are a fine lot, you Christians; are you getting this world made much better?" The Christian is obliged to own that it is not. I am not expecting it. I am looking to get men turned to God, and brought, by the Gospel, out of the world, which is only ripening rapidly for judgment. I admit I want your heart for Christ, but why, because that will fit you for His coming. You see, if I think of the world getting better, I have to inquire, Is it better? Is commercial morality higher to-day? Are morals more elevated? Is society more chaste? Are husbands more true, wives more loving, children more dutiful, friends more reliable, servants more faithful? I see lots of you shaking your heads. We have to admit that as regards the world it may be outwardly somewhat whitewashed, but when people talk of progress, I grant you it is progressing, but it is progressing towards judgment. But, thank God, before the judgment comes, Jesus comes. That is exactly what the Christian wants. We are going to be taken out of it.

Look how the apostle argues in the 2nd chapter of 2nd Thessalonians. He does not make a new revelation of the truth of the Lord's coming, but he draws a most beautiful argument from it. He says, " I beseech you, brethren, by the coming of our Lord Jesus Christ, and by our gathering together unto him." It is a wonderfully happy thing to get a good big gathering of Christians down here. What a warming your heart will get, one of these days, when we have this great big gathering. When that gathering comes, there will be no break up. Ah! you say, that will be glorious. You are right, it will be grand, to be gathered up, by and to the Lord. Look at the words, " I beseech you, by the coming of our Lord Jesus Christ, and by our gathering together unto him, that ye be not soon shaken in mind, or be troubled, neither by spirit nor by word, nor by letter as from us, as that the day of Christ is present (set in)." Why does he beseech them? The reason is simple. The

Thessalonians were passing through tremendous persecution; they had received the Gospel, they had owned it, they had confessed it, and young converts were preaching it. We are, however, I fear, all too fond of relegating to other people that which the Lord has committed to us, for if I receive Jesus as my own Saviour, it is my privilege, as well as my responsibility, to tell you about Him. What did Andrew do when he was converted? He went and brought Peter to Jesus. When the soul receives Christ, it communicates the good tidings. That is the way it spreads. Conversion is like scarlet fever. When it gets into a family, it is wonderful how it will spread. No doubt, the proper plan is to keep the fever out, but by all means let the conversion in, for if conversion gets into one member of the family, thank God, it will soon spread, because the heart that really receives Christ, will be telling the others about Him. So, when Paul came into Macedonia and Achaia to tell them the Gospel, they said, We have heard it already from these Thessalonians. A beautiful testimony, indeed, as to what their life was.

What is the next thing? Persecution comes, downright, bitter, stern, terrible persecution for Christ's sake. What then? The devil comes in, and he says to these young, uninstructed Thessalonians, "Ah! you have missed it, you have missed the coming of the Lord, and the day of the Lord has set in." Do you not think they knew what the day of the Lord meant? Do you know what the day of the Lord means? The apostle beseeches "that ye be not soon shaken in mind, or be troubled, neither by spirit, nor by word, nor by letter as from us, as that the day of Christ is set in." What is the day of Christ? The day of Christ is a terrible word for a wicked man. It will be a terrible day for the world in its ungodliness. What the devil was doing, was by means of false letters. Satan, at the best, is only an imitator. The first Epistle to the Thessalonians, had been written by the apostle to comfort them concerning the brethren that had fallen asleep. They thought that some who had fallen asleep would miss coming with Christ in His glory. No, he says, "them that sleep in Jesus will God bring with him." He will come with all His saints. But he goes on to tell them how it will happen, in order that they, who fall asleep, may come back with Him in glory. He, as it were, says, I will tell you something that never was revealed before, that the Lord is going to come into the air, that He is going to raise the dead, and take up the living that are His, and then, you and they, we all, shall come back again with the Lord when He comes, as Son of Man, and King of kings.

Well, comforted by this word of the apostle, they continue in their testimony, and then persecution comes, and now the devil, who hates all Christians, says,—I will terrify them. There is nothing the devil likes better than to terrify people. So he writes a letter to say that the day of the Lord has already set in. What did that mean to them? Said they, It is perfectly clear that we have missed the rapture; we have missed what we were looking for; and they got into a great state of anxiety. Paul, therefore, writes this second epistle to assure them that the day of the Lord had not come, because, as you will see, if you turn back to chapter i. of the 2nd epistle, the portion of the saint in that day is given in the 7th verse, — "*rest, when* the Lord Jesus shall be revealed from heaven with his mighty angels" (verses 6-9). Paul carries them on to the moment of the revelation. Christ comes in absolute glory, with His people, in that day. The day of the Lord is marked by this, that the righteous shine as the sun, and the wicked are troubled. But what was going on just then? Why, he says, you who are the righteous are troubled now, you are troubled by the wicked—the day of the Lord cannot have come, because the day of the Lord is marked by this, that the righteous are blessed, and the wicked are to be troubled, when "the Lord Jesus shall be revealed from heaven with his mighty angels, in flaming fire taking vengeance on them that know not God, and that obey not the gospel of our Lord Jesus Christ."

I should like just to clear the subject, by turning to one or two Old Testament passages, that you may distinctly see what "the day of Christ" means in Scripture. Turn to the 13th chapter of Isaiah, verse 6:—"Howl ye; for the day of the Lord is at hand; it shall come as a destruction from the Almighty. Therefore shall all hands be faint, and every man's heart shall melt: and they shall be afraid: pangs and sorrows shall take hold of them; they shall be in pain as a woman that travaileth; they shall be amazed one at another; their faces shall be as flames. Behold, the day of the Lord cometh, cruel both with wrath and fierce anger, to lay the land desolate: and he shall destroy the sinners thereof out of it. For the stars of heaven, and the constellations thereof, shall not give their light: the sun shall be darkened in his going forth, and the moon shall not cause her light to shine.

And I will punish the world for their evil, and the wicked for their iniquity; and I will cause the arrogancy of the proud to cease, and will lay low the haughtiness of the terrible. I will make a man more precious than fine gold; even a man than the golden wedge of Ophir."

Now look at another witness, Joel, 2nd chapter:—"Blow ye the trumpet in Zion, and sound an alarm in my holy mountain; let all the inhabitants of the land tremble; for the day of the Lord cometh, for it is nigh at hand; a day of darkness and of gloominess, a day of clouds and of thick darkness" (verses 1, 2). Mark its character—"a day of darkness and of gloominess; a day of clouds and of thick darkness." Then in the 11th verse:—"And the Lord shall utter his voice before his army; for his camp is very great: for he is strong that executeth his word: for the day of the Lord is great and very terrible; and who can abide it?" Who can abide it? None but a saint. I recommend you, sinner, not to risk it. The great day of His wrath is coming, and who shall be able to stand?

Look now at Amos:—"Woe unto you that desire the day of the Lord! to what end is it for you? the day of the Lord is darkness and not light. As if a man did flee from a lion, and a bear met him; or went into the house, and leaned his hand on the wall, and a serpent bit him. Shall not the day of the Lord be darkness, and not light? even very dark, and no brightness in it?" (v. 18.) No brightness! The day of the Gospel is all brightness, and light. Thank God we are in the day of the Gospel; thank God, we are here now, while bright light, and heavenly glory are streaming upon us. There is no gloominess now. Thank God. It is all brightness, and gladness, and peace, when you are brought to know the heavenly Saviour. This is the day of grace. But the day of the Lord—these scriptures surely will convince any grave person—will be an awful day for the ungodly.

Let us come back to 2 Thessalonians ii., and observe what precedes, and ushers in that day. The apostle goes on:—"Let no man deceive you by any means; for that day shall not come, except there come a falling away first, and that man of sin be revealed, the son of perdition" (ver. 3). Nothing could be plainer than that. The day of the Lord, the day of Christ, the day of which the Old Testament Scriptures speak so abundantly, that day, says the Spirit of God here, cannot come, until there come first of all a falling away—an apostasy—and that man of sin be revealed, the son of perdition. You have three things here,— an apostasy instead of Christianity; "the man of sin" instead of Christ; and you will find a little lower down in the chapter, the devil instead of the Holy Ghost. That is what is coming. You have apostasy instead of truth, the man of sin instead of the ministry, and presentation of the man of God—grace; and you have also the power of Satan, instead of the living power of the blessed Spirit of God. That is what is before Christendom; that is what will be the inevitable, manifested consequence of the rapture of the saints. By the "rapture," I mean the moment of the Lord's people being taken away to glory. Every Christian goes up; I mean every converted man. Every believer of the Gospel goes up; and then comes to pass the statement,— "truth is fallen in the street" (Isa. lix. 14).

The Lord has come into the air, and gathered out of the world His own people. And what is left? Apostasy. What a solemn thing! You say, What is that? It is really leaving first estate, giving up what God has conferred in goodness; but, in effect, it is the blinding judgment that God will pass over this land, and many another land, where the light of the Gospel has been, and where, alas! it has been neglected and slighted. Nothing can be more solemn than the way in which the Spirit of God describes Christendom's state here. It is the widespread giving up of the truth,—that is apostasy. What God has given to the Church in responsibility, that she utterly gives up. When the real saints are gone, when the true living believers are gone, what is left behind? The carcase of an effete, lifeless religiousness; and only judgment can fall on Christendom's wide area of lifeless, and utterly Christless profession. It is a dead system; and, after death, it is not long before it is a putrid corrupt thing. I know the devil will do his best to make people say things are all right, when they are all wrong; but God's Word shows that Christendom is the spot upon which the deepest and direst judgment of God must fall, because Christ, and truth have been refused, and slighted, and cast out.

The apostasy surely comes apace; and I do not think there is any sober person in this audience to-night, carefully looking for himself, who will be able to contradict the apostle's statement, as he says, lower down in our chapter (ver. 7), "The mystery of iniquity doth already work." I should like to ask some of you who have now grey hairs, What is the state of things, as regards the truth, compared with fifty years ago? You know how the very Scriptures of truth have been undermined in your own land. You know that some, whom you thought would be the conservators of the truth of God, are the very men, who, carried away by human reasoning, have ruthlessly taken the axe of modern scientific criticism, and cut out first one, and then another piece of the Word of God, until, if we were to believe these learned neologians, there would only be some small shreds of the Bible left for faith to feed upon. Thank God, faith knows better than dark unbelief what is of, and from God, and so it holds on to the blessed Book of books, from cover to cover. Nevertheless, this is the beginning of the end,—" the mystery of iniquity doth already work." But when the Lord comes, and the Spirit and the Bride are taken up out of the scene, things will ripen for evil with unprecedented rapidity. I believe that the world will proclaim a general holiday when they have got rid of every testimony for Christ. That is what the Holy Ghost speaks of here as the apostasy.

But you, who think that, if the Lord were to come, you might still get the Gospel afterwards, I would like you to weigh carefully what the Spirit brings out here. The testimony to a heavenly Christ has ceased ere the moment of the apparition of " the man of sin." Some one says, " But I thought the man of sin had appeared long ago." I do not deny the principle of it in the papacy, but that is not the fulfilment. Let us look at this " son of perdition." His names are pretty abundant in Scripture, and I would like just to indicate, what I believe to be the testimony of the Word of God, as to the person spoken of here,—the man of sin. He is antichrist,—the one who tries to arrogate to himself the divine attributes, and characteristics of Christ. There are a good many allusions to him in

Scripture, and under several names. Go to the Psalms, for instance; the 10th Psalm and 17th verse: "Lord, thou hast heard the desire of the humble; thou wilt prepare their heart; thou wilt cause thine ear to hear; to judge the fatherless and the oppressed, that the man of the earth may no more oppress." When antichrist comes, he is "the man of the earth," he is the true descendant of the first man. Look at Jesus. What does Jesus do? He comes from heaven, dies to fit you for heaven, and then takes you to heaven; He is the heavenly Man. But what about this man, he is "the man of the earth."

The Spirit of God describes him also in Isaiah xxx. 30, "Tophet is ordained of old; yea, for THE KING ALSO it is prepared: he hath made it deep and large; the pile thereof is fire and much wood; the breath of the Lord, like a stream of brimstone, doth kindle it." He is the "king" here, while his end is also predicted. This fully accords with, and in fact, I presume, is alluded to in the book of Revelation, chapter xix. 20, 21. Go to the 57th chapter of Isaiah, where he is again spoken of. God is reproaching His earthly people because of their idolatry, and departure from Him. Their greatest sin is this (9th verse), "And thou wentest to the king with ointment, and didst increase thy perfumes, and didst send thy messengers far off, and didst debase thyself even unto hell." This may allude to the incense offered to the idol, "the image to the beast" of Rev. xiii., for which the king will be responsible. Doubtless in the day when this is reached, the claims which antichrist will make, to be the long-looked-for Messiah, will have acted on many; and, regardless of the Lord's words, "If any man shall say unto you, Lo, here is Christ, or there; believe it not. For there shall arise false Christs and false prophets, and shall shew signs and great wonders" (Matt. xxiv. 23), there will be many going to the king with ointments.

If you now turn to the 11th of Daniel, you will again find him brought before you most strikingly. In the Old Testament, he is presented as "the king," because he will get his seat in Jerusalem, and he will have dominance, and kingly authority over the Lord's then earthly people, the Jews, who will have been brought back to their own land ere he arises. "And the king shall do according to his will; and he shall exalt himself, and magnify himself above every god, and shall speak marvellous things against the God of gods, and shall prosper till the indignation be accomplished: for that that is determined shall be done. Neither shall he regard the God of his fathers [Jehovah], nor the desire of women [Christ], nor regard any god: for he shall magnify himself above all" (Dan. xi. 36, 37). Here is another characteristic of him; he has no sense of his dependence upon God, the will of his own heart is that which governs and dominates him. Then in John v. our Lord Jesus Christ marks him out most distinctly. Pleading with the Jews, He had said to them that He had come that they "might be saved." They would not have Jesus, and refused every testimony to Him. The Lord cites the four-fold testimony to Himself, John the Baptist (ver. 33), His own works (ver. 36), the Father (ver. 37), and the Scriptures (ver. 39). He says then, "Ye search the scriptures; for in them ye think ye have eternal life: and they are they which testify of me. And ye will not come to me, that ye might have life" (verses 39, 40). "I am come in my Father's name [He had no business on earth, but the Father's will and wishes], and ye receive me not; if another shall come *in his own name,* him ye will receive" (ver. 43). Solemn prediction—antichrist comes in "his own name," and is received.

Then if we turn to the 1st Epistle of John, we shall find the Spirit of God indicating not alone the name and character, but the features and the action, of this one (chap. ii. 22)—"Who is the liar, but he that denieth that Jesus is the Christ? He is the antichrist, that denieth the Father and the Son." The first is what he will do in view of the Jew; there is what I may call Jewish infidelity. He denies that Jesus is the Christ, the Messiah, and God stamps him as a liar. Next, "he is the antichrist, that denieth the Father and the Son." That is what is now more than ever coming up,—the dark and ever-widening river of rationalism. It is the denial that we have a revelation from God. It is the denial of the revelation of the Father and the Son; and, in this being, this "man of sin," it will by-and-by all culminate. And what does he do? He denies the Father and the Son,— that is, he sweeps every remaining vestige of Christianity aside, for the great truth of Christianity is the Father and the Son. He denies the Father and the Son, and he denies that Jesus is the Christ. That is a setting aside of what is a special truth for the latter-day Jews; and now you will find that this exactly concurs with what the apostle Paul brings out in his wonderful description of this man,—for a man he is; it is not a system merely.

There are yet two other strikingly descriptive names that he gets. Turn to the book of Revelation, and you will see the closing testimony of the Spirit of

God as to this man (chap. xiii. 11):—"And I beheld another beast coming up out of the earth; and he had two horns like a lamb, and he spake as a dragon." He is the imitation of Christ,—"two horns like a lamb.' " And he exerciseth all the power of the first beast before him, and causeth the earth, and them which dwell therein, to worship the first beast, whose deadly wound was healed." You see he exercises immense power, and here he is called a "beast," a "wild beast" truly, though simulating the characters of Him who is God's Lamb, the Lord Jesus Christ.

If you look at the 19th chapter, you find his last title, and unspeakably awful doom. At the 20th verse we read,—" And the beast [the Roman imperial head] was taken, and with him *the false prophet* that wrought miracles before him, with which he deceived them that had received the mark of the beast, and them that worshipped his image. These both were cast alive into a lake of fire burning with brimstone." In the Old Testament there were two men—Enoch and Elijah—who went up to glory without death; in New Testament times there are two men who go to the lake of fire without death, and they are here. The beast with ten horns is the head of political opposition, and the false prophet the head of the ecclesiastical opposition, against God in that day. Why is he called a false prophet? It is very simple. There are three beautiful characters in which the Lord Jesus Christ is presented. He is prophet, priest, and king. When He was on earth, He was the prophet that Moses spake of; but now in glory, He is the priest; and by-and-by He is going to be the king. This one will imitate Him absolutely; he is the false prophet, the tyrant-king; and more than that, he will be, not exactly priest, but anti-priest—he goes utterly against the true people of God of that day.

This man seeks to arrogate to himself what belongs to Christ. And now, if you refer once more to 2nd Thessalonians, you will find, that it is not only that there is this daring simulation of the Lord Jesus Christ, but he has the audacity to take the place of God (ii. 4):—" Who opposeth and exalteth himself above all that is called God, or that is worshipped ; so that he, as God, sitteth in the temple of God, showing himself that he is God." He actually claims divine prerogative. " Remember ye not, that, when I was yet with you, I told you these things? And now ye know what withholdeth, that he might be revealed in his time." What is the hindrance now? I doubt not the hindrance, at the present moment, is the active working of the Holy Ghost. He is the hinderer, but the moment the completion of the Church, the body of Christ, arrives, and the rapture occurs, the Holy Ghost, who forms, and indwells that Church, is removed from the earth. He came down at Pentecost to form the Church, and He will go up with the Church.

When He who hinders the opening of all the floodgates of iniquity is "taken out of the way," and ceases to work in His present way, what takes place? The floodgates of wickedness are let loose, flung wide open, and out comes this "man of sin," who takes the place of Christ; nay more, sits in the temple of God. Let me say, in passing, that St Peter's at Rome was never the temple of God, nor ever will be. It has been called such, but it never could be. There will be a day when the Jews will rebuild Jehovah's temple at Jerusalem, and then this arrogant being springs up, and takes the place, not only of Christ—he asserts that he is Christ—but he usurps the place of God likewise. But what is his end? Isaiah xi. 4 foretells it briefly, while fuller detail is given here:—" Then shall that Wicked be revealed, whom the Lord shall consume with the spirit of his mouth, and shall destroy with the brightness of his coming." Oh! I love to think of that, of the One that is going in that day to deal with this proud oppressor of God's earthly people, who has deceived many, while denying the truth of Jehovah, and the truth of Christianity. Satan thought he had done a wonderful thing when he got the Jews cast out of Palestine; he will think he has done a better thing still, when he has got the truth cast out, and the Word of God set aside, and his man exalted to the uttermost.

But then comes the moment, when the One who was the humble, lowly, self-emptied, dependent man, comes out, and is the consumer and destroyer of this wicked one! Yes, it is Jesus, my Saviour, that is going to do that. Is he your Saviour? Mark, you will have to be on the Lord's side, or you may be among those that are caught in the snare of the devil in that sorrowful day. Read the verse once more,— " Then shall that Wicked be revealed, whom the Lord shall consume with the spirit of his mouth, and shall destroy with the brightness of his coming : even him, whose coming is after the working of Satan, with all power and signs, and lying wonders." Suppose the Lord came to-night, and you are left behind, unconverted, because unbelieving, do you think you will escape the snare? I do not believe it, because there will be such wonderful power and testimony. He will do what Jesus did. Compare Acts ii. 22—"Jesus of Nazareth, a man approved of God among you by miracles, and wonders, and signs, which God did by him"—and you will find that what Jesus did, this man essays with "the working of Satan, with all power, and signs, and lying wonders." The very same words are used in each case. Remember Elijah, with the prophets of Baal, when the question was put to them, "How long halt ye between two opinions? If Jehovah be God, follow him; but if Baal, then follow him." Let it be settled by fire, says Elijah,—"the God that answereth by fire, let him be God." The votaries of Baal cried and prayed all day, and cut themselves with knives, but no answer came. Then what happened? Why, Elijah builds his altar, and souses it with water, that there might be no appearance of deception, and he cries to the Lord, and fire comes out from heaven. This man will do the same (*see* Rev. xiii. 13).

You will not escape the snare, my friends, if you are on the earth in that day. I recommend you to believe the truth now, because the apostle says he shall come "with all power, and signs, and lying wonders." I believe that when the antichrist comes there will be a wonderful number of conversions. Have you heard the news? will be the query. What? Christ has come! The tidings will spread; the news will be gladly received of the advent of a wonderful Christ. But what about the judgment to come? Oh! that is all a delusion; that myth to frighten fools has long been exposed and exploded. *The* Christ has come, the world's Christ, the Christ that men want, and there is no word about judgment;

we may live as we like. Numbers of converts flock to the standard. They need not much persuasion; and, sinner, you, who might have been converted to the Christ of God, will be taken with the wiles and lies of a false Christ—the devil's Christ. If men will not believe the truth, they will have to believe a lie. Man is not self-supporting, or self-existing, and infidelity is such a dry, dreary, heartless thing, that in a while men will get tired of sheer infidelity; and when something comes with display and power, you will say, Oh! that is beautiful; that will suit me exactly. The bubble bursts, with appalling results. What results? "That they all might be damned who believed not the truth, but had pleasure in unrighteousness," is God's verdict, already gone out, against the hell-lured convert of antichrist. Let me say to you plainly, there is nothing but damnation ahead of you, if you do not turn to God, and get salvation through faith in the Lord Jesus Christ.

The coming of the Lord is the next thing for us who are saved; and then, if we are taken up—if the saints of God are called up,—there is nothing but this dark terrible delusion left for Christendom's Christless masses of unconverted professors of a Saviour they never have known, and then never can know! Do you suppose that if you have not believed God in the day of the Holy Ghost, if you have not believed the Gospel now, in the day when God is telling of His love, when the Holy Ghost is here working and pointing you to Jesus, if you do not receive the Gospel, and believe it now, when everybody is desirous for your blessing,—do you suppose that, when every possible influence and power under heaven, and out of hell, and on the earth, is against you,—do you suppose that you will believe the truth then? Listen. "That they all might be damned who BELIEVED NOT THE TRUTH, but had pleasure in unrighteousness." Oh, may God save you from this terrible, strong delusion. Far better have the truth now. Christ is the truth; and the apostle goes on to say, "We are bound to give thanks alway to God for you, brethren beloved of the Lord, because God hath from the beginning chosen you to salvation through sanctification of the Spirit and BELIEF OF THE TRUTH" (2 Thess. ii. 13).

How sweetly the warm-hearted apostle addresses the simple believers, and says, I have portrayed the dark future of the unbeliever, but I now turn with joy to what belongs to you. You have believed the truth, and you are entitled to know yourselves among the possessors of salvation. I would not stand here to-night, and not be a Christian, for ten thousand worlds, with all their wealth ten thousand times told. Nay, but I say to you to-night, if you never were a Christian before, come, seize your opportunity, turn to the Lord, believe in His name, rest on His blood, come to His loving open arms. Thus be ready for the Lord's return; and then, when He comes, you will be taken to be with Him, and you will be like Him, and with Him, for ever and ever. What a prospect! I say again, if you have been lingering or halting till to-night, come, and "join Christ's waiting band," for that band has a title to glory without a flaw, and a prospect without a cloud

THE TIMES OF THE GENTILES.

DANIEL ii.-vii.

Lecture III.

WHAT are we to understand by the expression, "the times of the Gentiles"? Turn to the scripture where the phrase occurs. It is found in the 21st chapter of Luke (ver. 24), where the Lord Jesus is describing to His disciples the imminent destruction of Jerusalem. It is the last day of His public life. When I say that, I mean the last day of His public ministry. If you have never gone over the last week of the Lord's life, I recommend you all to do it, and you will be wonderfully struck with the amazing amount of ministry which took place during that time. On the first day of the week He was anointed in Bethany (John xii. 1-11). He is made much of—and that is what we have the privilege of doing now—the first day of the week. The Jew gave Him the last day of the week, the Christian gives Him the first. The next day (Monday) He comes into Jerusalem in triumph, riding upon an ass, and a colt the foal of an ass (Mark xi. 1-11). The next day (Tuesday) He curses the fig-tree, and cleanses the temple (Mark xi. 12-19). The next day (Wednesday) occupies from Mark xi. 20 to verse 11 of chapter xiv. (see also Matt. xxii. to xxv., and Luke xx., xxi). The ministry that took place that day is simply enormous.

Into it I cannot go now; you must trace it out for yourselves; but from early morn to dewy eve, that day, the blessed Lord seems to have been pouring out His marvellous ministry.

What took place on the Thursday is given us in Mark xiv. 12-72. It is most noticeable that nothing is recorded, save what relates to the Passover being prepared—no ministry. He spent that day apparently with God alone till eventide. Then on Friday (Mark xv.) He died,—thank God, for me! In the grave He lay all the Sabbath day, and He rose, the triumphant Saviour, on the first day of the new week. It is on the Wednesday that He is telling His disciples what is coming on Jerusalem, and, as we get down towards the end of the discourse, we read,— " These be the days of vengeance, that all things which are written may be fulfilled. But woe unto them that are with child, and to them that give suck, in those days! for there shall be great distress in the land, and wrath upon this people. And they shall fall by the edge of the sword, and shall be led away captive into all nations: and Jerusalem shall be trodden down of the Gentiles, until THE TIMES OF THE GENTILES be fulfilled" (Luke xxi. 22-24). I need not stay to tell you how absolutely this solemn prediction was fulfilled. Jerusalem was soon after overthrown. God, in patient grace, waited a little, He did not destroy it the day after the death of His Son. Nay, for sixty years He waited on His rebellious people, who first rejected their Messiah, and then resisted the Holy Ghost (Acts vii. 51, 52). At length He sent forth His edict; and, if I may so say, the scavenger came upon the scene, and swept the carcase away. Judaism, as a system of religion, came to an end before God, when Christ was nailed to the cross (Col. ii. 14); but the Jews clung fast to their city and their religion, until the Romans, like the scavenger with the broom, came, and swept it and them away.

"Jerusalem shall be trodden down of the Gentiles, until the times of the Gentiles be fulfilled," was the Lord's statement, and every one knows what a bone of contention that city, and Palestine have been from that day to this. Almost all the fighting in Europe, and Asia, has been connected, in some way or other, with Jerusalem, and it has all along been trodden down, and will be till "the times of the Gentiles be fulfilled."

What, however, are we to learn from the expression "the times of the Gentiles"? Go back to the book of Daniel, because the prophecies of Daniel are a simple and distinct answer to that question. They unfold to us, in a remarkable way, what the Lord calls "the times of the Gentiles." Observe that Daniel opens with an account of Nebuchadnezzar destroying Jerusalem the first time. It was in the third year of the reign of Jehoiakim, King of Judah, that Nebuchadnezzar besieged it, and took it :—" And the king spake unto Ashpenaz, the master of his eunuchs, that he should bring certain of the children of Israel, and of the king's seed, and of the princes; children in whom was no blemish, but well-favoured, and skilful in all wisdom, and cunning in knowledge, and understanding science, and such as had ability in them to stand in the king's palace, and whom they might teach the learning and the tongue of the Chaldeans" (i. 3, 4).

I read these verses, because we have thus absolutely fulfilled the solemn prediction which, you will remember, God sent by the lips of Isaiah to King

Hezekiah, as recorded in the 39th chapter. Hezekiah had been sick, and when he recovered, the King of Babylon sent up letters and a present, and congratulated him upon his recovery,—a little bit of courtesy on the part of the world. It is ever a dangerous thing to a saint of God when the world begins to be courteous to him. What does Hezekiah do? He opens his house and shows the ambassadors the " precious things, the silver, and the gold, and the spices, and the precious ointment, and all the house of his armour, and all that was found in his treasures." Then Isaiah comes to Hezekiah and says, " Hear the word of the Lord of hosts ; behold, the days come, that all that is in thine house, and that which thy fathers have laid up in store until this day, shall be carried to Babylon ; nothing shall be left, saith the Lord. And of thy sons that shall issue from thee, which thou shalt beget, shall they take away ; and they shall be eunuchs in the palace of the king of Babylon " (Isa. xxxix. 5, 6).

"The times of the Gentiles," let me then repeat, begin with that which Daniel describes here, when Nebuchadnezzar, as the servant of God, went up and took the city,—where the throne of the Lord God had been, where the temple of God was, and where the worship of God was still nominally offered, —took it, and razed it to the ground, because of the sin, and iniquity of its inhabitants. God had forsaken His people. Ezekiel describes how the glory of the Lord gradually forsook the place (chapter x. 4, 18, 19) ; and then the next thing, in God's righteous government was, that He passed His earthly people, the Jews, into the hands of the enemy, and "the times of the Gentiles" began. That is why all through the book of Daniel you find God called "the God of heaven." He has given up the earth, and while I do not at all, for a moment, deny that there is a providence of God working now, as a matter of fact, God has left the earth alone, and the potsherds of the earth are striving with the potsherds thereof.

In the 2nd of Daniel it is to be noticed that, at the 18th verse, Daniel desires "mercies of the God of *heaven;*" 19th verse, "blesses the God of *heaven;*" 28th verse, declares "there is a God in *heaven* that revealeth secrets;" 37th verse, informs Nebuchadnezzar "the God of *heaven* hath given thee a kingdom;" and, 44th verse, prophesies, "In the days of these kings shall the God of *heaven* set up a kingdom." The reason of this is that Daniel, by the Spirit of God, is bringing out, for the instruction of God's people, the wonderfully solemn truth, that, for the time being, God's kingdom upon earth is in abeyance. He has retired—given up the earth. Well, but you say, Afterwards He sent His Son—Jesus came by-and-by. True, but what did man do? Sent Him back again, by the way of the cross. As far as the world is concerned, God has got no place in it. I quite admit that some people would be, and are, what is called religious, but if you go to the world, and talk about God, what will they do? They will very soon let you know what they think; "Not this man, but Barabbas," was the world's choice eighteen centuries ago, nor are things really different now. "Crucify him, crucify him!" That is the world expressing its heart—what it would like—viz., Get rid of Jesus. And I tell you more, what Scripture unfolds is this, that the day is drawing near, when apparently, they will get rid of every bit of testimony for God and His Son, and they will then delight in the thought, We have got rid of Him altogether; and that is just the moment when the storm bursts, and the God of heaven re-enters the scene.

Now here, then, we learn in Daniel that "the times of the Gentiles" begin in this way, by God retiring, and Jerusalem being captured; and when you come to chapter ii., you find Nebuchadnezzar commencing the history of the Gentile empire. I do not mean, of course, that there were not Gentile kingdoms before; but, to inaugurate "the times of the Gentiles," Nebuchadnezzar is suffered—yea, helped of God—to get into a place of absolute supremacy, and earthly power. That comes out distinctly in the 2nd chapter of Daniel.

I may say, for those who would like to study the book of Daniel a little carefully, that it is divided into two great parts—the first six chapters, and the last six. The first part gives us all Nebuchadnezzar's visions, what he saw, and Daniel's interpretation. God begins in the 7th chapter, and thenceforward we get what Daniel sees. It is what God reveals, and makes known to His servant. The reason seems to be this,—the first six chapters are occupied in showing what I may call the moral features of the Gentile empires, what they really were, and what they did. Beginning with the 7th chapter, God shows us the circumstantial appearance of these powers, how He looks upon them, what He sees in them, and thinks about them. Chapters ii. to vi. show what the kings think about themselves, and the 7th and succeeding chapters, what God thinks of them.

In chapter ii., Nebuchadnezzar dreamed dreams, and then forgot them, like many another person;

but, being a tyrant, he calls in his wise men, and says, Tell me my dream. They say, "Tell thy servants the dream, and we will show thee the interpretation." The king replies, "The thing is gone from me; if ye will not make known unto me the dream, with the interpretation thereof, ye shall be cut in pieces." Then they say they were never asked before to interpret a dream which they had not heard, and thereon the furious autocrat "commanded to destroy all the wise men of Babylon" (ver. 12). The news of this harsh decree gets abroad, and Daniel, being involved in it, goes to God in prayer. The Lord makes known to him what Nebuchadnezzar had dreamed. And what is the next thing he does? Runs away and tells the king? Oh, no! "Then Daniel blessed the God of heaven," and said, "Blessed be the name of God for ever and ever: for wisdom and might are his: and he changeth the times and the seasons: he removeth kings, and setteth up kings: he giveth wisdom unto the wise, and knowledge to them that know understanding; he revealeth the deep and secret things: he knoweth what is in the darkness, and the light dwelleth with him. I thank thee, and praise thee, O thou God of my fathers, who hast given me wisdom and might, and hast made known unto me now what we desired of thee: for thou hast now made known unto us the king's matter" (verses 19-23).

Daniel's course is beautiful. He first of all got hold of his brethren, and had a prayer-meeting. "He made the thing known to his companions" (ver. 17). But his resource was God. Then, instead of going straight off and telling all abroad what he had learned, he has, what I may venture to call, a worship meeting; he comes and thanks the Lord. Very fine this.

There is a great moral lesson here. First he thanks the Lord, saying, "Blessed be the name of the Lord for ever and ever." His heart runs over in thankfulness to the Lord first, and then he goes in to the king and says, I can tell you your dream.

"Thou, O king, sawest, and behold a great image. This great image, whose brightness was excellent, stood before thee, and the form thereof was terrible. This image's head was of fine gold, his breast and his arms of silver, his belly and his thighs of brass. His legs of iron, his feet part of iron and part of clay" (verses 31-33). It was deteriorating as it came down, and as to the figure there was no doubt as to its meaning, because he tells us what it is. He goes on, "Thou sawest till that a stone was cut out without hands, which smote the image upon his feet that were of iron and clay, and brake them to pieces. Then was the iron, the clay, the brass, the silver, and the gold, broken to pieces together, and became like the chaff of the summer threshing-floors; and the wind carried them away, that no place was found for them: and the stone that smote the image became a great mountain, and filled the whole earth. This is the dream; and we will tell the interpretation thereof before the king. Thou, O king, art a king of kings: for the God of heaven hath given thee a kingdom, power, and strength, and glory. And wheresoever the children of men dwell, the beasts of the field, and the fowls of the heaven, hath he given into thine hand, and hath made thee ruler over them all. Thou art this head of gold" (verses 34-38).

Mark, God did not give Nebuchadnezzar the fish of the sea. Why? Because the Man of the 8th Psalm had not yet come, who had the power over the fish of the sea. You must go to the 17th chapter of Matthew for that, where Peter was troubled, and wanted money for tribute. And the Lord said to him, "Go thou to the sea, and cast an hook, and take up the fish that first cometh up; and when thou hast opened his mouth, thou shalt find a piece of money: that take, and give unto them for me and thee" (Matt. xvii. 27). It was only the Lord Jesus, the Son of Man, who had power over the fish of the sea. Nebuchadnezzar's power and dominion was in that sense limited; but as regards the children of men, the beasts of the field, and the fowls of the heaven, he is told, "God hath made thee ruler over them all." It is very simple. God unfolds to Nebuchadnezzar the fact that, in His sovereignty, He would allow him to raise the Babylonian empire, in his own person, to universal supremacy, and we know as a matter of history it was so.

But Nebuchadnezzar is further informed, "After thee shall rise another kingdom inferior to thee"—the Medo-Persian; "and another third kingdom of brass, which shall bear rule over all the earth;" clearly Greece, as every schoolboy knows. "And the fourth kingdom shall be strong as iron: forasmuch as iron breaketh in pieces and subdueth all things; and as iron that breaketh all these, shall it break in pieces and bruise" (verses 39, 40). Here we have the last empire, the Roman, under which the Lord Jesus died,—because of course it was Pilate, as the official representative of Cæsar, who authorised the death of the Son of God, when His own people, the Jews, had delivered Him into his hands. Therefore the utmost importance, all the way through, is attached to the last kingdom, the last empire, and so we find, at the close, that the stone, cut out without hands, falls on the feet of the image. It is upon the last empire that the stone falls, and then becomes a great mountain, and fills the whole earth. Without doubt that is the kingdom of the Lord Jesus Christ, plainly foretold in the 44th verse, where we read, "And in the days of these kings shall the God of heaven set up a kingdom, which shall never be destroyed: and the kingdom shall not be left to other people, but it shall break in pieces, and consume all these kingdoms, and it shall stand for ever. Forasmuch as thou sawest that the stone was cut out of the mountain without hands, and that it brake in pieces the iron, the brass, the clay, the silver, and the gold ; the great God hath made known to the king what shall come to pass hereafter ; and the dream is certain, and the interpretation thereof sure" (verses 44, 45).

Thus quickly, and startlingly, will be introduced the kingdom of the Lord Jesus Christ, whom man has despised and cast out; He will yet come into this world, and come in a way that will mark the fact that God has sent Him. Though the Roman empire be the one He may first deal with, it is to be observed that all the other kingdoms will come under His solemn, and crushing judgment. In the gospels the Lord Jesus speaks of Himself as "the stone which the builders rejected" become "the head of the corner." He then adds, "Whosoever shall fall on this stone shall be broken; but on whomsoever it shall fall, it will grind him to powder" (Matt. xxi. 42, 44). The Jewish nation fell over Jesus, whom they could not receive in His humiliation, and lowliness, and was thus broken ; but it is the proud Gentile powers upon whom the crushing stone, the now rejected Christ

Jesus, will fall by-and-by. It is the proud infidel Gentile, that will not receive the gospel of a heavenly Saviour, upon whom that stone will fall, and grind him to powder. No figure of utter judgment could be more apt.

Nebuchadnezzar's first vision gives, then, in consecutive history, the four empires, terminating in the Roman; and the end is the introduction of the Son of Man, the Lord Jesus Christ, as King of kings, and Lord of lords. Thus, what I may call the general view of Gentile imperial power, or "the times of the Gentiles," you have developed before you in the 2nd chapter of Daniel.

Glance now, for one moment, at the four following chapters, because they give us, in detail, what we may call the moral features of these Gentile kingdoms. What marks them—what marks man when he gets earthly power away from God? In the 3rd chapter, you will find that Nebuchadnezzar, elated with the position of supremacy which God had given him, makes an image of gold, and demands that every one shall worship that image. In plain language, idolatry is the great salient point of that chapter. That is what is coming in again by-and-by. What will really bring down the crushing judgment of God upon antichrist, and Christendom, will be the solemn fact, that idolatry will spring up, once more, among those who profess to be the earthly people of God. In the 12th chapter of Matthew this is foretold by the Lord Jesus. He says,—" When the unclean spirit [idolatry] is gone out of a man, he walketh through dry places, seeking rest, and findeth none. Then he saith, I will return into my house from whence I came out; and when he is come, he findeth it empty, swept, and garnished. Then goeth he, and taketh with himself seven other spirits more wicked than himself, and they enter in and dwell there; and the last state of that man is worse than the first. Even so shall it be also unto this wicked generation" (Matt. xii. 43-45). Idolatry was repudiated by the Jews, when Jesus was here; but, as they refused to own Him (see Matt. xii.) who was their real God, as well as their Messiah, He shows that they would yet fall into the old trap of the enemy—idolatry—as Daniel (chaps ix. and xii.) also informs us. You may get rid of idolatry, but unless you really have the truth, though you have your house swept and garnished, it is empty, and Satan will bring in what is false to fill it; and therefore the Lord says, "the last state of that man is worse than the first." The point is this, idolatry will yet be revived in Israel.

Daniel's 3rd chapter shows the fact of compulsory idolatry; and you will find, in Revelation xiii. 15, that antichrist will "cause that as many as would not worship the image of the beast should be killed." The day is coming when the civil power in the world will compel idolatry. History simply repeats itself. Nebuchadnezzar gives us a prophetic picture of it. Shadrach, Meshech, and Abednego will not bow down; they are faithful to God. They are cast into the fiery furnace; but it only burned off their bonds, set them free, and put them in the company of the Son of God. Faithfulness toward God always leads to the deepest blessing to the soul.

In chapter iv., Nebuchadnezzar, conceited and full of his own thoughts, has visions of a great tree. Daniel alone is able to tell him what the meaning is. I do not now unfold it; but we read that what takes place is this:—"At the end of twelve months he walked in the palace of the kingdom of Babylon. The king spake, and said, Is not this great Babylon, that I have built for the house of the kingdom, by the might of my power, and for the honour of my majesty? While the word was in the king's mouth, there fell a voice from heaven, saying, O king Nebuchadnezzar, to thee it is spoken; The kingdom is departed from thee," &c. (verses 27-31). In the same hour he was driven from men, and became as a beast. It was a remarkable thing, but it was God's solemn way of dealing with the pride, and self-exaltation of man. When man gets into power, he exalts himself. There is only one Man that can really be trusted with power—the Lord Jesus Christ; and that is why, in the 5th chapter of Revelation, the song of the universe by-and-by is this:—"Worthy is the Lamb that was slain, to receive power, and riches, and wisdom, and strength, and honour, and glory, and blessing." Give any other man power, and what will he do with it? Give any other man riches, and what will he do with them? I love to think that the song in glory is this, that the only One worthy of what men are rushing after here—the only One worthy of all—is the Lord Jesus Christ. Here Nebuchadnezzar has power to exalt himself, and God abases him.

Now the next chapter goes a step further, we have there the grossest impiety and sacrilege. It is Belshazzar's banquet, and the solemn judgment in connection therewith. In that night Belshazzar dies,—God casts him down.

In the 6th chapter, we get apostasy. At the death of Belshazzar, Darius the Mede gets the kingdom, and they come up and say in terms to Darius, Now we want you to make an edict that nobody shall pray but to you ; and I have no doubt Darius was flattered, and he puts out the edict, that no prayer shall be made to any god, or man, but to himself, for thirty days. It will be exactly the same in the day that is coming. God has, so to speak, sketched the history in this book. In the 3rd chapter we have the idolatry that will come in compelled by civil power ; in the 4th, self-exaltation ; in the 5th, impiety ; and in the 6th, what I may call apostasy—that is, giving up first estate, and departing from all dependence upon God. That is the general view of " the times of the Gentiles,"— what man does when he possesses power given him by God.

In the 7th chapter—which I read this evening—we get God's view of these four empires. There you will see that these four consecutive kingdoms are brought before us again, in a different way. In the first vision of chapter vii. we have the three earlier kingdoms, the Babylonian, the Medo-Persian, and the Grecian, under the figures of the three beasts. The fourth kingdom is the subject of a separate vision: verse 7, " After this I saw in the night-visions, and behold a fourth beast, dreadful and terrible, and strong exceedingly ; and it had great iron teeth : it devoured and brake in pieces, and stamped the residue with the feet of it : and it was diverse from all the beasts that were before it ; and it had ten horns. I considered the horns, and, behold, there came up among them another little horn before whom there were three of the first horns plucked up by the roots : and, behold, in this horn were eyes like the eyes of man, and a mouth speaking great things." This fourth beast, I have

THE TIMES OF THE GENTILES. 59

no doubt at all, is the Roman empire,—not as it is now, but as it will be revived in the day that is very near at hand. You may turn and say, Where is the Roman empire now? It is at present non-existent; but it is a striking thing that in the 12th verse it says, "As concerning the rest of the beasts, they had their dominion taken away: yet their lives were prolonged for a season and time." I can show you the kingdom of Greece just now; I can show you the Shah of Persia; and I suppose in a certain sense there is that which might possibly be the vestige of the Babylonian kingdom. But where is the Roman? I will tell you what you can see,—you can discover the ten kingdoms into which the Roman empire was divided. It broke up, as you know, into that number. Daniel sees the ten horns—always in Scripture a symbol of kingly power; and now, if you read a little lower down in the chapter, you will see that it is in connection with this beast that Daniel sees the "thrones set up" (for this is the true reading, not "cast down") in the 9th verse. "I beheld till the thrones were set, and the Ancient of days did sit, whose garment was white as snow, and the hair of his head like the pure wool: his throne was like the fiery flame, and his wheels as burning fire. A fiery stream issued and came forth from before him: thousand thousands ministered unto him, and ten thousand times ten thousand stood before him: the judgment was set, and the books were opened. I beheld then, because of the voice of the great words which the horn spake I beheld even till the beast was slain, and his body destroyed, and given to the burning flame" (Dan. vii. 9-11).

I repeat, for the sake of clearness, the Roman empire does not exist at this moment. The ten kingdoms into which that empire was divided are existing, though difficult, perhaps, to exactly identify and delimit; but we see in the book of Revelation that they will all have a separate existence, as kings (chap. xvii. 12), while, at the same time, the empire will be revived, and reconstituted. Daniel sees the beast having ten horns; he saw it in its original character, and what it was going later to become; but in the book of Revelation, you will find that John sees it possessing imperial unity, while separate kingly power existed in the ten horns. It is revived and re-energised entirely by Satanic power. What is very striking in the 7th of Daniel is, that it is because of "the little horn" (ver. 8) that the judgment comes. He wields the beast. In Revelation xiii. you will see that there are two beasts coming, the one having ten horns (ver. 1), and the other two horns like a lamb (ver. 11). I have no doubt that the one having two horns is really antichrist. While there are two systems of wickedness, one political, the other ecclesiastical, they play into each other's hands. This "little horn" that Daniel sees, is the leader or head of the revived Roman empire, who works in conjunction with his tool, antichrist, to "change times and laws" (ver. 25), and practically speaking, he dominates the beast. It is all the doings of the little horn, and it is because of the wickedness of the little horn that the judgment falls upon the beast. "I beheld then, because of the voice of the great words which the horn spake: I beheld even till the beast was slain, and his body destroyed, and given to the burning flame" (Dan. vii. 11). There you have the same thing as we find in Revelation xix. 20, where the beast, and the false prophet, are cast into the lake of fire.

Coming again to the latter part of the 7th of Daniel, you will find that we get more light upon the subject. You always find in Scripture, that, whether it be a parable, or a direct statement of God, if He goes on to expound or explain, there is always something added; and this you will observe, when you come down to the 17th verse, where the interpretation is made known to Daniel. " These great beasts, which are four, are four kings, which shall arise out of the earth. But the saints of the most High shall take the kingdom, and possess the kingdom for ever, even for ever and ever. Then I would know the truth of the fourth beast, which was diverse from all the others, exceeding dreadful, whose teeth were of iron, and his nails of brass; which devoured, brake in pieces, and stamped the residue with his feet; and of the ten horns that were in his head, and of the other which came up, and before whom three fell; even of that horn that had eyes, and a mouth that spake very great things, whose look was more stout than his fellows. I beheld, and the same horn made war with the saints, and prevailed against them; until the Ancient of days came, and judgment was given to the saints of the most High; and the time came that the saints possessed the kingdom " (Dan. vii. 17-22).

Notice the words " brake in pieces." This feature is that which has marked the history of the Roman empire from first to last. By the " saints" here, we must not understand the saints that belong to the Church,—not the Christians of the present moment; because we shall all be carried out of the scene, we shall be with Jesus, in glory, before this scripture can be fulfilled; but in that day God will have some earthly saints. The Spirit of God will work again amongst the Jews, and it is against them that all the hatred and energy of this horn is expressed. We shall have to look at Scripture another night to see the great tribulation, and those who pass through it. They are the saints, I have no doubt, named here :—" Judgment was given to the saints of the most High ; and the time came that the saints possessed the kingdom." How remarkable is the language of Scripture! We all thought that by-and-by we were going to be judged ; but even the book of Daniel says, that so far from the saints being judged, they are going to be the judges. " Judgment was given to the saints, and the time came that the saints possessed the kingdom " (ver. 22).

Then he says, " The fourth beast shall be the fourth kingdom upon earth, which shall be diverse from all kingdoms, and shall devour the whole earth, and shall tread it down, and break it in pieces. And the ten horns out of this kingdom are ten kings that shall arise : and another shall rise after them ; and he shall be diverse from the first, and he shall subdue three kings. And he shall speak great words against the most High, and shall wear out the saints of the most High, and think to change times and laws : and they shall be given into his hand, until a time and times and the dividing of time. But the judgment shall sit, and they shall take away his dominion, to consume and to destroy it unto the end. And the kingdom and dominion, and the greatness of the kingdom under the whole heaven, shall be given to the people of the saints of the most High, whose kingdom is an everlasting kingdom, and all dominions shall serve and obey him. Hitherto is the end of the matter. As for me Daniel, my cogitations much troubled me, and my countenance changed in me: but I kept the matter in my heart" (verses 23-28).

There are three things that this horn does. (1.) He "shall speak great words against the most High," that is, he blasphemes God. (2.) He "shall wear out the saints of the most High." (3.) He shall "think to change times and laws," that is, the revived feasts, which the Jews will have, when they are gathered back into their own land, the Passover, &c. Now observe, "They shall be given into his hand,"—not the saints, thank God, no,—but God will let him have dominance for the time being, and he will delight to persecute the godly, and he will be able to change their "times and laws, and they shall be given into his hand, until a time and times and the dividing of time."

You have here what Daniel speaks about in connection with his seventieth week (see chap. ix. 27), where there is a sudden, and unlooked-for break of the covenant, and for three and a half years there is tribulation and distress. For the space of three and a half years—forty-two months (Rev. xi. 2), or twelve hundred and sixty days (Rev. xi. 3), or "a time, and times, and half a time" (Rev. xii. 14)—this "prince that shall come" will persecute the saints of God, and then "the judgment shall sit, and they shall take away his dominion, to consume and to destroy it unto the end" (Dan. vii. 26).

Thereupon you behold the introduction of the kingdom of Christ, "and the greatness of the kingdom under the whole heaven, shall be given to the people of the saints of the most High, whose kingdom is an everlasting kingdom, and all dominions shall serve and obey him." That is, there is a setting aside of all earthly power, by the introduction of the blessed kingdom — wonderful moment!—of our Lord and Saviour Jesus Christ.

What Daniel gives us briefly, and prophetically, the Spirit of God recounts in the book of Revelation in much detail. Look at chapter xiii.: "And I stood upon the sand of the sea, and saw a beast rise up out of the sea, having seven heads and ten horns, and upon his horns ten crowns, and upon his heads the names of blasphemy. And the beast which I saw was like unto a leopard, and his feet were as the feet of a bear, and his mouth as the mouth of a lion; and the dragon gave him his power, and his seat, and great authority. And I saw one of his heads, as it were wounded to death; and his deadly wound was healed; and all the world wondered after the beast. And they worshipped the dragon which gave power unto the beast; and they worshipped the beast, saying, Who is like unto the beast? Who is able to make war with him? And there was given unto him a mouth speaking great things, and blasphemies; and power was given unto him to continue forty and two months. And he opened his mouth in blasphemy against God, to blaspheme his name, and his tabernacle, and them that dwell in heaven. And it was given unto him to make war with the saints, and to overcome them: and power was given him over all kindreds, and tongues, and nations. And all that dwell upon the earth shall worship him, whose names are not written in the book of life of the Lamb slain from the foundation of the world. If any man have an ear, let him hear. He that leadeth into captivity shall go into captivity: he that killeth with the sword, must be killed with the sword. Here is the patience and the faith of the saints" (Rev. xiii. 1-10).

"The dragon gave him his power, and his seat, and great authority." The same empire is seen by John that Daniel saw, only a new feature is observable in the source of power—the dragon, Satan. In the 5th verse:—" There was given unto him a mouth speaking great things, and blasphemies ; and power was given unto him to continue forty and two months." Forty-two months is the same time as three and a half years. Now, in the 7th verse, " It was given unto him to make war with the saints, and to overcome them." That will be an awfully solemn day, " for all that dwell upon the earth shall worship him,"—idolatry again,—" whose names are not written in the book of life, of the Lamb slain, from the foundation of the world. If any man have an ear, let him hear."

Then in the 11th verse, John says, " I beheld another beast." That is antichrist. In various ways God presents him :—" He exerciseth all the power of the first beast before him, and causeth the earth, and them which dwell therein, to worship the first beast, whose deadly wound was healed. And he doeth great wonders, so that he maketh fire come down from heaven on the earth in the sight of men, and deceiveth them that dwell on the earth by the means of those miracles which he had power to do in the sight of the beast; saying to them that dwell on the earth, that they should make an image to the beast, which had the wound by a sword, and did live. And he had power to give life unto the image of the beast, that the image of the beast should both speak, and cause that as many as would not worship the image of the beast should be killed. And he causeth all, both small and great, rich and poor, free and bond, to receive a mark in their right hand, or in their foreheads: and that no man might buy or sell, save he that had the mark, or the name of the beast, or the number of his name. Here is wisdom. Let him that hath understanding count the number of the beast: for it is the number of a man; and his number is Six hundred threescore and six" (Rev. xiii. 12-18). If you are alive on the earth in that day, my unconverted hearer, there is one of two things before you. You will either have to bow down, and worship the image of the beast, or you will pay the penalty of your hardihood with your life; and I do not believe an unconverted man will do that—not a bit of it.

The "strong delusion" has gone out, and so great will be the glamour, and so wonderful will be the power, and so magnificent will be the display, that men will be caught, trapped, and carried away by that which appeals to the senses, and to the eye. There will be no Gospel then. You will have what people are aiming at now. You will have your continental Sunday; there will be no kirks, and no meetings; and you will have your fill of what the world wants, and what the devil will furnish; and you will have to do that which is most awful in the history of a man, viz., bow down, and worship before the image of another man, as sinful as yourself.

Now let us look at the 17th chapter, which shows the sequel of all this frightful condition of matters in that day. The 7th verse: — "And the angel said unto me, Wherefore didst thou marvel? I will tell thee the mystery of the woman, and of the beast that carrieth her, which hath the seven heads and ten horns. The beast that thou sawest was, and is not; and shall ascend out of the bottomless pit, and go into perdition: and they that dwell on the earth shall wonder (whose names were not written in the book of life from the foundation of the world), when they behold the beast that was, and is not—("*Was*," when John wrote, "*is not*" now)—but shall be present." That empire is non-existent, as I speak, but it will arise out of the bottomless pit. It will be revived; the Roman empire will be re-gathered again. You know, that Charlemagne strove for it; and it was the supreme object of the first Napoleon's life to get the Roman empire together again, and he very nearly did it. People told the late Napoleon that he was the "beast," and he was flattered. There is, however, coming a man, who will gather the Roman empire together again, in the sense of the Scripture here. It "shall ascend out of the bottomless pit, and go into perdition (true brother, and companion of Judas), and they that dwell on the earth shall wonder." Of course they will, when "they behold the beast who was, and is not, and shall be present." The "yet *is*" of verse 8 should be, "*shall be present.*"

This fallen empire will come up again, and look what follows :—" And the ten horns which thou sawest are ten kings, which have received no kingdom as yet; but receive power as kings one hour with the beast" (ver. 12). That is, God, by-and-by, will so work, that I have no doubt that these kings, who will be the leaders of the ten parts of the Roman empire, will all be made to bow down, and one of the ten will be exalted to imperial power, and that will be the moment when things will be headed up. The early part of this chapter shows, that upon the back of this beast, there was sitting a woman, and I have no doubt that you have there the false Church. Is that awful thing what we call the Church of God? Yes, and she is carried on by the world's power, till it turns and rends her. The fact is, beloved friends, men will get tired of priestcraft, and they will be tired by-and-by of everything except the energy of their own will. And what will be the result? They will hate the whore, and rob her first, and then eat her flesh, and burn her with fire. Already they are taking away as much as they can of church land. The stream has set in. Already the thing has begun; but by-and-by man will become utterly infidel, and say, No, no, away to the winds with everything that has even the semblance of God, or that bears the name of Christ upon it. The result will be that everything will be swept aside, and the apostasy become full-blown. The 18th chapter of Revelation shows you the fall of Babylon; and the 19th, the destruction of the beast, and the false prophet,—that is the Roman empire, and the antichrist. Then the Lord will come. Of that we will speak a little more fully another night.

I trust you have been able to see, from the Word of God, what is the meaning of "the times of the Gentiles." It is the period during which God puts earthly power into the hands of the Gentiles; and Scripture has shown us how man uses that earthly power, viz., to exalt himself, persecute the saints of God, blaspheme God Himself, and at length he falls completely into the power of Satan. The revived Latin empire, energised by Satan, is the full-blown expression of daring revolt against God, and His Christ.

THE GREAT TRIBULATION.

MATT. xxiv. 1-44; DAN. ix. 24-27.

Lecture IV.

THE subject before us this evening is the Jew in relation to the return of the Lord Jesus Christ.

The question is often raised, Has God cast off His ancient people? The apostle Paul answers most distinctly in the 11th of Romans, No, He has not, but they have come under His lash. They have come under His judgment for their guilt, and so will Christendom likewise come under the governmental judgment of God, in a day very near at hand, because of their sin. But the Jew is not "cast off" in the sense in which Scripture uses the word,—as final rejection,—because there is the most abundant testimony that the day is coming, when the Lord will re-gather His ancient people,—the house of Israel and the house of Judah,— and He will plant them in the land which He gave to them, and their fathers, for God has plainly said, "One king shall be king to them all," and " David my servant shall be king over them" (Ezek. xxxvii. 22, 24),— a beautiful allusion to Christ!

To-night, therefore, it will be my business to show you, if I can, from the Word of God, that this will really take place, as well as to point out the relation which this, at present, despised, and apparently cast-off people, has to the Lord Jesus, in the day of His reappearing. I have read these closing verses of the 9th chapter of Daniel for this reason, that they give us clearly, a bird's-eye view of the situation. I may say also, very simply, to any person in this audience, that if you and I do not understand the end of the 9th chapter of Daniel, we shall never understand the prophetic Scriptures. I have not got the key that unlocks to me the Old Testament prophetic Scriptures, just as in the New Testament, if I do not comprehend the definite import of the parables of the 13th of Matthew, I shall fail to understand the Scriptures that relate to the kingdom of heaven, and the Church. The 13th of Matthew is, dispensationally speaking, the key to the New Testament, and the end of the 9th of Daniel is the key that unlocks the storehouse of Old Testament prophecy with relation to the Jews. Therefore, I dwell just a moment on it, because it is impossible to get on, unless we have correct thoughts of what God is going to do. If we conclude, as many do, that God has cast off the Jew for ever, and that we—Christians—are only going to be blessed, we are running full in the face of, and practically counter to, the testimony of Old Testament Scripture.

What has led us into error is this, that we have been reading Old Testament Scriptures with New Testament spectacles on, and when we found something about the blessing and enlargement of Israel, we began to apply it to ourselves, instead of really seeing of whom God was writing. We do not need to poach upon Old Testament Scriptures for what our souls need. God has blessed us wonderfully—not the Gentiles generally, but the believers in Christ. You see the character of our blessing is most wonderful, because God brings us to heaven in Christ. The Jew will get blessing by-and-by, but what does he get? He gets the earth. We have got heaven, and that is far better. And so, I say that those who go to the Old Testament and say, "That applies to us," are very like poachers. You know poachers are never very easy in their work, they are always afraid of being disturbed; and so if I have to go to the Old Testament Scriptures to find what belongs to me, it is perfectly clear I am not distinct, in my own soul, as to what belongs to me as a believer.

But before going further, permit me just to ask you, Are you a Christian? Oh, you say, that is a very plain question. Then let it have an honest answer now. But what do you mean by a Christian? you ask. I mean by a Christian a person that really knows Christ—not a person that knows something about Him, but a person that really knows Christ as his own Saviour. A Christian man is one who knows the rejected and once slain, but now raised, and glorified Saviour at God's right hand, and is connected with, and united to, that risen Saviour, where He now is. A Christian is a man who is born again of God, whose sins are all forgiven—all blotted out, and who has received the Holy Ghost, and knows it. If you can only say, "I hope this is all mine," you are not a true Christian in the proper sense of the word; and, let me tell you frankly, you have not got hold of the real essence of Christianity yet.

A Christian is a man that is indissolubly connected with the victorious risen Saviour. He is linked to the One who went down first of all into death for him, bore his sins, blotted them all out, met all the claims of God, in righteousness, in respect of those sins, and that Saviour is risen without a single sin, and has gone into God's presence, to prepare a place, and take him to it.

The blessing of the believer is this—he knows his sins are forgiven, he knows he is saved, and knows God is his Father; he has the Holy Ghost dwelling in him, and he is a person standing on the other side of death and judgment, waiting, at the return of the Bridegroom, for glory. Do you not see, that if your heart is perfectly at peace before God, through faith in the Lord Jesus Christ, and in the enjoyment of what Christ has wrought for you, you are free to turn round then, and see how God is going to bless other people? The reason why we can happily think of Israel's restoration is because we know ourselves so wonderfully and absolutely blessed of God. If you are a believer in the Lord Jesus Christ you are loved eternally, and, more than that, you are fitted for glory, and you belong to that Saviour, who is coming to take you to the spot, where He Himself is. You see the Christian has everything perfectly clear for eternity, he has a title to glory without a flaw, and he has a prospect before him without a cloud. Are you, I repeat, a Christian? Have you that title to glory without a flaw? What is that title? The precious blood of Christ—nothing more, and nothing less. If you say, I am resting on that blood, then thank God that you have such a title. And there is something more—a prospect without a cloud. But, you say, there is judgment coming. Not for you and me, not for us. Whoever may go through the tribulation, the Church of Christ never will. The Lord's word is distinct upon that point. There is not a cloud in our horizon. Why? Because everything is settled. Every possible question that could be raised between the soul and God is settled, and the only thing we are waiting for, is the Saviour to come for us, and receive us to Himself. I do not want a better prospect. You cannot give me one. That is what entrances the heart.

I tell you that my Saviour may be here to-night, and that I may meet Him in the air. What can be more blessed than that? But if you do not know the Saviour, and do not possess that title, then your prospect has got nothing but clouds in it, and I am going to show you some of them. If you are an unsettled, and hesitating soul, if you do not yet know the Lord, remember, that while I speak of that which specifically relates to the Jews, it may have distinct application to you also. You will find that although the hottest bit of the furnace of tribulation may be at Jerusalem, yet the tip of the flame will touch all the world. There will be no mercy in that day for the man who has refused the Gospel. Now is the day of mercy. I recommend you to get it.

Turn now to the prophecy itself (Dan. ix. 24-27) for a moment, and we shall see what was unfolded to Daniel, as he was looking to God about his people. He hears this, " Seventy weeks are determined upon thy people." Look what an immense amount is to take place in these seventy weeks—I believe they are weeks of years, not weeks of days. You find, " Seventy weeks are determined upon thy people, and upon thy holy city, (1) to finish the transgression, (2) and to make an end of sins, (3) and to make reconciliation for iniquity, (4) and to bring in everlasting righteousness, (5) and to seal up the vision and prophecy, (6) and to anoint the most Holy,"—to replace everything that the godly Jew desired ; and as this opened out before Daniel's soul, I can imagine how his heart was filled, to have it all brought about in seventy weeks; the Temple rebuilt and the Holy of Holies there. But listen, "Know, therefore, and understand, that from the going forth of the commandment to restore and to build Jerusalem, unto Messiah the Prince, shall be seven weeks, and threescore and two weeks : the street shall be built again, and the wall, even in troublous times." When was that commandment issued? It was in the days of Nehemiah. It was in the twentieth year of Artaxerxes Longimanus, that this took place, four hundred and fifty-four years before the birth of Jesus. For the detail of this edict read the 2nd chapter of Nehemiah, verses 5-9. The first seven weeks (forty-nine years) were really occupied with the building of the city and the wall, "in troublous times," after the coming back of the remnant from Babylon. "And after the threescore and two weeks shall Messiah be cut off, and have nothing" (*margin*). That is, counting from the end of the first seven weeks, right on to the end of the sixty-ninth week, you come down to Messiah's death, four hundred and eighty-three years from the date of Nehemiah's commission.

Four hundred and eighty-three years from the going forth of the edict to build the wall, was the very time when was fulfilled the word, "Rejoice greatly, O daughter of Zion; shout, O daughter of Jerusalem: behold, thy King cometh unto thee: he is just, and having salvation; lowly, and riding upon an ass, and upon a colt the foal of an ass" (Zech. ix. 9). Jesus presented Himself thus to the Jewish nation, "lowly, and riding upon an ass," and was "cut off and had nothing." He came into Jerusalem fulfilling prophecy. He came in on the Monday of the last week of His life. He had been anointed in Bethany over night by Mary—she knew the King—and the children say, "Hosanna to the Son of David," but the chief priests and the scribes "were sore displeased." Ah, the children knew what the parents did not. Three days afterwards He was betrayed, and on the following day was slain, and what took place? Israel's hopes were dashed to the ground, for the Messiah was cut off, and had nothing.

The next prophecy evidently refers to the Romans and to Jerusalem, "And the people of the prince that shall come shall destroy the city and the sanctuary." Observe, it is "the people of the prince *that shall come.*" The prince, I apprehend, has not yet come, for he is to be the chief actor in the seventieth week, which has not yet arrived, but his people (the Romans), nevertheless, came and destroyed Jerusalem, but not until A.D. 70. "And the end thereof shall be with a flood, and unto the end of the war desolations are determined. And he shall confirm a (*not* the) covenant with the many for one week: and in the midst of the week he shall cause the sacrifice and the oblation to cease, and for the overspreading of abominations he shall make it desolate (or, a desolator), even until the consummation, and that determined shall be poured upon the desolate" (ix. 26, 27).

Now, you might turn and say, that week is fulfilled. No, because what Scripture brings out is this, that with the death of Christ, God ceases altogether to count time, God's relations with His earthly people were stopped, the link was snapped, the chain was divided, and there has come in the long interval of

Christianity, commencing with the descent of the Holy Ghost, and closing with the coming again of the Lord Jesus, as the Bridegroom, to gather up His bride, the Church, to meet Him in the air. When that takes place, when this parenthesis, in which you and I live, is over, you will find that Daniel's seventieth week will be fulfilled; the links of the broken chain are picked up, and God puts the two ends together, and what do you find then going on again? Israel's history. Get clearly and distinctly in your mind what I mean. I hope everybody understands. I have no doubt in my own mind as to what God means. The point to note, is this, that after the sixty-ninth week Messiah was cut off, and then Israel was for the time being set aside, and the secret thought of God from eternity—the Church—came out. God's work, since Pentecost, has been but little among the Jews—and that not nationally, but chiefly among the Gentiles, calling souls out of each, and forming them into "one new man,"—the Church; but the moment this work of grace is over, and there is brought in the last soul that believes the Gospel—and it might be this night that the last believer in Jesus is being laid hold of by the energy of the Spirit of God,—then the Lord Jesus will come again, and we who know Him, rise to meet Him in the air, the living changed, the dead taken out of their graves, and what then? Israel comes again to the front; God again picks up the chain, if I may say so, and the seventieth week of Daniel is fulfilled.

"The people of the prince that shall come, shall destroy the city and the sanctuary." It was the last empire, the Roman empire, that slew the Lord, and destroyed the city, and it will be the Roman empire, revived by Satanic power, that, in the day yet to come, will oppress the Jew, and will be the real foe of God's people in the time of which the seventieth week of Daniel so solemnly treats. I believe the prince in that verse has never arrived yet. He is the beast with the ten horns, the revived Imperial head of the Roman empire, who, along with the false prophet, antichrist, will yet crush down God's ancient people.

The end of verse 26 doubtless alludes to what took place shortly after the death of the Lord. That death broke the link between God and His people, and since then they have lost their national place. A perfect flood of troubles broke on them, as it says, "And the end thereof shall be with a flood, and unto the end of the war desolations are determined." Again, "The king . . . sent forth his armies, and destroyed those murderers, and burned up their city" (Matt. xxii. 7). This is no part of the seventy weeks.

The 27th verse carries us up to the close, and gives us the seventieth week. Here the long interregnum of Christianity ends, and we read, "He," that is the coming Roman prince—not the Lord Jesus—"shall confirm *a* covenant with *the* many for one week, and in the midst of the week he shall cause the sacrifice and the oblation to cease" (ver. 17). The Jews will be gathered back into their own land, with the temple rebuilt, the sacrifices re-established, and their old customs, feast days, and rites going on, and then they get under the protection of this western political power, that is, the revived Roman empire. A covenant is made with "*the* many," the mass of the nation; the remnant declining it, and having no part in it. "In the midst of the week" this covenant is broken. "He shall cause the sacrifice and oblation to cease." The object of this is plain. Antichrist having effected, first of all, the complete obliteration of every remaining trace in Christendom of what was, or pretended to be, the worship of Jesus—the Christian's God—will not be content till he has driven out of the earth every testimony to Jehovah, the God of the Jew. The Lord having come for the Church, and the Holy Ghost being removed, then the mystery of iniquity works, the man of sin appears, thenceforth every vestige of what you and I are accustomed to think of as Christianity will be set aside, and then the Lord will send them a strong delusion, and they will believe a lie.

But there is a portion of God's earth still left, where the name of Jehovah is known, and the God of the Jew still owned, and worshipped. The Jews are gathered to their own land, and they are worshipping the God of their fathers, according to their idea. What is the next thing? 'I must get rid of that also,' says Satan, and great will be his satisfaction when he can say, I have made clear riddance of every vestige of the testimony to Jehovah, I have got rid of Christ in Christendom, and I have replaced the true Christ by antichrist. When he shall have turned out every vestige of worship of the true God in Judæa, then he will be content. The enemy's great design appears to have succeeded, for a man—himself but Satan's tool and dupe—has usurped God's place upon the earth. That is the moment when God begins to assert His rights. The patience of God is wonderful. If either you or I had had the government of this world in our hands, we should have wound the business up long ago. There is not a man here to-night who would have gone on as long with it, for if he had had the power, he would have exercised it long ere this, and set things right according to his own mind. But I repeat, the patience of God is wonderful.

Now, however, when idolatry is once more upheld in what professes to be His temple, the long-suffering patience of God with man on the earth is ended. The reason is here given, " And for (or on account of) the wing of abominations, a desolator, even until the consummation, and that determined shall be poured upon the desolate." The covenant is broken, the sacrifice and oblation caused to cease, and the wing of protection flung over the "abomination"—the well-known Old Testament term for idolatry. In plain language, you have clearly predicted here the solemn fact, that there will yet be idolatry in the spot where Jesus died, in Jerusalem, and in what purports to be Jehovah's temple. Idolatry there will undoubtedly be, according to the 12th of Daniel (ver. 11) and our Lord's own words in Matt. xxiv. 15, 16: "When ye, therefore, shall see the abomination of desolation, spoken of by Daniel the prophet, stand in the holy place, (whoso readeth, let him understand), then let them which be in Judea flee into the mountains."

"The abomination that maketh desolate" is this: Antichrist, the beast with two horns, the simulator of Jesus, will make an image to the beast with ten horns (see Rev. xiii. 11-18). He will make the image of his friend, with whom he is working in confederacy, and he will have the power to make that image speak, and compel people to worship it. In plain language, compulsory idolatry springs up again, and then God sends, in retributive judgment, the "flood." What is called the "*flood*" in verse 26 is called the "desolator" in verse 27. I regard this as the Assyrian. Because idols are taken under the protection of "the princ that shall come," God sends "a desolator," "an overflowing scourge" on Jerusalem—here spoken of, as "the desolate." The prince, although he has broken the covenant, is still the patron and head of the nation, and his minion is the false prophet—antichrist—who will have his seat in Jerusalem, as the great arch-priest of the idolatrous worship offered to the image in the temple of God. As a result God sends down the "flood," or the "desolator." The one referred to by these two figures is the Assyrian, or "king of the north," the foe outside the land. Antichrist is the enemy of the righteous Jews within; the Assyrian, from without. Thus the remnant are exposed, so to speak, to a double fire of diabolical persecution.

Other scriptures speak of this moment, particularly Isa. xxviii. 2: "Behold, the Lord hath a mighty and strong one, which, as a tempest of hail, and a destroying storm, as a flood of mighty waters overflowing, shall cast down to the earth with the hand." This verse flings light on the 9th of Daniel. Further down in Isaiah xxviii., ver. 14, you find the covenant also spoken of: "Wherefore hear the word of the Lord, ye scornful men, that rule this people which is in Jerusalem. Because ye have said, We have made a covenant with death, and with hell are we at agreement; when the overflowing scourge shall pass through, it shall not come unto us: for we have made lies our refuge, and under falsehood have we hid ourselves. Therefore thus saith the Lord God, Behold, I lay in Zion for a foundation a stone, a tried stone, a precious corner stone, a sure foundation: he that believeth shall not make haste. Judgment also will I lay to the line, and righteousness to the plummet: and the hail shall sweep away the refuge of lies, and the waters shall overflow the hiding place. And your covenant with death shall be disannulled, and your agreement with hell shall not stand; when the overflowing scourge shall pass through, then ye shall be trodden down by it." That is, the Roman emperor will make a covenant with the ungodly mass of the restored Jews. That covenant is an unholy covenant, and he breaks it, and God will then step in, and bitterly chastise them, because of their sin, first of all, in the rejection of Jesus, as their Messiah, and secondly, because of their acceptance of antichrist. Mark it well, if men do not have the true Christ, they are bound to accept the false one. Man is not independent, and self-supporting, and therefore, when antichrist comes, with his delusions, and wiles, he will be accepted, and received, above all in Jerusalem, where, of course, his throne will be. God's indignation is thereon expressed against these last representatives of the Christ-rejecting portion of Israel, and on them will fall His dire judgments, the Assyrian being used as "the rod of mine anger" (Isa. x. 5).

But now what about the tribulation? Well, here is the whole point. It is because of the sad moral condition of the nation, at that moment, that God pours forth the judgment, of which Scripture thus speaks, and if any of you have any doubt as to this special time, I must refer you briefly to other scriptures, both in the Old and New Testaments, which point out this state of matters. Look first at the 30th chapter of Jeremiah, where you will find, first of all, the statement that God will restore His people, and then, what will be effected, when they are restored. "For, lo, the days come, saith the Lord, that I will bring again the captivity of my people Israel and Judah, saith the Lord; and I will cause them to return to the land that I gave to their fathers, and they shall possess it" (Jer. xxx. 3).

Concerning Israel and Judah, you must not forget that the kingdom, in the days of Rehoboam, the son of Solomon, had been divided. The ten tribes that went off with Jeroboam are usually spoken of, by the prophets of the Old Testament, as "Israel" or "Ephraim," and you will have pointed out, later in this course of lectures, that Scripture speaks most distinctly as to the different dealing of God with the ten tribes and the two tribes. Here we have merely the fact brought out, "I will bring again the captivity of my people Israel and Judah." The ten tribes were taken into captivity long before Judah. Where they are, at this day, I do not know, and no one knows. There has been a great effort to make out that the English-speaking race, and specially the Christians thereof, are the ten tribes, but I demur to this, because I do not think there is a shadow of ground, in Scripture, for this theory. I am quite willing to admit this, that if a man wants to prove any absurdity he can always get some wrested scripture, dislocated from its connection, to support him. But what destroys the whole force of the theory to me, is this, that the acme of the beauty and blessedness of Christianity is, that we are going to heavenly glory with Christ. We are not going to live on the earth. Thank God, no. When the time comes to go hence, the Lord has given us something far better than earth. Let the Jew have his portion, and we will give it to him freely, and therefore if anybody comes and says, You are the house of Israel, do not you believe it; because even if an Israelite were converted now, he ceases, as a believer in Jesus, to be a Jew, and becomes a member of the body of Christ.

I truly confess, beloved friends, that the day when I say "good-bye" to the earth, I shall say, from the bottom of my heart, Thank God. If the Lord came to-night, we should break out, as we left the earth behind, into that noble pæan, "O death, where is thy sting? O grave, where is thy victory? The sting of death is sin, and the strength of sin is the law. But thanks be to God, which giveth us the victory through our Lord Jesus Christ." We are going to be changed into the likeness of Christ, and to be with him for ever. Heaven, not earth, is our home. I would not be anything but a Christian for ten thousand worlds; and if you are not one, it is high time you became one.

But, with regard to the house of Israel, and the house of Judah, we read, "And these are the words that the Lord spake concerning Israel, and concerning Judah. For thus saith the Lord, We have heard a voice of trembling, of fear, and not of peace. Ask ye now, and see whether a man doth travail with child? wherefore do I see every man with his hands on his loins, as a woman in travail, and all faces are turned into paleness? Alas! for that day is great, so that none is like it: it is even the time of Jacob's trouble: but he shall be saved out of it" (Jer. xxx. 4-7). The time of Jacob's trouble is the time when the Jews, regathered, will be brought under this solemn judgment of God. "For it shall come to pass in that day, saith the Lord of hosts, that I will break his yoke from off thy neck, and will burst thy bonds, and strangers shall no more serve themselves of him: but they shall serve the Lord their God, and David their king, whom I will raise up unto them. Therefore fear thou not, O my servant Jacob, saith the Lord; neither be dismayed, O Israel: for, lo, I will save thee from afar, and thy seed from the land of their captivity: and Jacob shall return, and shall be in rest, and be quiet, and none shall make him afraid. For I am with thee, saith the Lord, to save thee: though I make a full end of all nations whither I have scattered thee, yet will I not make a full end of thee; but I will correct thee in measure, and will not leave thee altogether unpunished" (verses 8-11). Then in the 18th verse, "Thus saith the Lord, Behold I will bring again the captivity of Jacob's tents, and have mercy on his dwelling-places; and the city shall be builded upon her own heap, and the palace shall remain after the manner thereof. And out of them shall proceed thanksgiving, and the voice of them that make merry: and I will multiply them, and they shall not be few; I will also glorify them, and they shall not be small" (verses 18, 19). Abundant other scriptures give the same testimony as to their restoration, but this one I refer to because it speaks of the time of "Jacob's trouble," and of the solemn character of that day.

Now go to the 12th chapter of Daniel, and you will find the same time marked out. It is in the last, or seventieth week, at the close of the time spoken of as the forty-two months, the last half of the seventieth week of Daniel. "And at that time shall Michael stand up, the great prince which standeth for the children of thy people; and there shall be a time of trouble, such as never was since there was a nation even to that same time: and at that time thy people shall be delivered, every one that shall be found written in the book. And many of them that sleep in the dust of the earth shall awake, some to everlasting life, and some to shame and everlasting contempt. And they that be wise shall shine as the brightness of the firmament; and they that turn many to righteousness as the stars for ever and ever" (verses 1-3). Here, see, we have the remnant teaching the mass righteousness, if they will learn. But, some one says, I thought that was the resurrection. So it is, but it is not the resurrection of the body; it is the resurrection of the nation of Israel. This use of resurrection, as a figure of blessed restoration from national ruin, is not uncommon in Old Testament Scripture. Compare with this passage Isaiah xxvi., where Israel's trouble under Gentile lords is described. In verse 19 the Lord says, "Thy dead men shall live, together with my dead body shall they arise. Awake and sing, ye that dwell in dust: for thy dew is as the dew of herbs, and the earth shall cast out the dead." They are yet to be delivered from Gentile thraldom. Again, Ezekiel xxxvii. 1-14, speaks of Israel as not only dead, but buried nationally. There God says, "O my people, I will open your graves, and cause you to come up out of your graves, and bring you into the land of Israel" (ver. 12). Jeremiah shows us then the time of Jacob's trouble, whereas Daniel lets us know that it will be a time of trouble of which the like was never known before.

Now come to the scripture, which I read at the beginning of the meeting, Matthew xxiv., and you will find our Lord comments upon that time in the most remarkable way. Having detailed all the surrounding circumstances of that day, He says in verse 15, "When ye, therefore, shall see the abomination of desolation, spoken of by Daniel the prophet, stand in the holy place (whoso readeth, let him understand): then let them which be in Judea flee into the mountains: let him which is on the house-top not come down to take any thing out of his house: neither let him which is in the field return back to take his clothes. And woe unto them that are with child, and to them that give suck in those days! But pray ye that your flight be not in the winter, neither on the sabbath-day: for then shall be great tribulation, such as was not since the beginning of the world to this time, no, nor ever shall be. And except those days should be shortened, there should no flesh be saved: but for the elect's sake those days shall be shortened." What does the shortening of those days refer to? It carries you back to another scripture in the book of Daniel, chap. xii., verse 11, "And from the time that the daily sacrifice shall be taken away, and the abomination that maketh desolate set up, there shall be a thousand two hundred and ninety days." That is more than a thousand two hundred and sixty; it is three and a half years and one month more. That is, the end of the seventieth week will scarcely bring in the contemplated blessing, they must hold out in their trouble and wait thirty days longer; and then Daniel adds, "Blessed is he that waiteth, and cometh to the thousand three hundred and five and thirty days." That is another forty-five days further on. At that moment, when God puts His hand to things, He does not take very long about it. After the seventieth week closes, another month will produce wonderful effects, and at the end of the thousand three hundred and thirty-five days the reign of the Son of Man will be established.

But the Lord, in speaking to His disciples here in Matthew, says, "When ye therefore shall see the abomination of desolation, spoken of by Daniel the prophet, stand in the holy place, (whoso readeth, let him understand,) then let them which be in Judea flee into the mountains." The moment they see idolatry in Jerusalem, let them take refuge where they can, because He tells us in the 21st verse, " Then shall be great tribulation, such as was not since the beginning of the world to this time, no, nor ever shall be." There never has been such trouble, and there never shall again be such trouble, as at that moment, and for the reason that idolatry is sanctioned, maintained, and protected, in what is ostensibly the temple of God. But you may say, I thought Christians always had trouble. Well, no doubt, we do get it, and it does not do us any harm, but always good. Whenever there is a bit of sharp persecution, you will always find that the saints are very bright and happy, and very bold in their testimony for the Lord ; but when everything is quiet they are apt to go to sleep. It is quite true that "in the world ye shall have tribulation," for our Lord says so. What then are we to do? Run away from it? The Lord alone can guide us at the moment. Here, however, there is clear instruction for an earthly people, in peculiar circumstances, at a special moment of coming trial. "Woe unto them that are with child, and to them that give suck in those days ! But pray ye that your flight be not in winter, neither on the sabbath-day." Why not on the Sabbath day ? Because the Jew could not, under the law, go beyond a Sabbath day's journey—not quite half a mile—on the

Sabbath day. No Christian would think that there is anything wrong in travelling ten times that distance, on the Lord's Day, if it were to serve the Lord, say in preaching the Gospel. Not that the two days are identical, because I claim for the Lord's Day a far higher sanctity than ever was accorded to the Sabbath. The Lord's Day is the day that marks Christianity, and the Sabbath is what was connected with Judaism, and it is a remarkable fact that the Lord spent the Sabbath day in the grave.

There is great grace in the Lord's desiring that no obstacle might be in the way of those who were bid to flee then,—" For then shall be great tribulation, such as was not since the beginning of the world to this time, no, nor ever shall be," &c. He gives them further warning not to listen to this man, or that, because they have then distinctly to understand, that, at that moment, He is, Himself, coming to their rescue. " Immediately after the tribulation of those days," He says, " shall appear the sign of the Son of Man in heaven : and then shall all the tribes of the earth mourn, and they shall see the Son of Man coming in the clouds of heaven with power and great glory" (verses 29, 30). I know that expositors have attempted to explain these verses, by saying their fulfilment was the Romans taking Jerusalem. But on the very face of it, we cannot accept that. The Romans did not come from the east, but from the west,—" As the lightning cometh out of the east and shineth even unto the west, so shall also the coming of the Son of man be. For wheresoever the carcase is, there will the eagles be gathered together" (verses 27, 28). What is the carcase? Corrupt, dead Judaism.

If you turn now to the 13th of St Mark, you will

there find identical testimony as to the tribulation. " For in those days shall be affliction such as was not from the beginning of the creation which God created unto this time, neither shall be. And except that the Lord had shortened those days, no flesh should be saved : but for the elect's sake, whom he hath chosen, he hath shortened the days " (verses 19, 20). We have read two distinct statements in the Old Testament Scriptures as to this special time of trouble ; and you have the two evangelists, Matthew and Mark, each speaking of it, specifically, as a special time, and then, in the Revelation, you have confirmatory testimony. Turn there for one moment, and you will see exactly who they are who go through, and come out of " the great tribulation." Read the 7th chapter. The first half is occupied with telling you, that there were sealed twelve thousand of each of the twelve tribes of Israel —God will have His own testimony—and you have therefore this limited number—one hundred and forty-four thousand of Israel. Then in the 9th verse we read : —" After this I beheld, and, lo, a great multitude, which no man could number "—it is refreshing in its largeness—" of all nations, and kindreds, and people, and tongues, stood before the throne, and before the Lamb, clothed with white robes, and palms in their hands: and cried with a loud voice, saying, Salvation to our God which sitteth upon the throne, and unto the Lamb." I confess I do not like to have to spoil a happy, and pretty illusion, but truth demands it. Many—perhaps, at some time, all—of us have thought this was heaven, but we must give that thought up ; it is not a heavenly, it is an earthly, scene, and company.

But I hear some one saying, Oh, but I thought

this meant us Christians. Thank God, it is not us. We have something infinitely better. This scene is enacted on the earth. We see first, Israel's remnant blessed on the earth, and then we get those countless white-robed Gentile multitudes on the earth. They have to do with God now, in the enjoyment of His grace; they are in definite relationship with God, and they have also palms in their hands,—they are victorious. They are seen standing *before*, not around the throne, and they ascribe salvation to God, on the throne, and to the Lamb. Who the "elders" are here, you can learn from Revelation, 4th and 5th chapters. The four and twenty elders represent the heavenly saints. We are supposed to understand all about that day, for God is giving us light about it in this day. We are to know it now. The saint of Christ, the saint of heaven, is supposed to understand all about the earth, because his heart is so free, and happy, in the enjoyment of what he possesses himself, that he is able to think of, and be interested in, what is going on in the earth.

Now, in proof of this statement, observe,—"One of the *elders* answered, saying unto me, What are these which are arrayed in white robes? and whence came they? And I said unto him, *Sir, thou knowest*. And he said to me, These are they which came out of great tribulation, and have washed their robes, and made them white in the blood of the Lamb. Therefore are they before the throne of God, and serve him day and night in his temple: and he that sitteth on the throne shall dwell among them. They shall hunger no more, neither thirst any more; neither shall the sun light on them, nor any heat. For the Lamb, which is in the midst of the throne, shall feed them, and shall lead them unto living fountains of waters; and God shall wipe away all tears from their eyes" (Rev. vii. 13-17). They had come out of *the* great tribulation. They had been true to God, and faithful in it, and their robes were washed in the blood of the Lamb. They were cleansed ones, owned to be such, hence are always *before* the throne, a special class, and serve God day and night in His temple. This at once distinguishes them from the Church, the heavenly saints. There is no temple in Revelation xxi. 22, for the Lord God Almighty, and the Lamb are the temple. This white-robed multitude have a priestly place, in the temple, on this earth, and they will have the deep consolations of God, worth all the sorrows they have passed through. It is a lovely picture of how, after the tribulation, God brings them into perfect blessing on earth.

The Church of God, the body of Christ, will not go through the tribulation. There have not been wanting those who have asserted that she will, but to any simple believer the distinct, absolute statement of the blessed Lord, to the overcomer, in Philadelphia, settles that finally. In the 3rd chapter of Revelation and 10th verse, we get this lovely word—"Because thou hast kept the word of my patience, I also will keep thee *from* (*out of*, not *in*) the hour of temptation, which shall come upon all the world, to try them that dwell upon the earth. Behold, I come quickly: hold that fast which thou hast, that no man take thy crown." Thus while the 7th chapter distinctly brings out who will be passing through, and coming out of, the great tribulation,—viz., all those that are blessed of God in Israel, and likewise an innumerable company from among the Gentiles,—we see the other side in this 3rd chapter, and learn who will *not* go through it—the Church, the Bride of Christ. Will the Christian pass through it? No; "because thou hast kept the word of my patience, I also will *keep thee from the hour* of temptation." Jesus, as it were, says, You have known Me, you have loved Me, and I am going to come for you before that day sets in. "Behold I come quickly." Beloved friends, how blessed thus to hear His sweet voice speaking to us. I ask you, are you among this number, that have believed in His name, have heard His voice, and are waiting for the Lord Jesus Christ from heaven? Are you ready, are you prepared, are you His? If not, let me say as I close, Oh! turn to Him now, and escape that tribulation. Get into the very presence of God now, into the enjoyment of His own grace. Approach now, trust, and know the Lord Jesus, as the risen Saviour, and then wait for Him, as the coming Bridegroom.

THE SUN OF RIGHTEOUSNESS.

MALACHI iii. 16-18, iv.

Lecture V.

YOU will remember, dear friends, that on the first night we were together, we were looking, a little, at the blessed Lord in the character of "The Morning Star." You will further remember that it is in *the last* chapter of the New Testament, that the Lord Jesus says specifically, "I am the bright and morning star." Now is it not remarkable that the New Testament closes with the apparition of the Morning Star, whereas the Old Testament closes with the rising of the Sun, "the Sun of righteousness." Every one knows that the morning star is always visible before the sun. And you say, What is the Scripture meaning of that? Simply this, that what the last chapter of the New Testament brings before us, will be certainly fulfilled, before that which the last chapter of the Old Testament brings before us. It is but another illustration of the Scripture principle, "The last shall be first." Do you inquire what is the Morning Star? It is the Lord Jesus Christ. And what is the Sun of Righteousness? It is the Lord Jesus Christ, without doubt, but the Lord Jesus looked at in a totally different way. As "the morning star," He shows Himself in heavenly glory, as the One who says, "Behold I come quickly"; and He is coming. For whom? For those who are His own, His own redeemed people. If He came to-night, beloved friends, He would come for you and me, if we belong to Him. You say, But suppose I do not belong to Him? Well, you will get your portion in this last chapter of the Old Testament, and it is by no means a very bright outlook, for an unsaved man.

I do not deny, for a moment, that many a true and honest soul has looked at the " Sun of righteousness," as being the gospel of the grace of God, but such is not the meaning of it, I am persuaded. The context of Scripture will always explain its meaning, and if you will take the trouble to read the context of the passage, where the expression " the Sun of righteousness shall arise with healing in his wings," occurs, you will immediately see to whom it refers—a company of people, in terrible sorrow, but, who are marked by one lovely characteristic, viz.—" They that feared the Lord." I do not know whether you observed, as I read, that three times over the Spirit of God marks out a certain company by this characteristic—" Then they that feared the Lord," " Them that feared the Lord" (iii. 16), and " Unto you that fear my name " (iv. 2). What marks the people, to whom the Sun of Righteousness shall arise, is this, that they " fear the Lord." They are godly.

Now, I do not suppose your nearest friend supposes you to be a godly person, if you are not converted. No, I do not think that your nearest friend would exactly put that characteristic upon you, if you are an unconverted person, because of the ungodly it is said there is no fear of God before their eyes. The mark of the unregene. ate man is always this, the fear of God is not in him. The fear of hell may be, the fear of judgment, and torment may be, and ought to be there, but that is not the fear of God. Ah, beloved friends, it is a blessed thing to be a God-fearing person, whether in this present time—the Christian era—or in that of which the last of Malachi speaks. Are you a person that fears God? "Blessed is the man that feareth alway," says Scripture. The thief on the cross turned round to his wicked neighbour,—grace had opened his eyes and opened his heart, and saved his soul,—and he said, "Dost thou not fear God, seeing thou art in the same condemnation? And we indeed justly; for we receive the due reward of our deeds; but this man has done nothing amiss." Then he said unto Jesus, "Lord remember me when thou comest in thy kingdom. And Jesus said unto him, Verily I say unto thee, To-day shalt thou be with me in Paradise."

The man that fears the Lord is never forgotten by the Lord. These men, that Malachi speaks of, feared God, and I say, beloved friends, that there is nothing more blessed for a man than that. "The fear of the Lord is the beginning of knowledge" (Prov. i. 7). Again, "Fear the Lord and depart from evil" (Prov. iii. 7). It is ever a happy thing for a man when he fears the Lord. I do not doubt that many a man may have the fear of God, who may not have the full enjoyment of the Gospel; but the point in this chapter is that the Lord has His eye upon, and blessedly addresses, a certain company who feared Him. They are those whom He will save, whom He will deliver; nay, more, He says, "Ye shall tread down the wicked." Of course, they cannot be Christians, for no Christian would do that. No Christian would tread down the wicked man, it is foreign to the spirit and genius of Christianity, whose motto is "Bless them which persecute you: bless, and curse not" (Rom. xii. 14)

You may say, Who then are these? I spoke a little, last Lord's Day evening, of a certain company of godly Jews here upon the earth, who,—after the Lord has come into the air, after the Church of God is taken up, after antichrist has appeared, and the beast has made its appearance, and full Satanic power is manifest upon the earth,—come on the scene, pious earthly saints, and they speak of the things of the Lord. They fear the Lord, they delight in the Lord, and although they are passing through terrible persecution, and tribulation for the Lord's sake, they are not crushed. Here God speaks by Malachi, and says of them this—"They shall be mine in that day when I make up my jewels." I will read it again. "Then they that feared the Lord spake often one to another: and the Lord hearkened, and heard it; and a book of remembrance was written before him for them that feared the Lord, and that thought upon his name. And they shall be mine, saith the Lord of hosts, in that day when I make up my jewels; and"—look—"I will spare them, as a man spareth his own son that serveth him." This is a company of witnesses alive on earth when the Lord is coming to judge righteously, and about to deal with the earth. God says about them, "I will spare them."

Although many Christians might not take much interest in, or comfort out of, these last verses, I believe there is coming the day when there will be a good many saints upon the earth, who will take the deepest, and sweetest comfort out of them, because they will apply to them, in a moment, when they are passing through terrible persecution for the Lord's sake. I say again they are Jewish saints. Do you ask me, then, What means the rising of the Sun of Righteousness?

The Lord unfolds the meaning, plainly, and simply here. He says, "Behold, the day cometh, that shall burn as an oven; and all the proud, yea, and all that do wickedly, shall be stubble; and the day that cometh shall burn them up, saith the Lord of hosts, that it shall leave them neither root nor branch." That is not the Gospel day. The day in which your lot and mine is cast, is the day when the Gospel comes fresh down from glory, and the Spirit of God labours to bring your heart to the heavenly Saviour, to attract you to Him, and to save you. There is no "oven" in this day, but "the day cometh," says He, "that shall burn as an oven." Solemn prediction of what is coming! It is the day of the Lord. The day of the appearing of the Son of Man, the day when the Sun of Righteousness arises with healing in His wings, will be an awful day for the wicked man. Doubtless men will get on swimmingly till the Lord appears—grandly till the Son of Man appears. It will be a day when men will be rubbing their hands smoothly, and saying, "Peace and safety." Yes, but it is when they are *saying* this, that "then sudden destruction cometh upon them, as travail upon a woman with child (*i.e.*, it is inevitable), and they shall not escape" (1 Thess. v. 3). It will be the day when Satan governs and rules, when Christ is utterly ignored, and forgotten, and antichrist is owned in His place, and that which goes on in that day will suit the hearts of men of the world, it will suit you, my unconverted friend, absolutely. There will be no Gospel then. You will not have a godly mother praying for you, or anybody persuading you to go to a Gospel meeting, or any one thrusting a tract into your hand. You will be saying, Thank God, I have got rid of all those unwelcome interruptions to my happiness. You *will* have got rid of them all, and you will be in a fool's paradise, with the judgment of God just about to burst on your head. The Lord deliver you, my friend, yet unsaved, from the day of His wrath, by giving you now to know Himself, in the day of His grace.

Look then, the wicked are going to be dealt with by God, "But unto you that fear my name shall the Sun of righteousness arise with healing in his wings." That is very simple. The godly are looking for deliverance—for the appearing of the Saviour, the Messiah; looking, as many a man, who has gone through a black night of tempest, looks. Look at the mariner passing through a terrible storm at sea, in the darkness of night. How he longs for the morning, and he takes hope and says, It will not be long before daylight comes, and by-and-by the sun arises, and what a comfort there is in the light. Do you not think it will be a great comfort for the people of God upon earth in that day, when the Saviour—Jesus, their own Messiah, their Deliverer, comes? Immense comfort! "And so all Israel shall be saved; as it is written, There shall come out of Sion the Deliverer, and turn away ungodliness from Jacob" (Rom. xi. 26). It will be very wonderful comfort, and therefore the figure here, "the Sun of righteousness shall arise with *healing* in his wings."

I should not like to be misunderstood as to this point. It is not the Gospel of the grace of God, though I fully believe, that many an anxious soul has gone down on his knees, and cried with deep earnestness, that the Sun of Righteousness might arise to him, with healing in His wings, and the Lord has answered that prayer. God knew what the man wanted. He wanted the Gospel, and got it too, and, if you want the Gospel, you are welcome to it; yea, more welcome to it than to the air you draw into your lungs at this moment. Freer to you than the very air you breathe is God's precious salvation. Whatever you are, whatever you have been, and whatever you have done, God sends out now the word of salvation, and if you are anxious men, or troubled women, you are heartily welcome to it, but that is not the interpretation of the scripture before us.

This scripture means that Christ, in glory, and power, and majesty, and having everything in His hand, comes for the deliverance, and help, and healing of the godly amongst those who are His ancient people upon the earth—the Jews gathered back into their own land—restored. They are a little company, whom Scripture speaks of by a term, which, when once apprehended, will help you better to understand Old Testament Scriptures. I will therefore ask you to go to the 10th chapter of Isaiah, and you will there find that this company is designated by God as the remnant: "And it shall come to pass in that day, that *the remnant* of Israel, and such as are escaped of the house of Jacob, shall no more again stay upon him that smote them; but shall stay upon the Lord, the Holy One of Israel, in truth. *The remnant* shall return, even *the remnant* of Jacob, unto the mighty God" (verses 20, 21). This language brings out distinctly the fact, that there will be some saints upon earth, in the day after the Holy Ghost, and the Church are taken up, after the testimony of Christianity is over, and while the general apostasy is manifest, and antichrist is ruling. God, who never left Himself without a witness on earth, and never will, raises up in that day a company who testify to Jehovah, and who are spoken of in numberless passages of the Old Testament Scriptures: often by this term, "the remnant."

In the first instance they seem to belong only to the two tribes of Judah and Benjamin, and, if you want to learn more about them, turn to the 13th chapter of Zechariah. There again you find God speaking of them in another way: "And it shall come to pass, that in all the land, saith the Lord, two parts therein shall be cut off and die; but the third shall be left therein. And I will bring the third part through the fire, and will refine them as silver is refined, and will try them as gold is tried: they shall call on my name, and I will hear them: I will say, It is my people: and they shall say, The Lord is my God" (verses 8, 9). There is almost universal declension, and apostasy, and a giving up by the Jews generally, of all their own peculiar truth. But in spite of the idolatry in their midst, and the terrible power of the enemy against them, led on by the antichrist, and the beast, God has, as He always will have, a witness to Himself, in this "third part."

In this passage we see that only one-third escapes, the rest being cut off in judgment. The two tribes—Judah and Benjamin—were those that were in the land when the Lord Jesus Christ died. The ten tribes had been taken into captivity, long before the two tribes were carried away to Babylon. Out of the captivity of Babylon, a certain number came back into Judæa, in the days of Ezra, and Nehemiah. Their descendants were in the land when Jesus came, and Him they refused, and got Pilate to condemn to death, and they were glad when He died. They have lying against them, therefore, this grave and serious sin, that they murdered their Messiah. When again restored to their land, and evidences arise, indicating Messiah's return, this sin will press upon their conscience, for God says, " I will pour upon the house of David, and upon the inhabitants of Jerusalem, the spirit of grace and of supplications; and they shall look upon me whom they have pierced, and they shall mourn for him, as one mourneth for his only son, and shall be in bitterness for him, as one that is in bitterness for his firstborn. In that day shall there be a great mourning in Jerusalem, as the mourning of Hadadrimmon in the valley of Megiddon. And the land shall mourn, every family apart; the family of the house of David apart, and their wives apart; the family of the house of Nathan apart, and their wives apart; the family of the house of Levi apart, and their wives apart; the family of Shimei apart, and their wives apart; all the families that remain, every family apart, and their wives apart. In that day there shall be a fountain opened to the house of David, and to the inhabitants of Jerusalem, for sin and for uncleanness" (Zech. xii. 10-14, xiii. 1).

The repentance will be deep and real. Each, separately, will take part therein. A Nathan will not rebuke a David, as in days gone by (2 Sam. xii. 7-12), but will judge himself. Levi and Simeon, who were companions in murder (Gen. xxxiv. 25, 16) will repent apart.

I have little doubt that the tide has set in, at this moment, by which the Jews are going to be replaced in Palestine. Their return will begin, perhaps, as the outcome of political intrigue, and matters will go on swimmingly till they think themselves securely reestablished. If you refer to the 18th chapter of Isaiah you will find, in figurative language, the fact that they are put back in their land, but when everything seems to be all right, and happy, God blows upon the whole thing. "For afore the harvest, when the bud is perfect, and the sour grape is ripening in the flower, he shall both cut off the sprigs with pruning hooks, and take away and cut down the branches. They shall be left together unto the fowls of the mountains, and to the beasts of the earth : and the fowls shall summer upon them, and all the beasts of the earth shall winter upon them. In that time shall the present be brought unto the Lord of hosts of a people scattered and peeled, and from a people terrible from their beginning hitherto ; a nation meted out and trodden under foot, whose land the rivers have spoiled, to the place of the name of the Lord of hosts, the mount Zion" (Isa. xviii. 5-7). The Lord breaks up men's plans, because He is not going to have His people put back into His land, and theirs, as the outcome of man's political ideas.

When the Lord takes His people back, He will take them back Himself. He will, however, have to purge them. The two tribes are purged after they have reached the land. One-third is faithful to God, spite of antichrist's wiles and force, but "two parts therein shall be cut off and die." The two tribes are commonly called, in Scripture, the Jews. This is their technical term. The ten tribes are, on the other hand, spoken of as "the house of Israel." In Zechariah you find the two tribes returning, and being purged in the land. At a later date God will bring back the ten tribes. The two tribes come back *in unbelief*, and are purged, by God, in the land, and two-thirds are cut off in judgment. The ten tribes will be purged of God on their way to the land, whither the Lord Himself will gather them. They will be purged in the wilderness, as their fathers were. This is given to us in Ezekiel, "And I will bring you out from the people, and will gather you out of the countries wherein ye are scattered, with a mighty hand, and with a stretched-out arm, and with fury poured out. And I will bring you into the wilderness of the people, and there will I plead with you face to face. Like as I pleaded with your fathers in the wilderness of the land of Egypt, so will I plead with you, saith the Lord God. And I will cause you to pass under the rod, and I will bring you into the bond of the covenant: and I will purge out from among you the rebels, and them that transgress against me: I will bring them forth out of the country where they sojourn, and they shall not enter into the land of Israel: and ye shall know that I am the Lord" (Ezek. xx. 34-38).

Now, let us turn to the prophet Amos for confirmation, "Lo, I will command, and I will sift the house of Israel among all nations, like as corn is sifted in a sieve, yet shall not the least grain fall upon the earth. All the sinners of my people shall die by the sword, which say, The evil shall not overtake nor prevent us" (Amos ix. 9, 10). These scriptures make it abundantly plain, that the two tribes are purged, after they have got back into the land in unbelief, whereas the ten tribes are purged in the wilderness, while they are on their way to the land.

I ask you now to look a little bit into the book of Psalms, and for this reason,—that the question, Why does the Lord come in this character of the Sun of Righteousness? may be answered. Turn back to the 93rd Psalm, and you will find what is exceedingly interesting, and instructive. From the 93rd to the 100th Psalm — really a little book by itself — the Spirit of God shows us various of His activities in "the remnant," just at the moment that is characterised by the return of the First-begotten from the dead ; the Lord Jesus, as Jehovah, then coming back manifestly into the world. We do not get here the hope of the Church, nor the truth of the Bridegroom coming into the air, and the Bride meeting Him there. What we get is the return of the Messiah, who really is Jehovah, to the earth, for the deliverance, and help, and comfort of His ancient people. You will find in this little book of Psalms the whole series of coming events developed, with the utmost exactness.

The 93rd Psalm is prefatory to the rest. We will read it therefore, "The Lord reigneth ; he is clothed with majesty ; the Lord is clothed with strength, wherewith he hath girded himself : the world also is stablished, that it cannot be moved. Thy throne is established of old : thou art from everlasting. The floods have lifted up, O Lord, the floods have lifted up their voice ; the floods lift up their waves. The Lord on high is mightier than the noise of many waters, yea, than the mighty waves of the sea. Thy testimonies are very sure : holiness becometh thine house, O Lord, for ever." It is what I may call the anticipatory inauguration of Messiah's reign. He is coming, that is the point. Yes, He is coming, but what brings Him ? The 94th Psalm answers that question. Briefly, that Psalm is the fervent, earnest, longing cry of the remnant, of which I have been speaking, who, in their sorrow, and need, and distress, suffering keenly under the power of Satan, the pressure of antichrist, and tremendously persecuted by the enemies of the Lord, turn round to God, and cry to Him for deliverance.

We shall trace this as we read it. "O Lord God, to whom vengeance belongeth; O God, to whom vengeance belongeth, shew thyself" (*margin*, shine forth, see also Ps. lxxx. 1—they cry for, and await the rising Sun). "Lift up thyself, thou Judge of the earth; render a reward to the proud. Lord, how long shall the wicked, how long shall the wicked triumph? How long shall they utter and speak hard things? and all the workers of iniquity boast themselves? They break in pieces thy people, O Lord, and afflict thine heritage. They slay the widow and the stranger, and murder the fatherless. Yet they say, The Lord shall not see, neither shall the God of Jacob regard it." Ah! but He does, and lower down, in the 14th verse, you will see they have good reason for their cry. They say, "The Lord will not cast off his people, neither will he forsake his inheritance. But judgment shall return unto righteousness." Remarkable expression—"Judgment shall return unto righteousness." When did judgment depart from righteousness? Do you not remember? When this very people had dragged the Son of God to the bar of the Gentile governor. And do you not remember when Pilate had said, "I find no fault in him," they cried "Crucify him"? Yes, in Pilate's hall, over eighteen hundred years ago, judgment in the person of Pilate, and righteousness in the person of Jesus, parted company, and the innocent Man was condemned and slain. Thank God, that Man is my Saviour, I hope He is yours.

But the day is coming when "judgment shall return unto righteousness." Everything will be altered in that day. When the Lord returns in power and glory, "judgment shall return unto righteousness, and all the upright in heart shall follow it." Then the remnant say,—" Unless the Lord had been my help, my soul had almost dwelt in silence. When I said, My foot slippeth; thy mercy, O Lord, held me up. In the multitude of my thoughts within me thy comforts delight my soul;" and then they ask this question,—" Shall the throne of iniquity have fellowship with thee, which frameth mischief by a law?" (ver. 20.) Here we see how the godly Jew, by-and-by, will turn back to the 94th Psalm, and interpret his difficulties, under the pressure, and power, of antichrist's reign, with every semblance of Christianity gone, and all his own religious feasts, and rites set aside. Although they have rebuilt their temple, set up their altar, and resumed their sacrifices once more, all has been put aside. Hence the prayer and query,—" Shall the throne of iniquity have fellowship with thee, which frameth mischief by a law? They gather themselves together against the soul of the righteous, and condemn the innocent blood. But the Lord is my defence; and my God is the rock of my refuge. And he shall bring upon them their own iniquity, and shall cut them off in their own wickedness; yea, the Lord our God shall cut them off." It is the cry of the remnant, at that moment, that really causes their sun to "shine forth," and brings the Son of Man upon the scene, in answer to their cry, " Lord, how long shall the wicked triumph?" (ver. 3.)

Similarly, you hear their voice in the 6th chapter of Revelation, when John saw "under the altar the souls of them that were slain for the word of God, and for the testimony which they held: and they cried with a loud voice, saying, How long, O Lord, holy and true, dost thou not judge and avenge our blood on them that dwell on the earth? And white robes were given unto every one of them: and it was said unto them, that they should rest yet for a little season, until their fellow-servants also and their brethren, that should be killed as they were, should be fulfilled" (verses 9-11). God had been patient. The indignation which He had been pouring upon His people had not yet come to its full height, and therefore He tarries, and bids them be patient. But He will come, and they know it; and what therefore does this remnant do? They turn round, in Psalm xcv., to their brethren, yet unprepared, of the house of Israel, and say, Get ready. And then, in Psalm xcvi., to the Gentiles—the heathen generally—they say, Get ready. They render what I call a double testimony. It is a testimony on the one hand to their brethren, and, on the other, to the Gentiles, to get ready because the Messiah is coming.

Look at the 95th Psalm. It is a summons to Israel to get ready. "*O come.*" It is the earnest cry of the evangelists of that day—" O come, let us sing unto the Lord; let us make a joyful noise to the Rock of our salvation. Let us come before his presence with thanksgiving, and make a joyful noise unto him with psalms. For the Lord is a great God, and a great King above all gods. In his hand are the deep places of the earth; the strength of the hills is his also. The sea is his, and he made it; and his hands formed the dry land. O come, let us worship and bow down; let us kneel before the Lord our Maker. For he is our God: and we are the people of his pasture, and the sheep of his hand. To-day, if ye will hear his voice, (Ah! may I not say this unto you also, my unsaved friend? To-day, if ye will hear his voice,) harden not your heart, as in the provocation, and as in the day of temptation in the wilderness, when your fathers tempted me, proved me, and saw my work. Forty years long was I grieved with this generation, and said, It is a people that do err in their heart, and they have not known my ways: unto whom I sware in my wrath, that they should not enter into my rest." It is a beautiful, and simple, earnest, loving testimony, on the part of those godly saints of the Lord, to their Israelitish brethren, to get ready, because Messiah, Jehovah, is about to appear to "judge the world with righteousness, and his people with his truth."

Is that all? Nay, God puts it into their hearts to turn round in that day to the heathen. Read the 96th Psalm. The call is to "all the earth" now (ver. 1). We are not to forget the heathen, beloved friends, but if we do, they will be remembered in that day. People sometimes say, What will happen to all the heathen before the Lord comes? Well, the 96th Psalm is a very great comfort to my heart. Christians have made very little progress in converting the heathen, and we all ought to be far more earnest about that than we are. It is a sad reflection that a very much larger proportion of the earth's surface was Christian twelve hundred years ago, than is the case, at the present time. In the sixth century almost all China was Christian.

I rejoice to think the day is coming, when evangelists, who will be commissioned, and called of God to the work, and who will do the work magnificently, will go out to call the heathen. You may say, How do you know their work will succeed? We saw the fruit of their work last Lord's Day evening. Do you not recollect that "great multitude which no man could number, of all nations, and kindreds, and peoples, and tongues"? (Rev. vii. 9.) How were they converted? By hearing the preachers. Who the preachers are, is not there stated, but the effect of their preaching is palpable, and in Ps. xcvi. I believe we get the preachers. "O sing unto the Lord a new song; sing unto the Lord, all the earth. Sing unto the Lord, bless his name; shew forth his salvation from day to day. Declare his glory among the heathen, his wonders among all people. For the Lord is great, and greatly to be praised: he is to be feared above all gods. For all the gods of the nation are idols: but the Lord made the heavens. Honour and majesty are before him; strength and beauty are in his sanctuary. Give unto the Lord, O ye kindreds of the people, give unto the Lord glory and strength. Give unto the Lord the glory due unto his name: bring an offering, and come into his courts. O worship the Lord in the beauty of holiness; fear before him, all the earth. Say among the heathen, that the Lord reigneth" (Ps. xcvi. 1-10).

That is a splendid sermon, though I could not preach it, for the simplest reason possible, viz., that He does not reign yet. Nay, He is in heavenly glory now. He has been refused here, and has gone to heaven, but He is going to reign. In that day, these earnest souls go out, and say, "The Lord reigneth." What then? "The world also shall be established that it shall not be moved: he shall judge the people righteously. **Let the heavens rejoice, and let the earth be glad ; let the sea roar, and the fulness thereof. Let the field be joyful, and all that is therein ; then shall all the trees of the wood rejoice before the**

Lord ; for he cometh, for he cometh to judge the earth : he shall judge the world with righteousness, and the people with his truth" (Ps. xcvi. 10-13). They go out with this beautiful testimony to the earthly rights of the Messiah, the now rejected Jesus.

I should like to show you, in connection with this Psalm, two other scriptures. One of them is the 24th of Matthew, where we shall see what our Lord Jesus Christ says about this matter. There He is unfolding future events for Israel, and the Jew. He says distinctly, that there shall be unspeakable troubles and sorrows, and (12th ver.), " because iniquity shall abound, the love of many shall wax cold. But he that shall endure unto the end, the same shall be saved. And this gospel of the kingdom shall be preached in all the world, for a witness unto all nations ; and then shall the end come." *All the world* shall hear of Him, as the coming King. Thank God for that. Only a small portion of the world has had "the gospel of the grace of God" preached to it, in our day, but I comfort my heart, that within a very short time from this night, if the Lord were to come, and the Church to be taken up, and this blessed company, of what I may call earthly evangelists, appeared, a wonderful change would be manifest. "This *gospel of the kingdom* shall be preached in all the world for a witness unto all nations." Christ does not say, or mean, that all nations will be converted, because, I shall yet show you, that many will not be converted, but, nevertheless, they will have presented to them a clear distinct testimony.

But recollect, friends, that there will be no comfort for a lost man, who hears now the gospel of a heavenly Saviour, to remember by-and-by, that he might have been " saved " but for his folly, and unbelief, and there will be no excuse, for the nations of that day, if they come under the condemnation of the Son of Man, as given in Matthew xxv., where the nations are gathered together before Him, and judged. It will be no comfort for them to remember that they heard of the coming Messiah, and refused to bow the knee to Him. What they will hear is "the gospel of the kingdom." You may say to me, Are not the two identical? The two identical! The gospel of the grace of God, identical with the gospel of the kingdom— the announcement that the Son of Man is coming, by-and-by, to put things right by judgment! The difference between them is immense. The gospel of the grace of God is this, you may be saved to-night through simple faith in Jesus, who has come into this world, and has died for sinners on the cross. The work of atonement has been effected by Him, that whoever believes in Him might be saved, the moment there is faith in that precious Saviour. You are welcome to that Saviour, He wants you. That Saviour's voice rings through this earth, through this hall, and says to many a weary soul, " Come unto me, all ye that labour and are heavy laden, and I will give you rest." He brings you pardon, peace, life, forgiveness, justification, salvation, where you are, and as you are. The gospel of the grace of God takes your heart to heaven, whereas the gospel of the kingdom, if believed, will make a man very happy on earth eventually, because it is the assertion of the glory and rights of the Son of Man, about to come and purify the earth by His righteous judgment.

We see, then, that the gospel of the kingdom will go out to all nations, and then shall the end come.

This allegation is confirmed by another scripture—the 14th of Revelation. It is very remarkable that this latter chapter, which contemplates the time of the energy of antichrist, and the wrath of the beast, when persecution is going on apace, opens with this, "A Lamb stood on the Mount Sion, and with him a hundred and forty and four thousand, having his Father's name written in their foreheads. And I heard a voice from heaven, as the voice of many waters, and as the voice of a great thunder; and I heard the voice of harpers harping with their harps · and they sung as it were a new song before the throne, and before the four beasts, and the elders: and no man could learn that song but the hundred and forty and four thousand, which were redeemed from the earth. These are they which were not defiled with women; for they are virgins. These are they which follow the Lamb whithersoever he goeth. These were redeemed from among men, being the first-fruits unto God and to the Lamb. And in their mouth was found no guile: for they are without fault before the throne of God." Here again we have the remnant, seen on that which is the centre of dominion, and glory, in a renewed earth—Mount Sion, where the Lamb shall reign. They had suffered, but not unto death; suffered, as Christ had in His life, in owning God to be His Father. Hence His name, and His Father's is on their foreheads. It is clearly an earthly company of saints.

Now, a good many expositors of prophecy, in the present day, are most anxious to make out that the one hundred and forty-four thousand here spoken of, are a particularly bright, earnest, fervent set of *living* Christians, who alone are to be caught up to meet the

Lord in the air, when He comes. That I believe to be a thorough mistake, because it is an earthly scene, and there is not one word about their being caught up. The scene—Mount Sion, the seat of royal grace—is upon earth, and they are evidently an earthly company of Jews, who are standing firm, and faithful for God, in that day when truth has altogether been given up. They are the first-fruits of the new scene which God is about to inaugurate. They had not corrupted themselves when all others had. They neither loved nor made a lie, nor gave in to it. Hence, they are without fault, and they share the Lamb's earthly place and glory, being His companions whithersoever He goes in the manifestation of that glory.

The idea that the Lord, when He comes, is going to take up only one hundred and forty-four thousand bright, earnest Christians, is, I think, most curious, not to say mistaken. I most earnestly trust and hope that you, my Christian friends, will not be beguiled by such a poverty-stricken theory, as unworthy of Christ, and His grace, as could well be imagined. If the Lord Jesus came to-night a good many more than one hundred and forty-four thousand would go up to meet Him in the air. Why? Because all believers in Him are "members of his body, of his flesh, and of his bones" (Eph. v. 30), and the bride of Christ—not a bit of her only—must go up to meet the Bridegroom. What do you think of a man who only wants a bit of his bride on the marriage day? He wants her altogether—of course he does. And what a mercy to be numbered amongst those that compose that Bride. Such an idea, therefore, as I have indicated, I believe to be foreign altogether to Scripture, and, for this reason, that Scripture presents, as the hope of the whole Church, which is the Bride, the return of the blessed Lord Jesus Christ as the Bridegroom. No man can fix the date when He will come, but He is coming, and coming quickly, and when He comes He will take up all those "that are Christ's," the dead first, then those that are alive and remain. Therefore, I have no hesitation in saying—and you may charge me if you like with speaking dogmatically—that the idea is totally foreign to the sustained testimony of the Word of God.

A little careful perusal of the Scripture will show that the one hundred and forty-four thousand are an earthly company, and not a heavenly company at all. The "man-child" of Revelation xii. will have been "caught up unto God, and to his throne," before the scenes of chapter xiv. are enacted. But who is the man-child? Christ? Yes, but not Christ only. Those that are Christ's, I take it, are included in the expression. The man-child is going "to rule all nations with a rod of iron"; and in Rev. ii. 26, 27, we find the Lord promising this position to the overcomer in Thyatira. Hence, not only is it Christ, but those that belong to Christ, and who, like Himself, have been taken up to heaven.

Returning again to Revelation xiv., we find the connection between the position, and portion of the remnant, and the angelic testimony of verses 6 and 7, which are practically the carrying out of the statement of the Lord in Matthew xxiv. 14: "And I saw another angel fly in the midst of heaven, having the everlasting gospel to preach unto them that dwell on the earth, and to every nation, and kindred, and tongue, and people, saying with a loud voice, Fear God and give glory to him; for the hour of his judgment is come; and worship him that made heaven, and earth, and the sea, and the fountains of waters." There is the everlasting gospel—the testimony of Christ's power, from paradise onward, as in contrast with the special announcement of the glad tidings which relate to the assembly of God. Now I know very well that people often speak about the gospel of the grace of God as the everlasting gospel. I am by no means critical, nor anxious to make a man an offender for a word; but if you ask me whether the gospel of the grace of God is thus spoken of in Scripture, I unhesitatingly say, No, because the gospel of the grace of God is connected with the heavenly Saviour, who died, and rose again, and it calls the soul to have to do with Him where He now is. That gospel could only come out consequent on the incarnation of the Son of God, followed by His death, resurrection, and ascension to heaven, and it in no way resembles the everlasting gospel spoken of here. Nay more, supposing I were to stand up, and tell you, that your salvation depended upon this—your fearing God, and giving glory to Him,—and that you would be saved by that, I think you would tell me, with very good right, that I had better go and learn the gospel before preaching it—because there is therein no word about salvation, atonement, and the blood of Christ. No, that which is really characteristic of Christianity is conspicuous, by its absence, in this everlasting gospel; but, take the Scripture as it stands, read it in its just connection, and you soon see how, in view of the return of Him, who is the everlasting Son of God, to the earth—in view of the return of the Messiah, this godly little company goes out and asserts the rights of that coming One, ascribing to Him all that is His due, as they do in the 96th Psalm.

You see how perfectly simple it is. The remnant go out and call on the heathen to "give unto the Lord the glory due unto His name" because "He cometh to judge the earth." When that testimony goes out, what is at hand? The Lord is going to judge the earth. The "everlasting gospel" is heralded forth, apparently, by these Jewish evangelists, just before the Lord appears, in manifest glory, to sweep the earth of the godless, and to bless the righteous, and therefore I have no hesitation in saying, that I believe the 96th Psalm, the 24th of Matthew, and the "everlasting gospel" of the 14th of Revelation, are all connected with the same movement, in fact, are the same testimony presented in different aspects.

I now go back again to this little book of Psalms, for a brief space before I close. The 97th Psalm goes a step further, and the Spirit of God there leads us to the moment of Christ's appearing. I will repeat for the sake of clearness. The 93rd is prefatory; the 94th, is, O Lord, come; the 95th, Israel, get ready; the 96th, Gentiles, get ready; the 97th celebrates the very fact of His coming, and brings out the character of that coming—what that appearing of the Lord will be. "The Lord reigneth; let the earth rejoice; let the multitude of isles be glad thereof. Clouds and darkness are round about him: righteousness and judgment are the habitation of his throne." Do you suppose the coming of the Lord to the earth will be a joke? Do you suppose that the day, when the Son of Man comes back, will be a day of mirth for the world, a day of fun for the wicked? Oh, how plain is the word of God! "A fire goeth before him, and burneth up his enemies round about. His lightnings enlightened the world: the earth saw, and trembled. The hills melted like wax at the presence of the Lord, at the presence of the Lord of the whole earth." He is going to claim the earth then; He came once as King of the Jews, but when He comes another time He will come as "Lord of the whole earth." Then it is " that the heavens declare his righteousness, and all the people see his glory. Confounded be all they that serve graven images, that boast themselves of idols; worship him, all ye gods." The day of the utter, and lasting overthrow of idolatry has dawned.

"Worship him, all ye gods," is the Spirit's urgent call then, and if any of you have a doubt, whether that distinctly, and definitely, refers to the coming back of the Son of God, in this way, to the world, it must be immediately dissipated, by your turning over your Bible to the 1st chapter of Hebrews. There you find the Spirit of God, by the pen of Paul, makes absolutely certain the moment to which the 97th Psalm refers. He says in the sixth verse, "And again, when he bringeth in the first-begotten into the world, he saith, And let all the angels of God worship him." God will demand, in that day, that every one shall worship Jesus. Thank God for that, but I am not going to wait for that day to adore Him. No, no, for I know His love, and delight to bless and worship Him now. It is my joy to worship Him, Is it not yours also? But the point is this, that, in that day, the Spirit of God will command it, and will force it, and what will mark the day? He will be worshipped. When He came in grace, He came as the only-begotten Son; when He rose from the dead, the world never saw Him. The last the world saw of Him was hanging on the cross. The next time the world sees Him it will be as "the first-begotten" in glory, and then "Worship him, all ye gods," will be the word.

The 98th Psalm goes yet further, Israel there celebrate their deliverance. The Lord has come and answered the cry of the remnant. "O sing unto the Lord a new song; for he has done marvellous things: his right hand, and his holy arm, hath gotten him the victory. The Lord hath made known his salvation: his righteousness hath he openly showed in the sight of the heathen. He hath remembered his mercy and his truth toward the house of Israel: all the ends of the earth have seen the salvation of our God." He has come, and delivered them, delivered this broken-down remnant, and they are delighting in His grace. They are wonderfully happy; it is only delivered people that can really sing, and they sing in this Psalm with great joy. "Make a joyful noise unto the Lord, all the earth: make a loud noise, and rejoice, and sing praise. Sing unto the Lord with the harp; with the harp, and the voice of a psalm. With trumpets, and sound of cornet, make a joyful noise before the Lord, the King. Let the sea roar, and the fulness thereof: the world, and they that dwell therein. Let the floods clap their hands: let the hills be joyful together before the Lord: for he cometh to judge the earth: with righteousness shall he judge the world, and the people with equity." He has taken the kingly character—Israel is delivered, the Deliverer has come out of Zion, and His happy subjects are celebrating the joy of that moment.

The 99th Psalm goes a step further. "The Lord reigneth: let the people tremble: he sitteth between the cherubims; let the earth be moved. The Lord is great in Zion; and he is high above all people. Let them praise thy great and terrible name; for it is holy. The king's strength also loveth judgment: thou dost establish equity, thou executest judgment and righteousness in Jacob." He is now in Jerusalem. He is in the temple, judging peacefully, sitting between the cherubims, and everything is being done exactly as their hearts would desire ; and then comes in the 100th Psalm. Sometimes we are asked to sing it, but I say to my friends we shall have to wait a little before we can sing it to its own tune. It is scarcely the moment yet when it can be sung in the Spirit. "Make a joyful noise unto the Lord, all ye lands. Serve the Lord with gladness; come before his presence with singing. Know ye that the Lord he is God ; it is he that hath made us, and not we ourselves: we are his people, and the sheep of his pasture. Enter into his gates with thanksgiving, and into his courts with praise: be thankful unto him, and bless his name. For the Lord is good; his mercy is everlasting; and his truth endureth to all generations." *His mercy is everlasting*—that is always the key-note of Israel's song—His mercy is everlasting, and His truth endures. It will be a wonderful moment for the earth by-and-by, when that psalm is rightly sung, in full world-wide chorus.

What a grand thing it is that we can look into Scripture and see what is coming, and then can turn back, rejoicingly, to our own portion, because, bright and blessed, as is the day, that is coming for the earth, there is something far brighter, and better, belonging to you and me. We who have received the Lord Jesus Christ, know Him now as our Saviour, and we can rejoice in our hearts, and be glad, and look up, simply waiting to see that blessed Saviour face to face.

Is there no joy in your heart to think that the One who came, and had nothing but a borrowed cradle, a cross built for a robber, and another man's tomb—I say, is there no joy that God is going to give Him all His rights, and establish Him in them by-and-by? I freely confess it is a great joy to me, and I love to think that when He comes back I shall be there. We shall be sharers of His glory and joy, and our hearts will be glad to the full, because it is the day of the exaltation of our own Jesus, our own blessed Saviour.

Well, friends, if you have seen to-night what the everlasting gospel is, what the gospel of the kingdom is, do not for a moment hesitate to let the gospel of God s grace do what it desires—save *you*. Get this salvation of God, where you sit to-night, and then you will be able to sing suitably to the Lord now, while waiting patiently for the day when, the "Sun of righteousness" having arisen, the 100th Psalm will fill the earth with its charming melody, and heaven's arches re-echo its notes of joy.

THE STONE CUT OUT WITHOUT HANDS.

Dan. ii. 34-45. Rev. xix.

Lecture VI.

WE had occasion, beloved friends, on a previous night, to look at the 2nd chapter of Daniel, in connection with the times of the Gentiles, and many of you will remember, that we saw brought out in the book of Daniel, the history of Gentile power in this world, commencing in the person of Nebuchadnezzar, and successively passing from the Babylonian empire to the Medo-Persian, then to the Grecian, and finally to the Roman. Then, in Nebuchadnezzar's great image, we saw the head, of gold, the breast and arms, of silver, the belly and the thighs, of brass, the legs of iron, and the feet, part of iron, and part of clay. It was a tale of deterioration right down. Now you will observe, in the verses I read this evening, that the stone that fell, did not fall on the head, nor on the breast, nor on the belly, but on the feet, that is, that whatever might be designed by God as the interpretation of the feet, made part of iron, and part of clay, it was upon the feet that the stone fell.

I have no doubt, as before stated, that the image gives us a continuous view of "the times of the

Gentiles," that is, the time in which God gives the Gentiles power on the earth, the Jew, for the while, being set aside. But there is a moment coming when God will change everything, and we find it indicated here in the 44th and 45th verses. This really happens in the closing days of the Roman empire, the revived Roman empire, for it does not now exist as such. But we learn from Scripture that that empire, which has now ceased to dominate the world, will be revived by Satanic energy in a day, I believe, near at hand, and it will have immense power, particularly in Europe—where, of course, its seat will be.

It will have great power, and it will be a bitter foe to all that is connected with God, whether under the name of Christianity, or Judaism, and it is that power, which is first dealt with by the Lord, when He returns in glory. You must not forget that it was under the Roman power, and by its decree, that He died. It was the Roman governor that said, "What shall I do then with Jesus, whom ye call Christ?" You must not forget that it was the Roman authority that signed His death-warrant. It was under the Romans that Jesus died, and John suffered, and it will be that same power, revived, that will be dominating things very much in the world, when the moment arrives of which the 2nd chapter of Daniel speaks, and there comes this remarkable intervention of God, "the stone was cut out of the mountain without hands."

That stone falls, and smites the image upon his feet, and the result is that it is all reduced to powder, and the whole thing disappears. Then we find "the stone that smote the image became a great mountain, and filled the whole earth." I am perfectly well aware that many expositors of the Word of God have endeavoured to make out that this is the Gospel. I do not see how they make it out at all, because I do not think the Gospel is very destructive, as this falling stone most certainly is, and, moreover, I ask you this, Did the Gospel ever smite the image? Never, the image smote Christ. It was the Roman power that slew the Lord Jesus. The Gospel has never set aside the civil power in this world; on the contrary, the Gospel has always suffered, and will suffer right on to the end. But what we have here is, that there comes a power that sets aside every human empire, and then is introduced an everlasting kingdom. "And in the days of these kings shall the God of heaven set up a kingdom, which shall never be destroyed: and the kingdom shall not be left to other people, but it shall break in pieces and consume all these kingdoms, and it shall stand for ever." God sets up a kingdom which shall never be destroyed. There can be no shadow of a doubt this refers to what Scripture speaks abundantly of elsewhere, "The everlasting kingdom of our Lord and Saviour Jesus Christ" (2 Peter i. 11), in the moment when He comes back to earth, to assume the reins of government, which He alone is worthy to hold.

What we read in the 19th of Revelation carries us up to that point. That chapter introduces us to the moment when He, who is King of kings, and Lord of lords, returns, as Son of Man, to assert His rights, and when God will establish them, and there shall be brought in a kingdom that shall never pass away. I will speak another evening of the nature and character of that kingdom, but, to-night, I just want to show you, if I can, how it comes in, and what will be the salient features of that day. It is indeed a blessed character that God gives to the kingdom—it never passes away. The fact is that there never has been a king, in this world, that has not—sooner or later—lost his crown, and there never has been a kingdom but what has been upset, or is going to be; but what God is about to do is to bring in a King, who shall never be uncrowned, and a kingdom, that shall never be set aside. The kingdom shall extend from pole to pole, and the King does not lose the crown, nor have it taken from Him, either by a usurper, or by death. Nevertheless, the moment will come when that throne which He has filled so blessedly for a thousand years, He will abdicate, as man, and lay down the crown voluntarily, which, as man, His peerless brow has borne, unsullied, during the ages of His mediatorial and universal sway, so that God may be all in all, for eternity. The history of the first man is this, he sought to rise—to get up to God's level, and he fell to Satan's, he was abased. The history of the last Man is this, that when He comes to assert His rights as Son of Man, and has put down every foe, He gives all up, that God may be all in all.

Scripture speaks abundantly of the return of the Lord Jesus in this way. We must not, however, confound the coming of the Lord Jesus Christ for His heavenly people, with the appearing of the Lord Jesus Christ with His attendant hosts. That which we look for, as Christians, is the return of the Lord Jesus for us. We shall rise to meet Him, and we shall go and be with Him, in the Father's house, and then we shall come with the Lord, when He returns to the earth in power and glory. That He will so come there can be no manner of doubt. Just turn to one or two parts of Scripture by way of confirmation. In the 24th of Matthew, we have already seen the Lord distinctly speaking of His appearing—His revelation, verse 30, " And then shall appear the sign of the Son of man in heaven : and then shall all the tribes of the earth mourn, and they shall see the Son of man coming in the clouds of heaven, with power and great glory." He is about to come to the earth in that character. Then turn to Matthew xxvi., where He is standing before the high priest. They had Him, who is going to be the Judge of all the earth, dragged before man's bar, and see what takes place. " The high priest arose, and said unto him, Answerest thou nothing ? what is it which these witness against thee ? But Jesus held his peace. And the high priest answered and said unto him, I adjure thee by the living God, that thou tell us whether thou be the Christ, the Son of God. Jesus saith unto him, Thou hast said : nevertheless, I say unto you, Hereafter shall ye see the Son of man sitting on the right hand of power, and coming in the clouds of heaven " (verses 62-64). When the Lord is put upon oath, He answers. Up to that moment He was silent, but put upon oath He immediately responds. He, as Son of Man, was to come with every surrounding of power, and glory, conferred on Him by God, " Sitting on the right hand of power, and coming in the clouds of heaven." That moment has not yet come, but thank God, it is coming. When He does come in that character, of course it will be in relation to the earth, and in judgment thereof.

Turn now to the 19th of Revelation, and you will get a general view of what will be the characteristics of the appearing of the Lord Jesus. Recollect it is to deal with the earth, in order to put down all opposing power on the earth, and that is the great point that the Spirit of God brings out in the 19th chapter. But there are a few points that I must touch upon, before going into that, viz., what the early part of the chapter brings out.

You will observe that this chapter opens with a great movement in heaven—" After these things I heard a great voice of much people in heaven, saying, Hallelujah," &c. Now, what produced the praise? It is clearly the judgment of which the 18th chapter speaks—the fall of Babylon. You have there the judgment of the false Church—the false bride you may call it if you please—and you have now the coming out in glory of the real Bride, the Bride of Christ. In the 18th chapter the judgment, upon earth, of what is false, immediately precedes this moment, when the marriage of the Lamb takes place, and the Bridegroom and the Bride together appear, when He comes out, in kingly character, as Son of Man to deal with the earth.

It is important to bear in mind that, in the main, what the book of Revelation gives you, up to this point, are the providential judgments of God, that are preparatory to what the 19th chapter ushers in. I believe that in the opening of the seven seals, and the sounding of the seven trumpets (chaps. vi.-xi.), as well as in the pouring out of the vials (chap. xvi.), you have given to you—sometimes in mystical language—those desolating temporal judgments, with which this whole earth will be overwhelmed, previous to the appearing of the Son of Man; and if any of you are unsaved, and want to know what you are hastening on to, I recommend you, without delay, to read these chapters straight through, and you will have a very fair idea of what your portion is to be, if not caught up at the rapture. If the Lord Jesus came now, if the true saints were called up at this moment into glory, I will tell you what you would have to face immediately thereafter. You would find the first seal (chap. vi.) begun to be broken, before you were at all aware.

In the 4th of Revelation you have the creatorial glories of Christ. In the 5th you have the redemption glories of Jesus, and there you see Him, as the Lamb slain, in the midst of the throne. The cry is sent forth, "Who is worthy to open the book?" In the hand of God there is a roll. That roll contains the purposes and counsels of God with regard to the earth. There goes out this challenge, "Who is worthy? John says, "*I wept much.*" He knew he was not worthy himself, and he looked for some one to come up who was worthy. Would not Joseph, Moses, Samuel, or Elijah come? Nay, neither patriarch, priest, nor prophet was worthy; nor Peter, nor Paul, nor himself; and he "wept much." Then, what takes place? The Lion of the Tribe of Juda prevails. John turns round to look for the Lion, and he says, "Lo, in the midst of the throne, stood a Lamb as it had been slain." There you may see Jesus, the Saviour—my Saviour! Your Saviour? Oh, my friends, hurry to Him, if He is not yet your Saviour. Get ready for Him. But we read, "He came, and took the book out of the right hand of him that sat upon the throne." And as Jesus puts forth His hand to take the roll, what does heaven see? It sees the mark of the nail, that tells of His death on the cross, and all in heaven together bow, and sing, "Thou art worthy to take the book, and to open the seals thereof: for thou wast slain, and hast redeemed us to God by thy blood out of every kindred, and tongue, and people, and nation." What has led you to worship Jesus? Because He died for you.

There is no one worthy but Jesus to unfold the mind of God, or to execute the purposes of God. He therefore takes the book. I must not dwell upon that, but let me ask, Are you sure to be with Him when He takes the book, and breaks the seals? If you are not, whither are you going? As you sit to-night, you are either a glory-bound saint, or a hell-bound sinner. You say, That is drawing the line very fine. Well, grant it, but I am not drawing the line finer than God does. A glory-bound saint! Oh, how blessed! That is a remarkable expression; I like it —a man bound for glory through the grace of God. If I am not that, what am I? I am on my road to hell, as surely as I face you this night. Oh! say some people, we cannot be sure of salvation. Do not be deceived by the devil that way. You ought to be sure. If you never were sure before, I implore you to be sure now, because He died for us, and there is the song in glory—" Thou wast slain, and thou hast redeemed us to God by thy blood." Perhaps you say, They learned that up there. No, they learned it on earth, and if you do not learn that song on earth, you will never learn it. There is no redemption after death; there is no pardon in the tomb; and there is no forgiveness for the man, who has heard, and despised the Gospel, after the Lord has come, and the door is shut. You may, and you had better, learn that song now.

What is the next thing? The 6th of Revelation opens with the fact that the Lamb begins to break the seals. He is about to begin to deal with the earth. I believe, in point of fact, that what we have in Revelation iv. and v., and in chapters vi., vii., and viii., and onwards, are concurrent. Chapters iv. and v. are what I may call the high level, and the 6th, &c., give us the low level. The two are going on together. The one is a heavenly, and the other an earthly scene. The worship meeting in heaven of chapter v. is concurrent with the prayer-meeting on earth, of the 6th chapter of Revelation. But what is the prayer-meeting on earth? In verse 15 we find "And the kings of the earth, and the great men, and the rich men, and the chief captains, and the mighty men, and every bondman, and every free man, hid themselves in the dens, and in the rocks of the mountains; and said to the mountains and rocks, Fall on us, and hide us from the face of him that sitteth on the throne, and from the wrath of the Lamb: For the great day of his wrath is come; and who shall be able to stand?" I do not believe the day of the Lord really has come then, but conscience terrifies men into thinking it has come. I do not believe the "day of the Lord" has actually set in then, it is only the gathering of the clouds. But, O beloved friends, there is many a man in Christendom to-day, who never bent his knees at a prayer-meeting, that will be found at a prayer-meeting yet, beseeching—not God for mercy on his guilty soul, but—the rocks and the hills to fall upon him. These are God's solemn statements, and yet I repeat, not yet has the day of the Lord set in. It is only what is coming, acting on conscience, guilty conscience. Man wakes up, and feels he is in an awful case, and flies, if he can, to get away from God, in the dens of the earth. You remember our Lord

Jesus Christ prophesied this prayer-meeting in Luke 23rd, "Weep not for me, but weep for yourselves, and for your children. For, behold, the days are coming, in the which they shall say, Blessed are the barren, and the wombs that never bare, and the paps which never gave suck. Then shall they begin to say to the mountains, Fall on us; and to the hills, Cover us. For if they do these things in a green tree, what shall be done in the dry?" (verses 28-51.) What the Lord predicts, in the moment of His willing self-sacrifice for guilty man, that he might be saved from judgment, we find fully brought out in the 6th of Revelation.

From the 6th chapter to the end of the 18th, broadly speaking, you have brought before you the providential dealings of God, in judgment, with man upon the earth, which lead up to the final climax, which is the appearing of the Man that the world does not want to see. If you could only certify to the world that the Lord Jesus Christ, and His Father, the Living God, were dead, and buried, and never would have anything more to say to the earth, I believe that the world would take a general holiday.

But God yet lives, Jesus lives, and it is well to remind the world that God "hath appointed a day, in the which he will judge the world in righteousness, by that man whom he hath ordained; whereof he hath given assurance unto all men, in that he hath raised him from the dead" (Acts xvii. 31).

The One who died on the cross eighteen hundred years ago, died for our sins, and was raised for our justification, has passed into glory, and the heavens have concealed Him for eighteen long centuries. God has had long patience with man, but the day is

THE STONE CUT OUT WITHOUT HANDS. 131

appointed, and the Lord will come out again, according to the testimony of the 19th of Revelation, to which I again turn. Joy fills the arches of heaven's courts in that day, because the time has come when the whore with all her children are cast into the fire. That is her judgment. Babylon falls, in the 18th chapter, and then heaven rejoices, because the moment is coming of earth's deliverance.

Then, just before the Lord comes out, there is brought before our view something peculiarly blessed to the Christian. I cannot pass it over, because it is what I may call our own unique portion. A wonderfully blessed place will all believers in Jesus have in the day when the Lord comes out. Let us read it. "And a voice came out of the throne, saying, Praise our God, all ye his servants, and ye that fear him, both small and great. And I heard as it were the voice of a great multitude, and as the voice of many waters, and as the voice of mighty thunderings, saying, Alleluia: for the Lord God omnipotent reigneth. Let us be glad and rejoice, and give honour to him: for the marriage of the Lamb is come, and his wife hath made herself ready" (Rev. xix. 5, 6, 7). The great multitude anticipates what is coming, and heaven goes into an ecstasy, because they see that the moment has come, when the Lord is going to put forth His hand to clear sin from the earth, and set things right; and heaven, after six thousand years of patient waiting, says, "Hallelujah for the Lord our God, the Almighty, has taken to himself Kingly power" (ver. 6, New Trans.). But before He comes out in glory, they add, "Let us be glad and rejoice, and give honour to him: for the marriage of the Lamb is come, and his wife hath made herself ready" (ver. 7). What a wonderful thing, heaven goes into an ecstasy over the marriage of the Lamb. There was another time when heaven was equally moved, when the angelic messenger came and told the shepherds, " I bring you tidings of great joy, . . . for unto you is born this day . . . a Saviour which is Christ the Lord" (Luke ii. 10, 11). Immediately there was with the angel a multitude of the heavenly host, and they were all praising God. Heaven went into an ecstasy when Jesus was born, because it now saw a way for man to be saved. The problem of four thousand years, how man could be saved, was now settled by the birth of the Son of God, the Saviour, who was going to die for sinners like you and me. Yes, joy filled heaven that day, and here is the other side of it. He came down, He was born, He lived, He was refused, rejected, abhorred of the people, and despised of the Gentiles, and at length cast out. A robber was preferred to Jesus, the Son of God, a murderer rather than a Saviour. The world took Him forth, crowned with thorns, and slew Him on the tree. All that Jesus got from this world was to be born in one man's manger, to die on another man's cross, and to be buried in another man's tomb. The world has well-nigh forgotten His existence, and would entirely but for the Holy Ghost's testimony ; and now there comes a moment, after eighteen hundred years have gone by, when there is to be an end to His waiting, and a reward for His toil, and heaven is in deepest sympathy with His joy, and says, " Let us be glad and rejoice, and give honour to him : for the marriage of the Lamb is come, and his wife hath made herself ready. And to her was granted that she should be arrayed in fine linen, clean and white : for the fine linen is the righteousnesses of the saints " (Rev. xix. 7, 8).

A rapturous moment, for the Bridegroom and the Bride has come. Who is the Bride? I have no doubt who the Bride is. There are others looking on, who are called to the marriage supper of the Lamb (see verse 9), but these are the guests—they are not the Bride. But who is the Bride? There is not a believer in this hall to-night, that does not form part of the Bride of Christ; there has not been one believing soul on earth, from the day of Pentecost, right on to the moment when the Lord comes back for His people, that does not form an integral part of the Bride. On the day of the marriage, the heavenly Bridegroom wants the whole Bride, He does not take a part of her. If you are going to limit the Bride, as some would, to a few faithful *living* Christians, you have to leave Peter and Paul out. Are we going to leave them out? Nay, the Bride is composed of all that belong to the Lord, from the day of Pentecost, to the day of the rapture. When the last soul is converted, and, by being sealed with the Holy Ghost, is brought into the body of Christ, that body is complete. The Bride is also then complete, and observe, you will find always that the Bride is connected with glory. When I come to think of eternal glory, then it is, that we specially hear of the Bridegroom and the Bride, terms that call up, and foster in our hearts, those holy and blessed affections that befit such a relationship.

But observe how the Bride is apparelled here. She is "arrayed in fine linen clean and bright; for the fine linen is the righteousnesses of the saints" (ver. 8). What are we to learn from this? "Fine linen" or "white raiment" (Rev. iii. 18), would appear, in the Word, to be the figure of practical righteousness in the saint, as "gold" is divine righteousness, in which we stand before God. It is, I judge, connected with reward, though the fruit of perfect grace. " God is not unrighteous to forget your work and labour of love " (Heb. vi. 10). This will be the outcome of going before the judgment-seat of Christ, which precedes the marriage day. Although you and I, if believers, can never be judged for our sins—Jesus having been judged for them—yet, as believers, we shall have to give an account to the Lord, by and by, of all our actions here. We shall go before the judgment-seat of Christ, and if we have served the Lord, He will reward us. I believe that when our whole history has come under review before the Lord, we shall come out, deeply thankful, to have gone over it with Him.

I do not think you will be concerned about my history, but only about your own. I shall be very troubled about what will come out then, some one may say. Nay, I will tell you one thing that will come out, you will find that you have been put into glory, in the likeness of Christ. Will you have any objection to review that? Guilt can never be imputed to us, because it has been already imputed to Christ. He died for our sins, and Christ is, then, as now, our righteousness, and our ground for appearing in the presence of God. Nevertheless, when before the Lord, it will be a very blessed, though withal a very solemn thing, to review what His grace was to us here, in our earthly pathway. At that moment, when I get before the judgment-seat of Christ, the Lord will, I judge, take me over the whole of my history. Looking back on my life, as an unconverted man, I see, so to speak, a long, dark, black, inky river of nothing but self-will, and sin, and then I come to a point when His grace began to work in my heart, and I see a little bright silvery streak coming in, the first touch of the Spirit of God on my soul. And then the stream of grace begins to widen a little, and the inky stream of self-will, and active sin, to diminish. Thus I retrace the whole of my history, seeing my failures, and my faults, and the Lord's patience, and grace with me; what a fool I was here, and how grace helped me there, and then I come right up to the end of the double stream, and I say, Here I am with Christ in glory. Oh! what wondrous grace, me in glory! I think I shall turn and say, Where is my harp, that I may strike my hand across its strings, and praise the ever blessed, loving Lord, that brought *me* here. I would not miss that for worlds.

What we have been for Jesus here will be manifested there. Your service will come out there, and I tell you honestly, I believe I shall delight to look on then, and say, Look at that brother, what a blessed reward that saint has received, how brightly does his garment shine. Your practical righteousness here will follow you into heaven. This, you see, will make us careful down here as to our walk, and it is a very good thing that we should be careful. We are not trying to get salvation, or righteousness, to fit us for glory, we are only trying to be "rich in good works" (1 Tim. vi. 17-19), which will follow us there.

The marriage of the Lamb having taken place, the Son of Man comes out, and who is with Him? You and I, fellow-believer, will be with Him. Many an earthly bridegroom and bride, have had to be separated, but we are to be *for ever with the Lord;* with Him in the Father's house in glory, at the marriage supper, and when He comes out in majesty, and power, and glory. Will it not be deep joy to be with Him in that day?

The character of the Lord's appearing, as given here, is very striking. He comes out seated "on a white horse," the symbol in Scripture of victorious power, and similarly seated "upon white horses, clothed in fine linen, white and clean," the armies of heaven follow Him. He is called "Faithful and True ; and in righteousness he doth judge and make war. His eyes were as a flame of fire, and on his head were many crowns" (verses 11, 12). The last time the world saw Him He was naked. They had stripped Him, and had gambled for His garments, beneath His dying eyes. The next time the world sees Him, how will it be? Oh, sinner, it will be an awful time for you. Unsaved man, if you are caught in that day, it will be a terrible time for you. "He was clothed with a vesture dipped in blood ; and his name is called THE WORD OF GOD. . . . And out of his mouth goeth a sharp sword, that with it he should smite the nations ; and he shall rule [shepherd] them with a rod of iron" (verses 13-15).

When He rules we shall be with Him, in the day of His power. We who have known, and followed Him, in the day of His weakness, and rejection, shall be with Him, in the day of His manifested power, and glory.

But further, "He treadeth the wine-press of the fierceness and wrath of Almighty God." There is a difference seen clearly elsewhere in Scripture, between the harvest, and the vintage. Here He treads the *wine-press*. Turn back to Rev. xiv. 15, and we read, "And another angel came out of the temple, crying with a loud voice to him that sat on the cloud, Thrust in thy sickle, and reap : for the time is come for thee to reap ; for the harvest of the earth is ripe. And he that sat on the cloud thrust in his sickle on the earth ;

and the earth was reaped. And another angel came out of the temple which is in heaven, he also having a sharp sickle. And another angel came out from the altar, which had power over fire ; and cried with a loud cry to him that had the sharp sickle, saying, Thrust in thy sharp sickle, and gather the clusters of the vine of the earth ; for her grapes are fully ripe. And the angel thrust in his sickle into the earth, and gathered the vine of the earth, and cast it into the great wine-press of the wrath of God. And the wine-press was trodden without the city, and blood came out of the wine-press, even unto the horse bridles, by the space of a thousand and six hundred furlongs." You have there two things, the harvest and the vintage. What is the difference? The harvest clearly is connected with judgment, Christ reaps the earth—separating, gathering, and judging, but there is discrimination in the judgment of the Lord in that day. "There shall be two in one bed ; the one shall be taken, and the other left. Two shall be grinding together ; the one shall be taken, and the other left. Two shall be in the field; the one shall be taken, and the other left" (Luke xvii. 34-36). That is the principle of the harvest, because some righteous are to be found then. When the Lord treads the wine-press, He exercises unmingled vengeance upon the wicked, for the vintage is the moment when the final desolating judgment takes place, that is to say, the godly have been delivered, the harvest has been gathered, and what remains forms the vintage, and every bunch goes into the wine-press. It will be an awful day for the earth when the harvest is over. Then the rest are left to the judgment, that is expressed by the vintage.

I will here ask you to turn to other Scriptures,

merely to refer to what is going to take place in that day. Look at Joel iii. 9, where you will see clearly what the Lord will do. God summons the earth to try conclusions with Him. "Proclaim ye this among the Gentiles; prepare war, wake up the mighty men, let all the men of war draw near; let them come up: beat your ploughshares into swords, and your pruning-hooks into spears: let the weak say, I am strong. Assemble yourselves, and come, all ye heathen, and gather yourselves together round about: thither cause thy mighty ones to come down, O Lord. Let the heathen be wakened, and come up to the valley of Jehoshaphat: for there will I sit to judge all the heathen round about. Put ye in the sickle; for the harvest is ripe: come, get you down; for the press is full, the fats overflow: for their wickedness is great. Multitudes, multitudes in the valley of decision: for the day of the Lord is near in the valley of decision" (Joel iii. 9-14). It is a stupendous fact, that at that moment Jehovah comes, and deals with the nations of the earth, and men are obliged to bow down before God. There again we read that the "harvest is ripe," and "the press is full." Although a terrible, it will, at first, be a discriminating judgment.

Then look at Matt. xxv. 31-46, where you get, not the warrior judgment of Christ, but His sessional judgment, what you may call an assize. In this, His saints are associated with Him (Dan. vii. 22; 1 Cor. vi. 2, 3; Rev. xx. 4). In the warrior judgment Christ is alone. "I have trodden the wine-press alone; and of the people none was with me" (Isa. lxiii. 3).

The 19th of Revelation gives us the warrior judgment of Christ—overcoming power—while sessional judgment we find in chap. xx. from verse 4. Now we read on

"He hath on his vesture and on his thigh a name written, KING OF KINGS, AND LORD OF LORDS." He is thus publicly, and officially announced. "And I saw the beast, and the kings of the earth, and their armies, gathered together to make war against him that sat on the horse, and against his army. And the beast was taken, and with him the false prophet that wrought miracles before him, with which he deceived them that had received the mark of the beast, and them that worshipped his image. These both were cast alive into a lake of fire burning with brimstone. And the remnant were slain with the sword of him that sat upon the horse, which sword proceeded out of his mouth: and all the fowls were filled with their flesh" (Rev. xix. 19-21). The impiety and daring folly of man rises to its full height, as we see gathered against Him the beast and his tributaries, "to make war against him." There will be a tremendous effort on the part of man to resist God, but that effort results in nothing but overwhelming destruction. What takes place? The beast and the false prophet are taken, and are cast alive into the lake of fire. These two men—ringleaders in evil—get their final doom without death—they are cast into the lake of fire. That is not strange, for Enoch and Elijah were taken to heaven without death. That was in Old Testament times of feeble light, and knowledge of God. Alas! it is reserved for two men, in New Testament times, when grace is abundant, and has been despised, to be cast alive into the lake of fire. They receive their final judgment, the rest are judicially "slain with the sword of him that sat upon the horse."

In the 25th of Matthew, familiar to every one of us, the Lord commences His sessional judgment, "When the Son of man shall come in his glory, and all the holy angels with him, then shall he sit upon the throne of his glory: And before him shall be gathered all nations: and he shall separate them one from another, as a shepherd divideth his sheep from the goats: And he shall set the sheep on his right hand, but the goats on the left. Then shall the King say unto them on his right hand, Come, ye blessed of my Father, inherit the kingdom prepared for you from the foundation of the world: for I was an hungered, and ye gave me meat: I was thirsty, and ye gave me drink: I was a stranger, and ye took me in: naked, and ye clothed me: I was sick, and ye visited me: I was in prison, and ye came unto me. Then shall the righteous answer him, saying, Lord, when saw we thee an hungered, and fed thee? or thirsty, and gave thee drink? When saw we thee a stranger, and took thee in? or naked, and clothed thee? Or when saw we thee sick, or in prison, and came unto thee? And the King shall answer and say unto them, Verily I say unto you, Inasmuch as ye have done it unto one of the least of these my brethren, ye have done it unto me. Then shall he say also unto them on the left hand, Depart from me, ye cursed, into everlasting fire, prepared for the devil and his angels: for I was an hungered, and ye gave me no meat: I was thirsty, and ye gave me no drink: I was a stranger, and ye took me not in: naked, and ye clothed me not: sick, and in prison, and ye visited me not. Then shall they also answer him, saying, Lord, when saw we thee an hungered, or athirst, or a stranger, or naked, or sick, or in prison, and did not minister unto thee? Then shall he answer them, saying, Verily I say unto you, inasmuch as ye did it not to one of the least of these,

THE STONE CUT OUT WITHOUT HANDS. 141

ye did it not to me. And these shall go away into everlasting punishment, but the righteousness into life eternal" (Matt. xxv. 31-46).

It will be a wonderful moment, and a deeply impressive scene. All His angels, and all His saints, form His retinue, and there never has been such an assemblage since the world began, and there never will again be such a concourse in the world's history. The Son of man comes in His glory, and "then shall he sit upon the throne of his glory, and before him shall be gathered all nations." But, some one may say, that is the same judgment, as the great white throne, is it not? No, dear friend, nothing of the sort. They who are judged here, are gathered before the Lord in nations, but people do not so rise from the dead. There are four judgments spoken of in Scripture. You have the judgment of sin on the cross, the judgment of the works of the Christian in glory, with Christ, when we are like Him. Then, here, we get the judgment of the living nations, which corresponds exactly to the 3rd of Joel, " Gather together all the heathen," &c., and lastly, the judgment of the wicked dead, as given to us in Revelation xx. 11-15.

Clearly the sheep in Matthew xxv. are, in a certain sense, related to the Lord, and the goats are not, but both classes are living nations! Observe: "Inherit the kingdom prepared for you from the foundation of the world." Are these Christians? No, *our* blessing dates from "*before* the foundation of the world" (Eph. i. 4). These are blessed *from* the foundation of the world. Observe also the ground of the judgment, viz., the treatment of the king's *brethren*. The king answers and says unto the sheep, "Verily I say unto you, Inasmuch as ye have done it unto one of the least of these my brethren, ye have done it unto me." Who are the brethren? Christians? No, certainly not Christians, the day of Christianity has gone by, it is the day when the Son of Man is dealing with the nations upon earth, and in that day, you do not get the three classes, Jew, Gentile, and the Church of God. The day of the Church of God is over. She has gone up into glory before this day. But we have Jew and Gentile. I was showing you, in my last lecture, how the Jew will carry forth the Gospel of the kingdom in the end of the age. The brethren here, I conclude, are the messengers. These sheep, who will be witnesses of the return of the Son of Man, are the believing Gentile nations who bow to the truth, while the goats are those who refuse the truth. It is not the great white throne. It is the Son of Man on the throne of His glory, dealing with the living nations on the earth, and judging them according to the way they have treated His messengers. The judgment of the great white throne will come before us on another occasion.

In this way then is the kingdom of the Son of Man established. Every foe is put down; for "the Son of man shall send forth his angels, and they shall gather out of his kingdom all things that offend, and them which do iniquity. . . . Then shall the righteous shine forth as the sun in the kingdom of their Father. Who hath ears to hear, let him hear" (Matt. xiii. 41-43). The beast and the false prophet; the Roman empire and its minion, with all their confederates, we have seen dealt with, but there is yet another foe of Israel to be set aside, ere the stone, cut out without hands, can fill the whole earth. That I reserve for our next lecture.

ISRAEL AND THE ASSYRIAN.

Rom. xi. ; Ezek. xxxvi.–xxxix.

Lecture VII.

THE question with which the apostle opens the 11th of Romans is an exceedingly important, and interesting one, not only to Israel but to us. Of course, when he says, "Hath God cast away his people?" he is not talking of Christians now, but of His ancient people Israel. At once the apostle says, "God forbid. For I also am an Israelite, of the seed of Abraham, of the tribe of Benjamin." Then he states most emphatically, "God hath not cast away his people which he foreknew." Now, by casting them off, what the apostle has before his mind, clearly, is their being, as a nation, irrevocably rejected by God, to be no more taken up by Him. It is not a question of individual salvation here, in this part of Scripture; it is as a nation they are spoken of. Has He then cast them off? The answer is most distinct. "God hath not cast away his people which he foreknew," and the apostle goes on to quote a remarkable bit of their history in connection with Elijah, who, when he thought he was the only man standing for God, is reminded, that God had seven thousand men, who had not bowed the knee to Baal. "Even so then at this present time also there is a remnant according to the election of grace" (ver. 5).

The apostle says they have fallen (verses 11, 12), but they have not been cast off—they have fallen, and God has allowed them, in the meantime, as a nation, to stay where they have fallen. They have fallen under the power of the Gentiles, and by their fall salvation is come to the latter. This fall refers, clearly, to their national captivity. You remember how they were carried off. Two and a half tribes were first carried into captivity, by the Assyrian king, Tiglath Pileser (2 Kings xv. 29), because of their idolatry. Then seven and a half tribes, the rest of Israel, were carried away to Assyria, by Shalmaneser (2 Kings xvii. 6), and, about a hundred and forty years afterwards, Nebuchadnezzar carried off Judah, and Benjamin, the other two tribes, to Babylon, so that, in three sections, Israel as a nation was swept out of the land. A little remnant might, and did return in the days of Ezra, and Nehemiah; still, speaking broadly, Israel has fallen, they have been rejected, they are not in the land God gave to their fathers, and the question is this, Is God going to restore them? We shall see, clearly, that God is going to restore them, for "the gifts and calling of God are without repentance" (Rom. xi. 29).

Very beautiful is the way in which the apostle brings in, in this 11th chapter of Romans, our relation to Israel. The blessing of God comes to us Gentiles in the moment of, and because of, their rejection. He says in verse 11, "Through their fall, salvation is come unto the Gentiles." Why, beloved friends, you and I ought to go down on our knees, and thank God for what has happened. We should never have heard of the Saviour, if it had not been for the sin of Israel. When the Messiah came, had He been accepted, the kingdom would have been established in Jerusalem, and we should not have had the Gospel, as we have it now, but "through their fall, salvation is come unto the Gentiles." You see the Gentiles, the nations of the earth, were, in no sense, in relationship with God. Sinners of the Gentiles are stated to be "afar off," but first, as a consequence of the sin of Israel, that compelled God to judge them, and cast them out of their land, and secondly, because the remnant, when restored, rejected their Messiah,—God, as you know, had the temple destroyed, the city burned down, and the Jews were scattered to the four winds of heaven. God has, so to speak, dropped them for the time being, and He has turned round to the Gentiles. Thank God, indeed, for the news, that "Through their fall, salvation is come unto the Gentiles."

I should like to pause a moment, and ask whether you are saved? If you are not, you have somehow escaped what God is presenting to you, for "salvation *is come* unto the Gentiles." The Messiah crucified by Israel, God has raised and glorified, and the Holy Ghost has come down, and for eighteen centuries has the blessed Spirit of God been carrying out the testimony about Jesus, the exalted Saviour in glory, and been turning the eyes of sinners, on earth, to that Saviour in glory. But God is about to replace His ancient people in their land, and establish them there, for He promised Abraham, "Thy seed shall possess the gate of his enemies." That event is preceded by all the Lord's evangelists being called home. The Gospel of God's grace then ceases, but the Lord Jesus is still in heaven as I speak, the sweet note of the Gospel still rings out in this world, and if there should happen to be, in this room to-night, only one unsaved person, I would earnestly say to that soul, Join now the company of those that know the heavenly Saviour, who have believed, through infinite grace in Him, and received God's salvation. I know perfectly well you may reply, Nobody can know they are saved. But that reply is a mistake, for here the apostle says, "Through their fall salvation is come unto the Gentiles." Salvation you may know, you ought to know. The blessed news is this, that there is forgiveness, peace, pardon, and access to God, through Jesus Christ, for any poor sinner that is on earth at this moment.

There are fuller, and deeper, because heavenly, blessings to be had now, through the rejection of the Lord Jesus, than ever Israel will know, in the day of their revived glory, and their restored kingdom, under the King, of whom I will speak a little further on. Therefore, if there be a soul in this hall, that has not yet been saved, pause, think, and ask these questions, Why has God sent the Gospel to me? Why has God not yet sent back His Son, the Lord Jesus, to re-establish Israel in their land? Why is He tarrying? He is tarrying because "blindness in part has happened to Israel, until the fulness of the Gentiles be come in" (ver. 25). What does He mean? This. He delays till the last Gentile has been brought into the Church of God, till the last member of the body of Christ has been called, reached, converted, and baptized, by the Holy Ghost, into that body. Were you ever struck with the expression, "the fulness of the Gentiles"? We saw, on a previous evening, what was meant by "the times of the Gentiles," the time when the Gentiles rule, and the Jews are nowhere. "Blindness in part is happened to Israel until the fulness of the Gentiles be come in," has, however, a different significance, viz., that Israel will not be blessed until the Gospel has reached the last soul, that will listen to the testimony of this heavenly Saviour, and thus the body of Christ completed, the Bride of Christ is also complete, and the Bridegroom comes into the air and catches up His own people, to meet Him there.

The fulness of the Gentiles has then come. God will begin to put His hand upon the Jew once more, and the long night of their sorrow, and dispersal, will end in a morning of joy, and gladness, for here it is stated distinctly, " So all Israel shall be saved ; as it is written, There shall come out of Zion the Deliverer, and shall turn away ungodliness from Jacob : for this is my covenant unto them, when I shall take away their sins" (verses 26, 27). And the reason is this, " For the gifts and calling of God are without repentance" (ver. 29). He has let them drop for the time being, and they are under the chastening hand of the Lord, but the time is coming, and I believe in my heart rapidly drawing near, when God will show how true is His word, how faithful is He to His promises, and how blessedly His Son "Jesus Christ was" (and yet will be) "a minister of the circumcision for the truth of God, to confirm the promises made to the fathers" (Rom. xv. 8). Not one promise, that God has made, shall ever fail.

I now turn to some scriptures, to show the way in which the Word of God informs us, that He will yet gather, and lead His people, and plant them in the land, given to their fathers. The kingdom of Israel was broken up in the days of Rehoboam (1 Kings xii.). Two tribes, Judah and Benjamin, clave to the house of David, and they are spoken of in the Old Testament as Judah. The ten tribes who revolted, under Jeroboam, are spoken of constantly, in the historical books, as "the house of Israel," and in the prophets, under the title of Ephraim. Judah, and Ephraim, are the technical terms, used in the later books of the Old Testament Scripture, to express the two divisions of the nation. Now, we have already seen, that it was at the hands of the representatives of the two tribes, that the Lord Jesus died, and therefore, that in the judgment of God, the heaviest end of His lash must fall upon these two tribes, who were guilty of the murder of their Messiah. We have observed on a previous occasion, these words: "It shall come to pass, that in all the land, saith the Lord, two parts therein shall be cut off and die; but the third shall be left therein. And I will bring the third part through the fire, and will refine them as silver is refined, and will try them as gold is tried: they shall call on my name, and I will hear them: I will say, It is my people; and they shall say, The Lord is my God" (Zech. xiii. 8, 9). I have already pointed out, that we have presented to us there, the little company spoken of in the Psalms, and in the Prophets as "the remnant" of the two tribes, who, gathered back into their own land, will be looking to the Lord for deliverance. They are chastened in the land,—purged, so much so, that two-thirds will die. Only one-third shall escape the tribulation, which, elsewhere, is spoken of as God's "indignation," at that moment.

And what of the other ten tribes? It would appear that they are not restored to Palestine till a later date. So far as I can see from Scripture, the return of the Son of Man in power, and majesty, to the earth, will really take place before the mass of the ten tribes is recovered, and restored. Look at Matthew xxiv. in confirmation of that statement. Speaking of His

return, the Lord tells His disciples this: "Then shall appear the sign of the Son of man in heaven: and then shall all the tribes of the earth mourn, and they shall see the Son of man coming in the clouds of heaven, with power and great glory. And he shall send his angels with a great sound of a trumpet; and they shall gather together his elect from the four winds, from one end of heaven to the other" (Matt. xxiv. 30, 31). With this statement agrees that of the prophet Isaiah: "And it shall come to pass in that day, that the Lord shall beat off from the channel of the river unto the stream of Egypt, and ye shall be gathered one by one, O ye children of Israel. And it shall come to pass in that day, that the great trumpet shall be blown, and they shall come which were ready to perish in the land of Assyria, and the outcasts in the land of Egypt, and shall worship the Lord in the holy mount at Jerusalem" (Isa. xxvii. 12, 13). It appears to me that only the remnant of repentant Judah will welcome the Messiah, when He does return in glory, but, having returned, He will have the great trumpet blown by His many angels, and thus will regather His elect of Israel.

By way of confirmation of these passages, turn back to the 11th of Isaiah, where we find a fuller prophetic statement by the Spirit of God (ver. 10). "And in that day there shall be a root of Jesse, which shall stand for an ensign of the people; to it shall the Gentiles seek: and his rest shall be glorious. And it shall come to pass in that day, that the Lord shall set his hand again the second time to recover the remnant of his people, which shall be left from Assyria, and from Egypt, and from Pathros, and from Cush, and from Elam, and from Shinar, and from Hamath, and from the islands of the sea. And he shall set up an ensign for the nations, and shall assemble the outcasts of Israel, and gather together the dispersed of Judah from the four corners of the earth. The envy also of Ephraim shall depart, and the adversaries of Judah shall be cut off; Ephraim shall not envy Judah, and Judah shall not vex Ephraim" (Isa. xi. 10-13). The two tribes and the ten are to dwell together in amity.

Now go to the last chapter of Isaiah, and you will find further testimony to the same point. It contemplates the moment when the Lord has come to the earth. You read at the 18th verse—"It shall come, that I will gather all nations and tongues; and they shall come, and see my glory. And I will set a sign among them, and I will send those that escape of them unto the nations, to Tarshish, Pul, and Lud, that draw the bow, to Tubal and Javan, to the isles afar off, that have not heard my fame, neither have seen my glory: and they shall declare my glory among the Gentiles. And they shall bring all your brethren for an offering unto the Lord, out of all nations, upon horses, and in chariots, and in litters, and upon mules, and upon swift beasts, to my holy mountain Jerusalem, saith the Lord, as the children of Israel bring an offering in a clean vessel into the house of the Lord. And I will also take of them for priests and for Levites, saith the Lord" (Isa. lxvi. 18-21). Again, you have indicated that He gathers His people Israel from all nations, and, therefore, I think the idea, that the British nation is the ten tribes, is foreign to Scripture. I think this expression, "out of all nations," should at once dispel the illusion. The truth is that no one knows where they are, save God Himself, and when the time comes, He will find them, and bring them, in His own way.

The Book of Ezekiel gives us, in much detail, the subject before us. "As I live, saith the Lord God, surely with a mighty hand, and with a stretched-out arm, and with fury poured out, will I rule over you ; and I will bring you out from the people, and will gather you out of the countries wherein ye are scattered, with a mighty hand, and with a stretched-out arm, and with fury poured out. And I will bring you into the wilderness of the people, and there will I plead with you face to face. Like as I pleaded with your fathers in the wilderness of the land of Egypt, so will I plead with you, saith the Lord God. And I will cause you to pass under the rod, and I will bring you into the bond of the covenant: and I will purge out from among you the rebels, and them that transgress against me ; I will bring them forth out of the country where they sojourn, and they shall not enter into the land of Israel : and ye shall know that I am the Lord. As for you, O house of Israel, thus saith the Lord God. . . . I will accept you with your sweet savour, when I bring you out from the people, and gather you out of the countries wherein ye have been scattered : and I will be sanctified in you before the heathen. And ye shall know that I am the Lord, when I shall bring you into the land of Israel, into the country for the which I lifted up mine hand to give it to your fathers" (Ezek. xx. 33-39, 41, 42). The statement is clear. God is going to gather them out, and bring them into their own land ; but, observe, He purges them on the way. There is this difference between the two tribes, and the ten. The two tribes go into Palestine in unbelief, and are purged in the land. The ten tribes are brought out of the nations in unbelief, but they are purged, by God, on their way to the land. Just as their fathers fell in the wilderness, so will God test the children, in the time to come.

Turning now to another prophet, we find that the truth Ezekiel affirms, Amos glowingly corroborates. "Behold, the eyes of the Lord God are upon the sinful kingdom, and I will destroy it from off the face of the earth; saving that I will not utterly destroy the house of Jacob, saith the Lord. For, lo, I will command, and I will sift the house of Israel among all nations, like as corn is sifted in a sieve, yet shall not the least grain fall upon the earth. All the sinners of my people shall die by the sword, which say, The evil shall not overtake nor prevent us. In that day will I raise up the tabernacle of David that is fallen, and close up the breaches thereof; and I will raise up his ruins, and I will build it as in the days of old: that they may possess the remnant of Edom, and of all the heathen, which are called by my name, saith the Lord that doeth this. Behold, the days come, saith the Lord, that the plowman shall overtake the reaper, and the treader of grapes him that soweth seed; and the mountains shall drop sweet wine, and all the hills shall melt. And I will bring again the captivity of my people of Israel, and they shall build the waste cities, and inhabit them; and they shall plant vineyards, and drink the wine thereof; they shall also make gardens, and eat the fruit of them. And I will plant them upon their land, and they shall no more be pulled up out of their land which I have given them, saith the Lord thy God" (Amos ix. 8-15). He is going to gather them out of the nations, and, although He chastens them,— "the sinners shall die,"—that is the very moment that He raises up the tabernacle of David, and closes up the breaches thereof. He restores Israel to their pristine glory—even greater glory than under the reign of Solomon.

I would like now to turn to Ezekiel once more, to see the elaborate care that God takes, by His Spirit, to make all this plain and certain for the faith of His ancient people. I am going to ask you to look at the close of this prophecy, a little in detail, because it is exceedingly interesting. Let us look at the 34th chapter, and you will read, "For thus saith the Lord God, Behold I, even I, will both search my sheep, and seek them out. As a shepherd seeketh out his flock in the day that he is among his sheep that are scattered; so will I seek out my sheep, and will deliver them out of all places where they have been scattered in the cloudy and dark day" (verses 11, 12). Oh what a cloudy and dark day has Israel known, for over two thousand five hundred years, but if I could only speak to those twelve tribes, I would say, There is a good time coming for you—there is at hand a moment when the Lord will redeem this wonderful statement on His part. "And I will bring them out from the people, and gather them from the countries, and will bring them to their own land, and feed them upon the mountains of Israel, by the rivers, and in all the inhabited places of the country. I will feed them in a good pasture. [Oh, friends, God is a wonderful God.] And upon the high mountains of Israel shall their fold be; there shall they lie in a good fold, and in a fat pasture shall they feed upon the mountains of Israel. I will feed my flock, and I will cause them to lie down, saith the Lord God. I will seek that which was lost"—blessed be His name—" and bring again that which was driven away, and will bind up that which was broken, and will strengthen that which was sick ; but I will destroy the fat and the strong ; I will feed them with judgment" (verses 13-16). God will break down and judge the guilty in Israel, just as He does the Gentile. You will find that God will break you down, hardy sinner that you are, very soon, if you are not brought to repentance, and faith in the Lord Jesus Christ. Here, in the midst of beautiful promises, I find God saying, "I will destroy the fat and the strong." I know perfectly well that expositors want to apply these scriptures to Christians. Nay, they do not belong to us. I do not object to the application of a scripture, but I want the meaning, and interpretation, of those blessed, and beautiful promises, which are to me exquisitely lovely.

Pass now to Ezekiel xxxvi. and xxxvii, which run together, even as xxxviii. and xxxix. go together. I do not say they are absolutely consecutive, though I conclude they are, for I do not see how that which chapters xxxviii.and xxxix. bring out, could take place, until that which chapters xxxvi. and xxxvii. unfold has transpired. To them I now turn your attention, assured that you will be filled with admiration of the goodness, the mercy, and the long-suffering patience of God, as you look at what He states there.

"Also, thou son of man, prophesy unto the mountains of Israel, and say, Ye mountains of Israel, hear the word of the Lord. Thus saith the Lord God, Because the enemy hath said against you, Aha! even the ancient high places are ours in possession : therefore prophesy and say, Thus saith the Lord God, Because they have made you desolate, and swallowed you up on every side, that ye might be a possession unto the residue of the heathen, and ye are taken up in the lips of talkers, and are an infamy of the people: Therefore, ye mountains of Israel, hear the word of the Lord God; Thus saith the Lord God to the mountains, and to the hills, to the rivers, and to the valleys, to the desolate wastes, and to the cities that are forsaken, which became a prey and derision to the residue of the heathen that are round about; Therefore thus saith the Lord God, Surely in the fire of my jealousy have I spoken against the residue of the heathen, and against all Idumea, which have appointed my land into their possession with the joy of all their heart, with despiteful minds, to cast it out for a prey." God says, I know what you think. You think you are going to possess the land. I will tell you what I am going to do—" Prophesy therefore concerning the land of Israel, and say unto the mountains and to the hills, to the rivers and to the valleys, Thus saith the Lord God, Behold, I have spoken in my jealousy, and in my fury, because ye have borne the shame of the heathen: Therefore, thus saith the Lord God, I have lifted up mine hand, Surely the heathen that are about you, they shall bear their shame. But ye, O mountains of Israel, ye shall shoot forth your branches, and yield your fruit to my people of Israel; for they are at hand to come. For, behold, I am for you, and I will turn unto you, and ye shall be tilled and sown. And I will multiply men upon you, all the house of Israel, even all of it: and the cities shall be inhabited, and the wastes shall be builded: and I will multiply upon you man and beast; and they shall increase and bring fruit: and I will settle you after your old estates, and will do better unto you than at your beginnings; and ye shall know that I am the Lord." That is like God. It is better at the end, after Israel has sinned, than before they sinned. It is exactly the same with us. After we have sinned, and are on our road to hell, what does God do? He opens up heaven, and says, Come this way.

But, in continuation of God's words to the land, we read, "Yea, I will cause men to walk upon you, even my people Israel; and they shall possess thee, and thou shalt be their inheritance, and thou shalt no more henceforth bereave them of men. Thus saith the Lord God, Because they say unto you, Thou land devourest up men, and hast bereaved thy nations: therefore thou shalt devour men no more, neither bereave thy nations any more, saith the Lord God" (Ezek. xxxvi. 1-14). You recollect that when the spies went up to the land (Num. xiii. 31-33), they, with the exception of Joshua and Caleb, said it was "a land that eateth up the inhabitants thereof"—so barren that people could not live on it. You see that is exactly what Palestine is now. Many cannot live therein, as they do not yet get "the first and the latter rain," and, until that comes, it will not be able to feed the people. But the Scripture says, "I will give you the rain of your land in his due season, the first rain and the latter rain, that thou mayest gather in thy corn, and thy wine, and thine oil" (Deut. xi. 14). It will yet bring forth abundantly, for the curse will be removed, and Jesus will be there. In that day "the plowman shall overtake the reaper, and the treader of grapes him that soweth seed." It is a very remarkable statement, but it is only God's way of showing how wonderfully fruitful everything is to be in the day here spoken of.

It is the land that the Lord first addresses, and further down in this chapter He talks to those who shall be the people thereof. "For I will take you from among the heathen, and gather you out of all countries, and will bring you into your own land. Then will I sprinkle clean water upon you, and ye shall be clean : from all your filthiness, and from all your idols, will I cleanse you. A new heart also will I give you, and a new spirit will I put within you; and I will take away the stony heart out of your flesh, and I will give you an heart of flesh. And I will put my Spirit within you, and cause you to walk in my statutes, and ye shall keep my judgments, and do them. And ye shall dwell in the land that I give to your fathers ; and ye shall be my people, and I will be your God" (verses 24-28). I know that people say, We thought that was only a figure of what the Gospel is. Does not the Lord Jesus make allusion to this scripture when he says to Nicodemus, "If I have told you earthly things, and ye believe not, how shall ye believe if I tell you of heavenly things?" I have no doubt that the Lord did allude to this, along with other scriptures, when He said to Nicodemus, "Except a man be born of water and of the Spirit, he cannot enter into the kingdom of God" (John iii. 5). That is exactly what will take place in Israel.

Scripture abounds in figures, hence I do not understand by water, either in this scripture, or in Isaiah xliv. 3, what we are accustomed to think of as the material water that men wash in. It is a figure of the Word of God, applied in the energy and power of the Spirit of God, by which men will be blessed. New birth is ever, and only, by the Word of God, of which water is the figure, and that such is so is abundantly plain in the New Testament. The Lord Jesus says to Nicodemus, "Except a man be born of water and of the Spirit, he cannot enter into the kingdom of God." Some have thought that to mean baptism. I do not believe it at all. There is no word about baptism in either chapter. In Ezekiel xxxvi., what God says is, " I will sprinkle clean water upon you, and ye shall be clean." He takes away the heart of stone, and gives them the Spirit. It is the new birth through which they are to pass—even as you and I have to pass through it now, if we are to enter God's kingdom. It is plain that it is not baptism, by the fact of our blessed Lord taking water, and washing all His disciples' feet, and then saying, " Ye are clean, but *not all*" (John xiii. 10). Later on the same eventful night He says to His disciples, " Now are ye clean " —through the water I used before Judas went out? *No.* " Now are ye clean through *the Word* which I have spoken unto you " (John xv. 3).

With this also fully agrees that which we read in Ephesians, " Christ also loved the church, and gave himself for it ; that he might sanctify and cleanse it with the washing of water by the word " (Eph. v. 25, 26). Again, in St James we read, " Of his own will begat he us with the word of truth " (Jas. i. 18), and in St Peter, " Being born again, not of corruptible seed, but of incorruptible, by the word of God, which liveth and abideth for ever " (1 Pet. i. 23). In plain language the water is the figure of the Word of God, by which the Lord converts the soul, whether of the godless Gentile now, or of the repentant Israelite in the day yet to come. The word enters and is the means of cleansing. " Wherewithal shall a young man cleanse his way? By taking heed thereto according to thy word " (Psa. cxix. 9). It is only by the Word of God that the soul is new-born. Whether you are new-born I do not know, but I desire to remind you of the universal applicability, of what the Lord says to Nicodemus, as well as to you, and to me also, "Ye must be born again." Doubtless the Lord knew it would surprise his listener a bit—and many others since—and therefore He said, "*Marvel not* that I said unto you, *ye must be born again.*" Whether in the day of Israel's restoration, or in the present day, the new birth is an absolute moral necessity if we are to be blessed of God. Jesus tells you how it can be. The Son of Man is lifted up on the cross, and you have to believe in the dying Saviour, in order to get life to your dead soul.

Well, now, it is perfectly plain what God will do. Israel will be converted to God, new-born, and they will possess the Holy Ghost—not in the same way as the Christian does now, but the Spirit of God will be within them. Thus the new birth, and the possession of the Spirit will lead them into relationship with God, known in grace. "Ye shall be my people, and I will be your God" (ver. 28).

Passing now to the 37th chapter, we come to a passage familiar, I doubt not, to everybody in this room. The valley of dry bones has been, no doubt, before you many times, as the subject of a Gospel address. I should like, however, to show you what I believe to be God's meaning in the scripture. "The hand of the Lord was upon me, and carried me out in the Spirit of the Lord, and set me down in the midst of the valley which was full of bones, and caused me to pass by them round about; and, behold there were very many in the open valley; and lo, they were very dry." *Dry*, that is exactly what the sinner is; you are very dry, you have not got a bit of life, or sap in you. Dry bones may very well describe your spiritual state, if you are an unconverted sinner, no matter what your profession may be. "And he said unto me, Son of man, can these bones live? And I answered, O Lord God, thou knowest. Again he said unto me, Prophesy upon these bones, and say unto them, O ye dry bones, hear the word of the Lord." I have no objection at all to the extraction of the Gospel here, and I know that dear old Dr Guthrie preached lovely sermons from this chapter, and got many a conversion through it too, but then you see the application, and the interpretation of a scripture, are two totally different things. Well, "hear the word of the Lord. Thus saith the Lord God unto these bones, Behold, I will cause breath to enter into you, and ye shall live: and I will lay sinews upon you, and will bring up flesh upon you, and cover you with skin, and put breath in you, and ye shall live; and ye shall know that I am the Lord. So I prophesied as I was commanded: and as I prophesied there was a noise, and, behold, a shaking, and the bones came together, bone to his bone. And when I beheld, lo, the sinews and the flesh came up upon them, and the skin covered them above: but there was no breath in them. Then said he unto me, Prophesy unto the wind, prophesy, son of man, and say to the wind, Thus saith the Lord God, Come from the four winds, O breath, and breathe upon these slain, that they may live. So I prophesied as he commanded me, and the breath came into them, and they lived, and stood up upon their feet, an exceeding great army. Then he said unto me, Son of man, these bones are"—what? Poor Gentile sinners converted by the Gospel? No. "Son of man, these bones are *the whole house of Israel:* behold, they say, Our bones are dried, and our hope is lost: we are cut off for our parts." That is what they are saying to-day, We are cast off, we are rejected of the Lord. "Therefore prophesy, and say unto them, Thus saith the Lord God; Behold, O my people, I will open your graves, and cause you to come up out of your graves, and bring you into the land of Israel. And ye shall know that I am the Lord, when I have opened your graves, O my people, and brought you up out of your graves, and shall put my spirit in you, and ye shall live, and I shall place you in your own land: then shall ye know that I the Lord have spoken it, and performed it, saith the Lord" (Ezek. xxxvii. 1-14).

The grave here, clearly, is their national grave, and corresponds exactly with the last chapter of the book of Daniel, where you recollect it says (1st verse),—"And at that time shall Michael stand up, the great prince which standeth for the children of thy people: and there shall be a time of trouble, such as never was since there was a nation even to that same time: and at that time thy people shall be delivered, every one that shall be found written in the book. And many of them that sleep in the dust of the earth shall awake, some to everlasting life, and some to shame and everlasting contempt." That is, in that day, I do not think all will be saved, but when the word of the Lord comes out, the nation will be revived, and the people, whom nobody can put their hand upon now, God will put His hand upon, and will find them, and restore them, and the whole house of Israel will be replaced, by the hand of the blessed God, in their own land.

It is very beautiful to note the way that God repeats

a truth, thereby to cause the faith of His people to be confirmed. In the 36th chapter you have the doctrine of Israel's restoration, in the 37th you have a striking figure of their national resurrection, and then you get another view of it in the two sticks. God comes to great detail, in the latter half of chapter xxxvii.: " The word of the Lord came again unto me, saying, Moreover, thou son of man, take thee one stick, and write upon it, For Judah, and for the children of Israel his companions; then take another stick, and write upon it, For Joseph, the stick of Ephraim, and for all the house of Israel his companions: and join them one to another into one stick; and they shall become one in thine hand. And when the children of thy people shall speak unto thee, saying, Wilt thou not shew us what thou meanest by these? say unto them, Thus saith the Lord God, Behold, I will take the stick of Joseph, which is in the hand of Ephraim, and the tribes of Israel his fellows, and will put them with him, even with the stick of Judah, and make them one stick, and they shall be one in mine hand. And the sticks whereon thou writest shall be in thine hand before their eyes. And say unto them, Thus saith the Lord God, Behold, I will take the children of Israel from among the heathen, whither they be gone, and will gather them on every side, and bring them into their own land: and I will make them one nation in the land upon the mountains of Israel; and one king shall be king to them all: and they shall be no more two nations, neither shall they be divided into two kingdoms any more at all: neither shall they defile themselves any more with their idols, nor with their detestable things, nor with any of their transgressions: but I will save them out of all their dwelling-places, wherein they have sinned, and will cleanse them ; so shall they be my people, and I will be their God." Oh! glorious promises, for this ancient, and down-trodden people. But more : " And David my servant shall be king over them ; and they all shall have one shepherd. . . . And they shall dwell in the land that I have given unto Jacob my servant, wherein your fathers have dwelt ; and they shall dwell therein : even they, and their children, and their children's children, for ever ; and my servant David shall be their prince for ever " (Ezek. xxxvii. 15-25).

But, who is David ? I have no doubt he is the Lord Jesus. You say, Why David ? and why not Solomon ? David is a type of Jesus as a king, but a king who is patient with his enemies. Solomon judged his immediately. I have no doubt that when the Lord reproduces the kingdom, He will do as David did, He will not put His hand on His foes, in the tremendous hurry, that you, or I, would do. He is patient. Why it is David, is this, that it is more in the shepherd character, and because he did not deal with, and judge all his enemies, when he might have so done. There were several enemies left when David died, and it was Solomon, who executed righteous judgment, upon those godless men.

Our chapter concludes, " My tabernacle also shall be with them : yea, I will be their God, and they shall be my people. And the heathen shall know that I the Lord do sanctify Israel, when my sanctuary shall be in the midst of them for evermore " (Ezek. xxxvii. 27, 28). They are re-established in the land, and Christ reigns over them, and every promise of God is fulfilled. What a happy, and glorious day, for Israel will that indeed be !

No sooner is Israel possessed of the land in peace, than they are again, and finally, assaulted by Gog and Magog (chaps. xxxviii., xxxix.). These must not be confounded with those spoken of in Revelation xx. The Gog, and Magog, of Revelation are not brought into view until the millennium has passed by. And they come, "from the four quarters of the earth." Here, clearly, Gog and Magog are a huge host, gathered from comparatively contiguous lands to Palestine, and led on, I have no doubt, by the antitype of Israel's ancient, and ruthless foe, the Assyrian, or "King of the North." You, who are conversant with the Old Testament, will remember, that as long as Israel were in outward relationship with God, and were owned by Him as His people, and were living in the land He had given them, when they were Ammi, *i.e.*, my people (Hosea ii. 1), it was the Assyrian that oppressed them. It was when they were cast off by God, and called Lo-Ammi, *i.e.*, not my people (Hosea i. 9), that the power of Rome came in, at length completely subjugating the Jews, destroying their city and temple, and scattering them to the winds of heaven, as we have seen. The beast and the false prophet, the fourth empire, revived in Satanic energy, will yet again oppress the Jews, who get back to Palestine, before Messiah returns. The Assyrian oppressed Israel while they were in, and before they, as the fruit of their sins, lost, the land, at the time of their captivity. The Spirit of God gives us here a prophetic picture, of what will be yet attempted, by the old foe. No sooner are they replaced in their own land, than the old desire of the Assyrian, to despoil God's people, and possess their land, breaks forth again, and the remarkable details of the 38th, and 39th chapters, come before us.

"And the word of the Lord came unto me, saying, Son of man, set thy face against Gog, the land of Magog, the prince of Rosh, of Meshech and Tubal, and prophesy against him, and say, Thus saith the Lord God, Behold I am against thee, O Gog, prince of Rosh, Meshech, and Tubal" (Ezek. xxxviii. 1-3). The expression rendered in your English bible, "chief prince," is the Hebrew word ראש (Pώs), which learned, and perfectly competent men, of all nations, and schools of thought, agree in telling us, is the old proper name for Russia. Gog is the name of the leader, of this threefold band of Gentiles, from the north, and east, and south, while his territory is called the land of Magog—the Scythia of the ancients. Impelled by territorial greed, this Prince of Rosh (Russia), Meshech (Muscovy), and Tubal (Tobolsk), the three great divisions, of the vast European, and Asiatic possessions, of the Russian empire, leads his countless hosts against the Holy Land, saying, "I will go up to the land of unwalled villages" (ver. 11). He goes, but only to his utter destruction, as we shall see. You know that the great desire of Russia is territorial aggrandisement, and for centuries she has been making her plans to get possession of India. Peter the Great said his children were never to rest, until they possessed India, and Constantinople, with Turkey in Europe. There are remarkable reasons for that; it is not only that they would have the countries named, as added bits of land, but then, he thought, they would be able completely to dominate the Holy Land. To possess the land where the Lord Jesus lived and died, would gain for them a character for sanctity, which would admirably suit a power, whose superstition is as notorious as its greed. That land has for nearly two thousand years been a bone of contention. It was the cause of all the crusades. It, however, specially belongs to God, and His earthly people, Israel, and they will yet enjoy it.

"Thus saith the Lord God, In that day when my people of Israel dwelleth safely, shalt thou not know it. And thou shalt come from thy place out of the north parts, thou, and many people with thee, all of them riding upon horses, a great company, and a mighty army" (xxxviii. 14, 15). Lured by the apparently defenceless condition of Israel, and ignorant that God is there, Gog puts forth his mighty hand, with a desire to annex that land, and the history of the invasion is given in these two chapters, telling alike his folly, and utter overthrow. Gog comes with his hosts and allies, an overwhelming army, and God cuts off five-sixths of them (xxxix. 2). So mighty is the multitude, with bows, and arrows, that we read: "They that dwell in the cities of Israel shall go forth, and shall set on fire and burn the weapons, both the shields and the bucklers, the bows and the arrows, and the handstaves and the spears, and they shall burn them with fire seven years: so that they shall take no wood out of the field, neither cut down any out of the forests: for they shall burn the weapons with fire: and they shall spoil those that spoiled them, and rob those that robbed them, saith the Lord God" (verses 9, 10). Tremendous, indeed, must be the number of warriors that come against them, since Scripture says they will not need to cut firewood for seven years, and it will take seven months to bury the dead in their appointed graveyard, the valley of Hamon-gog (verses 11-15).

In conclusion, let me, at this point, connect one or two passages, to show you the place which the

Assyrian—who is the forerunner and type of Gog—holds in Scripture. In Isaiah x. you find this mighty power spoken of in relation to Israel: "O Assyrian, the rod of mine anger, and the staff in thine hand is mine indignation" (ver. 5). God used this power, as His rod, to chasten His people. Again: "It shall come to pass, that, when the Lord hath performed his whole work upon mount Zion and on Jerusalem, I will punish the fruit of the stout heart of the king of Assyria, and the glory of his high looks. For he saith, By the strength of my hand I have done it, and by my wisdom; for I am prudent: and I have removed the bounds of the people, and have robbed their treasures, and I have put down the inhabitants like a valiant man: and my hand hath found, as a nest, the riches of the people: and as one gathereth eggs that are left, have I gathered all the earth; and there was none that moved the wing, or opened the mouth, or peeped. Shall the axe boast itself against him that heweth therewith? or shall the saw magnify itself against him that shaketh it? as if the rod should shake itself against them that lift it up, or as if the staff should lift up itself, as if it were no wood" (verses 12-15). God, so to speak, says to this mighty power, I am using you to chastise my erring people, but if you lift up yourself against Me, then I must bring you down. Again: "Therefore thus saith the Lord God of hosts, O my people that dwellest in Zion, be not afraid of the Assyrian: he shall smite thee with a rod, and shall lift up his staff against thee, after the manner of Egypt. For yet a little while, and the indignation shall cease, and mine anger in their destruction" (verses 24, 25).

With the fall of the Assyrian, with the crushing of the

power of Eastern Europe, in that day put down by the Son of Man, will cease the chastening, by the Lord, of His people. The last foe to be judged is the one who was their earliest—the Assyrian. This is fully predicted in Isaiah xiv.: " I will break the Assyrian in my land, and upon my mountains tread him under foot; then shall his yoke depart from off them, and his burden from off their shoulders" (ver. 25). Then there is further testimony in Isaiah xxx.: "For the Lord shall cause his glorious voice to be heard, and shall shew the lighting down of his arm, with the indignation of his anger, and with the flame of a devouring fire, with scattering, and tempest, and hailstones. For through the voice of the Lord shall the Assyrian be beaten down, which smote with a rod. And in every place where the grounded staff shall pass, which the Lord shall lay upon him, it shall be with tabrets and harps: and in battles of shaking will he fight with it. For Tophet is ordained of old; yea, for the king also it is prepared: he hath made it deep and large; the pile thereof is fire and much wood; the breath of the Lord, like a stream of brimstone, doth kindle it " (verses 30-33).

The prophet Micah, also, speaks of the Assyrian being overthrown by Christ. " And he shall stand and feed in the strength of the Lord, in the majesty of the name of the Lord his God; and they shall abide, for now shall he be great unto the ends of the earth. And this man shall be the peace when the Assyrian shall come into our land: and when he shall tread in our palaces, then shall we raise against him seven shepherds, and eight principal men. And they shall waste the lands of Assyria with the sword, and the land of Nimrod in the entrances thereof: thus shall he deliver us from the

Assyrian when he cometh into our land, and when he treadeth within our borders" (Micah v. 4-6).

We get further light on this in Daniel xi.: "And at the time of the end shall the king of the south push at him: and the king of the north shall come against him like a whirlwind, with chariots, and with horsemen, and with many ships; and he shall enter into the countries, and shall overflow and pass over" (ver. 40). "The king" spoken of in verse 36, is antichrist, reigning in the Holy Land. Against him comes, first "the king of the south," or Egypt, which lies south of Palestine. He is soon followed by "the king of the north," that Syrian district, north of Palestine, now belonging to Turkey in Asia, but which will eventually fall into the hands of the great north-eastern power— Gog—which we have been looking at in Ezekiel. These two powers both oppose antichrist, "the king," and each other, but "the king of the north" appears to be victorious, for "he shall enter also into the glorious land, and many countries shall be overthrown; but there shall escape out of his hand, even Edom, and Moab, and the children of Ammon" (ver. 41). "The king" we hear no more of here. His fate we have seen elsewhere (Rev. xix. 20). "The king of the north" seems to triumph everywhere, but Edom, Moab, and Ammon escape his clutches. Why? The answer is found in Isaiah xi. 14. Blood relations, and among the earliest enemies of Israel, God will not let their chastisement come from any hands but from those they have so needlessly injured. They are shortly after entirely subjugated by the victorious Israelites.

"He shall stretch forth his hand also upon the countries: and the land of Egypt shall not escape. But he shall have power over the treasures of gold and of silver, and over all the precious things of Egypt: and the Libyans and the Ethiopians shall be at his steps" (verses 42, 43). This clearly shows that "the king of the north" is inimical to "the king of the south," and in fact ravages his kingdom, apparently much changed from what it now is—Egypt, then, being as rich, as she is now notoriously poor. "But tidings out of the east and out of the north shall trouble him: therefore he shall go forth with great fury to destroy, and utterly to make away many. And he shall plant the tabernacles of his palace between the seas in the glorious holy mountain; yet he shall come to his end, and none shall help him" (verses 44, 45). What the tidings are, out of the east, and out of the north, that trouble him, we are not told. Whatever they be, he hastens back from Egypt, plants the tabernacles of his palace "between the seas"—the Mediterranean and the Dead Seas—and there comes to his end, cut off, not by man, but by God.

With this scripture, I would just connect, what we get in the close of Zechariah (chaps. xii. and xiv.), where Jerusalem is made "a burdensome stone for all people." Against it all nations gather—and at first victory seems to lie with the foe, for the city is taken, and half of the city goes into captivity. This may be possibly connected with the downward march of the king of the north. Thereafter the Lord appears, and goes forth "to fight against these nations." Then it is, that "his feet shall stand in that day upon the Mount of Olives" (Zech. xiv. 4), which will be cloven in twain—and the word shall be fulfilled, "At evening time it shall be light" (ver. 7).

The way is now clear for the reign of the Son of

Man. All is indeed wonderful that has led up to it. The Church is gathered out, and the Lord coming in the air, every believer is caught up. The sleeping saints raised, the living changed, are all caught up in His likeness. And what is the next thing? The Jews restored, and purged, are seen waiting for the coming of the Son of Man. The Son of Man comes, and then all Israel is brought back to the land, and every foe is set aside. The moment is drawing near now when many a prophetic scripture will have its fulfilment, and at that time the Lord will fill the earth with gladness. We may well say in our hearts, Lord, hasten that day. If you are not on the Lord's side, let me once more implore you now. Do not hesitate, because the Lord is coming. Perhaps this is the last Gospel call that you will ever hear. Before to-morrow's sun rises, we may have gone up, and you who are not His, will be left behind, to mourn your folly for ever.

A KING SHALL REIGN IN RIGHTEOUSNESS.

2 SAM. xxiii. 1-7; PS. lxxii.

Lecture VIII

ONE is in no sense surprised that the last words of David should be true, to life, of Him, who is David's Son, and David's Heir, although He was also the Root of David, and David's Lord. I think no person can have the slightest difficulty in seeing, that the One of whom David speaks, in the third verse of the 23rd of 2nd Samuel—although the principle, of course, ought to apply to every ruler—in truth can be none but Jesus, and Jesus in that blessed moment of which the 72nd Psalm has already spoken to us this evening—when He shall rule and reign over this earth. In no part of Scripture can I put my hand upon a passage, which brings out more beautifully, and sweetly, what will be the character of that day, than that which we have read—" He that ruleth over men must be just, ruling in the fear of God : and he shall be as the light of the morning, when the sun riseth, even a morning without clouds; as the tender grass springing out of the earth by clear shining after rain."

Now turn to the 32nd chapter of Isaiah, where we get a remarkable expression with regard to the Lord Jesus Christ, which I desire to point out to you,—

"Behold, a king shall reign in righteousness, and princes shall rule in judgment. And a man shall be as an hiding place from the wind, and a covert from the tempest; as rivers of water in a dry place, as the shadow of a great rock in a weary land. And the eyes of them that see shall not be dim, and the ears of them that hear shall hearken" (verses 1-3). Then lower down in the same chapter we read, "Until the Spirit be poured upon us from on high, and the wilderness be a fruitful field, and the fruitful field be counted for a forest" (ver. 15). That is the change, in the external aspect of the world, at that moment—the wilderness becomes a fruitful field, and what men had, till then, counted a fruitful field, in that day, will be thought a forest—the character of things will be so changed. Reading on, you further find what marks the moment: "Then judgment shall dwell in the wilderness, and righteousness remain in the fruitful field. And the work of righteousness shall be peace: and the effect of righteousness, quietness and assurance for ever. And my people shall dwell in a peaceable habitation, and in sure dwellings, and in quiet resting places" (verses 16-18). Thus you see the Lord distinctly unfolds to His people, by the pen of Isaiah, what will mark that day when the King shall reign in righteousness.

Now, beloved friends, it is very important for us to see, distinctly, the relationship, in which we, as Christians, stand to the Lord, as compared with that of the people, Isaiah writes about here. I know perfectly well, it is a very common thing, for people to speak, poets to write, and preachers to preach about the Lord Jesus, as our King. Scripture, however, is quite silent upon this term, used in relation to the saints of the present dispensation — Christians. In fact, I daresay, it may a little interest you, if I say, that the Lord Jesus, in the whole of His earthly pathway, never spoke of Himself as a king, save once. That once was in the 25th of Matthew, where He is speaking of the future day, of which this 32nd of Isaiah speaks also, when, as King, He will sit upon the throne of His glory, and "then shall the king say unto them on his right hand, Come, ye blessed of my Father, inherit the kingdom prepared for you from the foundation of the world." It is surely not without interest to us, to see, that the Saviour never speaks of Himself as a King, in the whole of His pathway here, save in that passage, and the reason is very simple. It is not as King that the believer knows Him now. It is not, of course, but that the Lord has authority over him, but the moment of the manifestation of the kingship of Christ has not yet come. The expression "King of saints" (Rev. xv. 3) should be "King of nations," as the margin rightly gives it. When the Lord was upon the earth, He was a prophet, and now interceding before God, He is the great High-priest, but, in the day to come, He is to be a King.

What, then, is our relationship to the Lord Jesus? It is one of a much deeper, and far more blessed nature, than that of a subject to a king. Do not we, as believers in the Lord Jesus Christ, stand in a wonderfully nearer relationship to Him, than that of subjects to a king? There is, of necessity, no love between a subject and a king. It is merely a relationship of authority and subjection—exaltation on the part of the king, and subjection on the part of a subject. But the blessed truth of Christianity is this, that if you and I are brought, through grace, to know the Lord Jesus

Christ now, as our Saviour, we are washed in His blood, and redeemed to God, through the work that He accomplished on the cross. We stand in the same relationship to God, as He does, as Man. He is now set down as the risen Man, the exalted Man in glory, and then, and never till then, did He become what Scripture asserts that He is, viz., "the head of the body—the Church." But now that He is in glory, the Holy Ghost comes down from Him there, and believers, Jew and Gentile, are first of all born of the Spirit, and then indwelt of the Spirit, and are so "baptized by one Spirit into one body," of which the Lord Jesus, in glory, is the living head. We are thus made members of Christ, and members one of another.

It is not by faith, nor by possessing life, but by having the Holy Ghost, that we become united to Christ. But what has that to do with the Lord's coming? A great deal. Another night I hope to show you, that they who are in union with Christ, as members of His body—hence composing the Bride—will have a wonderful place, by-and-by, in the millennial day. I do not purpose this evening taking up that side of the truth, but I will say this, that those who belong to Jesus now, who are united to Him, as Head of the Church, will have a marvellous place in the millennial reign of the Lord Jesus Christ. You will find all this fully unfolded in the 21st, and 22nd of Revelation, where the New Jerusalem, the Bride, the Lamb's wife, is depicted, and portrayed, and her relation to a delivered earth fully brought out. The importance of knowing the Saviour now, and our relationship with that Saviour, is very far reaching, because it is of that day, that the Lord Himself speaks, when He says, "The glory which thou gavest me I have given them; that they may be one, even as we are one: I in them, and thou in me, that they may be made perfect in one; and that the world may know that thou hast sent me, and hast loved them, as thou hast loved me" (John xvii. 22, 23). And by-and-by, when the world sees the blessed Lord, and owns Him, it will be a wonderful thing for you and me, to find ourselves in association with Christ, not as subjects merely, but as sharers of the glory, which He inaugurates, and will maintain for a thousand years, over the delivered earth. It is a happy thing to be a Christian, there is nothing brighter or better, if one thinks of it now, or for the time to come.

Here, then, we get plainly enough the divine statement that a King shall reign in righteousness. Now turn to a scripture which definitely states what the period of the reign will be—Revelation xx. 4-6. On a previous occasion we looked at the 19th chapter, and saw how the Lord comes as King of kings, and Lord of lords, from heaven, and how the beast and the false prophet will be put down by Him, when, as a warrior judge, He comes again to the earth. "And I saw an angel come down from heaven, having the key of the bottomless pit and a great chain in his hand. And he laid hold on the dragon, that old serpent, which is the Devil, and Satan, and bound him a thousand years."

The very first thing the true King does, before He commences His reign of peace upon the earth, is to bind the usurper of God's rights, and place, in this world, from the Garden of Eden downwards. Satan is "bound for a thousand years." He is called here the dragon, but also the old serpent. He was the source of all the evil, and sorrow, in the morning of man's day on earth (Gen. iii.), and every name, that Scripture gives him elsewhere, is introduced here, that there might be no mistake whatever as to his personality. The angel " cast him into the bottomless pit, and shut him up, and set a seal upon him, that he should deceive the nations no more, till the thousand years should be fulfilled; and after that he must be loosed a little season" (ver. 3). The time of his incarceration in the bottomless pit endures then for one thousand years.

Then John says, "I saw thrones, and *they*" (the heavenly saints, who came out with the Lord in chapter xix., the Church, I have no doubt, but more than the Church, all the heavenly saints) " sat upon them, and judgment was given unto them : and I saw the souls of them that were beheaded for the witness of Jesus, and for the word of God" (the early martyrs of the book of Revelation, see chapter vi.), " and those which had not worshipped the beast, neither his image, neither had received his mark upon their foreheads, or in their hands" (that is the later company of martyrs, spoken of in the 13th, and 15th chapters) ; " and they lived and reigned with Christ a thousand years." They have full association with the Lord in the day of His earthly glory. " But the rest of the dead lived not again until the thousand years were finished. This is the first resurrection. Blessed and holy is he that hath part in the first resurrection : on such the second death hath no power ; but they shall be priests of God and of Christ, and shall reign with him a thousand years. And when the thousand years are expired, Satan shall be loosed out of his prison" (verses 4-7).

I speak not now of Satan's release, but you see that for a thousand years—the millennium—the prime mover of all evil is cast out of the scene. Some person might say, Why a thousand years? Well, Scripture distinctly says it shall be a thousand years, and, I have little doubt in my mind that, the thousand years is connected very beautifully with the faithfulness of God. Do you not remember what God said, when He re-formed this earth, and put man upon it? Turn back to the first of Genesis, and you will at once see another instance of how all Scripture hangs together most wonderfully. "In the beginning God created the heaven and the earth." Then we read, "the earth was without form and void." Do you think that is the way God made the earth? Do you think God turned this earth out, a rude, shapeless mass, like that? Impossible, no! There is no mistake about that. Just turn to the 45th of Isaiah, verse 18, and you will find a remarkable statement as to this point. There the Spirit of God says, "Thus saith the Lord that created the heavens; God himself that formed the earth, and made it; he hath established it, he created it not in vain; he formed it to be inhabited."

What does "in vain" mean? It is the very same Hebrew word rendered "without form, and void" in Genesis i. 2. So you see that you have here, a great sidelight flung on Genesis i. In the beginning God created the earth. When thus created, it was *not* created "without form, and void." How it became "without form, and void," is not told us in Scripture. We are only told, that God did not *so* create it, but that eventually it was reduced to that condition, and therefore, I have little doubt, that between the 1st and 2nd verses of Genesis i., in other words, between "the beginning," when God created the earth, and the time when it is seen to be "without form, and void," we have that necessarily vast period, during which all the varied strata of the earth's crust were formed, of which the geologists instruct us, and, for the deposition of which, they demand such unlimited ages. In the interval between these two verses you have space for all that geology demands. Let me say, in passing, you had better believe Scripture before geology. Geology sometimes speaks a little bit widely. Science, and geology especially, is rather like a noisy baby, it is very apt to make a great noise when it first appears, but as it gets older it gets quieter. We had better listen to God than to geologists, if they state what is counter to Scripture. We have lived long enough, some of us, to know that the theories of fifty years ago have all been exploded to-day, but the Word of God abides. Geologists tell us that there were at least twenty-nine epochs, and twenty-nine immense convulsions of the earth's crust. Well, be it so, and what do you find? We discover the granite, which was formed at the bottom, brought to the top, and you build your houses thereof, and the coal, that you are glad to warm yourselves with in winter, though formed infinitely lower than where it is found to-day by your miners, was, by the very influence, that rendered the earth "without form, and void," brought near the surface, or they could never get at it at all.

Let me repeat, then, that there is room, for all that geology wants, between verses 1 and 2, and then we can take the six days to be, as I believe them to be, days of twenty-four hours, in which God prepared the earth for man. It might have taken one hundred years for an oak tree to grow, but it would not take a carpenter one day to cut that tree, and make it into some useful article. That is what is meant, I take it, when it is said of the earth, that God "*formed* it to be inhabited." He put to His hand, and formed the earth for man, and then "God saw everything that he had made, and, behold it was very good" (Gen. i. 31). Then we read, "And on the seventh day God ended his work which he had made, and he rested on the seventh day from all his work which he had made; and God blessed the seventh day and sanctified it, because that in it he had rested from all his work which God created and made" (Gen. ii. 2, 3).

We have, then, God working six days, and He appoints the seventh as the day of rest. That is the second of Genesis, and you know what took place in the third. I do not know that the fall of man took place on the very day that God did rest, but He had made man, and put a helpmeet by his side—a lovely type of Christ and His Church. Then the next thing we find is, that the serpent enters, and this happy scene is defiled by the enemy's power. Man falls, and the rest of God is broken, and from that day till this, the earth has been marked by the trail of the serpent, the sin of man, and the absence of rest. That has gone on for nearly six thousand years. About four thousand years elapsed before Christ was born, and we are now in A.D. 1891, which makes 5891. We are not, however, quite sure of our chronology, and I am thankful for that too, for we may be rather nearer the end of the six thousand years, than people are aware of. Earth has been robbed of her Sabbaths for six thousand years, but God is faithful, and will give them to her, all in a lump, by-and-by, and so, I have little doubt, that the seventh thousand, will be the thousand years of which the 20th of Revelation speaks; for, as six days of labour, are to one of rest, so are six thousand years of sin, and sorrow, under the rule of the devil, to the thousand years, of rest, and peace, under the blessed Lord Jesus.

The next thing before us is the rapture of the saints, the Church is taken to glory, and then the Lord appears, Satan is cast into the bottomless pit, and the reign of the righteous King begins. The 72nd Psalm, to which I will turn you, is exceedingly beautiful, as unfolding what will be the character of that reign. All the Lord's enemies are judged, and He gathers out of His kingdom all things that offend, and then He rules, and reigns over the earth, in absolute righteousness. In this Psalm you will see one particular feature of the Lord's reign, that is exceedingly beautiful. He thinks of the poor especially. In the 4th verse we find, "He shall judge the poor of the people, he shall save the children of the needy, and shall break in pieces the oppressor. They shall fear thee as long as the sun and moon endure, throughout all generations. He shall come down like rain upon the mown grass; as showers that water the earth. In his days shall the righteous flourish; and abundance of peace so long as the moon endureth. He shall have dominion also from sea to sea, and from the river unto the ends of the earth. They that dwell in the wilderness shall bow before him; and his enemies shall lick the dust. The kings of Tarshish and of the isles shall bring presents: the kings of Sheba and Seba shall offer gifts. Yea, all kings shall fall down before him; all nations shall serve him. For he shall deliver the needy when he crieth; the poor also, and him that hath no helper" (Ps. lxxii. 4-12).

Every kind of injustice will be remedied, by His blessed hand, immediately, for He reigns in righteousness. There are three spheres where righteousness is found. In the present moment, if I think of God's dealings with men, I learn this, that grace reigns through righteousness—it is divine grace upon a righteous basis that saves men to-day. But from another point of view, now is the day when righteousness *suffers*. From the day of the rejection of the Lord Jesus, in fact from Abel downwards, righteousness has always suffered. You just try to be practically a righteous person, and you will suffer. I do not deny at all that in the long run "Honesty is the best policy," but nevertheless the honest one will have to suffer. You may suffer for "conscience toward God" (1 Pet. ii. 19); or, "for righteousness sake" (1 Pet. iii. 14); or, "as a Christian" (1 Pet. iv. 16). In the millennial day righteousness *reigns;* and as regards eternity we read of "new heavens and a new earth, wherein *dwelleth* righteousness" (2 Pet. iii. 13). It is perfectly at home, so to speak, there. In the day when righteousness reigns upon the earth, it does not appear that everybody will be converted. The millennial reign of the Lord Jesus does not, necessarily, involve the absolute conversion to God, of every soul upon earth, although, thank God, the mass will be converted. There may be, even in that day, when the Lord is manifesting His glory so wonderfully, those, who may break out in opposition to Him. When the Lord appears by-and-by, in power, and majesty, with every attribute of glory connected with Him, it will be a magnificent, marvellous, and appalling sight for the world. Sinners will think then, that they had better bow down to Him, but whether they all will do so, in reality, is a question.

In proof of this, I ask you to turn to the 18th Psalm. It describes the moment when the Lord **is** made "the head of the heathen." "Thou hast delivered me from the strivings of the people; and thou hast made me the head of the heathen: a people whom I have not known shall serve me. As soon as they hear of me they shall obey me: the sons of the stranger [*see* margin] shall yield feigned obedience [margin] unto me" (verses 43, 44). This is not a very remarkable thing; the fathers will be all right, but the sons unchanged; just, as to-day, you will find a godly father, and, alas! an ungodly son. Again, in Psalm lxvi. we read—"How terrible art thou in thy works; through the greatness of thy power shall thine enemies submit themselves unto thee," or as in the margin, "lie, or yield feigned obedience" (ver. 3). That is, in the presence of the unmistakable power, and divine authority of the Lord Jesus, in that day, there will be an apparent subjection to Him, that may not be real, and that being so, one is prepared for that which the 20th of Revelation gives us,—namely, that after the thousand years, there is found Gog and Magog—a large company, who yield themselves to Satan, when, being loosed, he emerges from the bottomless pit.

I would now like you to look at some of the salient features of the millennium.

(1.) *Death will be a rare thing.* Turn to Isaiah lxv. "Behold, I create new heavens, and a new earth! and the former shall not be remembered, nor come into mind. But be ye glad and rejoice for ever in that which I create; for behold I create Jerusalem a rejoicing, and her people, a joy. And I will rejoice in Jerusalem, and joy in my people: and the voice of weeping shall be no more heard in her, nor the voice of crying. There shall be no more thence an infant of days, nor an old man that hath not filled his days: for the child shall die an hundred years old; but the sinner being an hundred years old, shall be accursed" (verses 17-20). You see from this passage that death will be a rare thing. To-day death is the rule; "death reigned from Adam to Moses," and right onward too; but in that day it will be the exception. We, believers in the Lord Jesus Christ, are looking for the return of the Bridegroom, and we look to go to heaven, without death, and, thank God, some of us will—I do not say you and I will—but, certainly, some of the Lord's saints will be alive when He comes. You remember Methuselah, whose life was nine hundred and sixty-nine years. That was not very much short of the thousand; but in the thousand years of the peaceful reign of Jesus, man will live out the full limit, which God has designed for him. What is meant then by saying that "the child shall die an hundred years old"? Well, supposing you had a little one of seven, and it died, you say it died a child. Supposing next week the grandfather dies, and his age is seventy, you say he was an "old man." He was only seventy, and as seven is to seventy, so is an hundred to a thousand. Seven is the child's age in our day, while it will be an hundred in that day. In our day seventy is the old man's age, while in that day one thousand years will many an old man see. I take it that death will only be, as the result of the governmental dealing of God, upon some open, and distinct act of sin, against the Lord.

But I hear an objector saying, If people are not going to die, how will you get them fed; the population of the earth will overstep the possibility of its supplying food for its inhabitants?

(2.) *The curse will be removed from the earth.* In that day God will change the very aspect of things upon the earth. I wonder if you have ever observed another verse in our chapter. "They shall build houses, and inhabit them, and they shall plant vineyards and eat the fruit of them" (ver. 21). Man is in the most happy, and blessed relations with God possible, in that day, and God will blessedly undertake for him then. We have looked already this evening at the 3rd of Genesis, where the curse came in. The head of creation, Adam, fell, and, for his sake, the ground was cursed. It did not yield its increase. It is by the sweat of the brow that man has had to earn his bread since, and I suppose there never was a day, when people, in this land, felt more the pressure of the curse than now, when agriculture has so failed, and competition is so keen. Every year comes out the cry that the land cannot be made to bring forth food, to feed the people thereof; and it is a question of importing from all quarters, to keep people alive, at least where you and I live.

Now observe what is going to happen in that day? The curse is to be removed entirely. It was partially alleviated in the day of Noah, but it will be completely abrogated in Messiah's day. This is plainly stated in Isaiah xxxv.: "The wilderness and the solitary place shall be glad for them; and the desert shall rejoice and blossom as the rose. It shall blossom abundantly, and rejoice even with joy and singing; the glory of Lebanon shall be given unto it, the excellency of Carmel and Sharon, they shall see the glory of the Lord, and the excellency of our God. . . . in the wilderness shall waters break out, and streams in the desert. And the parched ground shall become a pool, and the thirsty land, springs of water; in the habitation of dragons where each lay, shall be grass, with reeds and rushes. . . . And the ransomed of the Lord shall return, and come to Zion with songs, and everlasting joy upon their heads; they shall obtain joy and gladness, and sorrow and sighing shall flee away" (verses 1, 2, 6, 7, 10). The Lord puts His hand upon the face of creation in that day.

Look at Amos ix.: " Behold, the days come, saith the Lord, that the plowman shall overtake the reaper, and the treader of grapes him that soweth seed; and the mountains shall drop sweet wine, and all the hills shall melt. And I will bring again the captivity of my people of Israel, and they shall build the waste cities, and inhabit them; and they shall plant vineyards, and drink the wine thereof; they shall also make gardens, and eat the fruit of them. And I will plant them upon their land, and they shall no more be pulled up out of their land which I have given them, saith the Lord thy God" (verses 13-15). In Isaiah 32nd, the same testimony comes out, when "the wilderness shall be a fruitful field, and the fruitful field be counted for a forest" (ver. 15). The sweet Psalmist of Israel also anticipates this moment when he says, " Then shall the earth yield her increase; and God, even our own God, shall bless us" (Ps. lxvii. 6). Very wonderful will be the change over the face of creation, and all a testimony to Christ.

(3.) *The animal creation will undergo a radical change.* Turn for a little again to Isaiah lxv., "The wolf and the lamb shall feed together, and the lion shall eat straw like the bullock: and dust shall be the serpent's meat. They shall not hurt nor destroy in all my holy mountain, saith the Lord" (ver. 25). The only creature, from which God does not remove the curse, is the serpent. Even in that day the recollection will be in Jehovah's mind, of the part the serpent played, in producing the ruin He is now remedying, and therefore we have that sentence, "dust shall be the serpent's meat."

Then in Isaiah xi. we have a glowing picture of the reign of the Messiah. He comes forth as a rod out of the stem of Jesse—a branch growing out. Then we get the character of His reign. "But with righteousness shall he judge the poor, and reprove with equity for the meek of the earth: and he shall smite the earth with the rod of his mouth, and with the breath of his lips shall he slay the wicked. And righteousness shall be the girdle of his loins, and faithfulness the girdle of his reins. The wolf also shall dwell with the lamb, and the leopard shall lie down with the kid; and the calf, and the young lion, and the fatling together; and a little child shall lead them. And the cow and the bear shall feed: their young ones shall lie down together: and the lion shall eat straw like the ox. And the sucking child shall play on the hole of the asp, and the weaned child shall put his hand on the cockatrice den. They shall not hurt nor destroy in all my holy mountain: for the earth shall be full of the knowledge of the Lord, as the waters cover the sea" (verses 4-9). A marvellous day for the earth, and the, at present, groaning creation, will it be. It will be the fulfilment of the statement, "The creature itself also shall be delivered from the bondage of corruption into the liberty of the glory of the children of God. For we know that every creature groaneth and travaileth in pain together until now" (Rom. viii. 21, 22). We shall then have the curse removed, and the brute creation—at least as far as "my holy mountain" extends—brought into touch with the mind of God, and all will be equally fitting, and beautiful.

(4.) *Jerusalem, in more than pristine glory, will be the world's metropolis.* Jerusalem, which was so trodden down of the Gentiles, will occupy a wonderful place in that day, and, her recovered glory, as much eclipse the past, as the glory of Christ as King, will surpass that of Solomon. I refer you to the closing verses of Isaiah lix.: "So shall they fear the name of the Lord from the west, and his glory from the rising of the sun. When the enemy shall come in like a flood, the Spirit of the Lord shall lift up a standard against him. And the Redeemer shall come to Zion, and unto them that turn from transgression in Jacob, saith the Lord" (verses 19, 20). Then (chap. lx.) there is the beautiful call, to a long down-trodden nation, to wake up to their glory. "Arise, shine; for thy light is come, and the glory of the Lord is risen upon thee." Who is the light? It is Christ.* When He did come as the light of Israel, they refused Him, but when He appears again, they will own Him, and acknowledge Him, and now the Spirit of God calls upon them to wake up and see what God is going to give them. "For, behold, the darkness shall cover the earth, and gross darkness the people: but the Lord shall arise upon thee, and his glory shall be seen upon thee. And the Gentiles shall come to thy light, and kings to the brightness of thy rising. Lift up thine eyes round about, and see: all they gather themselves together, they come to thee: thy sons

---

* Possibly here, Christ, and the Church, are indicated. (See Lecture IX., The New Jerusalem, pages 213, 214).

A KING SHALL REIGN IN RIGHTEOUSNESS.

shall come from far, and thy daughters shall be nursed at thy side. Then thou shalt see, and flow together, and thine heart shall fear, and be enlarged; because the abundance of the sea shall be converted unto thee, the forces of the Gentiles shall come unto thee. . . . And the sons of strangers shall build up thy walls, and their kings shall minister unto thee: for in my wrath I smote thee, but in my favour have I had mercy on thee. Therefore thy gates shall be open continually; they shall not be shut day nor night; that men may bring unto thee the forces of the Gentiles, and that their kings may be brought. For the nation and kingdom that will not serve thee shall perish; yea, those nations shall be utterly wasted. The glory of Lebanon shall come unto thee"—the Jew knew what that meant—"the fir tree, the pine tree, and the box together, to beautify the place of my sanctuary; and I will make the place of my feet glorious. . . . Violence shall no more be heard in thy land, wasting nor destruction within thy borders: but thou shalt call thy walls Salvation, and thy gates Praise. The sun shall be no more thy light by day; neither for brightness shall the moon give light unto thee: but the Lord shall be unto thee an everlasting light, and thy God thy glory. Thy sun shall no more go down; neither shall thy moon withdraw itself: for the Lord shall be thine everlasting light, and the days of thy mourning shall be ended" (Isa. lx. 1-5, 10-13, 18-20).

Then let us go to the 62nd chapter: "For Zion's sake will I not hold my peace, and for Jerusalem's sake I will not rest, until the righteousness thereof go forth as brightness, and the salvation thereof as a lamp that urneth. And the Gentiles shall see thy righteousness, and all kings thy glory: and thou shalt be called by a new name, which the mouth of the Lord shall name. Thou shalt also be a crown of glory in the hand of the Lord, and a royal diadem in the hand of thy God. Thou shalt no more be termed Forsaken; neither shall thy land any more be termed Desolate: but thou shalt be called Hephzi-bah (*i.e.*, my delight is in her), and thy land Beulah (*i.e.*, married): for the Lord delighteth in thee, and thy land shall be married. For as a young man marrieth a virgin, so shall thy sons marry thee: and as the bridegroom rejoiceth over the bride, so shall thy God rejoice over thee. I have set watchmen upon thy walls, O Jerusalem, which shall never hold their peace day nor night: ye that make mention of the Lord, keep not silence, and give him no rest, till he establish, and till he make Jerusalem a praise in the earth" (Isa. lxii. 1-7). Nothing could be more clear than these statements of God's faithful word to His people.

Look now at Zephaniah, chapter iii., "In that day it shall be said to Jerusalem, Fear thou not; and to Zion, Let not thine hands be slack. The Lord thy God in the midst of thee is mighty; he will save, he will rejoice over thee with joy; he will rest in his love; he will joy over thee with singing. I will gather them that are sorrowful for the solemn assembly, who are of thee, to whom the reproach of it was a burden. Behold, at that time I will undo all that afflict thee; and I will save her that halteth, and gather her that was driven out; and *I will get them praise and fame in every land* where they have been put to shame. At that time will I bring you again, even in the time that I gather you: for I will make you *a name and a praise among all people of the earth*, when I turn back your captivity before your eyes, saith the Lord" (verses 16-20). That has nothing in the world to do with the Church, it is Israel's blessing, and Israel's day of glory.

(5.) *The Temple will be rebuilt, and its services restored with great magnificence.* This we get unfolded in Ezekiel, chapters xl. to xlvi., which I am, from lack of time, unable to touch to-night, and you can peruse at your leisure. You will find this comes out, that Jerusalem is not only the joy of all the earth, but God owns that place as the spot where His temple is, and you have the temple rebuilt, in more than pristine glory, while the sacrifices are renewed, and the veil of the temple again exists in that day. That might seem to some of us a little retrograde, but I think you will find this, that, as the Old Testament sacrifices were anticipatory, the sacrifices of that day will be commemorative, because Israel's salvation, like our own, is based on the blood of the Lord Jesus Christ.

(6.) *Jerusalem becomes the centre of earthly worship—all nations flow to it.* Israel will have their temple rebuilt, and its services reinstituted, we have seen, but not only will Jehovah have their worship, but the whole earth will turn to Jerusalem, as its centre of worship. In proof of this, I shall quote here but two scriptures —"The word that Isaiah the son of Amoz saw concerning Judah and Jerusalem. And it shall come to pass in the last days, that the mountain of the Lord's house shall be established in the top of the mountains, and shall be exalted above the hills; *and all nations shall flow unto it.* And many people shall go and say, Come ye, and let us go up to the mountain of the Lord, to the house of the God of Jacob; and he will teach us of his ways, and we will walk in his paths: for out of Zion shall go forth the law, and the word of the Lord from Jerusalem" (Isa. ii. 1-3). Nothing could be plainer. Then in Zech. xiv., which, in its early verses, states, "I will gather all nations against Jerusalem to battle," and then, that the Lord has come to the Mount of Olives, fought against them, and delivered her, we read, "And every one that is left of all the nations which came against Jerusalem, shall even go up from year to year to worship the King, the Lord of hosts, and to keep the feast of tabernacles; and it shall be that whoso will not come up of all the families of the earth unto Jerusalem to worship the King, the Lord of hosts, even upon them shall be no rain. And if the family of Egypt go not up, and come not, that have no rain, there shall be the plague wherewith the Lord will smite the heathen that come not up to keep the feast of tabernacles. This shall be the punishment of Egypt, and the punishment of all nations that come not up to keep the feast of tabernacles" (Zech. xiv. 16-19).

The Feast of Tabernacles is the Old Testament feast, in Israel, which was typical of the millennial day of the Lord Jesus Christ. They had three great feasts, the Passover, the Feast of Weeks, and the Feast of Tabernacles; and it is very striking to see, that, while the Passover, which has its fulfilment in the death of Christ, and the Feast of Tabernacles, which is a figure of the coming glory of Christ, will be kept, Ezekiel is most careful to omit the Feast of Weeks, because that feast has found its antitype in Pentecost—the coming down of the Holy Ghost, and the forming of the Church. Israel will not keep it in that day, because the Church, so to speak, absorbed into herself what the Feast of Weeks meant. In that day Israel will keep the Passover (Ezek. xlv. 21), and the Feast of Tabernacles, and all the nations of the earth will come up, and join them, at least in the latter, and worship the Lord. A happy and blessed day for the earth will that be. A wonderful day indeed will it be for this poor sin-stained earth. Well may we pray, Lord, hasten that day.

THE NEW JERUSALEM.

REV. xxi. 9-27, xxii. 1-5.

Lecture IX.

WE were looking, last Lord's Day evening, at the earthly side of the millennial reign of the Lord Jesus. There passed before us the testimony of Scripture as to what the nature, and character of that day would be, with every foe, and every adverse power, subjugated to the Lord Jesus, Satan in the bottomless pit, and "neither adversary nor evil occurrent." We saw that those, under that beneficent reign, will be indeed blessed. We saw that death is to be a rare thing, the curse to be removed, the earth to be fruitful, the earthly Jerusalem to be rebuilt, and re-established in more than her pristine glory; the temple to be rebuilt, the sacrifices re-established, and Jerusalem to be the metropolis of a renewed, and absolutely blessed earth. The Jew—now despised, looked down upon, and often treated with contempt—in that day will be "the head, and not the tail" (Deut. xxviii. 13). Jerusalem will be the joy of the earth, and from Zion will come out streams of deepest blessing, and all the earth will rejoice under the sway of Jesus. And where shall we Christians be in that day? I believe the scripture, which I have read this evening, answers that question most distinctly. What I desire to bring before you now, is, what I may call, the heavenly side of the kingdom of the Son of Man, the heavenly side of the millennial reign of the Lord Jesus, and to show how the Church—it is a wonderful thing, and an unspeakable favour, to belong to the Church of God, the Body of Christ—will be in distinct relation to the renewed earth. In the scripture which I have just read, God gives us much light and information, of an exceedingly interesting, and very blessed character, upon this point.

Before I touch this subject, bear with me a moment, while I point out that, which I think may help some students of Scripture, in regard to this passage, and its position in the book of Revelation. I can easily understand a person saying, Are not the subjects of these chapters in Revelation consecutive? I believe they are not. The book is, in a certain sense, a book of drama, and you find, every now and then, the curtain drops, and something entirely new will come before you—a new scene. Commencing with the 19th chapter, we find the marriage of the Lamb,—the Bride, the Lamb's wife, gets herself ready, and the marriage takes place. The next thing is this, the Lord Jesus comes out from heaven, as King of kings, and Lord of lords, attended by the armies of heaven, on white horses; the heavenly saints attend their Lord; the Bride is with the Bridegroom, when He comes to deal with the earth. The next thing is, that every foe is put down; the beast, and antichrist are cast alive into the lake of fire, and their armies overwhelmed, and Satan bound, and cast into the bottomless pit. Then (chap. xx.) the reign of the Lord is established; the heavenly saints, and two martyred companies, live, and reign, with Christ, a thousand years, and, at the end of that time, Satan is let loose.

Gog and Magog come to his hand, fire comes down from God, their destruction follows, and then the great white throne is set up. Time is over, the judgment is set, and you are carried, in the first few verses of chapter xxi., into the eternal state, the description of which closes with the 8th verse of the chapter. We have here, then, a consecutive, descriptive account of events, commencing with the Lord's appearing, and coming to earth, with His people, right on, through the millennial day, to the great white throne; and then into the eternal state; and with the 8th verse of chapter xxi. the prophecy of the book of Revelation closes, for you cannot get further than the eternal state. We have the history of God's dealings, with man upon the earth, absolutely closed in chapter xx., and in the first eight verses of chapter xxi. we have the relationship of God, to man, in eternity. The eternal state is there most fully, and beautifully described, and the curtain, so to speak, drops. The question before us to-night is, Why does it rise once more?

Why does the Spirit of God commence an altogether new subject in the 9th verse of chapter xxi., which is carried on to the close of the 5th verse of chapter xxii.? Because He would give us, and, in order to do so, turns back again, into time, to give us, details about a certain being—a certain company of people if you like the expression better—who will be in relation to the Lord of the earth, in the millennial day, and who will be in relation to the earth itself, in that day. In the verses read, I have no doubt we get the distinctive relation of the Church,—the heavenly people of the Lord, that belong to Jesus now,—to the renewed earth in that day. Some one may say, That is a very arbitrary way of dealing with Scripture. No, it is the way of the Spirit of God. You will find in numberless places in Scripture, that God's Spirit will, first of all, give you a little summary, and then turn back again, and give detail. Revelation xxi. 9-27, xxii. 1-5, is not any exception, because you will find that, in another part of this same book, you have absolutely the same line of descriptive treatment by the Spirit of God, not with regard to the Church—the true Bride of Christ—but with regard to what calls itself the church—the false bride—Babylon, the Mother of Harlots.

Turn back, for proof of this, to the 14th chapter of this book, where the Spirit of God brings out seven distinct points, of, as yet, unfulfilled prophecy. The first thing that John sees is the one hundred and forty-four thousand, the earthly company. That brings us down to the end of verse 5. Then in verse 6, we get a second point, the preaching of the everlasting Gospel. In the 8th verse, we get the third point, " Babylon is fallen." Now Babylon's fall comes here, as the third of the seven, and you will see what follows. Next, we get what will be the judgment of those who worship the beast (verses 9-12). That is the fourth point. The fifth point is how blessed it will be then to "die in the Lord" (ver. 13). Then (sixth), in verses 14 to 16, Christ comes, with a sharp sickle in His hand, and we have the harvest of the earth—discriminating judgment. Then (verses 17 to 20) another angel comes out, and we have (seventh) the vintage described—the unmistakable vengeance of God, upon a guilty, blood-stained earth. Here, then, we see a summary of earthly events, commencing with the manifestation of the Jewish remnant, and closing with the final pre-millennial judgments. Now observe, Babylon was mentioned there in one verse (the 8th), but we do not get Babylon portrayed, and her fall described, till chapters xvii. and xviii., where you will find her characteristics delineated, viz., idolatry, corruption, worldliness, and persecution, as well as her destruction, given in detail.

The same mode of treatment is found in the part of Scripture before us to-night. We have first a summary of events, and then, for a particular purpose, the Spirit of God turns back, and gives us an immense amount of detail—not about the false bride, but about the true. Babylon is the false church; the new Jerusalem is the real thing. We have only to read these two scenes to see how strong, and doubtless purposed, is the analogy between the two passages. Nay more, if we observe the way, in which John is invited to behold the glory of the new Jerusalem, you will find, it is exactly similar to the way in which he is invited to look at the fall of Babylon. "And there came unto me one of the seven angels which had the seven vials full of the seven last plagues, and talked with me, saying, Come hither, I will show thee the Bride, the Lamb's wife" (xxi. 9). Again: "And there came one of the seven angels which had the seven vials, and talked with me, saying unto me, Come hither; I will show unto thee the judgment of the great whore, that sitteth upon many waters" (xvii. 1). Do not suppose that Babylon is a built city, or the New Jerusalem either. Both are figures. They have an immense meaning to the student of Scripture, and "the new Jerusalem" teems with thoughts of the Bride's glory, and happiness, to any one who understands the meaning of the term. I say this to show, that I am not taking unwarrantable liberties with the Word of God. I rather wish to show how absolutely the Scriptures hang together.

How beautiful that the Spirit of God should turn back then, in this 21st chapter, and show, that in the millennial day of the reign of the Lord Jesus, those who have followed a despised Saviour, those who have known an earth-rejected Saviour, those who have shared in His loss, and shame, and contempt, and scorn, during the long night of His rejection, and absence, will be identified with Him, in His glory. The Spirit of God delights to spend almost a whole chapter, in describing, and unfolding, what will be the beauty to the eye of God, what the joy to the heart of the Lord, and what the displayed glory to the eye of the world, in that day, of those, who have followed Jesus in the time of His rejection, and, hence, share with Him in His glory, and shine with Him, in the day, when the whole earth basks in the sunshine of His blessed favour. In figurative language here, the Spirit of God is bringing out that which had already fallen from the lips of the Saviour Himself, when He was here upon the earth. He shows us the moment of incomparable glory for the Church.

But who is the Church, the Bride? "I will show thee the Bride, the Lamb's wife." To see the Bride, I invite you, dear fellow-Christians, to look at yourselves to-night. I do not often do so. It is very rarely that I ask a Christian to look at himself, or herself—I always say, Look at Christ. But God is going to let us look, this evening, at ourselves, not as we are, but as He is going to make us, in Christ, in a day yet to come. Who, then, will compose that Bride? Let me ask you a question Do you think you are a part of the Bride? I know, through infinite grace, that I am, so also are all sinners saved by grace; sinners of the Gentiles, sinners of the Jews, called by the sovereign grace of God, touched by His blessed Spirit, converted, and brought to know the Saviour, in the night of His absence. I can see before me to-night scores that I know form a part of that Bride. Are you, however, sure that you belong to it? If not, I would most strongly urge you to come to Jesus at once. Come as a sinner, as you are to-night, and you will find, that He will give you a title to glory, that will never fail. Come to the One who died, and rose again. Cast yourself upon the mercy, and grace of that blessed Saviour, and He will not cast you out, because "it is a faithful saying, and worthy of all acceptation, that Christ Jesus came into the world to save sinners" (1 Tim. i. 15). The passage before us shows that we are saved, gloriously, grandly saved. I would not miss it for ten thousand worlds, ten thousand times told. I shall have yet to show you what will be your portion, if you do miss what God now offers, but I say, with all the love, and energy of my soul, Do not miss it. Get washed in the blood of the Lamb, believe in the Lord Jesus Christ, and you will find that you are a stone in this city, so to speak. I see a great many of the stones before me to-night. The Lord will have them all beautifully polished by-and-by—the same stones that are sitting down here to-night, will form part of this holy city, in that wonderful day. You have only to come to the Saviour, the Living Stone, and believe in Him, and you will find yourself a living stone also (1 Pet. ii. 4, 5), a member of the Church, the Bride.

By the Church, I mean sinners, brought to know the

heavenly Saviour, since the day of Pentecost, born of the Spirit, washed in the blood of the Son of God, indwelt by the Spirit of God, baptized into that "one body," of which Christ, in glory, is the head. The Church is the body of Christ. He went into death for it. He has made it His own by dying for it, as it says, "Christ also loved the church, and gave himself for it; that he might sanctify and cleanse it with the washing of water by the word; that he might present it to himself a glorious church, not having spot, or wrinkle, or any such thing; but that it should be holy, and without blemish" (Eph. v. 25-27). The Church, then, is composed of poor sinners, washed in the blood of Jesus, and led through grace to believe in Him. Anything down here, that man may call the Church, is neither here, nor there, in this respect. Being baptized, or a communicant, is utterly useless, for what I am speaking of to-night. These ordinances, most valued, and blessed, as they are in their place, never did, nor can, put a soul into Christ. The only real Church is composed of sinners, saved by grace, through faith in the Lord Jesus Christ. If you can truly say, I believe in Jesus, I rest upon His blood, then I believe, I shall see you, by-and-by, shining in the very glory of God. You may have many a doubt, though you ought not to, for the Lord leaves no room for such, when He says to every simple believer in Him, "Where I am, there ye shall be also."

Well, now, this Church, formed by the Holy Ghost, is united to her living Head in glory, and she is to appear, with Christ, in the character which is unfolded here. "Come hither, I will shew thee the Bride, the Lamb's wife." It is not the first time she is brought before us, for we saw (chap. xix. 7) that she got herself ready for the marriage day. In the 2nd and 3rd verses of chapter xxi., where she is again seen, the moment is really later on, in the ways of God, than the 9th verse. John is carried away in the Spirit now, to a great and high mountain, and is shown "the holy city, Jerusalem." The word "great" should be left out. It is not there as God wrote the verse. Babylon is called "that great city," Babylon, "that mighty city." Yes, man always wants something "great," but God does not call His Church great. No, another adjective suits her better—"holy." Babylon loves greatness, but we read of "the *holy city, Jerusalem*, descending out of heaven from God, having the glory of God." In the 9th and 10th verses, she is seen descending out of heaven from God. She is descending, but she has not got down to earth, whereas in the 3rd verse you find that she is resting on earth, for "the tabernacle of God is with men." In eternity it will be God and men together, and the tabernacle of God, which is the Church, is with men. By His Spirit, God has tabernacled in the Church from the day of Pentecost, but the world has not believed it. In the millennial day God will compel the world to believe, that He has been dwelling in the bosom of the Church, all through the long dark night of the absence of Jesus; and, further, He will make the world in that day to rejoice in the light of His glory. But in verses 10 and 11, she is only descending—it is, in fact, the position which the Church holds in the millennium. She is between heaven and earth, over the earth, clearly connected with Christ, but linked to the earth. What the character or extent of the communication between the heavenly Jerusalem, and the earthly may be, I do not know. Scripture is silent, and therefore we must not speak. This much we know, that we shall judge, both angels, and the world. "Do ye not know that the saints shall judge the world? . . . Know ye not that we shall judge angels?" (1 Cor. vi. 2, 3.) What, then, do the angels do? They will be uncommonly happy to be the doorkeepers of this holy city, because "unto the angels hath he not put in subjection the world to come" (Heb. ii. 5)—the future habitable earth. It is Man who is going to reign over the new earth, Man, in the person of Jesus, and His Bride in association with Him.

When the lowly Nazarene reigns over the earth, and blesses it, those who belong to Him in the day of His rejection, will reign with Him, in the moment of His glory. In the 10th verse, the city is not again called the New Jerusalem, because there is no necessity. She *is* the *new* Jerusalem, that is her nature and character, and there is no need to emphasise that again. She comes down from heaven. Her origin is divine, her nature, her character, is heavenly—"out of heaven from God." One is reminded of the scripture, "As is the heavenly, such are they also that are heavenly. . . . We shall also bear the image of the heavenly" (1 Cor. xv. 48, 49). Do you not know that the Christian is a heavenly being? Yes, he belongs to heaven, he is taken out of the earth. The world says now, of a devoted, unworldly, Christ-loving, and Christ-serving saint, What a fool that man is! but it will alter its judgment, in the day, when it sees the Bride, the Lamb's wife, the holy city "descending out of heaven from God, having the glory of God."

Turn to the 17th chapter of John for a moment, to which this scripture necessarily carries one's mind. The Son is there unbosoming Himself to the Father, and we find Him saying in the 20th verse—" Neither pray I for these alone." He was not only praying for the apostles, but He was likewise praying for us—for all them that believe. There may be a very great difference between the members of the family of God, but there is one feature, which marks the whole family of God—that is identical,—they all believe. The Lord says therefore, " Neither pray I for these alone, but for them also which shall believe on me through their word." Blessed Lord ! He was thinking of you and me, and He unfolds what belongs to us. "That they all may be one : as thou, Father, art in me, and I in thee, that they also may be one in us : that the world may *believe* that thou hast sent me." If the Church had been one, the world might have believed, but now it thinks it has very good ground for its unbelief because Christians are not one, but split into endless sects. But listen, he goes on—" And the glory which thou gavest me, I have given them ; that they may be one, even as we are one : I in them, and thou in me, that they may be made perfect in one: and that the world may *know* that thou hast sent me, and hast loved them as thou hast loved me " (John xvii. 20-23). That will be the day, when the world sees the Church coming down, out of heaven from God, and it will then say, Ah! those Christians were right after all. We thought they were only deluded when they talked of being one with Christ, and the possessors of eternal life, but we know now they were right. The world will know it when too late to believe it. What the Lord prays for in the 21st verse is that the world might believe, but in the 23rd, He asks that the world may know, " that thou hast sent me, and hast loved them, as thou hast loved me," and the world will know, then, that the believer in Jesus now, is accepted in, and is one with, God's beloved Son.

In that day the world will know this wondrous fact, that "the glory which thou gavest me, I have given them." It is the glory which God gave His Son, as man, not the incommunicable glory, which belongs to the Lord Jesus, in the Godhead,—this never can be given. But the glory which the Son of Man has acquired, on the ground of redemption, He can, and, blessed be His adorable name, He does, share with His loved, and blood-bought Bride. But He says more. "Father, I will that they also, whom thou hast given me, be with me where I am; that they may behold my glory, which thou hast given me; for thou lovedst me before the foundation of the world" (John xvii. 24). We shall see that glory; we shall be like Him, in that day of His glory, and more than that, we shall also appear with Him, in glory. Little wonder that the Spirit of God says here, " I saw the New Jerusalem descending out of heaven from God, having the glory of God." You and I, as sinners, are unfit for that glory, for "All have sinned, and *come short* of the glory of God," we read, in Rom. iii. 23. Then in Rom. v. 1, 2, we get, "Being justified by faith, we have peace with God through our Lord Jesus Christ; by whom also we have access by faith into this grace wherein we stand, and rejoice *in hope* of the glory of God." Revelation xxi. says John saw the city " descending out of heaven from God, *having* the glory of God." We are now made perfectly fit for it, through the work of the Lord Jesus Christ, then we shall possess, and enjoy it.

"And her light was like unto a stone most precious, even like a jasper stone, clear as crystal" (verse 11). The jasper stone is used in Scripture, for that which is expressive of the glory of God (chap. iv. 3), which can be seen by the creature, for He has a glory, which no man can approach unto. "The building of the wall of it was jasper" (verse 18). That which is used to express the glory of God Himself, this city is seen to have. Her wall (verse 18), and first foundation (verse 19), are jasper. The glory of God is the foundation, and protection, as well as the light, and beauty of the heavenly city, for the Church is glorified, with Christ, in the glory of God. She belongs to God. The Christian is born of God, and has the divine nature imparted to him, through the new birth. There is only what is the fruit of grace visible in this chapter, all is "clear as crystal."

The city is divinely secure also, for it "had a wall great and high, and had twelve gates, and at the gates twelve angels, and names written thereon, which are the names of the twelve tribes of the children of Israel. . . . And the wall of the city had twelve foundations, and in them the names of the twelve apostles of the Lamb" (verses 12-14). Another has said:[*] "It has twelve gates. Angels are become the willing doorkeepers of the great city, the fruit of Christ's redemption-work in glory. This marked the possession too, by man, thus brought, in the assembly, to glory, of the highest place in the creation and providential order of God, of which angels had been previously the administrators. The twelve gates are full human perfectness of governmental administrative power. The gate was the place of judgment. . . . There were twelve foundations, but these were

---

[*] "Synopsis of the Book of the Bible," Vol. V., p. 614, 2nd edition.

the twelve apostles of the Lamb. They were, in their work, the foundation of the heavenly city. Thus the creative, and providential display of power, the governmental (Jehovah), and the Church once founded at Jerusalem, are all brought together in the heavenly city, the organised seat of heavenly power. It is not *presented* as the Bride, though it be the Bride, the Lamb's wife. It is not in the Pauline character of nearness of blessing to Christ. It is the Church as founded at Jerusalem under the twelve—the organised seat of heavenly power, the new, and now heavenly capital of God's government."

The place which angels hold here is interesting. They are now, and have ever been, the servants of the saints, as we read: "Are they not all ministering spirits, sent forth to minister for them who shall be heirs of salvation" (Heb. i. 14), and when the Church is seen, by-and-by, in effulgent glory, they will be delighted to be the doorkeepers of the heavenly city. God, too, does not then forget His earthly people (Israel), nor the names of the twelve apostles of the Lamb. The world is not to forget that the twelve apostles who served the Lord, and suffered in the earthly Jerusalem, are they, who, by their ministry, founded the heavenly Jerusalem, and thus it is only seemly, that the names of the apostles should be found in the twelve foundations of the city. In Ephesians we are told that we "are built upon the foundation of the apostles and prophets, Jesus Christ himself being the chief corner stone; in whom all the building, fitly framed together, groweth unto an holy temple in the Lord" (Eph. ii. 20, 21), which has its full answer, I apprehend, in the new Jerusalem.

The city is alike vast, and perfect, and measured, and

owned of God. "He measured the city with the reed, twelve thousand furlongs. The length and the breadth and the height of it are equal" (ver. 16). It was a cube. Now a cube is the most perfect figure, being equal on every side—finite perfection. It has what you call finality, it is the most comprehensive, and holds the most—nothing contains as much as a cube—and therefore, it is given here, as the expression of perfection. Observe, it is finite perfection, divinely given. I do not say it is divine perfection, because that is God Himself; but it is divinely given perfection, and therefore it is spoken of as a cube. The Spirit of God delights to show, the absolute perfection of the place in glory, which the saints have before God, on the ground of Divine righteousness.

"And the building of the wall of it was of jasper; and the city was pure gold, like unto clear glass. And the foundations of the wall of the city were garnished with all manner of precious stones. The first foundation was jasper; the second, sapphire; the third, a chalcedony; the fourth, an emerald; the fifth, sardonyx; the sixth, sardius; the seventh, chrysolite; the eighth, beryl; the ninth, a topaz; the tenth, a chrysoprasus; the eleventh, a jacinth; the twelfth, an amethyst. And the twelve gates were twelve pearls; every several gate was of one pearl: and the street of the city was pure gold, as it were transparent glass" (Rev. xxi. 18-21).

To again quote the words of another,[*] "The city was formed in its nature, in divine righteousness and holiness—gold transparent as glass. That which was now, by the word, wrought in, and applied to men below, was the very nature of the whole place (compare

---

[*] *Loc. cit.*, p. 615.

Eph. iv. 24). The precious stones, or varied display of God's nature, who is light, in connection with the creature (seen in creation, Ezek. xxviii. 13; in grace, in the high-priest's breastplate, Exod. xxviii. 15-21), now shone in permanent glory, and adorned the foundations of the city. The gates had the moral beauty which attracted Christ in the assembly, and in a glorious way. That on which men walked, instead of bringing danger of defilement, was itself righteous, and holy; the streets, all that men came in contact with, were righteousness, and holiness—gold transparent as glass." Gold all through Scripture is Divine righteousness. White linen is practical human righteousness. When the Bride puts on the white raiment (Rev. xix. 8), it is her practical righteousness. If you were to put a little bit of white linen into the fire, it would soon be destroyed, but put a bit of gold in, and it stands the test. That is the whole point. Gold is Divine righteousness, and you, and I, stand before God, on the ground of Divine righteousness, in Christ.

"And the foundations of the wall of the city were garnished with all manner of precious stones." As we have seen, we have these precious stones in Scripture three times. In the garden of Eden they are seen in connection with creation; then in Exodus xxviii., where they are seen in the breastplate of the high-priest, it is evidently a question of grace for a failing people; but, when we see these same stones, in the foundation of the heavenly city, the thought suggested is permanent glory. Those many-hued stones bring out the varied qualities of God, made known through His people. There will be different rays of His glory reflected through them, illustrated by these different precious stones, which are the emblems employed, to set forth the lustre of God's saints, in heavenly glory, and the way, in which He displays, the beauty, which He sees in them. Put a light through an emerald, and it is quite different from that of the ruby, and although we are all partakers of the grace of God, that grace will shine through each differently, and no two are alike. It would be an immense pity if all the saints were like a cartload of bricks—all the same shape, and colour. Just as there are not two leaves of the forest alike, so there are not two saints of God alike. All are alike in being saved by grace, but all are different in the expression of that grace.

"And the twelve gates were twelve pearls; every several gate was of one pearl." Why was every gate a pearl? You remember the heavenly merchantman, in Matthew xiii., "seeking goodly pearls; who, when he had found one pearl of great price, went and sold all that he had and bought it" (ver. 46). You may say, That is a sinner seeking the Saviour. Indeed! a sinner selling? What has a sinner got to sell but his sins? Nay, the pearl of great price is not Christ, but the Church—the Church in its unity. Christ went and sold all that He had, truly, and gave up all for the Church. The pearl is the Church in her unity, beauty, and completeness as viewed in God's mind, that so fascinated the Lord Jesus, that He parted with "all that he had," to get that pearl.

"And the street of the city was pure gold, as it were transparent glass." When you walk through the streets of man's city, you get your feet defiled. But what do I find there? Nothing to defile; nothing of that sort can by any possibility enter. We are there on the ground of Divine righteousness.

"And I saw no temple therein: for the Lord God

Almighty and the Lamb are the temple of it. And
the city had no need of the sun, neither of the moon,
to shine in it: for the glory of God did lighten it,
and the Lamb is the lamp thereof" (verses 22, 23).
There being no temple is a great thing. There is no
concealment of God's glory. A temple would speak
of concealment, or of a special place, where God could
be known, by those who drew near to worship. All
this has gone by. Even now, we Christians, have fullest
access to the holiest (Heb. x. 19-22). In the heavenly
city God is fully displayed. The Lord God Almighty,
and the Lamb, are the temple. They are approached
in their own nature and glory, as another has sweetly
sung—

> "The Lamb is there, my soul—
> There, God Himself doth rest,
> In love divine diffused through all,
> With Him supremely blest.
>
> God and the Lamb—'tis well,
> I know that source divine,
> Of joy and love no tongue can tell,
> Yet know that all is mine.
>
> But who that glorious blaze
> Of living light shall tell,
> Where all His brightness God displays,
> And the Lamb's glories dwell.
>
> God and the Lamb shall there
> The light and temple be,
> And radiant hosts for ever share,
> The unveil'd mystery."

There will be a temple in the earthly Jerusalem. Any
architect, with a fair knowledge of his profession, might
go to Palestine, and build Ezekiel's temple to-day;
God has given the measurements, and plans, so plainly,

that Ezekiel's temple could be easily built. But there is here no temple—oh, no, because a temple always implies the thought of God being hidden, being in an inner place. In a certain sense it is all temple—*i.e.*, the Lord God and the Lamb pervade the city, and the saints are in the nearest contiguity to the Lord, in the closest relationship to the Lamb, enjoying the light, and basking in the sunshine, of the presence of the blessed Lord. Oh, what a contrast to the darkness of that eternal hell, which is the lot of the man who dies in his sins. God save you, if you are yet in your sins. Do not miss this scene of blessedness, and rest, and joy. There is no need for the sun, and the moon in that day. Why? Because "the glory of God did lighten it, and the Lamb is the lamp thereof." The glory of the divine nature illumines all, and the Lamb is the Lamp—the Light-bearer. God, fully displayed, supersedes all created light. The sun at mid-day was put out by a brighter light, when Saul was converted (Acts ix.). Even so will it be in this city. "The glory of God did lighten it." It comes, shaded for us, through the person of the Lord Jesus Christ.

Although this city is the Church, brought out for millennial view, and gives our relationship to the millennial earth, it is the Church really in her eternal state, though the figure of "the city" ceases in the eternal state. What she is, she is going to be for ever, but, first of all, set in relation to earth, as a visible and glorious object over it. Therefore we read, "And the nations shall walk by the light of it." Only the redeemed nations will enjoy that privilege, and blessing I apprehend. Suspended above the earthly Jerusalem, the holy city will transmit the rays of the glory of God, by which it is absolutely permeated, and encompassed.

The light which it will then transmit, and shed on to the earth, will render it a magnificent luminary, of an altogether unknown quality, and the nations will walk in, and enjoy its light. This wonderful glory of God shines among, and through His own people. The city enjoys the direct light within, the world gets the transmitted light of the glory, and "the kings of the earth do bring their glory and honour *unto* (not *into*) it." They thereby acknowledge the heavens, and the heavenly kingdom, to be the source of all they possess, and enjoy; they render homage to Him, who is the Source.

"And the gates of it shall not be shut at all by day; for there shall be no night there" (ver. 25). The poet has said,—

> "And sing of Thy glory above,
> In praises by day and by night."

I never sing that, for there is no night there, and the gates are ever open. Evil cannot enter in. Blessed thought. Divine security guards against this. No falsehood, no idol—"whatsoever worketh abomination, or maketh a lie" (ver. 27), no defilement can ever enter. Neither Satan's deceit, nor man's evil, can again produce corruption.

This glorious description of the New Jerusalem, forcibly reminds us of a passage, before quoted, in the Old Testament (Isa. lx.), where the earthly Jerusalem is addressed. "Arise, shine; for thy light is come, and the glory of the Lord is risen upon thee" (ver. 1). Again,—"Therefore thy gates shall be open continually; they shall not be shut day nor night: that men may bring unto thee the forces of the Gentiles, and that their kings may be brought" (ver. 11). If the nations of the earth will not bow down to Jerusalem they will perish. But further,—"Violence shall no more be heard in thy land, wasting nor destruction within thy borders: but thou shalt call thy walls Salvation, and thy gates Praise. The sun shall be no more thy light by day; neither for brightness shall the moon give light unto thee: but the Lord shall be unto thee an everlasting light, and thy God thy glory. Thy sun shall no more go down; neither shall thy moon withdraw itself: for the Lord shall be thine everlasting light, and the days of thy mourning shall be ended" (verses 18-20). What is the meaning of that? The light that streams through the heavenly city—having God's glory—would appear to irradiate the earthly, and we have the heavenly, and earthly, Jerusalem, in touch one with the other. You have reached "the dispensation of the fulness of times" when God will "gather together in one all things in Christ, both which are in heaven, and which are on earth" (Eph. i. 10). Jacob's dream is realised—"A ladder set up on the earth, and the top of it reached to heaven" (Gen. xxviii. 12). The two spheres are in intimate relation, and accord. The night of evil has passed away, and the day of glory has set in. The affections of the soul are moved, as one also reads, that "only they which are written in the Lamb's book of life" enter in to the city. Sovereign grace is at the bottom of all blessing for man.

The first five verses of chapter xxii. give us yet lovely details, as to the connection of the holy city with the earth, although not on it. "He showed me a pure river of water of life, clear as crystal, proceeding out of the throne of God and of the Lamb. In the midst of the street of it, and on either side of the river, was there the tree of life, which bare twelve manner of fruits, and yielded her fruit every month: and the leaves of the tree were for the healing of the nations." The city is refreshed by the river of God, and the fruits of the tree of life—always ripening—are for its inhabitants. The fruit, only the glorified saints eat, whereas the leaves—that which is visible without—are for the blessing of those on earth. Observe there is only one river here, and only one tree. You recollect in Genesis ii. there were four rivers, and two trees—the tree of the knowledge of good, and evil, and the tree of life. When man sinned, he was driven out, that he might not touch the tree of life. But when driven out of the earthly paradise, God opens a heavenly one to him. In Eden there were four rivers, and with two of them, Hiddekel, or Tigris, and Euphrates, are connected some of the most sorrowful passages of the history of God's earthly people. On the Tigris, was built Nineveh, the capital of Assyria, which carried captive the ten tribes. On the Euphrates, Babylon was built, whither the two tribes were taken. When we come to the last chapter of Scripture, we have but one river, the river of life, and one tree, the tree of life, and that seen on both sides of the river. The tree of the knowledge of good, and evil, is for ever gone. The day of man's responsibility, and testing, is, for ever, over, and everything is settled absolutely according to divine sovereign grace in Christ. There may be trouble on the earth, to begin with, but the Lord will put all right, in that day, for "the leaves of the tree were for the healing of the nations." It must be borne in mind that these are only God's figures of fullest blessing. There will not be any real river, or visible tree, I take it, but, the river of water of life symbolises the superabundance of life, and blessing, which will flow through the city—*i.e.*, the Bride, the Lamb's wife—and, clearly, we are on millennial ground, in this chapter, for, in eternity, there are no nations or kings.

Then comes the climax. "There shall be no more curse: but the throne of God and of the Lamb shall be in it; and his servants shall serve him" (xxii. 3). Sometimes we are hindered here, but, thank God, there will be no hindrance in that day, nothing to hinder the heart going out to the Lord, to the fullest. "And they shall see his face." Yes, we are going to see the face of the blessed One, who died for us on the tree. "And his name shall be on their foreheads." On the forehead, of many a man on earth, will the name of the beast have been imprinted, but here, everybody delights to own, I belong to Jesus. "And there shall be no night there; and they need no candle, neither light of the sun; for the Lord God giveth them light: and they shall reign for ever and ever" (ver. 5). There is no night, nor need of light, for the Lord God gives it. The "candle" man makes, and the "sun" God has made, but neither are required there. All that suits, and is needed in, this world, is past, for the heavenly saints,—the Bride, the Lamb's wife,—and they "shall reign for ever and ever." We shall pass into eternity, in the unclouded enjoyment, of that which the Spirit of God brings before us in these verses. Oh, what a day for the Church, what a day for Christ, what a day of unmingled, unparalleled glory, and what a great mercy for you, and me, if we can say now, "I belong to the Saviour." If you are His now, then you will be most certainly His, in that day

THE ETERNAL STATE.

Rev. xx., xxi. 1-8.

Lecture X.

FOR the last two Lord's Day evenings, we have been looking at the testimony of Scripture, as to the nature, and character, of the thousand years, of which the 20th chapter of Revelation speaks particularly. I need not, therefore, detain you with many remarks about it, because, what is before us this evening, is that which is subsequent to the millennial reign of the Lord Jesus. That He will reign for a thousand years, has been conclusively proved from the Word of God, and here in the scripture before us (4th ver.), we find three distinct companies, that lived, and reigned, with Christ, for one thousand years. "But the rest of the dead lived not again until the thousand years were finished. This is the first resurrection" (ver. 5). The first resurrection, which includes Christ, and all that are His, is pre-millennial. It is marked off, by its own peculiarities, from the moment when "the rest of the dead" again live. This solemn event is not here called the second resurrection, because the separate taking out of the wicked, from their graves, for judgment, and the lake of fire, the Spirit of God would not, in this connection, call, by that blessed word, resurrection. He calls it the second death. "The rest of the dead lived not again until the thousand years were finished. This is the first resurrection. Blessed and holy is he that hath part in the first resurrection : on such the second death hath no power ; but they shall be priests of God and of the Christ, and shall reign with him a thousand years " (verses 5, 6).

We have been looking at this blessed period, as given in Scripture, and we have seen the earth renewed, and blessed, under the sway of Jesus, and heaven, joining with earth, in owning, and praising Him. And now the Spirit of God carries us to the time, subsequent to this blessed millennial reign. "When the thousand years are expired, Satan shall be loosed out of his prison" (ver. 7). The thought in the minds of many is, that if the millennium came in, then, of course, everything would be fixed, and settled for ever. But not so. There is a period, fixed and limited, during which the blessed Son of Man, will have His mediatorial reign over the earth, but it comes to a close, for a reason which I shall show you presently, and now when it is ended, the first thing we find is this, that Satan is loosed out of his prison.

I understand, from this chapter, perfectly well, why the book of Revelation is so little read. I think I see clearly, why, even Christians, so little give themselves, to the study of this wonderful book. They often say, Oh, it is very difficult, and so full of figurative language, that we cannot comprehend its meaning. But that is not the reason. Do you think the devil likes that you, and I, should ponder, carefully, a book, that speaks, first of all, of himself and his angels, being cast out of heaven (chap. xii. 9), and then of his being cast, solitary, into the bottomless pit (xx. 1-3), and then, finally, hurled into the lake of fire (xx. 10)? Do you think the devil likes, that you and I should be occupied with his threefold fall, till, at length, he finds himself the most miserable wretch in creation, for such, indeed, he will be, as, in eternity, he reviews the sorrow he has wrought through pride, terminating in endless shame? Nay, nay, you would not put into the hands of a man, a book that told of your downfall. You would put it at the back of the fire if you could. But there is yet another reason. This is the book that brings out the final issues of all things, and the book, that shows, what is to be the end of the pathway of that lowly, self-humbled, blessed One, whom the world refused. This book shows His final exaltation, and glory, His reign over a Satan-delivered earth, for a thousand years, and then His dealing finally, and definitively, with the great adversary of man. Little wonder that Satan has persuaded Christians, that the book of Revelation, is a book that had better not be opened. It is remarkable, however, that in the first chapter, as well as in the last (i. 3, xxii. 6, 7, 10, 18, 19), God speaks of the blessing connected with reading, and keeping the sayings, of this book, so I fervently commend it to your attention, henceforth.

We now see, then, that Satan is "loosed a little season" (verses 3-7). He at once resumes his old tactics, the practice of which, for six thousand years, has rendered him an adept, and, for the last time, he goes out to "deceive the nations which are in the four quarters of the earth, Gog and Magog, to gather them together to battle : the number of whom is as the sand of the sea." The reign of Jesus has been marked by peace, plenty, and prosperity, and all, outwardly, have owned the Lord, but not every heart really, for we saw, on a previous occasion, in Psalms, xviii. 44, and lxvi. 3, that "the sons of the stranger shall lie."

While the manifest glory of Christ is irradiating the earth, they are quiet. So long as Satan—the prime mover of all evil—is off the scene, men are apparently not prompted to disobey, but, at this point, it would seem, that the Lord retires from the earth, veils His glory again, for a moment, and Satan is let loose. And what does he find? Alas! Gog and Magog, ready to his hand, and he will " gather them together to battle : the number of whom is as the sand of the sea."

These hosts must not be confounded with the Gog and Magog, of Ezekiel xxxviii. and xxxix., the old historic enemy of Israel—the Assyrian. They appear, and fall before the millennium, whereas, what is given us here, is post-millennial. Those pre-millennial hordes came only from Russia, and contiguous Eastern countries, but here, they come from " the four quarters of the earth." Satan brings from east, west, north, and south, against Palestine, all that are opposed to the Lord Jesus Christ. He easily manages again to " deceive the nations." It is his old business. He was a deceiver from the beginning, and he carries his character right on to the close (verses 3, 8, 10). This is the last trial of man, a needed trial, because the natural heart had not been tested, where all spoke of Christ ; and present blessing—long life on the earth— was the part of those, who owned a visible, glorious Christ. To have been unfaithful to Him then, meant to be cut off (Isa. lxv. 20). There was nothing to tempt them. But, alas, not even having seen Christ, basked in the sunshine of His glory, and enjoyed the fruits thereof, can secure the heart of man—mere, natural man. He is not to be depended on, and falls as soon as tempted. God they could not finally enjoy in that state, as proved by the ready way they fall into Satan's hands. It is the final effort of man, led on by Satan, to get rid of God from His own earth. This concludes man's history in responsibility. His last act is rebellion, even as his first (Gen. iii. 11).

"And they went up on the breadth of the earth, and compassed the camp of the saints about, and the beloved city" (ver. 9). The saints spoken of here are clearly the millennial saints, those who had been on earth, in the enjoyment of the love of the Saviour, through that thousand years. Attacked by the enemy, they are, apparently, left to be surrounded by their foe. They are tested, not only by seduction, but by violence—Satan's two great weapons with man. Had the Lord appeared visibly, Gog and Magog would, doubtless, not have come up, but the thoroughness of the trial, proves the faithfulness of the saints, who refuse Satan's seductions. The attack of the foe is once more upon the land, from which the eye of the Lord has never been withdrawn. Against that land the enemy goes up, determined, if possible, once more to sweep away the testimony to God, and His Son. Jehovah has been universally worshipped, and owned, and Jerusalem, "the beloved city," has been the very metropolis of the new earth, according to Isaiah lxv. 17, 18. The enemy comes up against the metropolis, and we read, "Fire came down from God out of heaven, and devoured them." The last open revolt of man upon earth, in time, is judged, by God, in the most solemn way possible. Fire from heaven devours them. What an excessively solemn thing!

Nothing, even on the new earth, but being converted to God will do for man. Not even a thousand years of displayed glory, prosperity, peace, and blessedness, under the reign of Jesus, will touch his heart, and, at the end of the thousand years, if the Lord retire, and Satan reappear, what material does the enemy find, of which to compose his hosts? It is only too true, that find, or put man, where you will, unless he be the subject of absolute grace, there is nothing in his heart but downright opposition to God. Affecting thought, opposition to God! Yes, my friends, opposition to God. If you are not a converted man, you are opposed to God. Till God, in His grace, converted me, over thirty years ago, I was opposed to Him. If you had then told me that plain, solemn, truth, in an unvarnished style, I have no doubt I should have been angry, but the truth would have been the same. "The carnal mind is enmity against God" (Rom. viii. 7), and, "The friendship of the world is enmity with God" (Jas. iv. 4). One sees here the end of it all, that unless grace has really touched the heart, what it is, in its hidden springs, is sure to be made apparent, as in this final, and unsurpassingly solemn, exhibition of enmity against God.

But the patience of God is exhausted, and fire—always the figure, in Scripture, of God's judgment—comes down from heaven, and destroys Gog, and Magog. Thus they perish, but for their leader, untouched by this divine judgment, is reserved a worse fate, for "the devil that deceived them was cast into the lake of fire and of brimstone, where the beast and the false prophet are, and shall be tormented day and night for ever and ever" (ver. 10). Thus God describes the final disposal, and overthrow, of His, and man's adversary. I know that pretty flights of fancy, about Satan's rule in hell, have been indulged in, and we have heard the phrase, "Better to reign in hell, than serve in heaven," but do you think he really reigns in hell? I believe, that if there be one being, more miserable than another, in the lake of fire, for all eternity, Satan is that one. Therefore I say to you, most affectionately, do not, as you value your being, as you value eternity, as you value your immortal, precious soul, be his companion. There is only one way in which you can ensure not being his companion—it is by being the companion of Christ. If you are going to be the companion of Christ, in eternal glory, you must know the love of the Lord Jesus Christ in your earthly pathway. Whether you are a converted person yet I do not know. If you never have been, let me beseech you to turn to the Lord now. Bow to the Saviour now, because the day is coming, when you must bow to that blessed One. Here God describes the end of the one, who has deceived man from first to last,—he is "tormented day and night for ever." The fate of his companions is no better. Do not then, I beseech you, be his companion.

Now the Spirit of God carries us beyond the limits of time. Every earthly enemy of God has been judged. The last foe, in that sense, has been dealt with by the hand of the Lord, and we come to a moment of unspeakable solemnity. "I saw a great white throne, and him that sat on it, from whose face the earth and the heavens fled away; and there was found no place for them" (ver. 11). Observe, the heaven, and the earth, fly from the face of Him, that sits on the throne, and I may ask, Who is it that sits there? Scripture leaves us in no doubt as to that point. It is clearly the Lord Jesus Christ. The One, who fills that throne, is without doubt the Son of Man. Have you any doubt about the point? Let us hear what Scripture says. In John v. you will find to whom is committed the judgment. "For the Father judgeth no man, but hath committed all judgment unto the Son" (ver. 22). Again: "As the Father hath life in himself, so hath he given to the Son to have life in himself; and hath given him authority to execute judgment also, because he is the Son of man. . . Marvel not at this: for the hour is coming, in the which all that are in the graves shall hear his voice, and shall come forth; they that have done good, unto the resurrection of life; and they that have done evil, unto the resurrection of judgment" (verses 26-29).

Nothing can be plainer than, that it is the Lord Jesus Christ, who is going to be the judge. All judgment is committed to the Son. Nay more, He is given authority to execute judgment, because He is the Son of Man. Why, because He is the Son of Man? Because He has come into the scene where man is a sinner, under judgment, and He, who has come into this scene—the blessed Son of God—became man, a man on whom death had no claim, absolutely, and perfectly holy. He it is, that, by-and-by, is to be the judge. And another reason, too. Man took occasion, so to speak, by the humiliation of the Lord Jesus—for He emptied Himself, and took upon Him the form of a servant—to put Him yet lower. They cast Him out, and preferred a robber, and a murderer to the Saviour. And what is God's answer to this? "Wherefore God also hath highly exalted him, and given him a name which is above every name, that at the name of Jesus every knee should bow, of heavenly, and earthly, and infernal beings, and that every tongue should confess that Jesus Christ is Lord" (Phil. ii. 9-11). As man, He is worthy to receive, and shall receive, what he can claim as God, in Isa. xlv. 23. All judgment is committed unto the Son, but He has to execute judgment, because He is the Son of Man. Some one may, however, say, Shall we not all be called out, by-and-by, together, to stand before the Lord? No, the Word of God is very plain, and in this 5th chapter of John, we find that the character of the resurrection is different. There is the "resurrection unto life," and the "resurrection unto judgment,"—the resurrection unto blessing, and the resurrection unto sorrow. We have already seen, this evening, that there is an interval of a thousand years, between these two resurrections. The first resurrection—and blessed and holy is he that hath part in it—is before the thousand years, but "the rest of the dead lived not again until the thousand years were finished."

In Acts xvii. we also see that the Lord Jesus is distinctly marked out, as the One who will be the judge, inasmuch as God "hath appointed a day, in the which he will judge the world in righteousness by that man whom he hath ordained, whereof he hath given assurance to all men, in that he hath raised him from the dead" (ver. 31). Another scripture is found in 2nd Timothy: "I charge thee therefore before God, and the Lord Jesus Christ, who shall judge the quick and the dead at his appearing and his kingdom" (iv. 1). He judges the quick—the living—before the millennium, and the dead, at the end thereof. Mark, it is the very last act of the kingdom, this solemn work of judging the dead. You have doubtless observed, that in the 5th chapter of John, to which I have alluded, the Lord Jesus speaks of two hours: "The hour is coming, and now is, when the dead shall hear the voice of the Son of God: and they that hear shall live" (ver. 25). That is the hour of blessing, the hour of grace, and salvation, the hour in which the Son of God is now calling men to come to Himself. That hour began with Jesus' life ministry, and goes on up to this moment. It is the hour in which men are getting saved; but that hour is coming to a close, for He adds immediately: "Marvel not at this: for the hour is coming" (*not* now, is) "in which all that are in the graves shall hear his voice, and shall come forth; they that have done good unto the resurrection of life; and they that have done evil unto the resurrection of judgment" (verses 28, 29). The first hour has lasted for nearly two thousand years, but I am persuaded the moment is drawing near, when, to use a figure, the hour-glass is going to be turned. The hour of grace, and life-giving, is rapidly drawing to a close, and the next thing is, the setting in of the hour of judgment. Oh, my friend, get ready, believe on the Lord Jesus, get to know the Lord, be decided for Him, for, if you are not one of those, who have part in the first resurrection, then you must have your part, in that which comes out here, at this great white throne.

Jesus sits upon that throne. He, who is now the Saviour, must then be the Judge. God has put all authority into His hand, once pierced for our sins, and He there sits, and wields the sword. The throne is called "*great*" because of the dignity of the One who fills it. It is called "*white*" because of the absolute purity of the judge. Everything must be according to the unsullied holiness of the nature, of Him who sits upon the throne. Now observe—" I saw a great white throne and him that sat on it, from whose face the earth and the heaven fled away, and there was found no place for them." People have sometimes spoken of this as the Lord's second coming to the earth. But observe, there is no coming at all here. Why? Because there is no earth to come to. Heaven and earth have fled away, consequently the Lord Jesus must have come to earth, before this epoch, or He can never come at all. Evidently time is no more, and the relation of man to the earth, as it now is, ended. Hence, there is no thought of any coming here. Nay, heaven and earth flee from the face of Him, who sits on that throne, so solemn, so appalling, is the sight.

But, let us see, what takes place at that moment. You may get fuller light by listening to what St Peter has to say. "The day of the Lord will come as a thief in the night; in the which the heavens shall pass away with a great noise, and the elements shall melt with fervent heat; the earth also, and the works that are therein, shall be burned up" (2 Pet. iii. 10). God has but one way of purifying this sin-stained earth, and it is by fire. It will be a terrible day, indeed, when "the earth also, and the works that are therein, shall be burned up." How it will be caused, it is not for me to say, but you all know that we live on the crust of a ball, whose interior consists of molten material, and flame. Whether God will let these mighty forces of nature then come into play, is for Him to decide, but all that Scripture says is this, "the earth also, and the works that are therein, shall be burned up." So that, on the mightiest monuments of man's skill, and ingenuity, faith sees written in indelible characters, the words, "Reserved unto fire" (2 Pet. iii. 7). It will be an awful day for the man who is not saved. This thought, therefore, leads the apostle to add:

"Seeing then that all these things shall be dissolved, what manner of persons ought ye to be in all holy conversation and godliness; looking for and hasting the coming of the day of God, wherein the heavens, being on fire, shall be dissolved, and the elements shall melt with fervent heat." This last clause, you observe, is repeated, that there might be no mistake whatever, as to the way in which God will cleanse the earth, and the heavens too. "Nevertheless, we, according to his promise, look for new heavens and a new earth, wherein dwelleth righteousness" (2 Pet. iii. 12-13). What Peter says he looks for, John writes that he saw. "We look for new heavens and a new earth," says Peter; but says John, "I saw a new heaven and a new earth," and you will find all about them in the 21st chapter of Revelation. Peter reveals them disappearing, in flame, and smoke, and John shows them reappearing, in all the beauty of the new creation, for eternity.

Jesus sits, then, on that great white throne, the earth and the heaven flee from His face, and now there comes a moment, unparalleled in its solemnity, in the history of men. "I saw the dead, small and great, stand before God." It is the closing moment of the second hour of the 5th of John. Is there any resurrection of the blessed here? Clearly not; they have been already raised more than a thousand years, and taken part in the millennial reign. The two resurrections are separated, as to time, by at least one thousand years, but they are separated more than that, by their utterly different character. "They that have done good" have already come forth "unto the resurrection of life." If the Lord came this evening, every sleeping believer would be so raised. But what about the unbelievers? They are left for this day—left for the "resurrection unto judgment" here, before the great white throne. It is a judgment of persons, not deeds, though they be judged according to their deeds—a judgment only of unbelievers—and though standing before the throne, they are all spoken of as "dead." They have been delivered from the grip of the first death, only to taste the second death, hence, they are still called dead.

"I saw the dead, small and great, stand before the throne, and the books were opened: and another book was opened, which is the book of life" (ver. 12). It is an assize; there is no hurry, there is no haste; and I may say more, if you stand there, you will have no advocate then, you will have no barrister to plead your case; further, you will have no plea. These dead—who are they? Those who have lived in sin, died in their sins, been buried in their sins, and now they are raised in their sins. Clearly they are raised in the body, but raised for judgment. But shall not we all be there? No, dear fellow-Christian, you will not be there—not a believer will be there. Nowhere, in Scripture, do we read of a general resurrection, and a general judgment. Not for ten thousand worlds, ten millions times told, would I be, in the class here described, for all are lost. If you are an unconverted sinner, you are in imminent danger of being in that class. Let me affectionately urge you now to step over the boundary line, from the power of Satan to God, and yield your heart to Jesus the Saviour, lest you have to stand before Him, as the Judge, in that day.

"The books were opened, and another book was opened, which is the book of life; and the dead were judged out of those things which were written in the books, *according to their works.*" Observe that. Will the Christian's place in heavenly glory be determined by his works? No, God forbid. We get that place, through grace, on the ground of the death, and resurrection of the Lord Jesus Christ for us, as poor sinners. There is, on the other hand, no doubt that we shall appear before the Lord (2 Cor. v. 10), and our position, in the kingdom of Christ, will differ, according to the character of our earthly service to the Lord, since we have known Him as our Saviour, but that is a different thing altogether. Here they are judged according to their works. The ground of judgment is twofold—positive and negative. Their works witness against them, and their names are not found in the book of life. Ah, is there not a single word to be said in favour of those trembling wretches that stand before the throne? Is there not one word of extenuation in favour of yon trembling, guilty, sin-stained company of unbelieving souls, from Cain downwards, that have come forth—yea, been compelled to come from their graves—by the voice of the Son of Man, which they would not pay heed to, when He said, "Come unto me, all ye that labour, and are heavy laden, and I will give you rest"? Not a syllable! They heeded Him not, in the day of grace, when He called them, to give them life, but they must heed, and obey Him, in the day when He calls them to judgment.

There will be no mistake *then*, because the books will show the truth. I do not know what your name may be. There may be ten thousand men, of the same name as yourself, but when the Lord puts His hand upon the book, it will be your book, and that of nobody else. What you are, what you have done, and not done, what you have been, the whole record of your life, will be there, and what a solemn record for a sinner, who dies now, in Gospel days, unconverted! Born in a Christian land, early sent to a Sunday school, perhaps "joined the Church" so called, but really loved the world, thought only of the world, put off repentance, and conversion, till a day that never came, never came to Christ, and at length, cut down, by some sudden judgment, at the hand of God, died, as you had lived, in your sins. As the book is opened, and the pages slowly turned over, on which is the record of your life, oh what an awful moment, for you, will it be, and if your blanched lips part, it will be but to confess—True, true. God have mercy on you, my friend, where you sit to-night, if you are still unsaved. By the blessings of the heavenly Gospel now pressed on you, and the certainty of coming judgment, I implore you not to miss God's salvation, while it is offered now. Do not let this scene, of which Scripture speaks so solemnly, ever be enacted in your case. Why should it be? I beseech you, come to the Saviour as you are, in your sins, all shall be forgiven, and you will be among those—holy and blessed—that have part in the first resurrection. Come to the Saviour now, all shall be pardoned, and you may henceforth go on your way, a happy believer, serving the Lord, and, in the day of glory, be the recipient of a full reward at the hand of the blessed Lord.

But not so is it here. "The dead were judged out of those things which were written in the books, according to their works. And the sea gave up the dead which were in it." The sea, which has engulfed so many, and been the cause of the sorrow of such countless thousands, the sea must give up the dead in it.

You may say, They have passed beyond the reach, and the ken of men. Quite true! How many a body has been brought to shore that nobody could identify, and how many have never been cast up. But God will be able to identify every one at that time, and the sea will cast him up, for God's identification, at the great white throne.

" And death and Hades delivered up the dead which were in them : and they were judged every man according to their works. And death and Hades were cast into the lake of fire. This is the second death." Now what does God mean by that remarkable expression, " Death and Hades were cast into the lake of fire"? Death held the body, Hades being the condition of the disembodied spirit; but then, as the wicked are brought to life again, Hades is no more inhabited in that sense, and Death no longer holds the body. They are no longer needed. They are here personified, as the enemies of God, and man, and are thus cast into the lake of fire. Oh! pitiful doom of every unsaved soul, taken out of the first death, which sundered him from his fellows, to meet, and taste " the second death,"— eternal separation from God. We come here to the point where death is annulled. " The last enemy that shall be destroyed is death." That is fulfilled by the raising of the wicked dead.

" And whosoever was not found written in the book of life was cast into the lake of fire" (ver. 15). This is a touching allusion to the wonderful grace of God, because the fact is, that if grace has not written our names in the Lamb's book of life, we shall find ourselves along with the number judged according to their works. Nothing but sovereign grace will do for you, or for me. Another has well stated it thus

*" Sovereign grace alone has saved according to the purpose of God. There was a book of life. Whosoever was not written there was cast into the lake of fire. But it was the finally closing, and separating scene for the whole race of men, and this world. And though they were judged every man according to his works, yet sovereign grace only had delivered any; and whosoever was not found in grace's book was cast into the lake of fire. The sea gave up the dead in it; death and Hades the dead in them. And death and Hades were put an end to, for ever, by the divine judgment. The heaven and earth passed away, but they were to be renewed; but death and Hades never. There was for them only divine destruction and judgment. They are looked at as the power of Satan. He has the power of death, and the gates of Hades; and hence they are for ever destroyed judicially. They will never have power again. They are personified; but of course there is no question of tormenting them, or of punishing them; when the devil himself is cast in, there is. But death was not then destroyed; for the wicked dead had not been raised for judgment. Now they had, and the last enemy is destroyed. The force of the image, I doubt not, is that all the dead now judged (the whole contents of Hades, in whom the power of death had been), were cast into the lake of fire, so that death and Hades, which had no existence but in their state, were entirely and judicially ended, by their being cast in. The saints had long since passed out of them, but they subsisted in the wicked. Now these were, consequent on the judgment of the white throne, cast into the lake of fire—the second death. The limit and measure of escape was the book of life."

---

* *Loc. cit.* (p. 612).

The Spirit of God now opens up eternity—the end of all God's dealings with men. The final destiny of all unsaved souls, has come before us—they are apportioned the lake of fire. I know many may say to me, I do not believe that. Beloved friends, I do believe it, for when God says, "Whosoever was not found written in the book of life was cast into the lake of fire," He means what He says. God never tells lies, although men may. When He speaks, He speaks solemnly, and truly. But turn now and see how beautiful is that which follows, "And I saw a new heaven and a new earth" (xxi. 1). A few verses before, John saw them fleeing away from the face of the Lord, now he sees them coming out, in all the radiance, and blessedness of this ever new, because eternal, condition of matters—"a new heaven and a new earth." Here you have them, just as the Christian will appear, by-and-by, in a real body—the resurrection body. What sort of body I do not know, but I know my body will undergo a wonderful change, for it will be "a spiritual body." In the same way, I take it, God carries the heaven, and the earth, through that scene of fire, and they come out "new"—in a new character—altogether suited to, and fitted for God, with every trace of the serpent's trail, and man's sin, removed from them. They come out "a new heaven and a new earth, wherein *dwelleth* righteousness."

Now, righteousness *suffers*, in the millennial day it *reigns*, but in the eternal day it *dwells* happily, it is quite at home. "I saw a new heaven and a new earth; for the first heaven and the first earth were passed away, and there was no more sea." This is not what Isaiah alludes to (lxv. 17). His new heavens, and new earth, are only new, in a moral sense, as suiting the millennium, and the sea also exists, for he speaks of "the isles afar off," but here, every bit of the new earth is seen, brought into relationship with every other part, for "there was no more sea." This would be impossible, as things now are, for man's life. Of course, there must then be a wonderful change in the character of our life, because, as things now exist, we could not get on without the sea. It is the great reservoir, from whence comes the moisture, that is necessary for man, and the earth. I do not know what the change will be, but God brings out here, that which is very simple, and plain, and which faith delights to contemplate, "a new heaven, and a new earth, and no more sea." God, if I might so say, in the new scene, will efface everything, that could bring to memory, the sorrows of man's heart down here.

"And I John saw the holy city, new Jerusalem, coming down from God, out of heaven, prepared as a bride adorned for her husband." Last Lord's Day evening we were occupied in looking at this holy city—the Bride—the Church. Then we saw that she was merely descending from heaven, towards earth, but now she comes right down to earth, because the new earth is divinely suited to this heavenly city. Look how she comes out? In the 19th chapter we saw the marriage of the Lamb, to His Bride, on the nuptial day, preparatory to the millennial reign. But now John sees her coming down, out of heaven, at the end of the thousand years. And how does she look? I have seen a good many brides in my day, and I have met them a few years after, and what furrows are on the brow, what cares evident on the countenance, and how soon grey hairs have appeared. A very few years will do it, in this scene down here,

But what does John see? He sees, coming down from heaven, her, who has been the Lamb's wife, for one thousand years, and she looks as bright, and as beautiful, and as fresh, as the day she went up. Not a grey hair, not a wrinkle, can be seen; her condition is what I may call perennial joy. No change can ever be, thank God. The Christian is going to fixed happiness, and unchangeable blessedness with Christ. This is all told out in the lovely words, "coming down . . . as a bride adorned for her husband." "And I heard a great voice out of heaven, saying, Behold the tabernacle of God is with men, and he will dwell with them, and they shall be his people, and God himself shall be with them, and be their God." The moment has come when God takes up His place, upon this earth, in happy relationship with men—not paying them a visit, as He did to Adam, in the garden of Eden, but tabernacling with them, and the tabernacle is the Church, the assembly, the body of Christ, those who are, through grace, now united to the blessed Lord.

Observe, it is not now a question of nations—of Jews and Gentiles — distinctions which had to do with time, and are now all gone by. It is God dwelling with men, as being their God, and therefore, for that reason, in these first eight verses of Revelation xxi., where you have eternity brought in, you have no mention of the Lamb. Jesus as the Lamb does not appear here. His mediatorial kingdom is over. It is all God—God is all in all. The moment, of which 1st Corinthians xv. speaks, has arrived: "Then cometh the end when he gives up the kingdom to him who is God and Father; when he shall have annulled all rule, and all authority and power. For he must reign until he put all enemies under his feet. The last enemy that is annulled is death. For he has put all things in subjection under his feet. But when he says that all things are put in subjection, it is evident that it is except him who put all things in subjection to him. But when all things shall have been brought into subjection to him, then the Son also himself shall be placed in subjection to him who put all things in subjection to him, that God may be all in all" (N.T., 1st Cor. xv. 24-28).

The blessed Saviour has already reigned, as man, over a renewed earth, and a thousand years have gone by; the righteous are blessed, the wicked are judged, and every foe subdued. And what now? He surrenders His earthly kingdom, and thenceforward is Himself subject. We know, there never was a king in this world, that did not lose his crown, and his kingdom, either by some usurper stepping in, or by death sweeping him off, sooner, or later; but here is a king, who, after a reign of a thousand years, takes the crown from His brow, as man, and gives up the kingdom to Him who is God and Father. He who does this is God, but He has been a man, and while we joyfully remember, that His essential deity ever remains untouched, what we learn is, that Jesus passes into the eternal state as man, and He will never cease to be a man, and you and I, beloved fellow-believers, are going to be with Him for ever. God Himself—Father, Son, and Holy Ghost—shall tabernacle with men, they, as delighted to have God's company, as He to be with them. Blessed moment, that God has ever looked on to, and that faith looks on to now! Then see what follows. " And he shall wipe away all tears from their eyes;

and there shall be no more death, neither sorrow, nor crying, neither shall there be any more pain ; for the former things are passed away." Oh how familiar you and I are with these terms. I see many dressed, in deepest mourning, as I speak, and you sorrowfully rejoin, Death has come into my house, and robbed me of the one that I loved best. Thank God, there shall be no more death, no more pain. Man's history on earth is all expressed in these four words—death, sorrow, crying, and pain, but then " the former things are passed away."

"And he that sat upon the throne said, Behold, I make all things new. And he said unto me, Write ; for these words are true and faithful. And he said unto me, It is done, I am the Alpha and the Omega, the beginning and the end."

Extremely beautiful are the verses that follow, as though God saw, that the description would make the soul, that heard about it, for the first time, desire to be a participator in that blessed scene. He therefore weaves in the Gospel, in the loveliest way possible, as He now says—" I will give unto him that is athirst of the fountain of the water of life freely. He that overcometh shall inherit these things; and I will be his God, and he shall be my son." He gives the water of life! Yes, but more than that. I will give of the fountain, I will take you up to the source of it—my own heart. He that overcometh, who is that? The man that turns to Christ, and believes in the Lord, that turns his back, through grace, on all the deception, and guile, through which he is passing, and sets himself to follow the truth. "Who is he that overcometh the world, but he that believeth that Jesus is the Son of God?" (1 John v. 5.) Will not

THE ETERNAL STATE. 239

Satan hinder you? Of course he will. He puts countless obstacles in every man's way, before he gets life, and blessing. But God would cheer, and encourage, and stimulate the believing soul, so He adds, "He that overcometh shall inherit these things; and I will be his God, and he shall be my son." Blessed promise!

And now we reach the most solemn "*But*" in all Scripture, as the Spirit of God gives a categorical description of those who, alas, are not blessed. " But the fearful, and the unbelieving, and the abominable, and murderers, and whoremongers, and sorcerers, and idolaters, and all liars, shall have their part in the lake which burneth with fire and brimstone, which is the second death " (ver. 8).

I should like, as I close, to ask you this,—If God sent down, from heaven to-night, an angel, with the commission, to visit Edinburgh, and write on his tablet the names, or the characters of the persons, who most surely, by-and-by, will be in the lake of fire, where would he begin? Do you fancy that that angel's visit would be to the slums of naked sin, or to the scenes of debauchery, that are, alas, too common? Nay, he would not begin his list there. And if he came into this hall, would the man, who is most sure to be in the lake of fire, be a notorious sinner? No! the list of the lost here commences with this,—" the fearful," the person who is afraid to confess Christ. Now, there is many a person in this hall to-night, who is not a murderer, an idolater, or a liar—nay, he is a person of a good character, but, up to this hour, never has he boldly confessed Jesus, as his Lord, and Saviour. I call your earnest attention to this, that it is the fearful, the timid, and the cowardly, the person who is afraid to come out for Jesus, whose name is first given in this list of the lost.

If, my friend, you have been a timid person, until this hour, may God, by His grace, drive out your timidity, by the sense of His love. When you have got in your heart the sense that the Lord loves you, then your fear of owning Jesus will all go. I tell you what it is, there is nothing grander, or brighter, or more blessed, under the sun, than to be a Christian, and if you have not been a Christian, up to this hour, you have missed a grand opportunity. But, thank God, you have still time, and I say, now turn to Him, drink of the living water, believe His grace, and then go on your way rejoicing. Then I shall meet you in glory. I shall never meet you in hell, mind that. I shall not be there through grace. I charge you, beloved friends, meet me yonder with Jesus, meet me in the air, when the Saviour comes.

We have only now to wait, and watch for Him. He is coming for us, coming out from heaven, the Bright and Morning Star, who will take us up to be for ever with Himself. The Lord keep us waiting, and watching for Him, and serving Him, till He come, for His own precious, and blessed name's sake